# *1989*
# FamilyCircle
## COOKBOOK

The Editors of Family Circle

*Other Books by Family Circle:*

The Best of Family Circle Cookbook
1986 Family Circle Cookbook
1987 Family Circle Cookbook
1988 Family Circle Cookbook

Family Circle Busy Cook's Book

Family Circle Christmas Treasury
1987 Family Circle Christmas Treasury
1988 Family Circle Christmas Treasury

Family Circle Favorite Needlecrafts

Family Circle Hints, Tips & Smart Advice

To order **FamilyCircle** books, write to Family Circle Books,
110 Fifth Avenue, 4th Floor, New York, NY 10001

To subscribe to **FamilyCircle** magazine, write to Family Circle Subscriptions,
110 Fifth Avenue, New York, NY 10011.

## Editorial

*Editor, Book Development—Carol A. Guasti*
*Editorial/Production Coordinator—Kim E. Gayton*
*Project Editor—JoAnn Brett-Billowitz*
*Book Design—Bessen, Tully & Lee*
*Illustrations—Lauren Jarrett*
*Typesetting—Gary S. Borden, Alison Chandler, Helen Russell*
*Special Assistants—Kristen J. Keller, Victoria A. Wachino, Molan Wong*

## Marketing

*Manager, Marketing & Development—Margaret Chan-Yip*
*Promotion/Fulfillment Manager—Pauline MacLean Treitler*
*Administrative Assistant—Lynne Bertram*

*Cover Photo—Ronald G. Harris*
*Photographers—David Bishop, Michele Clement, Ronald G. Harris, Richard Jeffrey, Jenifer Jordan, James Kozyra, Bill McGinn, Jeff Niki, Geoffrey Nilsen, Richard Simpson, Michael Skott, Ben Swedowsky, John Usher, Rene Velez.*
*Special Thanks to Jim Fobel*

Published by The Family Circle, Inc.
110 Fifth Avenue, New York, NY 10011

*Copyright® 1988 by The Family Circle, Inc.*

*Manufactured in the United States of America*

10 9 8 7 6 5 4 3 2 1

Library of Congress Cataloging in Publication Data
Main entry under title:

1989 Family circle cookbook.
Includes index.
1.Cookery.        I.Family circle (Mount Morris, Ill.)
TX715.B485555        1985        641.5        86-4465
ISBN 0-933585-10-1
ISSN 0890-1481

# 1989
# FamilyCircle
# COOKBOOK

The Editors of Family Circle

# Table of Contents

# Introduction

**W**hat's better than a year's worth of delicious recipes?

What can beat a plethora of useful cooking information all in one place?

What could be more useful than hundreds of recipes with complete nutrition analysis?

The answer: A book that has it all. The 1989 Family Circle Cookbook.

This year, we zero in on important eating trends, and offer a slew of low-calorie recipes. There's a special section of microwave recipes (as well as recipe adaptations throughout the book), a chapter on entertaining, as well as cooking tips and nutrition pointers.

There are traditional favorites as well. You'll find wonderful recipes for home-baked breads and enticing appetizers, terrific main courses and side dishes, plus oven-fresh pies, yummy cookies and frozen treats.

Each recipe is coded to help make meal planning easier. Quick recipes require an hour or less from prep time to serving; make-ahead means that the recipe, or part of it, can be prepared beforehand (from an hour to several weeks; each recipe specifies the time). Low-cost recipes generally cost $1.00 or less per serving, and recipes for entertaining feature ingredients or preparation techniques that make them especially elegant or unique.

Enjoy—and happy cooking!

## COOKING GUIDES

Each recipe is coded by type, indicated by the following symbols:

**⚡ Quick**

**◀◀◀ Make-Ahead**

**Y Entertaining**

**💲 Low-Cost**

Keep in mind that:
1. **Baking powder** is double action.
2. **Brown sugar** is firmly packed.
3. **Corn syrup,** unless specified, can be either light or dark.
4. **Doubling recipes** is not recommended unless otherwise instructed. It is best to make the recipe a second time.
5. **Eggs** are large.
6. **Egg, slightly beaten** means to just break the yolks.
7. **Eggs, lightly beaten** means to create a smooth mixture.
8. **Flour,** cake or all-purpose: most commercial brands of flour come presifted from the manufacturer. Some of our recipes indicate additional sifting to produce a lighter product.
9. **Heavy cream** for whipping is 40 percent butterfat.
10. **Herbs and spices** are dried unless noted otherwise.
11. **Measurements** are level.
12. **Milk** is whole homogenized.
13. **Vegetable shortening** is used for greasing pans.
14. **Vinegar** is white distilled unless otherwise noted.

## DAILY NUTRITION COUNTDOWN CHART

| | **Average Healthy Adult** | |
| | Women | Men |
| --- | --- | --- |
| **Calories[1]** | 2,000 | 2,700 |
| **Protein[2]** | 44 gms (176 cal.) | 56 gms (224 cal.) |
| **Fat[3]** | 66 gms (594 cal.) | 90 gms (810 cal.) |
| **Sodium[4]** | 1,100-3,300 mg | 1,100-3,300 mg |
| **Cholesterol[5]** | 300 mg | 300 mg |

Calories (cal.) that do not come from protein or fat should be derived from complex carbohydrates found in whole grains, fresh fruits, vegetables, pasta, etc.

[1]RDA [2](12% of calories) RDA [3](30% of calories) Amer. Heart Assoc. and Nat'l Acad. of Science [4]USDA [5]Amer. Heart Assoc.

Rapid growth rate and body changes during the developmental years account for the variations in a child's nutritional needs as compared to those of an adult.

To insure that a child is consuming sufficient amounts from the basic food groups, an adult should closely monitor a child's daily dietary intake. This will help to develop a lifetime of healthy eating habits and insure a well balanced diet. Consult a registered dietitian or qualified doctor to obtain the specific dietary needs of a healthy child.

## IMPORTANT MEASURES

| | |
| --- | --- |
| Dash | under ⅛ teaspoon |
| ½ tablespoon | 1½ teaspoons |
| 1 tablespoon | 3 teaspoons |
| 1 ounce liquid | 2 tablespoons |
| 1 jigger | 1½ ounces |
| ¼ cup | 4 tablespoons |
| ⅓ cup | 5 tablespoons plus 1 teaspoon |
| ½ cup | 8 tablespoons |
| ⅔ cup | 10 tablespoons plus 2 teaspoons |
| ¾ cup | 12 tablespoons |
| 1 cup | 16 tablespoons |
| 1 pint | 2 cups |
| 1 quart | 2 pints |
| 1 gallon | 4 quarts |
| 1 pound | 16 ounces |

## TAKING MEASURES

### Flour
Measure the all-purpose flour called for in most of the recipes in this book by spooning flour from the bag or canister into a dry measuring cup, heaping slightly. (*Note:* The top of the cup should be flat; there is no spout on a dry measure, as there is on a liquid measuring cup.)

Place the heaping cup of flour over the bag of flour or canister and run the flat side of a long knife across the top to level off the cup. (*Note:* Also use this technique to measure granulated sugar.)

### Brown Sugar
Measure light or dark brown sugar by packing it firmly into a dry measuring cup, using the back of a tablespoon.

### Shortening, Butter and Margarine
Measure vegetable shortening by scooping it with a rubber scraper into a dry measuring cup; run the flat blade of a long knife over the top, then scoop it out of the cup with the rubber scraper into a mixing bowl. Shortening can be measured before or after it is melted.

One stick of butter or margarine equals 4 ounces; 4 sticks equal 1 pound or 2 cups.

### Casserole Measurement Chart
Casserole recipes are imported from all over the world, and each country has its own system of measurements. The chart below will help you to convert your casserole's measurements from one system to another, so you can be assured your recipe will turn out perfectly.

| Cups | = | Pints | = | Quarts | = | Liters |
|------|---|-------|---|--------|---|--------|
| 1 | | ½ | | ¼ | | 0.237 |
| 2 | | 1* | | ½* | | 0.473 |
| 4 | | 2* | | 1* | | 0.946 |
| 6 | | 3 | | 1½ | | 1.419 |
| 8 | | 4 | | 2 | | 1.892 |
| 10 | | 5 | | 2½ | | 2.365 |
| 12 | | 6 | | 3 | | 2.838 |

*In Canada, 1 pint = 2½ cups; 1 quart = 5 cups.*

### Measuring Liquids
Place a liquid measuring cup on a flat surface and bend over until you are at eye level with the cup. Pour the liquid to the desired measure printed on the side of the cup. (*Note:* When measuring a sticky syrup, such as molasses or honey, first grease the cup with butter or margarine; the syrup will then pour out easily.)

## OVEN TEMPERATURES
It is not necessary to preheat an oven for most meat, vegetable and casserole dishes. A dish that requires a preheated oven will have a direction to that effect in the recipe, allowing for the 15-minute margin needed to preheat either a gas or electric oven.

| | |
|---|---|
| **Very Slow** | 250°-275° |
| **Slow** | 300°-325° |
| **Moderate** | 350°-375° |
| **Hot** | 400°-425° |
| **Very Hot** | 450°-475° |
| **Extremely Hot** | 500°+ |

## GOOD MEALS, GOOD HEALTH

*Always try to eat a variety of foods, in moderation, to insure a complete range of vitamins and minerals. Select foods that provide plenty of complex carbohydrates, such as whole grains, fruits and vegetables, for energy and high-fiber content. Try to avoid foods containing large amounts of fat, cholesterol, sodium and sugar.*

*The nutrient value per serving is included with each recipe in this book, to help you plan daily menus that are well balanced and healthful. Refer to the Daily Nutrition Countdown Chart on page 2, for the daily dietary requirements of the average adult man and woman.*

# EMERGENCY INGREDIENT SUBSTITUTES

| When The Recipe Calls For | You May Substitute |
| --- | --- |
| 1 square unsweetened chocolate | 3 tablespoons unsweetened cocoa powder plus 1 tablespoon butter, margarine or vegetable shortening |
| 1 cup sifted cake flour | ⅞ cup sifted all-purpose flour (1 cup less 2 tablespoons) |
| 2 tablespoons flour (for thickening) | 1 tablespoon cornstarch |
| 1 teaspoon baking powder | ¼ teaspoon baking powder plus ⅝ teaspoon cream of tartar |
| 1 cup corn syrup | 1 cup sugar and ¼ cup liquid used in recipe |
| 1 cup honey | 1¼ cups sugar and ¼ cup liquid used in recipe |
| 1 cup sweet milk | ½ cup evaporated milk plus ½ cup water |
| 1 cup buttermilk | 1 tablespoon vinegar plus enough sweet milk to make 1 cup |
| 1 cup sour cream (in baking) | ⅞ cup buttermilk or sour milk plus 3 tablespoons butter |
| 1 egg (for custards) | 2 egg yolks + 1 tablespoon water |
| 1 cup brown sugar (packed) | 1 cup sugar or 1 cup sugar plus 2 tablespoons molasses |
| 1 teaspoon lemon juice | ¼ teaspoon vinegar |
| ¼ cup chopped onion | 1 tablespoon instant minced onion |
| 1 clove garlic | ⅛ teaspoon garlic powder |
| 1 cup zucchini | 1 cup summer squash |
| 1 cup tomato juice | ½ cup tomato sauce plus ½ cup water |
| 2 cups tomato sauce | ¾ cup tomato paste plus 1 cup water |
| 1 tablespoon fresh snipped herbs | 1 teaspoon dried herbs |
| 1 tablespoon prepared mustard | 1 teaspoon dry mustard |
| ½ cup (1 stick) butter or margarine | 7 tablespoons vegetable shortening |

# EMERGENCY BAKING DISH AND PAN SUBSTITUTES

If you do not have the specific-size baking pan or mold called for in a recipe, substitute a pan of equal volume from the list below.
• If the pan you are substituting is made of glass, reduce the baking temperature by 25°.

• If you are substituting a pan that is shallower than the pan in the recipe, reduce the baking time by about one-quarter.
• If you are substituting a pan that is deeper than the pan in the recipe, increase the baking time by one-quarter.

## COMMON KITCHEN PANS TO USE AS CASSEROLES WHEN THE RECIPE CALLS FOR:

**4-cup baking dish:**
9-inch pie plate
8 x 1¼-inch round layer-cake pan—C
7⅜ x 3⅝ x 2⅝-inch loaf pan—A

**6-cup baking dish:**
10-inch pie plate
8 or 9 x1½-inch round layer-cake pan—C
8½ x 3⅝ x 2⅝-inch loaf pan—A

**8-cup baking dish:**
8 x 8 x 2-inch square pan—D
11 x 7 x 1½-inch baking pan
9 x5 x 3-inch loaf pan—A

**10-cup baking dish:**
9 x 9 x 2-inch square pan—A
11¾ x 7½ x 1¾-inch baking pan
15½ x10½ x 1-inch jelly-roll pan

**12-cup baking dish and over:**
13½ x 8½ x 2-inch glass baking dish (12 cups)
13 x 9 x 2-inch metal baking pan (15 cups)
14 x 10½ x 2½-inch roasting pan (19 cups)

**Three 8-inch-round pans:**
two 9 x 9 x 2-inch square cake pans

**Two 9-inch-round layer-cake pans:**
two 8 x 8 x 2-inch square cake pans, or 13 x 9 x 2-inch pan

**9 x 5 x 3-inch loaf pan:**
9 x 9 x 2-inch square cake pan

**9-inch angel-cake tube pan:**
10 x 3¾-inch Bundt® pan, or 9 x 3½-inch fancy tube pan

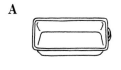

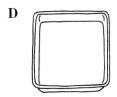

## TOTAL VOLUME OF VARIOUS SPECIAL BAKING PANS

**Tube pans:**

| | |
|---|---|
| 7½ x 3-inch Bundt® tube pan — K | 6 cups |
| 9 x 3½-inch fancy tube or Bundt® pan—J or K | 9 cups |
| 9 x 3½-inch angel-cake or tube pan — I | 12 cups |
| 10 x 3¾-inch Bundt® or Crownburst® pan — K | 12 cups |
| 9 x 3½-inch fancy tube mold—J | 12 cups |
| 10 x 4-inch fancy tube mold (Kugelhopf)—J | 16 cups |
| 10 x 4-inch angel-cake or tube pan—I | 18 cups |

**Melon Mold:**

| | |
|---|---|
| 7 x 5½ x 4-inch mold—H | 6 cups |

**Springform Pans:**

| | |
|---|---|
| 8 x 3-inch pan — B | 12 cups |
| 9 x 3-inch pan — B | 16 cups |

**Ring Molds:**

| | |
|---|---|
| 8½ x 2¼-inch mold—E | 4½ cups |
| 9¼ x 2¾-inch mold—E | 8 cups |

**Charlotte Mold:**

| | |
|---|---|
| 6 x 4¼-inch mold—G | 7½ cups |

**Brioche Pan:**

| | |
|---|---|
| 9½ x 3¼-inch pan—F | 8 cups |

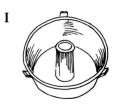

# FOOD EQUIVALENTS

| | |
|---|---|
| **Berries,** 1 pint | 1¾ cups |
| **Bread** | |
| Crumbs, soft, 1 cup | 2 slices |
| Cubes, 1 cup | 2 slices |
| 1 pound, sliced | 22 slices |
| **Broth** | |
| Beef or Chicken, 1 cup | 1 teaspoon instant bouillon, 1 envelope bouillon, 1 cube bouillon, dissolved in 1 cup boiling water |
| **Butter or Margarine** | |
| ½ stick | ¼ cup or 4 tablespoons |
| 1 pound | 4 sticks or 2 cups |
| **Cream and milk** | |
| Cream, heavy, 1 cup | 2 cups, whipped |
| Milk, evaporated, small can | ⅔ cup |
| Milk, sweetened condensed, 14-ounce can | 1⅔ cups |
| Milk, nonfat dry, 1 pound | 5 quarts liquid skim |
| **Cheese** | |
| Cream, 8-ounce package | 1 cup |
| Cottage, 8 ounces | 1 cup |
| Cheddar or Swiss, 1 pound, shredded | 4 cups |
| Blue, crumbled, 4 ounces | 1 cup |
| Parmesan or Romano, ¼ pound grated | 1¼ cups |
| **Chocolate** | |
| Unsweetened, 1 ounce | 1 square |
| Semisweet pieces, 6-ounce package | 1 cup |
| **Coconut** | |
| Flaked, 3½-ounce can | 1⅓ cups |
| Shredded 4-ounce can | 1⅓ cups |
| **Cookies** | |
| Chocolate wafers, 1 cup crumbs | 19 wafers |
| Vanilla wafers, 1 cup fine crumbs | 22 wafers |
| Graham crackers, 1 cup fine crumbs | 14 square crackers |
| **Dried Beans and Peas** | |
| 1 cup | 2¼ cups, cooked |
| **Eggs** (large) | |
| Whole, 1 cup | 5 to 6 |
| Yolks, 1 cup | 13 to 14 |
| Whites, 1 cup | 7 to 8 |
| **Flour** | |
| all-purpose, sifted, 1 pound | 4 cups |
| cake, sifted, 1 pound | 4¾ to 5 cups |

| | |
|---|---|
| **Gelatin** | |
| unflavored, 1 envelope | 1 tablespoon |
| **Nuts** | |
| Almonds, 1 pound, shelled | 3½ cups |
| Peanuts, 1 pound, shelled | 3 cups |
| Walnuts, 1 pound, shelled | 4 cups |
| Pecans, 1 pound, shelled | 4 cups |
| **Pasta** | |
| Macaroni, elbow, uncooked, 8 ounces | 4 cups, cooked |
| Spaghetti, 8 ounces, uncooked | 4 cups, cooked |
| Noodles, medium width, 8 ounces, uncooked | 3¾ cups, cooked |
| Noodles, fine width, 8 ounces, uncooked | 5½ cups, cooked |
| **Rice** | |
| Long-grain white rice, uncooked, 1 cup | 3 cups, cooked |
| Enriched precooked rice, uncooked, 1 cup | 2 cups, cooked |
| **Sugar** | |
| Granulated, 1 pound | 2 cups |
| Brown, firmly packed, 1 pound | 2¼ cups |
| 10X (confectioners' powdered), sifted, 1 pound | 3⅓ to 4 cups |
| **Vegetables and Fruits** | |
| Apples, 1 pound | 3 medium size |
| Bananas, 1 pound | 3 medium size |
| Carrots, 1 pound, sliced | 2½ cups |
| Cabbages, 1 pound, shredded | 4 cups |
| Herbs, chopped fresh, 1 tablespoon | 1 teaspoon dried |
| Lemon, 1 medium size, grated | 2 teaspoons rind |
| Lemon, 1 medium size, squeezed | 2 tablespoons juice |
| Orange, 1 medium size, grated | 2 tablespoons rind |
| Orange, 1 medium size, squeezed | ⅓ to ½ cup juice |
| Onions, yellow cooking, 1 pound | 5 to 6 medium size |
| Onions, small white silverskins, 1 pound | 12 to 14 |
| Potatoes, all-purpose, 1 pound | 3 medium size |
| Peaches, 1 pound | 4 medium size |
| Mushrooms, 1 pound, sliced | 3 cups |
| Tomatoes, 1 pound: | |
| Large | 2 |
| Medium size | 3 |
| Small | 4 |

# MAXIMUM CUPBOARD STORAGE TIMES

Use foods within the times recommended in this chart. Foods stored longer than recommended are still good to eat, but may be less flavorful and nutritious.

| | | | | |
|---|---|---|---|---|
| *Baking powder* | 18 months | | *Nonfat dry milk powder* | 6 months |
| *Baking soda* | 18 months | | *Oil** | |
| *Barbecue sauce** | 12 months | | Olive | 1 month |
| *Bouillon cubes, instant* | 12 months | | Vegetable | 3 months |
| *Cake Mixes* | 12 months | | *Olives/pickles** | 12 months |
| *Canned foods** | 12 months | | *Pancake mixes* | 6 months |
| Fruit, gravy, sauce, meat, poultry, milk, seafood, soup, vegetables | | | *Pasta* | 12 months |
| | | | *Peanut butter* | 6 months |
| | | | *Pie crust mixes* | 6 months |
| *Casserole mixes* | 18 months | | *Potato mixes*, or instant | 18 months |
| *Catsup** | 12 months | | *Pudding mixes* | 12 months |
| *Cereal* | 6 months | | *Rice* | |
| *Chili sauce** | 12 months | | Brown, wild | 12 months |
| *Chocolate*, for cooking | 12 months | | Regular long-grain | 24 months |
| *Coconut** | 12 months | | *Salad dressing** | 6 months |
| *Coffee** | | | *Shortening* | 8 months |
| In vacuum-packed cans | 12 months | | *Soup mixes* | 6 months |
| Instant | 6 months | | *Sugar* | |
| *Flour**, all types | 12 months | | Brown or 10X (confectioners') | 4 months |
| *Frosting*, mixes or cans | 8 months | | Granulated | 24 months |
| *Fruit**, dried | 6 months | | *Syrup**, Corn or Maple | 12 months |
| *Gelatin*, plain and sweet | 18 months | | *Tea* | |
| *Herbs/spices* (refrigerate red spices) | | | Bags or loose | 6 months |
| Ground | 6 months | | Instant | 12 months |
| Whole | 12 months | | *Vegetables* | |
| *Honey* | 12 months | | Onions and potatoes | 1 to 2 weeks |
| *Jam/jelly** | 12 months | | Winter squash | 1 to 3 months |
| *Molasses* | 24 months | | *Yeast*, active dry | follow package date |

*Refrigerate after opening.*

# MAXIMUM FREEZER STORAGE TIMES

Use foods within the times recommended in this chart. Foods stored longer than recommended are still good to eat, but will be less flavorful and nutritious.

### What Not To Freeze
Most foods *can* be frozen, but some suffer at freezer temperatures: • Canned hams become watery and soft; • cooked egg white becomes rubbery; • mayonnaise or salad dressings seperate (unless in very small amounts in a mixture); • milk sauces curdle; • fresh salad ingredients wilt; • processed meats (such as cold cuts) have a high salt content which speeds rancidity; • cooked white potatoes become mealy; • gelatin-based dishes "weep" upon thawing; • cream pie fillings become watery and lumpy. *Note: Never* refrigerate or freeze home-stuffed whole poultry (still on carcass); it will become contaminated due to slow freezing or thawing.

| | |
|---|---|
| **Appetizers** | |
| (Canapes, hors d'oeuvres) | ½ to 1 month |
| **Breads, Quick** | |
| Muffins, biscuits and quick breads | 2 to 3 months |
| Rich fruit, nut or spicy quick breads | 1 to 2 months |
| Unbaked dough | 1 month |
| **Yeast** | |
| Baked bread and rolls | 3 months |
| Danish pastry | 3 months |
| Doughnuts, cake or yeast | 3 months |
| Half-baked (brown 'n serve) | 2 or 3 months |
| Rich sweet breads | 2 months |
| Unbaked dough | 1 month |
| **Cakes** | |
| Butter cake,* frosted or unfrosted | 4 to 6 months |
| Angel or chiffon | 2 months |
| Fruit | 12 months |
| **Cooked Combination Dishes** | |
| Casseroles, pasta or rice base | 2 to 4 weeks |
| Pizza | 2 to 4 weeks |
| Sauces, stews | 1 to 3 months |
| **Cookies** | |
| Baked | 6 to 8 months |
| Unbaked, refrigerator | 6 months |

| | |
|---|---|
| **Dairy Products** | |
| Butter | 6 months |
| Margarine | 12 months |
| **Cheese** | |
| Cottage, uncreamed | 2 to 3 months |
| Cream cheese, for use in cooking | 2 months |
| Natural Cheddar and Swiss | 1½ months |
| Processed cheese** | 4 months |
| **Cream** | |
| Heavy cream (may not whip) | 2 months |
| Half-and-half | 2 months |
| Whipped cream | 1 month |
| **Desserts** | |
| Cream puffs or eclairs | 1 to 2 months |
| Fruit | 2 to 4 months |
| Ice cream, sherbet | 6 months |
| **Eggs** | |
| Whole or separated | 12 months |
| **Fish and shellfish, raw** | |
| Lean (bass, cod, perch, pike, sunfish) | 6 to 8 months |
| Oily (catfish, herring, salmon) | 2 to 3 months |
| Shrimp (unbreaded) | 9 to 12 months |
| **Fish, cooked** | 3 months |

**Meats, raw**
**Beef**

| | |
|---|---|
| Ground beef | 2 to 4 months |
| Steaks, roasts | 8 to 12 months |
| Stew meats | 2 to 4 months |

**Lamb**

| | |
|---|---|
| Chops | 3 to 4 months |
| Roasts | 4 to 8 months |

**Pork**

| | |
|---|---|
| Chops | 3 to 4 months |
| Cured (bacon, ham) | 2 months |
| Roasts | 4 to 8 months |
| Sausage | 1 to 3 months |

**Veal**

| | |
|---|---|
| Roasts, cutlets, chops | 6 to 9 months |

**Meats, cooked and processed**

| | |
|---|---|
| Bologna and luncheon meats | Not recommended |
| Casseroles, pies, prepared dinners | 3 months |
| Frankfurters | 3 months |
| Gravy, broth | 2 to 3 months |
| Loaves | 2 to 3 months |

**Nuts**

| | |
|---|---|
| Unsalted | 9 to 12 months |
| Salted | 6 to 8 months |

**Pastries**
**Pastry dough**

| | |
|---|---|
| Unbaked | 1½ to 2 months |
| Baked | 6 to 8 months |

**Pies††**

| | |
|---|---|
| Unbaked | 2 to 4 months |
| Baked | 6 to 8 months |
| Chiffon | 2 months |

**Poultry, raw**
**Chicken**

| | |
|---|---|
| Cut up | 9 months |
| Livers | 1 month |
| Whole | 12 months |

**Duckling,** whole — 6 months

**Turkey**

| | |
|---|---|
| Cut up | 6 to 9 months |
| Whole | 12 months |

**Poultry, cooked**

| | |
|---|---|
| Casseroles, pies, prepared dinners | 6 months |
| Fried | 4 months |
| Stuffing† | 1 month |
| Without gravy or broth | 1 month |
| Whole, unstuffed† | 6 months |

**Sandwiches**

| | |
|---|---|
| Meat, poultry, cheese, jelly or jam mixtures | 1 to 2 months |

**Soups**

| | |
|---|---|
| Including concentrated and stock | 1 to 3 months |

**Vegetables, blanched**

| | |
|---|---|
| Most | 12 months |

*Do not freeze cakes filled with custard or cream.*
**Processed cheese is identified on the label. If it is not so designated, it is natural cheese.*
†Never freeze home-stuffed poultry, because of the danger of bacterial contamination; freeze meat and stuffing seperately, well wrapped.*
††Do not freeze custard or cream pies, or those with a meringue topping.*

# CHAPTER 1

# Fresh From The Oven

*Fragrant breads, plump muffins, waffles, scones — coming straight from the hearth!*

*Herringbone Coffee Cake (recipe pages 16-17)*

**I**nhale deeply —the aroma of freshly baked bread is one of our favorites, one that conjures up pleasant memories of home. And now, with these recipes, it doesn't have to be just a memory.

Breads fall into two groups: yeast breads and quick breads. Yeast breads take longer because of their rising time, but they do offer therapeutic kneading. And they won't take as long as in Grandma's day: with rapid-rising yeast, rising time is cut in half. Do they taste as good? A slice of our Braided Seed Round *(recipe, page 30)* or Savory Herb Bread *(recipe, page 14)* will answer the question.

Quick breads are a cinch to prepare. Here, the rising power is delegated to leavening agents such as baking powder and baking soda, combined with even heat. And talk about variety! Muffins, tea breads, scones, pancakes and waffles all fall into this category. We're especially fond of Carrot 'n Spice Bread *(recipe, page 35)* and Peach Pecan Muffins *(recipe, page 38)*.

Homemade bread, fresh from the oven, is a wonderful treat for the family, or a great way to remember someone special—for a birthday, anniversary, holiday gift or just a heartfelt "thank you". ∎

# Yeast Breads

◀◀◀

## Monkey Bread

*Perfect picnic fare! Once they're baked, just pull them apart — no knives needed.*

Bake at 350° for 30 to 40 minutes.
Makes one 9-inch bread (48 tiny rolls).

*Nutrient Value Per Serving: 103 calories, 2 g protein, 5 g fat, 12 g carbohydrate, 146 mg sodium, 25 mg cholesterol.*

| | |
|---|---|
| 1 | **cup milk, scalded** |
| 1/3 | **cup sugar** |
| 2 | **teaspoons salt** |
| 1/4 | **cup (1/2 stick) butter or margarine, softened** |
| 2 | **envelopes active dry yeast** |
| 1/4 | **cup warm water (105° to 115°)** |
| 1 | **teaspoon sugar** |
| 2 | **eggs, beaten** |
| 5 | **cups all-purpose flour** |
| 1 | **cup (2 sticks) butter or margarine, melted** |

1. Combine the milk, the 1/3 cup of sugar, the salt and the 1/4 cup of butter or margarine in a large bowl. Stir until the butter melts and the sugar dissolves. Let stand until lukewarm.
2. Meanwhile, sprinkle the yeast over the warm water mixed with the 1 teaspoon of sugar in a 1-cup measure (warm water should feel comfortably warm when dropped on your wrist) and let stand for 5 minutes, or until the yeast dissolves.
3. Add the yeast to the milk mixture; stir with a wooden spoon until well blended. Stir in the eggs, then 3 cups of the flour, beating well. Add enough of the remaining flour to make a soft dough.
4. Turn out the dough onto a lightly floured surface. Knead for 8 to 10 minutes, or until the dough is smooth and elastic. Place the dough in a greased large bowl and turn the greased side up. Cover; let rise in a warm place, away from drafts, for 1 hour, or until doubled in bulk.
5. Punch down the dough, turn out onto a board, cover with a bowl and let rest for 10 minutes.
6. Shape the dough into a long cylinder and cut into 48 equal-size pieces. Shape each piece of dough into a ball and roll the balls in the melted butter or margarine.
7. Place a layer of balls in the bottom of a greased and floured 9-inch round cake pan, leaving space between them. Layer the remaining rolls successively on top.
8. Let rise in a warm place, away from drafts, for 40 minutes, or until the rolls have almost doubled in bulk. Meanwhile, preheat the oven to moderate (350°). Lightly brush the rolls with the remaining melted butter or margarine.
9. Bake in the preheated moderate oven (350°) for 30 to 40 minutes, or until the bread is golden brown. Let cool in the pan on a wire rack for 10 minutes, then gently remove from the pan to the rack.

**Note:** *If the bread cools completely, it may not separate into neat balls.*

## *KNEADING DOUGH CORRECTLY*

  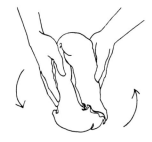

*1.* Turn out the soft dough onto a floured board. Flour your hands lightly and pat the dough to flatten it slightly. Begin to knead: Pick up the edge of the dough with your fingers and fold it over toward you.

*2.* Push the dough away from you with the heels of both hands. If the dough sticks to the board, have a metal spatula handy to scrape the board clean. Re-flour the board and continue.

*3.* Give the dough a quarter turn and repeat folding, pushing, turning. As you knead, you will develop your own speed. You'll find that well-kneaded bread dough is satiny, elastic and smooth.

## *BEAUTIFUL BREAD: SHAPE IT UP*

*1.* To shape a loaf of bread: Pat or roll out the dough into a rectangle with the short side equal to the length of a bread pan. Roll up the dough jelly-roll style, pressing the turns firmly.

  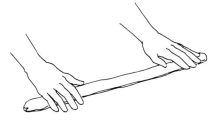

*2.* When the loaf has been shaped, make sure the dough is even on both ends. With your fingers, pinch the long seam firmly to seal it and keep it from unrolling.

*3.* To smooth the ends of the loaf, press the dough down on each end of the loaf with the side of your hand. Tuck the thin strips formed under the loaf. Lift the loaf into the pan, seam side down, without stretching the shape.

*4.* To shape a long loaf of bread: roll up jelly-roll style, pinching the seam, as in Fig. 2. Then, with the palms of your hands, taper the ends by rolling the loaf back and forth on a board.

## Food for Thought . . .

**Oats** *The grain of a grasslike plant in the cereal family, a grain of oats generally is covered with a husk that is removed (although there are some varieties that are hull-less). Oats are used to make rolled oats and oatmeal.*

*To make rolled oats, the grains are cleaned, sorted, dried (to loosen the hulls and develop flavor), hulled and sterilized. The hulled, sterilized grains then are flattened into flakes. To make oatmeal, the hulled grains are cut into coarse to fine textures. The word oatmeal should be used for the ground meal of the grain, but it commonly is used to describe the cooked cereal.*

*Oats are available as rolled (also known as old-fashioned) oats, quick-cooking and instant oatmeal. Scotch oatmeal is made by cutting the oat grains with stone rather than steel rollers, which creates a coarse texture.*

*Oats cannot be used alone in making breads because they contain no gluten; combine them with all-purpose flour for baking.*

*Oats are one of the most nutritious grains, containing some protein, fat and minerals and a high fiber content.*

### AVOID THE DRAFT: RAISING DOUGH RIGHT

*For a warm, draft-free place to let dough rise, use your oven. If the oven is electric, warm to 200°, turn off and let cool for 5 minutes, keeping the oven door closed. If the oven is gas, leave the oven door slightly ajar and the pilot light will keep the dough warm.*

# Savory Herb Bread

Bake at 375° for 45 minutes.
Makes 2 loaves (24 slices).

*Nutrient Value Per Serving: 230 calories, 6 g protein, 7 g fat, 35 g carbohydrate, 302 mg sodium, 28 mg cholesterol.*

- 2 **cups scalded milk**
- ½ **cup plus 1 teaspoon sugar**
- 1 **tablespoon salt**
- ½ **cup shortening**
- 2 **cups quick-cooking oats**
- 2 **eggs, beaten**
- 2 **envelopes active dry yeast**
- ¼ **cup warm water (105° to 115°)**
- 6 **to 6½ cups flour**
- 1 **cup finely chopped onions**
- ½ **cup celery leaves, chopped**
- ½ **cup chopped parsley**
- 2 **tablespoons butter**
- ½ **teaspoon thyme**
- 1 **teaspoon rosemary**

1. Combine the milk, the ½ cup of sugar, the salt and shortening and stir until melted. Add the oats and let stand until cooled. Add the eggs.
2. Soak the yeast in the warm water with the remaining 1 teaspoon of sugar (warm water should feel comfortably warm when dropped on your wrist) and add the milk mixture. Add enough of the flour to make a soft dough. Turn out the dough onto a board and knead until smooth. Place in a greased bowl and turn the greased side up. Cover with a buttered piece of wax paper. Let rise in a warm place, away from drafts, until doubled in bulk, for about 25 minutes.
3. Preheat the oven to moderate (375°).
4. Meanwhile, sauté the onion, celery and parsley in butter until softened. Add the thyme and rosemary. Divide dough into 2 portions; roll out each and spread with half the herb mixture. Roll up jelly-roll style. Place, seam side down, in two greased 9 x 5 x 3-inch loaf pans. Let rise again until doubled, for about 25 minutes.
5. Bake in the preheated moderate oven (375°) for 45 minutes, or until golden brown. Remove from the pans to cool.

# BAKE LIKE A PRO: SECRETS TO PERFECT COFFEE CAKES

### The Right Mix
When making a yeast coffee cake, first make sure the yeast is active *(see tip for testing yeast, page 21)*. Any milk mixture used should be cool to lukewarm, the temperature a low, low 85°. (A candy or water thermometer is a great help until you can judge temperature for yourself.) Baking powder coffee cakes are quick-mix—everything in one bowl.

### Kneading Know-How
Follow the step-by-step instructions found in the chart on page 13. Since part of the kneading in some of our coffee cake recipes is done with an electric mixer, the kneading time is fairly short.

### Rolling Along
Roll out the dough on a lightly floured surface. Make a neat square by rolling out the dough with steady pressure from the center outward, with occasional strokes from the center to the corners. Measure the dough; tug the corners gently to square off. Cover the dough during any pauses—rolling, shaping, rising—to prevent crusting.

### Fill 'Er Up
Dust juicy fillings with fine, dry bread crumbs or cake crumbs. Dab a tiny dot of the filling near the end of the sealed roll for easy identification.

### Rising Right
Keeping the dough warm is essential. Put the bowl of dough on top of (not in) a large pot of hot tap water. Cover with buttered wax paper and a towel; put the bowl and pot in an unheated oven *(see tip, page 14)*. The rising time varies depending on the temperature of the dough at the start of rising: covered, room-temperature dough will take about 45 minutes to double in size; cool rolls will take longer. Coffee cakes that have risen can be safely removed to the countertop while the oven is heating.

### It's Too Darn Hot!
A too-hot oven will overbrown your cake before it is baked; an oven thermometer assures accuracy. Baking powder cakes should go into a preheated oven without delay so the leavening can do its job.

### Baker's Secrets
For a shiny crust, brush the coffee cakes with an Egg Wash *(recipe, page 21)* just before baking. Bake in a preheated moderate oven (350°) for 20 to 25 minutes—two cakes per large baking sheet. Spread the Icing *(recipe, page 21)* on the warm cakes for a smooth glaze, or drizzle the Icing from a spoon onto cool cakes for zigzags or a lace effect. Add trims, such as nuts or glacé cherries before the Icing hardens.

### It's A Wrap
Thoroughly wrap cooled coffee cakes in plastic wrap or aluminum foil—this will keep them fresh for several days at room temperature. Omit icings if you plan to freeze coffee cakes (ice them after reheating). Wrap them tightly in foil, then overwrap in freezer-weight plastic wrap or bags. Store baked coffee cakes in the freezer for up to 3 months. To reheat, remove the plastic and reheat them in their foil wrapping on a baking sheet: 10 to 20 minutes, depending on their size, in a preheated moderate oven (350°).

### Make Now—Bake Later!
If you're making a batch of dough ahead of time, place each filled roll on a large baking sheet, lightly dusted with flour, leaving 2 inches between each. As you finish each roll, cover it loosely with plastic wrap and place it on the baking sheet in the refrigerator. When the batch is filled and rolled, wrap the rolls securely. You can refrigerate unbaked rolls for up to 2 days or freeze them, wrapped airtight and sealed, for up to 2 weeks. Defrost rolls in their wrappings in the refrigerator overnight, or until they are softened enough to shape.

## 4-STEP BASIC COFFEE CAKE

*First, carefully read the basic Sour Cream Sweet Dough recipe (at right), the directions for the 13 variations (pages 17-20), the Filling recipes (pages 20-21) and the Topping and Additions recipes (page 21). Then follow the four steps below:*

*1. Prepare the basic Sour Cream Sweet Dough. Refrigerate the dough for at least 4 hours, or for up to 2 days.*
*2. Prepare any fillings, toppings or additions for your coffee cakes.*
*3. Prepare the 6 filled rolls according to the specific variation directions.*
*4. For immediate use, shape the rolls, let rise, bake in a preheated moderate oven (350°) for 20 to 25 minutes, remove from the baking sheets to wire racks to cool, and decorate with the selected toppings. Or: Refrigerate the unbaked rolls overnight or for up to 2 days, or freeze for up to 2 weeks. Then proceed as for immediate use.*

## THE BASIC ROLL

• *Punch down the risen dough. Turn out onto a lightly floured surface and knead briefly. Divide dough into 6 equal parts. Shape into 4-inch squares. Cover; let rest up to 20 minutes.*
• *Roll out one portion at a time on a lightly floured surface into a 10-inch square. Keep the remaining portions covered and in a cool place.*
• *Spread the selected filling evenly over the dough to within ½ inch of the edges. Sprinkle with one of the additions.*
• *Roll up tightly, jelly-roll style.*
• *Pinch the long seam and ends to seal.*
• *Shape the roll into one of the 13 variations, or hold for baking later.*

## Sour Cream Sweet Dough

Makes enough dough for 6 coffee cakes.

*Nutrient Value For Dough, Per 1 Plain Cake: 772 calories, 17 g protein, 27 g fat, 115 g carbohydrate, 598 mg sodium, 150 mg cholesterol.*

2  envelopes active dry yeast
¾  cup warm water (105° to 115°)
½  cup sugar
½  cup (1 stick) unsalted butter or margarine, melted
1  cup dairy sour cream
2  eggs
1½  teaspoons salt
½  teaspoon ground nutmeg
1  tablespoon grated orange rind (from 1 medium-size orange)
6  cups unsifted all-purpose flour

1. Stir the yeast into the warm water in a small bowl with 1 tablespoon of the sugar until dissolved (warm water should feel comfortably warm when dropped on your wrist). Let stand for 10 minutes.
2. Combine the melted butter or margarine, the sour cream, eggs, salt, nutmeg, orange rind and the remaining sugar in a large bowl with an electric mixer and beat until well mixed. Add 2 cups of the flour and beat until well blended. Add the yeast mixture and 2 more cups of the flour. Beat for 2 minutes at medium speed, scraping down the side of the bowl occasionally. Gradually stir in the remaining 2 cups of flour to make a medium-soft dough. (The dough should be softer than bread dough.)
3. Turn out the dough onto a lightly floured surface. Knead for 5 minutes, or until smooth.
4. Shape the dough into a ball. Place in a lightly oiled large bowl and turn the oiled side up. Cover loosely with plastic wrap. Refrigerate for at least 4 hours, overnight or up to 2 days.

# A BAKER'S DOZEN—FAVORITE COFFEE CAKES

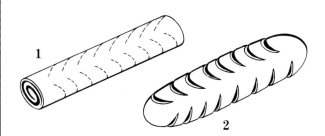

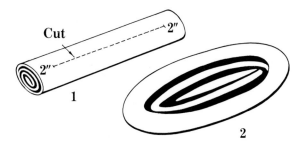

## 1. Herringbone

Gently flatten a filled roll to a 3-inch width. Place the roll on a greased baking sheet. With scissors, make 1-inch diagonal cuts, 1 inch apart, on both sides of the roll (1). Cover and let rise until doubled in volume (2). Brush with the Egg Wash *(recipe, page 21)*. Bake as per Basic Coffee Cake directions. Remove from the baking sheet to a wire rack to cool. Drizzle with the Icing *(recipe, page 21)*. Place pecan halves on top, if you wish.

## 2. Streusel Split Surprise

Flatten a filled roll slightly. Place the roll on a greased baking sheet. With scissors or a pizza cutter, make a deep slit lengthwise down the center, starting and ending 2 inches from each end (1). Cover and let rise until doubled in volume (2). Brush with the Egg Wash *(recipe, page 21)*. Sprinkle with the Streusel topping *(recipe, page 21)*. Bake as per Basic Coffee Cake directions. Remove from the baking sheet to a wire rack to cool. Dust with 10X (confectioners' powdered) sugar or drizzle the top with the Icing *(recipe, page 21)*. Sprinkle with sliced almonds, if you wish.

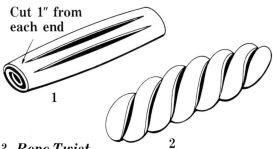

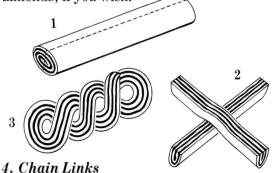

## 3. Rope Twist

Flatten a filled roll slightly. Place the roll on a greased baking sheet. With a sharp knife, make 2 parallel lengthwise slits all the way through the roll, starting and ending 1 inch from each end (1). Twist the roll a few times so that the filling shows (2). Cover and let rise until doubled in volume. Brush with the Egg Wash *(recipe, page 21)*. Bake as per Basic Coffee Cake directions. Remove from the baking sheet to a wire rack to cool. Glaze with the Icing *(recipe, page 21)* while the roll is still warm. Sprinkle with walnuts or sliced almonds, if you wish.

## 4. Chain Links

Flatten a filled roll slightly with a rolling pin and gently stretch the roll to about 15 inches. Cut the roll in half lengthwise (1). With the cut sides facing *up*, cross the 2 parts on a greased baking sheet to form an "X" (2). Loosely entwine the bottom of the "X," then entwine the top, keeping the cut sides up. Pinch the ends together to seal the chain (3). Cover and let rise until doubled in volume. Brush with the Egg Wash *(recipe, page 21)*. Bake as per Basic Coffee Cake directions. Remove from the baking sheet to a wire rack to cool. Glaze with the Icing *(recipe, page 21)* while still warm.

# FAVORITE COFFEE CAKES—CONTINUED

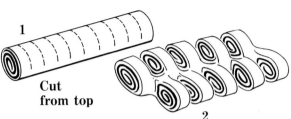

**Cut from top**

**Slightly touching**

**Flatten for totem pole shape**

## 5. Stepping Stones

Flatten a filled roll slightly. Place the roll on a greased baking sheet. With scissors held vertically (points down), make cuts from the top, 1 inch apart, almost going through the roll (1). Draw every other slice to one side, leaving the alternate slice in place; do not turn the slices (2). Cover and let rise until doubled in volume. Brush with the Egg Wash *(recipe, page 21)*. Bake as per Basic Coffee Cake directions. Remove from the baking sheet to a wire rack to cool. Glaze with the Icing *(recipe, page 21)* while still warm. Top each section with a pecan half.

## 6. Totem Pole

Cut a filled roll into 8 to 10 slices (1). Arrange the slices in a diagonal row, *cut side up*, on a greased baking sheet, with the sides barely touching (2). Brush with water between the slices. Lay wax paper on top and flatten the lined-up slices to half their original thickness (3). Cover and let rise until doubled in volume. Brush with the Egg Wash *(recipe, page 21)*. Bake as per Basic Coffee Cake directions. Remove from the baking sheet to a wire rack to cool. Drizzle circles of the Icing *(recipe, page 21)* on the slices to emphasize the shaping. Sprinkle with chopped glacé cherries.

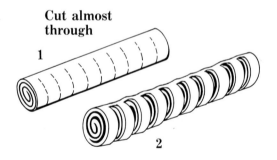

**Cut almost through**

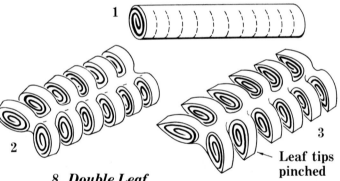

**Leaf tips pinched**

## 7. Single Leaf

Flatten a filled roll slightly. Place the roll on a greased baking sheet. With scissors, make cuts, 1 inch apart, along one side and not quite through to the other side (1). Lift each slice and slant it, *cut side up*, so that the slices overlap evenly and expose some of the filling (2). Keep the uncut side straight with a ruler. Cover and let rise until doubled in volume. Brush with the Egg Wash *(recipe, page 21)*. Bake as per Basic Coffee Cake directions. Remove from the baking sheet to a wire rack to cool. While still warm, outline the outer edge of each slice with the Icing *(recipe, page 21)*. Sprinkle with chopped nuts.

## 8. Double Leaf

Flatten a filled roll slightly. Place the roll on a greased baking sheet. Place a ruler against the roll to keep it straight. With scissors, make 11 cuts not quite through to the other side (1). Twist the slices alternately, *cut side up*, to show the filling—one slice to the left, one slice to the right—down the length of the roll (2). Cover and let rise until doubled in volume. With a moistened finger, pinch each 'leaf' to a point (3). Brush with the Egg Wash *(recipe, page 21)*. Bake as per Basic Coffee Cake directions. Remove from the baking sheet to a wire rack to cool. While still warm, glaze each slice with the Icing *(recipe, page 21)*.

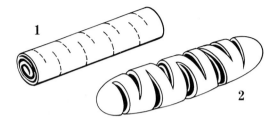

### 9. Fruited Double Leaf

Flatten, shape and let rise as in the Double Leaf *(directions, page 18)*. After 15 minutes' baking time, remove the loaf from the oven. Spoon slightly drained, prepared pie filling down the center *or* place a scant teaspoon of filling on each section (1). Return the loaf to the oven and bake for 10 minutes longer, or until done. Remove from the baking sheet to a wire rack to cool.

### 10. Corkscrew

Flatten a filled roll slightly. Place the roll on a greased baking sheet. With scissors, make cuts three-quarters through to the other side, 1 inch apart, cutting first from one side, then from the other (1). Twist the slices slightly so that the filling shows. Cover and let rise until doubled in volume (2). Brush with the Egg Wash *(recipe, page 21)*. Bake as per Basic Coffee Cake directions. Remove from the baking sheet to a wire rack to cool. While still warm, glaze with the Icing *(recipe, page 21)*.

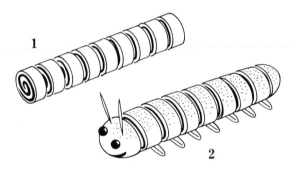

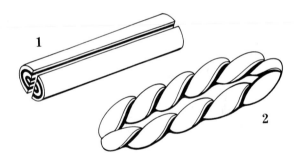

### 11. "Wooly Bug"

Place a filled roll on a greased baking sheet. Cut the roll into 1½-inch sections. Separate the sections, leaving ¼ inch, *not more*, between the pieces (1). Brush with the Egg Wash *(recipe, page 21)*. Insert pecan halves firmly at the bottom of each section on both sides for "feet," but leave the head end plain. Sprinkle with the Streusel topping *(recipe, page 21)*. Insert glacé cherry halves for "eyes" and a strip of cherry for the "mouth" (2). Cover and let rise until doubled in volume. Bake as per Basic Coffee Cake directions. Remove from the baking sheet to a wire rack to cool. Dust with 10X (confectioners' powdered) sugar. Insert 2 brightly colored swizzle sticks, straws or licorice strips for "feelers."

### 12. Twin Twists

Flatten a filled roll slightly. Cut the roll in half lengthwise (1). Twist each half 5 to 6 times, keeping both halves equal in length. Place ¼ inch apart on a greased baking sheet. Pinch the ends together and turn under (2). Cover and let rise until doubled in volume. Brush with the Egg Wash *(recipe, page 21)*. Bake as per Basic Coffee Cake directions. Remove from the baking sheet to a wire rack to cool. While still warm, glaze with the Icing *(recipe, page 21)*. Sprinkle with chopped nuts.

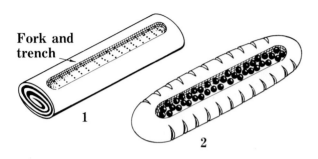

Fork and trench

1

2

### 13. Fancy Fruit Strip

Flatten a filled roll to a 3-inch width. Place on a greased baking sheet. Cover and let rise until doubled in volume. Brush with the Egg Wash *(recipe, page 21)*. With a fork, punch holes down the center, starting and ending 1 inch from each end. With a floured finger, press a deep trench about ¾ inch wide down the center of the roll (1). Spoon in drained, prepared pie filling. With scissors, cut ½-inch snips all around the sides (2). Bake as per Basic Coffee Cake directions. Remove from the baking sheet to a wire rack to cool. Fill in the trench with extra pie filling, if necessary.

# FABULOUS FILLINGS

## 1. Apricot Pecan Filling

*Nutrient Value Per Cake: 376 calories, 2 g protein, 10 g fat, 75 g carbohydrate, 3 mg sodium, 0 mg cholesterol.*

Combine 1 cup of apricot butter, ¼ cup of chopped pecans and 1 teaspoon of Cinnamon Sugar *(recipe, page 21)*. Fold in ½ cup of chopped, peeled apple.
*Makes enough to fill 2 coffee cakes.*

## 2. Apple Butter Filling

*Nutrient Value Per Cake: 360 calories, 2 g protein, 7 g fat, 78 g carbohydrate, 38 mg sodium, 9 mg cholesterol.*

Combine 1 cup of apple butter, ¼ cup of Streusel topping *(recipe, page 21)* and ¼ teaspoon of ground allspice.
*Makes enough to fill 2 coffee cakes.*

## 3. Cheese Filling

*Nutrient Value Per Cake: 304 calories, 17 g protein, 14 g fat, 36 g carbohydrate, 88 mg sodium, 20 mg cholesterol.*

Mix together a 7½-ounce package of farmer cheese, ¼ cup of sugar, ½ teaspoon of grated lemon rind, 1 teaspoon of lemon juice and 1 egg yolk in the container of an electric blender or a food processor. Then whirl until well combined. Stir in 2 tablespoons of dried currants.
*Makes enough to fill 2 coffee cakes.*

## 4. Walnut Filling

*Nutrient Value Per Cake: 992 calories, 19 g protein, 81 g fat, 63 g carbohydrate, 88 mg sodium, 20 mg cholesterol.*

Mix together 2 cups of ground walnuts, ¼ cup of sugar, ¼ cup of golden raisins, 1 tablespoon of dark rum and ¼ teaspoon of ground cinnamon in a small bowl until well blended. Heat ¼ cup of milk and 1 tablespoon of butter just to the boiling point and stir into the nut mixture.
*Makes enough to fill 2 coffee cakes.*

## 5. Almond Filling

*Nutrient Value Per Cake: 496 calories, 16 g protein, 37 g fat, 32 g carbohydrate, 42 mg sodium, 137 mg cholesterol.*

Whirl 1 cup of whole blanched almonds in the container of an electric blender or a food processor until very finely chopped. Add 3 tablespoons of sugar, 1 egg and ¼ teaspoon of almond extract.
*Makes enough to fill 2 coffee cakes.*

## 6. Raisin Nut Filling

*Nutrient Value Per Cake: 637 calories, 6 g protein, 42 g fat, 69 g carbohydrate, 243 mg sodium, 62 mg cholesterol.*

Spread a rolled square of dough with 2 tablespoons of melted butter. Combine ⅓ cup of raisins, ¼ cup of chopped nuts and 2 tablespoons of Cinnamon Sugar *(recipe, below right)* in a small bowl. Sprinkle the mixture over the dough.
*Makes enough to fill 1 coffee cake.*

**Note:** *Prepared pastry fillings are available in many supermarkets in flavors such as poppyseed, prune, almond and cherry.*

---

### YEAST: THE FRESH TEST

*All packages of yeast are dated. To insure the best final product, use the envelope before the expiration date. As a double check to be sure the yeast is alive and well, mix it with a bit of sugar while it is dissolving in warm water (105° to 115°). A fresh envelope of yeast will bubble nicely within 10 minutes. If not, start over with another envelope; you'll avoid wasting any of the other ingredients—or your time.*

# TO TOP IT OFF

## 1. Streusel

*Nutrient Value Per ¼ Cup: 195 calories, 2 g protein, 11 g fat, 24 g carbohydrate, 70 mg sodium, 18 mg cholesterol.*

Combine ⅔ cup of sugar, ⅔ cup of flour, ⅓ cup of butter (cut up) and 2 teaspoons of ground cinnamon in the container of an electric blender or a food processor and whirl until crumbly. Add ½ cup of walnuts and whirl until the walnuts are finely chopped. Streusel freezes well.
*Makes about 2¼ cups.*

## 2. Egg Wash

*Nutrient Value Per ¼ Cup: 79 calories, 6 g protein, 6 g fat, 60 g carbohydrate, 69 mg sodium, 274 mg cholesterol.*

Stir together 1 egg and 1 tablespoon of water in a small cup until well blended.
*Makes about ¼ cup.*

## 3. Icing

*Nutrient Value Per Cup: 976 calories, 1 g protein, 5 g fat, 240 g carbohydrate, 17 mg sodium, 26 mg cholesterol.*

Combine 2 cups of 10X (confectioners' powdered) sugar, 2 tablespoons of warm milk or water, 1 teaspoon of vegetable oil and ¼ teaspoon of vanilla in a small bowl. Stir until smooth; add a little more liquid, if necessary. Cover with damp paper toweling while working to keep the icing from drying out. Store covered. Warm the icing over hot tap water.
*Makes about 1 cup.*

## 4. Cinnamon Sugar

*Nutrient Value Per Teaspoon: 16 calories, 0 g protein, 0 g fat, 4 g carbohydrate, 0 mg sodium, 0 mg cholesterol.*

Mix together 1 cup of sugar and 1½ teaspoons of ground cinnamon in a small bowl until well blended.
*Makes 1 cup.*

## 5. Additions
Chopped nuts (except peanuts), grated orange, lemon or lime rind, glacé cherries, raisins or currants, coconut.

◀ ☍ $

# Cinnamon Bunny Bread

Bake large bunnies at 350° for 20 minutes, small bunnies for 15 minutes.
Makes 6 large bunnies (4 servings each), or 12 small bunnies (2 servings each).

*Nutrient Value Per Serving: 212 calories, 5 g protein, 6 g fat, 35 g carbohydrate, 115 mg sodium, 69 mg cholesterol.*

1  **cup milk**
½  **cup (1 stick) unsalted butter, sliced**
½  **cup warm water (105° to 115°)**
¾  **cup sugar**
2  **envelopes (¼ ounce each) active dry yeast**
5  **to 6 cups unsifted all-purpose flour**
1  **tablespoon ground cinnamon**
1  **teaspoon salt**
5  **eggs, at room temperature**
1  **tablespoon cold water**
    **Decorator Frosting (recipe, page 23)**
    **Small round candies or jelly beans**

1. Combine the milk and the butter in a small saucepan. Place over low heat until the butter melts. Remove from the heat and cool to lukewarm (110°).
2. Stir together the warm water and 1 tablespoon of the sugar in a small bowl (warm water should feel comfortably warm when dropped on your wrist). Sprinkle the yeast over the water and let soften for 1 minute. Stir to dissolve. Let stand until foamy, for about 5 minutes.
3. Combine 4 cups of the flour with the remaining sugar, the cinnamon and salt in a large bowl. Add 4 of the eggs, the yeast mixture and warm milk mixture. Stir with a wooden spoon until blended. Stir in enough of the remaining flour to make a soft but not sticky dough.
4. Knead the dough on a lightly floured surface or in a bowl using the dough hook of an electric mixer until smooth and elastic, for 8 to 10 minutes. Place the dough in a lightly oiled bowl and turn the oiled side up. Cover and let rise in a warm place, away from drafts, until

doubled in bulk, for 1 to 1½ hours.
5. Punch the dough down. Knead briefly. Cover and let rest for 10 minutes. Grease 2 large baking sheets.
6. **For Large Bunnies:** Cut the dough into 6 equal parts. Use one part for each bunny. If the kitchen is warm, keep the unused dough, covered, in the refrigerator.
7. Using one piece of dough, pinch off about ½ cup for the body and roll into a ball, slightly elongating it into the shape of an egg. Place on a baking sheet. Pinch off about ¼ cup from the remaining dough for the head and roll into a smooth ball, making it elongated and pointed at one end. Dip the point into water (have some handy in a small bowl) and tuck the point under the ball on the baking sheet. Pinch off a tiny piece for the nose. Roll into a ball, dip the bottom into the water and place in the center of the face.
8. Divide the remaining dough into 6 equal pieces. Roll 4 pieces into balls for paws, making them slightly pointed and elongated at one end. Dip the point of each into the water and tuck under the body in four places to make the paws. Roll the remaining 2 pieces into logs for ears, making a point at one end and flattening the other end of each log. Dip the flattened end of each into the water and tuck under the head for ears.
9. Repeat with the remaining 5 pieces of dough for 5 more bunnies, placing on the baking sheets with about 3 inches between each bunny bread. Cover with plastic wrap and let rise in a warm place, away from drafts, until doubled in bulk, for 30 minutes to 1 hour.
10. Position an oven rack in the center of the oven. Preheat the oven to moderate (350°).
11. Whisk together the remaining egg and the cold water in a small bowl to make a glaze. Uncover the bunny breads and brush with the egg glaze. Brush each a second time.
12. Bake in the preheated moderate oven (350°) for 20 minutes, or until the breads

are golden and sound hollow when tapped with your fingertips. Remove the breads from the baking sheets to wire racks. Let cool completely before decorating.

13. **For Small Bunnies:** Divide the dough into 12 equal parts. Assemble as directed for large bunnies in Steps 6, 7, and 8, but use half the amounts for each part. Brush with the glaze as directed for large bunnies in Step 11.
14. Bake in the preheated moderate oven (350°) for 15 minutes, or until the breads are golden and sound hollow when tapped with your fingertips. Remove from the baking sheets to wire racks. Let cool completely before decorating.
15. Prepare the Decorator Frosting.
16. **To Decorate:** Place the Decorator Frosting in a pastry bag fitted with a medium writing tip. Squeeze out "beads" on each face for eyes and top with jelly beans or candies. Squeeze out 3 fine lines radiating from each side of the nose for whiskers. Draw on a mouth. To decorate the bodies, space polka dots of frosting evenly all over and attach tiny candies for dots. Or make rows of buttons down the center fronts. Let the decorations air-dry for 30 minutes to 1 hour to harden the frosting.

**Decorator Frosting:** Combine 1 egg white and ⅛ teaspoon of cream of tartar in a small bowl. Beat with an electric mixer until frothy. Add 1½ cups of sifted 10X (confectioners' powdered) sugar and beat until fluffy and stiff, for about 5 minutes. If the frosting is too stiff, add a few drops of water and beat until it reaches the proper consistency. Keep covered with a damp cloth at all times or the frosting will harden.

## BAKE LIKE A PRO: THE BEST BREAD

- *Use the specified pan size called for in the recipe. A pan that is too large will yield a flat bread. Too small a pan will cause the dough to overflow.*
- *The material the pan is made of can affect the baking time. Uncoated metal pans need longer baking. Glass and enamel pans need a lower oven temperature: Reduce the oven temperature called for in the recipe by 25 degrees.*
- *Bake breads in a preheated oven. The final rising of the dough takes place during the first 10 to 15 minutes of baking time.*
- *When baking two loaves, place them on the center rack in the oven; for four loaves, use two racks, placed in the bottom and next to highest positions.*
- *For a shiny crust on a loaf of yeast bread, brush it with an egg beaten with a little water. For a soft crust, rub it with softened butter or margarine just after the bread is removed from the pan to cool.*
- *Breads should be checked for doneness near the end of the suggested baking time.*
- *Breads are done when nicely browned and hollow sounding when tapped lightly on top with your fingertips. Remove loaves from the pans so they do not become soggy. Cool completely on wire racks.*

## WHOLESOME WHOLE WHEAT

*Whole wheat flour is a coarse-textured flour ground from the entire kernel. This flour has a small amount of gluten, so baked products tend to be heavier and denser than those made with all-purpose flour. For better baking results, combine whole wheat with white flour. Whole wheat flour is rich in B-complex vitamins, vitamin E, fat, protein and some minerals. It is more susceptible to spoilage than other flours because of the fat in the wheat germ.*

## HOLD THAT DOUGH!

*If you're interrupted while making a yeast bread, don't worry. Here's where and how to stop without damaging the bread: If you've just prepared the dough, cover the bowl very securely with plastic wrap and refrigerate it without punching it down. The dough will stay perfectly fresh for up to 18 hours. If the dough has already risen and you have to leave it before it's formed, punch it down, cover securely and refrigerate.*

## Whole Wheat Batter Bread

Bake at 375° for 50 minutes.
Makes 1 loaf (16 slices).

*Nutrient Value Per Slice: 163 calories, 5 g protein, 5 g fat, 26 g carbohydrate, 163 mg sodium, 5 mg cholesterol.*

| | |
|---|---|
| 2 | **envelopes active dry yeast** |
| 1/3 | **cup nonfat dry milk powder** |
| 1/3 | **cup firmly packed light brown sugar** |
| 1 | **teaspoon salt** |
| 1/4 | **cup vegetable oil** |
| 2 | **cups very warm milk** |
| 2 | **cups sifted all-purpose flour** |
| 1½ | **cups unsifted whole wheat flour** |

1. Grease a 10-cup Kugelhopf mold or 9-inch angel-cake tube pan.
2. Combine the yeast, milk powder, brown sugar, salt and oil in a large bowl. Stir in the very warm milk (very warm milk should feel comfortably warm when dropped on your wrist). Beat the mixture until well blended, for about 30 seconds.
3. Mix together the all-purpose and whole wheat flours in a medium-size bowl. Stir 1½ cups of the flour mixture into the yeast mixture. Beat with an electric mixer at medium speed for 2 minutes. Stir in another ½ cup of the flour mixture and beat for 1 minute. Stir in the remaining flour until well mixed; the dough will be heavy and sticky.
4. Turn the dough into the prepared pan. Cover with a buttered piece of wax paper and a towel. Let rise in a warm place, away from drafts, until doubled in bulk, for about 20 minutes. Preheat the oven to moderate (375°).
5. Bake in the preheated moderate oven (375°) for 50 minutes, or until the loaf sounds hollow when tapped on the bottom. Remove the bread from the pan and cool on a wire rack.

# Whole Wheat Barley Bread

*An extremely soft bread that holds up well in sandwiches.*

Bake at 325° for 1¼ hours.
Makes 2 loaves (24 slices).

*Nutrient Value Per Slice: 185 calories, 6 g protein, 2 g fat, 38 g carbohydrate, 104 mg sodium, 3 mg cholesterol.*

| | |
|---|---|
| ⅓ | **cup barley** |
| 4 | **cups water** |
| 2 | **envelopes active dry yeast** |
| ⅓ | **cup firmly packed light brown sugar** |
| ¼ | **cup warm water (105° to 115°)** |
| 2 | **tablespoons butter or margarine** |
| 1 | **teaspoon salt** |
| 3 | **cups unsifted whole wheat flour** |
| 5 | **to 6 cups unsifted all-purpose flour** |

1. Rinse the barley in a coarse strainer under cold running water, turn into a large saucepan and cover with the 4 cups of water. Cover the saucepan with a lid or plastic wrap. Let stand overnight at room temperature.
2. Next day, bring the barley and the soaking liquid to boiling. Lower the heat and simmer for 45 minutes, or until the barley is tender. Reserve 2 cups of the barley water; drain and discard the remaining water.
3. Place the barley in the container of an electric blender. Cover, whirl until smooth and reserve.
4. Sprinkle the yeast and 1 teaspoon of the brown sugar over the ¼ cup of warm water in a 1-cup glass measure (warm water should feel comfortably warm when dropped on your wrist). Stir to dissolve the yeast. Let stand until bubbly, for about 10 minutes.
5. Heat the reserved barley water, the butter or margarine, the remaining brown sugar and the salt in a medium-size saucepan until the butter melts. Pour into a large bowl, add the reserved puréed barley and cool to lukewarm. Stir in the yeast mixture.
6. Stir in the whole wheat flour until smooth. Beat in enough of the all-purpose flour to make a soft dough.
7. Turn out the dough onto a lightly floured surface. Knead until smooth and elastic, for about 10 minutes, adding only as much of the remaining all-purpose flour as is needed to keep the dough from sticking.
8. Place in a buttered large bowl and turn the buttered side up. Cover with a damp towel. Let rise in a warm place, away from drafts, for 1 hour, or until doubled in bulk.
9. Punch the dough down, turn out onto a lightly floured surface and knead a few times. Invert a bowl over the dough and let rest for 10 minutes.
10. Grease two 9 x 5 x 3-inch loaf pans. Divide the dough in half and knead each half a few times. Shape into two loaves. Place the loaves in the prepared pans. Cover with a damp towel.
11. Let rise again in a warm place, away from drafts, for 45 minutes, or until doubled in bulk.
12. Place a rack in the lowest position in the oven. Preheat the oven to slow (325°).
13. Bake in the preheated slow oven (325°) for 1¼ hours, or until the loaves are golden brown and sound hollow when tapped on the bottom. Cover the loaves loosely with aluminum foil after 30 minutes of baking to prevent over-browning. Remove from the pans to wire racks to cool completely.

## TO SIFT OR NOT TO SIFT?

*Most commercial brands of flour come already sifted from the manufacturer, making additional sifting unnecessary in most cases. Some of our recipes indicate additional sifting in order to produce a lighter product. Do **not** sift unless it is called for in the recipe.*

# Parmesan Skillet Bread

*This bread is excellent at room temperature or when reheated in a 350° oven for 5 to 10 minutes.*

Bake at 375° for 25 minutes for two 9-inch breads, 35 minutes for one 10-inch bread. Makes two 9-inch or one 10-inch round bread (12 servings).

*Nutrient Value Per Serving: 224 calories, 7 g protein, 5 g fat, 37 g carbohydrate, 116 mg sodium, 9 mg cholesterol.*

| | |
|---|---|
| 2 | *tablespoons sugar* |
| 2 | *envelopes active dry yeast* |
| 2 | *cups warm water (105° to 115°)* |
| 2 | *tablespoons butter or margarine, softened* |
| ½ | *cup plus 2 tablepoons freshly grated Parmesan cheese* |
| 1 | *tablespoon leaf basil, crumbled* |
| ½ | *teaspoon leaf oregano, crumbled* |
| 1 | *clove garlic, finely chopped* |
| 1 | *teaspoon salt* |
| ¼ | *teaspoon pepper* |
| 4¼ | *cups* **unsifted** *all-purpose flour* |
| 1 | *tablespoon olive oil* |

1. Sprinkle the sugar and the yeast over the warm water in a large bowl (warm water should feel comfortably warm when dropped on your wrist). Stir to dissolve the yeast. Let stand until bubbly, for about 10 minutes.
2. Add the butter or margarine, the ½ cup of Parmesan cheese, the basil, oregano, garlic, salt, pepper and 3 cups of the flour. Beat with an electric mixer at low speed for 2 minutes, scraping down the side of the bowl occasionally. Gradually beat in the remaining 1¼ cups of flour with a wooden spoon until well blended. Cover with a buttered piece of wax paper. Let rise in a warm place, away from drafts, until doubled in bulk, for about 45 minutes.
3. About 10 minutes before the end of the rising time, preheat the oven to moderate (375°). Place two 9-inch or one 10-inch well-seasoned cast-iron skillet(s) in the oven to heat for 10 minutes. Using a pot holder, remove the skillet(s) from the oven. Lightly grease each with ½ tablespoon of the olive oil.
4. Stir down the batter and beat vigorously for 30 seconds. Divide the batter equally between the two 9-inch skillets or place in the one 10-inch; spread the batter evenly over the entire bottom(s). Sprinkle the top of each 9-inch with 1 tablespoon of the remaining Parmesan cheese, or sprinkle the 10-inch with 2 tablespoons.
5. Bake in the preheated moderate oven (375°) for about 25 minutes for the 9-inch or 35 minutes for the 10-inch, or until the bread is golden brown and sounds hollow when tapped with your fingertips. Remove the bread from the skillet(s) to a wire rack to cool. Serve warm or at room temperature.

---

## SEPARATE AND NOT EQUAL!

*Do not substitute vegetable shortening or diet margarine for butter or margarine, unless called for in the recipe—shortening will change the flavor, and diet margarine will alter the baking process.*

---

# Onion Batter Bread

Bake at 375° for 35 to 40 minutes. Makes 1 large loaf (20 slices).

*Nutrient Value Per Slice: 155 calories, 4 g protein, 3 g fat, 26 g carbohydrate, 146 mg sodium, 22 mg cholesterol.*

| | |
|---|---|
| 1 | *cup chopped onion (1 large onion)* |
| ¼ | *cup (½ stick) butter or margarine* |
| 2 | *envelopes active dry yeast* |
| 4 | *tablespoons light brown sugar* |
| ½ | *cup warm water (105° to 115°)* |
| 1½ | *cups milk* |
| 1 | *teaspoon salt* |
| 1 | *egg, slightly beaten* |
| 5 | *cups sifted all-purpose flour* |
| | *Melted butter* |

1. Grease a 2-quart soufflé dish or glass casserole.
2. Sauté the onion in the butter or margarine in a medium-size skillet, stirring often, until lightly browned. Reserve.
3. Sprinkle the yeast and 2 tablespoons of the brown sugar over the warm water in a 2-cup glass measure (warm water should feel comfortably warm when dropped on your wrist). Stir to dissolve the yeast. Let stand until bubbly, for about 10 minutes.
4. Heat the milk in a small saucepan until bubbles appear around the edge. Combine the milk, salt and the remaining 2 tablespoons of brown sugar in a large bowl. Cool to room temperature.
5. Add the yeast mixture, the reserved onion, the egg and flour to the milk mixture in the bowl. Mix with an electric mixer at low speed until blended; beat at medium speed for 3 minutes longer. Spread the batter in the prepared dish. Cover with a buttered piece of wax paper and a towel. Let rise in a warm place, away from drafts, until doubled in bulk, for about 45 minutes. Preheat the oven to moderate (375°).
6. Bake in the preheated moderate oven (375°) for 35 to 40 minutes, or until the loaf sounds hollow when tapped on the bottom. Remove the loaf from the dish to a wire rack. Brush the top with the melted butter. Serve warm.

## THE FLOUR STORE

*Regular all-purpose flour can be stored in an airtight container at room temperature. Whole wheat flour and rye flour should be stored in the freezer, in airtight freezer bags or containers, if they will not be used right away.*

## Food for Thought . . .

**Cornmeal** *This dried white or yellow corn is coarsely ground between steel rollers. The process uses hulled corn with the germ removed, which enables the corn to withstand the high temperatures of the process. Cornmeal produced by this method keeps well; since the fat-containing germ is not ground in, the cornmeal does not become rancid. Popular opinion holds stone-ground cornmeal, which uses the entire kernel, to be more flavorful and nutritious.*

## Down Home Cornbread

Bake at 350° for 35 minutes.
Makes 1 loaf (12 slices).

*Nutrient Value Per Slice: 162 calories, 4 g protein, 5 g fat, 24 g carbohydrate, 244 mg sodium, 46 mg cholesterol.*

½ **cup water**
3 **tablespoons sugar**
1 **teaspoon salt**
¼ **cup (½ stick) margarine, at room temperature**
1 **envelope active dry yeast**
½ **teaspoon sugar**
¼ **cup warm water (105° to 115°)**
1¾ **cups unsifted all-purpose flour**
¾ **cup yellow cornmeal**
2 **tablespoons nonfat dry milk powder**
2 **eggs, slightly beaten**

1. Grease an 8½ x 4¼ x 2½-inch glass or ceramic loaf pan.
2. Combine the ½ cup of water, the 3 tablespoons of sugar, the salt and margarine in a small saucepan. Heat over low heat, stirring, just until the margarine is melted. Cool to lukewarm.
3. Sprinkle the yeast and the ½ teaspoon of sugar over the warm water in a 1-cup

---

glass measure (warm water should feel comfortably warm when dropped on your wrist). Stir to dissolve the yeast. Let stand until bubbly, for about 10 minutes.

4. Stir together the flour, cornmeal and milk powder in a large bowl. Add the eggs, margarine mixture and yeast mixture; beat until well blended. Turn the batter into the prepared pan. Cover with a buttered piece of wax paper and a towel. Let rise in a warm place, away from drafts, until doubled in bulk, for about 1 hour. Preheat the oven to moderate (350°).

5. Bake in the preheated moderate oven (350°) for 35 minutes, or until the loaf is browned on top. Remove the bread from the pan to a wire rack to cool. Serve warm or at room temperature.

---

### Food for Thought . . .

**Caraway** This fragrant herb, native to southeastern Europe and western Asia, has been used for thousands of years. Caraway is a biennial plant and a relative of the carrot. It has an edible fleshy yellowish-white root and small white flowers. After flowering, seeds develop. Only the seeds are commercially available.

Caraway seeds are widely used in breads, rolls and biscuits, and provide the flavoring for the liqueur kummel. Use caraway in coleslaw, sauerkraut, potato salads, noodles or soups.

## Caraway Rye Round

*We've eliminated the hard work, kneading, by preparing the dough in a food processor.*

Bake at 350° for 30 minutes.
Makes 1 round loaf (12 slices).

---

*Nutrient Value Per Slice: 127 calories, 3 g protein, 3 g fat, 23 g carbohydrate, 140 mg sodium, 0 mg cholesterol.*

---

2 **cups unsifted all-purpose flour**
⅔ **cup unsifted rye flour**
2 **tablespoons dark brown sugar**
2 **tablespoons vegetable oil**
1 **teaspoon caraway seeds**
¾ **teaspoon salt**
1 **envelope active dry yeast**
1 **cup beer**

1. Process 1 cup of the all-purpose flour, the rye flour, brown sugar, oil, caraway seeds, salt and yeast in a food processor until mixed, for 5 seconds.
2. Heat the beer in a small saucepan until very warm (120° to 130°). With the processor running, add the beer all at once through the feed tube. Process until blended, for 30 seconds.
3. With the processor on, add the remaining cup of all-purpose flour, ¼ cup at a time, through the feed tube. Process for 5 to 10 seconds after each addition.
4. Pour the batter into a greased 1½-quart round casserole and smooth the top. Brush with additional oil. Cover and let rise in a warm place, away from drafts, until almost doubled in bulk, for about 45 minutes. Preheat the oven to moderate (350°).
5. Bake in the preheated moderate oven (350°) for 30 minutes, or until a wooden pick inserted in the center comes out clean.
6. Let the bread stand in the casserole on a wire rack for 10 minutes. Remove the bread from the casserole to the rack and cool to room temperature.

*Caraway Rye Round*

## Food for Thought . . .

**Rye Flour** *This flour is milled from the entire rye kernel. It is available in three grades: white, medium and dark. Rye flour produces gluten of low elasticity. Therefore, it should be combined with white flour in bread recipes to produce a better loaf.*

## QUICK-START YEAST

*Yearn for the flavor of old-fashioned yeast breads but can't spare the time? Substituting fast-rising dry yeast will reduce dough rising time by at least one third and as much as one half. Follow the list of suggestions below when using fast-rising yeast.*
- *Always include water in the ingredients. If the recipe calls for milk or a liquid other than water, decrease the amount of liquid by ¼ cup per envelope of fast-rising yeast used and substitute an equal amount of water.*
- *Combine the yeast with about two thirds of the flour (instead of one third as with regular active dry yeast) and the other dry ingredients in a large bowl; there's no need to dissolve the yeast in liquids first.*
- *Heat the liquids and the solid or liquid fats, but not the eggs, in a saucepan until comfortably hot to the touch, 130°. This is hotter than the 105° to 115° usually required if yeast is being dissolved directly in a liquid.*
- *Stir the hot liquids into the dry ingredients. Add the eggs, if using. Blend at low speed with an electric mixer, then beat at medium speed for 3 minutes. Stir in enough of the remaining flour to make a soft dough.*
- *Follow the recipe directions for kneading and rising. Start checking the dough halfway through the suggested rising time if you're using a recipe that calls for regular yeast.*

## THE BRAIDING GAME

*When braiding a bread, begin braiding in the middle—it makes for a more attractive loaf or round.*

## Braided Seed Rounds

Bake at 350° for 20 to 25 minutes.
Makes 2 loaves or rounds (12 slices per round).

*Nutrient Value Per Slice: 182 calories, 4 g protein, 2 g fat, 36 g carbohydrate, 106 mg sodium, 3 mg cholesterol.*

**7   cups sifted all-purpose flour**
**2   tablespoons sugar**
**1   teaspoon salt**
**2   envelopes fast-rising dry yeast**
**2   cups hot water (125° to 130°)**
**2   tablespoons butter, softened**
**2   tablespoons poppy seeds**
**2   tablespoons sesame seeds**
**2   tablespoons wheat germ**
**1   egg white**
**1   teaspoon water**

1. Reserve ½ cup of the flour. Combine the remaining 6½ cups of flour, the sugar, salt and yeast in a bowl. Stir in the hot water and the butter (hot water should feel comfortably hot to the touch). Beat until smooth. Gradually stir in enough of the reserved flour to make a soft dough.
2. Knead the dough on a floured surface until smooth and elastic, for 3 to 5 minutes. Invert a bowl over the dough and let rise for 15 minutes.
3. Grease and flour two 9-inch round layer-cake pans.
4. Divide the dough in half. Set half aside, under the bowl. Divide the remaining dough into 3 equal pieces. Roll each piece into a 16-inch-long rope.
5. Cut 3 pieces of wax paper, each 18 inches long. Spread the poppy seeds on one, the sesame seeds on another, the wheat germ on the third. Beat the egg white with the 1 teaspoon of water in a bowl.
6. Brush one rope with the egg wash and roll in the poppy seeds. Brush another rope with the wash and roll in the sesame seeds. Brush the third with the wash and roll in the wheat germ. Set aside the remaining seeds and wheat germ.

7. Lay the ropes, side by side, on a flat surface. Braid together gently, trying not to shake off the seeds. Coil the braid into one of the prepared pans. Spoon any excess seeds and wheat germ into the seedless areas on the braid. Cover loosely and refrigerate overnight. Repeat with the remaining dough.
8. Preheat the oven to moderate (350°).
9. Bake the bread in the preheated moderate oven (350°) for 20 to 25 minutes, or until firm to the touch and golden brown. Cool the bread in the pans on a wire rack for 10 minutes, then remove from the pans to cool completely.

# Whole Wheat Burger Buns

Bake at 350° for 20 to 25 minutes.
Makes 12 buns.

*Nutrient Value Per Bun: 335 calories, 9 g protein, 8 g fat, 58 g carbohydrate, 842 mg sodium, 17 mg cholesterol.*

| | |
|---|---|
| 4 | **cups unsifted unbleached flour** |
| 2½ | **cups whole wheat flour** |
| ⅓ | **cup nonfat dry milk powder** |
| 2 | **teaspoons salt** |
| 2 | **envelopes fast-rising dry yeast** |
| 1¼ | **cups water** |
| ⅔ | **cup Dijon-style mustard** |
| ⅓ | **cup butter or margarine** |
| ¼ | **cup honey** |
| 1 | **tablespoon butter or margarine, melted** |

1. Reserve 1 cup of the unbleached flour. Mix together the remaining 3 cups of unbleached flour, the whole wheat flour, milk powder, salt and yeast in a large bowl.
2. Combine the water, mustard, the ⅓ cup of butter or margarine and the honey in a medium-size saucepan. Heat to 130° (the mixture should feel comfortably hot to the touch). Mix into the dry ingredients. Stir in enough of the reserved unbleached flour to make a fairly stiff dough.

---

## Food for Thought . . .

**Mustard** *Prepared mustard, dry mustard, mustard seeds and mustard greens are all products derived from varieties of the mustard plant — a pungent herb belonging to the vast Brassica or cabbage family.*

*Prepared mustard, which can be hot or mild, spicy or sweet, is made by grinding mustard seeds and adding vinegar, water and seasoning. Dry mustard is blended from a variety of mustard seeds and can also be hot or mild. The blending of the seeds allows the mustard to achieve its full flavor.*

*In making prepared or dry mustard, the degree of hotness comes from the varieties of mustard seed used as well as the portion of the seed used. The two varieties of mustard seed commonly used are the black and the white or yellow mustard seed. The layer under the skin or hull of a mustard seed is hotter than the center of the seed.*

*Black mustard seed is yellowish-brown in color and has a very pungent flavor. White or yellow mustard seed is pale yellow with a less pungent taste than the black variety. Mustard seeds are used primarily when making pickles at home.*

---

3. Turn out the dough onto a lightly floured surface. Knead until smooth and elastic, 8 to 10 minutes. Cover; let rest 10 minutes.
4. Divide dough into 12 pieces and form each into a smooth ball. Place 2 inches apart on greased baking sheets; flatten slightly. Cover; let rise in a warm, draft-free place, until doubled, 35 to 45 minutes.
5. Meanwhile, preheat oven to 350°.
6. Brush tops of rolls with melted butter.
7. Bake in the oven (350°) for 20 to 25 minutes, or until buns are browned and sound hollow when tapped with your fingertips. Cool on wire racks.

# Quick Breads

## Food for Thought . . .

**Scone** *A traditionally triangular or diamond-shaped, biscuit-like tea cake of Scottish origin. Pronounced SKAHN, it is baked on a griddle or in a hot oven.*

## Currant Scones

*For a bit of Old English hospitality, try an afternoon tea party. Add a touch of elegance with our delicious scones, topped with raspberry jam and clotted cream.*

Bake at 425° for 10 to 15 minutes.
Makes 10 scones.

*Nutrient Value Per Scone: 183 calories, 4 g protein, 7 g fat, 26 g carbohydrate, 256 mg sodium, 56 mg cholesterol.*

| | |
|---|---|
| 2 | **eggs** |
| 1/3 | **cup milk** |
| 2 | **cups unsifted all-purpose flour** |
| 1 | **tablespoon sugar** |
| 1 | **tablespoon baking powder** |
| 1/2 | **teaspoon salt** |
| 1/4 | **cup vegetable shortening** |
| 1/2 | **cup currants** |
| | **Raspberry jam** |
| | **Clotted cream** |

1. Grease 2 baking sheets. Preheat the oven to hot (425°).
2. Beat together the eggs and the milk in a 1-cup glass measure until well blended. Transfer 2 tablespoons of the egg mixture to a small cup and reserve to use as a glaze just before baking.
3. Stir together the flour, sugar, baking powder and salt in a large bowl. Cut in the shortening with a pastry blender until the mixture is crumbly. Sprinkle in the flour mixture along with the currants. Pour in the egg and milk mixture. Stir with a fork until the dough is soft enough to gather into a ball but not stick to your fingers. Add several additional tablespoons of milk if the dough is too dry. Try not to overhandle the dough.
4. Divide the dough in half. Roll out half the dough on a lightly floured surface to a ½-inch thickness. With a 3-inch round cookie cutter, cut out as many scones as you can. Carefully transfer to the prepared baking sheets using a metal spatula. Space the scones 2 inches apart. Repeat with the remaining dough. Reroll the scraps of dough and cut out as many scones as you can. Brush the tops of the scones with the reserved 2 tablespoons of egg mixture.
5. Bake in the preheated hot oven (425°) for 10 to 15 minutes, or until the scones are golden. Remove with the spatula to a wire rack. When cool enough to handle, slice the scones in half horizontally. Serve with raspberry jam and clotted cream.

### CURRANT EVENTS

*Currants are small, seedless raisins from the Mediterranean region.*

*Currant Scones*

# FAST FACTS: A STUDY ON QUICK BREADS

### Speedy Action

Quick breads are made with fast-acting leavening agents, such as baking powder or baking soda. Air, steam and a combination of baking soda and an acid liquid, such as buttermilk or sour milk, also can cause the leavening action during baking.

Quick breads include loaves, muffins, biscuits, doughnuts, scones, shortcakes, dumplings, pancakes, waffles, popovers and spoon breads. Each differs in appearance and flavor but all are considered quick breads because they have similar leavening action and are easy to make, fast-rising, light and porous.

### Batter Up!

Quick bread batters are of three types: soft dough, drop batter or pourable batter. Soft dough can be rolled and shaped by hand. Biscuits, scones and doughnuts are examples of soft dough. Thick drop batter (muffins, cornbread, loaves, dumplings) need only be spooned into a baking pan to take the shape of the pan utensil. Pourable batter, such as waffles, pancakes, Yorkshire pudding and popovers, is made with a thin batter.

### Quick Tips

• When preparing a quick bread, mix the dry and liquid ingredients separately. Once the leavening agent (the baking powder or baking soda) comes in contact with the liquid, the leavening begins and within a short time will be spent. Add the fruit, vegetables and nuts last. To prepare the ingredients ahead, mix the dry ingredients and the liquid ingredients separately, then combine before baking.

• Mix the batter thoroughly but gently with a wooden spoon, just until the ingredients are moistened.

• Allow the breads to cool for 10 minutes in their pans, then remove and cool them completely on a wire rack before wrapping in aluminum foil or plastic wrap.

• Make the entire recipe for muffins and freeze the extras.

• Freeze quick breads for up to six months. To thaw, heat in aluminum foil wrapping in a slow oven (300°) for 25 minutes, or until heated.

### Fast Flavor

• Try adding up to ¼ cup of shredded carrot, apple, pear or mashed banana to your favorite muffin or sweet bread recipe for extra flavor.

• You can substitute pears for apples in most muffin and bread recipes.

• Try substituting cranberries for blueberries in some recipes. Cut cranberries in half and roll in granulated sugar before adding.

• For extra zest, include grated lemon, orange or lime rind in your favorite bread or muffin recipe. Try about two teaspoons per recipe at first, then increase to taste.

# Fruity Nut Bread

*A moist, lightly spiced loaf that is delicious spread with softened butter.*

Bake at 350° for 1 hour and 5 minutes.
Makes 1 loaf (8 slices).

*Nutrient Value Per Slice: 358 calories, 7 g protein, 13 g fat, 56 g carbohydrate, 518 mg sodium, 85 mg cholesterol.*

| | |
|---|---|
| 1½ | **cups sifted all-purpose flour** |
| 1 | **teaspoon baking powder** |
| 1 | **teaspoon baking soda** |
| 1 | **teaspoon salt** |
| 1 | **teaspoon ground cinnamon** |
| ½ | **teaspoon ground nutmeg** |
| ⅔ | **cup firmly packed light brown sugar** |
| 1 | **cup quick oats, uncooked** |
| ½ | **cup coarsely chopped pecans** |
| ½ | **cup raisins** |
| 2 | **eggs** |
| ¼ | **cup milk** |
| ¼ | **cup butter or margarine, melted and cooled** |
| 2 | **medium-size apples (¾ pound), halved, cored and coarsely shredded (1½ cups)** |

1. Preheat the oven to moderate (350°). Lightly grease and flour an 8½ x 4½ x 2¾-inch loaf pan.*
2. Sift together the flour, baking powder, baking soda, salt, cinnamon and nutmeg into a large bowl. Stir in the brown sugar, oats, pecans and raisins.
3. Mix together the eggs, milk and butter or margarine in a small bowl and add all at once to the oatmeal mixture. Add the apples and stir lightly with a fork just until the liquid is absorbed and the mixture is thoroughly moistened (do not overmix). Spoon into the prepared pan.
4. Bake in the preheated moderate oven (350°) for 1 hour and 5 minutes, or until a wooden pick inserted in the center comes out clean. Cool in the pan on a wire rack for 10 minutes. Loosen the edges of the loaf with a knife and remove from the pan to the rack. Cool completely. Wrap and store overnight.

*\*Note: The bread can be baked in a 9 x 5 x 3-inch loaf pan. Bake in a preheated moderate oven (350°) for 55 minutes, or until a wooden pick inserted in the center comes out clean.*

## A-PEELING APPLES

*Grate apples with the skin because the skin contains more fiber and vitamins and gives more flavor than the flesh.*

# Carrot 'n Spice Bread

*Chock full of carrots, walnuts and raisins, spiced with cinnamon, nutmeg and cloves — a slice of this loaf is especially scrumptious when spread with softened butter or cream cheese.*

Bake at 350° for 45 minutes.
Makes 1 loaf (12 slices).

*Nutrient Value Per Slice: 217 calories, 4 g protein, 11 g fat, 27 g carbohydrate, 215 mg sodium, 46 mg cholesterol.*

| | |
|---|---|
| 1½ | **cups unsifted all-purpose flour** |
| ½ | **cup sugar** |
| 1 | **teaspoon baking powder** |
| 1 | **teaspoon baking soda** |
| 1 | **teaspoon ground cinnamon** |
| ½ | **teaspoon salt** |
| ¼ | **teaspoon ground nutmeg** |
| ¼ | **teaspoon ground cloves** |
| 2 | **eggs** |
| 6 | **tablespoons vegetable oil** |
| 1 | **teaspoon vanilla** |
| 1¼ | **cups grated carrots (about 8 ounces)** |
| ½ | **cup walnuts, chopped** |
| ⅓ | **cup raisins** |
| | **Pecan halves (optional)** |

1. Preheat the oven to moderate (350°). Grease an 8½ x 4½ x 2⅝-inch loaf pan.
2. Stir together the flour, sugar, baking powder, baking soda, cinnamon, salt, nutmeg and cloves in a small bowl to mix well.

3. Beat the eggs in a large bowl until well blended. Add the oil, vanilla and carrots; beat until well mixed. Stir in the flour mixture until well blended. Fold in the walnuts and the raisins. Turn into the prepared pan. Place a row of pecan halves down the top center, if you wish.
4. Bake in the preheated moderate oven (350°) for 45 minutes, or until a wooden pick inserted in the center comes out clean. Cool the bread in the pan for 10 minutes. Remove from the pan to a wire rack to cool to room temperature.

*Note: This loaf slices better if it is wrapped and stored overnight.*

## Food for Thought . . .

**Buttermilk** *Originally buttermilk was the liquid remaining after the fat was removed from the milk or cream used to churn butter. Cultured buttermilk, found on supermarket dairy shelves, is made from pasteurized skimmed or partially skimmed milk inoculated with a suitable culture of lactic acid bacteria. It is left to ferment to a thickened consistency, at which time salt may or may not be added. It is a highly nutritious product with very few calories. One cup (8 ounces) has 90 calories, 9 grams of protein and is a good source of calcium and riboflavin. A shelf-stable dried buttermilk powder is available as a convenient substitute.*

# Irish Soda Bread

Bake at 400° for 40 minutes.
Makes 1 round loaf (12 slices).

*Nutrient Value Per Slice: 190 calories, 6 g protein, 1 g fat, 41 g carbohydrate, 377 mg sodium, 1 mg cholesterol.*

| 4 | cups sifted all-purpose flour |
|---|---|
| 1 | tablespoon sugar |
| 1½ | teaspoons salt |
| 1 | teaspoon baking soda |
| 1 | cup dried currants |
| 1½ | cups buttermilk |

1. Preheat the oven to hot (400°). Sift together the flour, sugar, salt and baking soda into a large bowl. Stir in the currants to coat with the flour.
2. Stir in the buttermilk just until the flour is moistened. Knead the dough 10 times in the bowl with lightly floured hands.
3. Turn out the dough onto a lightly floured baking sheet and shape into an 8-inch round. Cut a cross into the top with a floured knife.
4. Bake in the preheated hot oven (400°) for 40 minutes, or until the loaf turns golden and sounds hollow when tapped with your fingertips. Cool the loaf completely on a wire rack before slicing.

## BAKING SODA BULLETIN

*Baking soda works only when combined with an acid substance, such as in baking powder mixtures, or when an acidic liquid—buttermilk, sour milk, chocolate, honey, corn syrup, molasses or yogurt—is used.*

## Lemon Blueberry Muffins

*Nonfat plain yogurt keeps this muffin moist, low-calorie and great tasting.*

Bake at 400° for 25 to 30 minutes.
Makes 12 muffins.

*Nutrient Value Per Muffin: 113 calories, 3 g protein, 2 g fat, 20 g carbohydrate, 205 mg sodium, 23 mg cholesterol.*

  *Nonstick vegetable cooking spray*
1½ *cups unsifted all-purpose flour*
1 *teaspoon baking powder*
1 *teaspoon baking soda*
¼ *teaspoon salt*
3 *tablespoons reduced-calorie margarine*
¼ *cup firmly packed light brown sugar*
1 *egg, slightly beaten*
1 *cup nonfat plain yogurt*
2 *teaspoons lemon juice*
1½ *teaspoons grated lemon rind*
¾ *cup frozen dry-pack unsweetened blueberries (do not thaw)*
1 *tablespoon granulated sugar*

1. Preheat the oven to hot (400°). Spray muffin-pan cups, measuring 2½ inches in diameter, with nonstick vegetable cooking spray. Sift together the flour, baking powder, baking soda and salt onto wax paper.
2. Beat together the margarine and the brown sugar until light and fluffy. Beat in the egg until well blended.
3. Beat in the yogurt, lemon juice and 1 teaspoon of the lemon rind until smooth. Stir in the dry ingredients just until moistened. Stir in the frozen blueberries.
4. Spoon the batter into the prepared cups, filling each two thirds full. Sprinkle with a mixture of the granulated sugar and the remaining ½ teaspoon of lemon rind.
5. Bake in the preheated hot oven (400°) for 25 to 30 minutes, or until a wooden pick inserted into the centers comes out clean. Remove the muffins from the cups to a wire rack to cool slightly. Serve warm.

## Blueberry Spice Muffins

Bake at 400° for 18 to 20 minutes.
Makes 24 muffins.

*Nutrient Value Per Muffin: 195 calories, 3 g protein, 8 g fat, 28 g carbohydrate, 163 mg sodium, 47 mg cholesterol.*

3½ *cups all-purpose flour*
1 *tablespoon baking powder*
1 *teaspoon salt*
1 *teaspoon cinnamon*
½ *teaspoon grated nutmeg*
½ *teaspoon cloves*
1½ *cups sugar*
¾ *cup vegetable shortening*
4 *eggs*
1 *cup milk*
2 *cups fresh blueberries, washed and drained OR: frozen blueberries (do not thaw)*

1. Place paper liners in 24 large muffin-pan cups, or grease the cups. Preheat the oven to hot (400°). Sift together the flour, baking powder, salt, cinnamon, nutmeg and cloves onto wax paper.
2. Beat together the sugar and the shortening in a large bowl with an electric mixer at high speed for 3 minutes, or until light.
3. Add the eggs, one at a time, beating after each addition. Lower the mixer speed. Beat in the dry ingredients.
4. Slowly add the milk and mix just until blended. Fold in the blueberries. Do not overmix.
5. Spoon the batter into the prepared cups, dividing evenly.
6. Bake in the preheated hot oven (400°) for 18 to 20 minutes, or until the muffins are golden brown. Serve warm.

## ◪ Cranberry Orange Muffins

Bake at 400° for 18 to 20 minutes.
Makes 24 muffins.

*Nutrient Value Per Muffin: 205 calories, 3 g protein, 9 g fat, 27 g carbohydrate, 162 mg sodium, 47 mg cholesterol.*

3⅓ cups all-purpose flour
1 tablespoon baking powder
1 teaspoon salt
1 teaspoon cinnamon
½ teaspoon grated nutmeg
1½ cups sugar
¾ cup vegetable shortening
4 eggs
1 tablespoon grated orange rind
1 cup milk
1 cup fresh or frozen cranberries, coarsely chopped
½ cup coarsely chopped pecans

1. Place paper liners in 24 large muffin-pan cups, or grease the cups. Preheat the oven to hot (400°). Sift together the flour, baking powder, salt, cinnamon and nutmeg onto wax paper.
2. Beat together the sugar and the shortening in a large bowl with an electric mixer at high speed for 3 minutes, or until light.
3. Add the eggs, one at a time, beating after each addition. Lower the mixer speed. Beat in the dry ingredients. Stir in the orange rind.
4. Slowly add the milk and mix just until blended. Fold in the cranberries and the pecans. Do not overmix.
5. Spoon the batter into the prepared cups, dividing evenly.
6. Bake in the preheated hot oven (400°) for 18 to 20 minutes, or until the muffins are golden brown. Serve warm.

## ◪ Peach Pecan Muffins

*You can substitute one 16-ounce can of cling peaches, drained, and omit the sugar called for in the purée.*

Bake at 400° for 18 to 20 minutes.
Makes 21 muffins.

*Nutrient Value Per Muffin: 336 calories, 9 g protein, 8 g fat, 58 g carbohydrate, 843 mg sodium, 17 mg cholesterol.*

2½ cups all-purpose flour
½ cup firmly packed light brown sugar
1 tablespoon plus 2¼ teaspoons baking powder
½ teaspoon salt
¾ teaspoon ground cinnamon
4 ripe peaches or nectarines, peeled and pitted (about 1½ pounds)
⅓ cup granulated sugar
2 eggs
1⅓ cups wheat bran cereal
1 cup milk
½ cup vegetable oil
1 cup chopped pecans

1. Place paper liners in 21 muffin-pan cups, or grease the cups. Preheat the oven to hot (400°). Stir together the flour, brown sugar, baking powder, salt and cinnamon in a medium-size bowl. (With your fingertips, break up any lumps of brown sugar that form.)
2. Slice 2 of the peaches or nectarines into the container of an electric blender or a food processor fitted with the metal blade. Add the granulated sugar. Cover the container and process on high speed until the peaches are puréed.
3. Beat the eggs slightly in a large bowl. Add the cereal, milk, oil and puréed peach mixture. Chop the remaining 2 peaches directly into the mixture. Stir to blend. Let stand for about 10 minutes, or until the cereal is softened. Stir again.
4. Add the flour mixture to the peach mixture, mixing with a wooden spoon just until combined. Do not overmix. Fold in the pecans.

5. Spoon the batter into the prepared cups, dividing evenly. Fill the remaining 3 cups in the muffin-pan with water, so they are not damaged during baking.
6. Bake in the preheated hot oven (400°) for 18 to 20 minutes, or until the muffins are golden brown. Serve warm.

*Notes: These muffins are extra moist when served fresh from the oven. To prepare in advance and retain the moistness, mix the peach mixture and stir together the dry ingredients, but do not combine until just before baking.*

*If you can find really ripe fresh apricots, they can be used in this recipe, too. Use 1½ pounds of apricots.*

## Spicy Nut Muffins

*Lightly spiced and crunchy with nuts — these muffins are a great way to wake up.*

Bake at 400° for 20 minutes.
Makes 12 muffins.

*Nutrient Value Per Muffin: 145 calories, 4 g protein, 9 g fat, 219 g carbohydrate, 192 mg sodium, 37 mg cholesterol.*

1 **cup sifted all-purpose flour**
½ **teaspoon salt**
1 **teaspoon baking powder**
½ **teaspoon baking soda**
½ **teaspoon ground cinnamon**
½ **teaspoon ground ginger**
¼ **teaspoon ground nutmeg**
¾ **cup stirred whole wheat flour**
⅓ **cup firmly packed light brown sugar**
1 **egg**
1 **cup buttermilk**
⅓ **cup unsalted butter or margarine, melted**
½ **cup chopped walnuts**

1. Preheat the oven to hot (400°). Grease the bottoms only of twelve 2½-inch muffin-pan cups.
2. Sift together the all-purpose flour, salt, baking powder, baking soda, cinnamon, ginger and nutmeg into a large bowl. Stir in the whole wheat flour and the brown sugar.
3. Lightly beat the egg in a small bowl. Beat in the buttermilk and the butter or margarine. Stir in the walnuts. Pour all at once into the flour mixture. Stir briskly with a fork just until all the dry ingredients are moistened. Do not overstir. The batter will look lumpy.
4. Fill each prepared cup two thirds full with batter, using a large spoon and a rubber spatula.
5. Bake in the preheated hot oven (400°) for 20 minutes, or until the muffins are golden brown. Remove the pan to a wire rack. Loosen the muffins with the spatula and remove from the pan at once to prevent steaming. Serve piping hot.

## Blueberry Pecan Waffles

*The word "waffle" comes from the German word "wabe,"*
*which means honeycomb.*

Makes 6 waffles.

*Nutrient Value Per Serving: 382 calories, 8 g protein, 22 g*
*fat, 38 g carbohydrate, 374 mg sodium, 98 mg cholesterol.*

| | |
|---|---|
| 2 | **cups sifted all-purpose flour** |
| 2 | **tablespoons sugar** |
| 2 | **teaspoons baking powder** |
| ½ | **teaspoon salt** |
| 2 | **eggs, separated** |
| 1¼ | **cups milk** |
| ⅓ | **cup vegetable oil** |
| ½ | **cup coarsely chopped pecans** |
| 6 | **tablespoons blueberries, washed and dried** |

1. Sift together the flour, sugar, baking powder and salt onto wax paper.
2. Beat the egg whites until stiff, but not dry, in a small bowl and set aside.
3. Beat the egg yolks well in a medium-size bowl and stir in the milk.
4. Add the dry ingredients and mix just enough to blend. Add the oil and the pecans. Fold in the egg whites.
5. Pour the batter into a waffle iron following the manufacturer's directions. Sprinkle each waffle with just a few of the blueberries.
6. Bake in a moderately hot waffle iron for 4 to 5 minutes until crisp and brown, or following the iron manufacturer's directions. Serve hot with butter and syrup or honey.

## PANCAKE PERFECTION

***1.*** *Stir the batter as little as possible, just enough to get the dry ingredients mixed in.*
***2.*** *Pour the batter on a hot, but not smoking, griddle. A griddle is preferable to a skillet or pan with sides for ease in flipping.*
***3.*** *Cook until tiny bubbles appear on the top surface and the batter has lost its sheen. Flip and cook the second side for about half as long.*

## Buttermilk Pancakes

Makes about 8 pancakes.

*Nutrient Value Per Serving: 185 calories, 7 g protein, 6 g*
*fat, 26 g carbohydrate, 460 mg sodium, 71 mg cholesterol.*

| | |
|---|---|
| 2 | **cups sifted all-purpose flour** |
| 1 | **tablespoon sugar** |
| 1 | **teaspoon baking soda** |
| 1 | **teaspoon salt** |
| 2 | **eggs** |
| 2 | **cups buttermilk** |
| 2 | **tablespoons vegetable oil** |

1. Sift together the flour, sugar, baking soda and salt onto wax paper.
2. Beat together the eggs and the buttermilk in a medium-size bowl. Add the dry ingredients to the buttermilk mixture and beat until smooth. Stir in the oil.
3. For each pancake, pour about ⅓ cup of the batter onto a lightly greased, medium-hot griddle, or an electric fry pan preheated to moderate (350°). When the top and edges look dry and bubbly, turn and brown the second side. Keep warm and repeat with the remaining batter.

## Food for Thought...

***Flour*** Flour is one of the least standardized commercial products. A bag of all-purpose flour purchased in the South is not the same as a bag bought in the Northeast, although the brand may be the same. Flour sold in the Northeast may have a higher proportion of hard wheat to soft wheat. In the South, where more biscuits and cakes are baked than breads, the flour tends to have more soft wheat than hard.

The moisture or lack of moisture in the air affects flour and makes a notable difference in how recipes turn out. Flour will behave differently according to its ability to absorb liquids. That's why a recipe made with mostly flour may not always work. Since the variable factors are in the flour itself, there are no simple ways to counteract the effects in recipes of those differences. Some recipes will provide a range for the amount of flour to use, but it is still the expertise and working knowledge of the baker that will determine success or failure.

***All-purpose flour*** is a combination of soft and hard wheats. It is available bleached or unbleached. Unbleached flour is off-white in color, bleached flour is chemically whitened. They can be used interchangeably in recipes. However, unbleached flour has a higher nutritional value. Both flours are enriched with iron and B-complex vitamins—the nutrients lost with the removal of the bran and germ. All-purpose flour is suitable for most baking purposes.

***Cake flour*** is milled from soft wheat. It is especially suitable for cakes, cookies and pastries. Soft wheat contains less gluten-forming protein. Gluten is the substance that gives structure and elasticity to batters and doughs.

***Bread flour*** has a high gluten content. Gluten holds in the gas produced by the yeast or baking powder and builds the structure of breads. Bread flour is ground from the endosperm of the wheat kernel.

***Self-rising flour*** is all-purpose flour with salt and leavening added. One cup of self-rising flour contains 1½ teaspoons of baking powder and ½ teaspoon of salt. It can be used in place of all-purpose flour in a recipe if you reduce the amounts of salt and baking powder according to the above proportions.

CHAPTER 2

# In The Beginning

A heavenly start to your meal—appealing appetizers, sensational soups and salads.

Oriental Turkey Salad (recipe, page 121); Mushroom and Asparagus Salad (recipe, page 55); Best Butter Cake (recipe, page 165); Monkey Bread (recipe, page 12); Pasta Pesto Salad (recipe, page 129)

**P**ity the poor appetizer. It always seems neglected: never really a part of weekday meals, and brought out only on special occasions—when friends drop in, over the holidays, when you want to "make an impression". And if you're watching calories, appetizers are usually the first to go—even before dessert!

Let's start with soups. Instead of the run-of-the-mill variety, try a refreshing, chilled Spicy Tomato Vegetable Soup *(recipe, page 48)* or a soul-warming French Onion Soup with Cheese Croutons *(recipe, page 52)*. A hearty soup, paired with a crisp salad and fresh bread can make a wonderful (and calorie-smart!) lunch or supper.

Speaking of salads, you can expand your repertoire of ingredients by trying Five Greens Salad with Walnut Vinaigrette *(recipe, page 61)* or colorful, crunchy Snow Peas and Sprout Salad *(recipe, page 62)*. It's not all iceberg and Boston lettuce out there!

Finally, we come to hors d'oeuvres. They really *can* be dazzlers, for the eye as well as the palate. Case in point: Summer Vegetables with Tomato Cream Cheese Dip *(recipe, page 44)*. Sample our Chick Pea Spread *(recipe, page 44)* or Cucumber Mustard Dip *(recipe, page 45)* with raw veggies, too.

Have we convinced you to include appetizers with your meals? If our words don't, our recipes will. Give them a try! ■

# Appetizers, Dips & Such

## Summer Vegetables with Tomato Cream Cheese Dip

Makes 12 servings.

*Nutrient Value Per Serving: 146 calories, 3 g protein, 12 g fat, 7 g carbohydrate, 85 mg sodium, 39 mg cholesterol.*

2 **pounds assorted summer vegetables, such as green beans, broccoli, carrots, radishes, cucumbers, sweet peppers, zucchini**

***Tomato Cream Cheese Dip:***
½ **cup heavy cream**
1 **package (8 ounces) cream cheese, softened**
½ **cup dairy sour cream**
2 **teaspoons tomato paste**
1 **small clove garlic, pressed or finely chopped**
2 **to 3 tablespoons chopped fresh herbs, such as rosemary, basil or thyme**

1. Trim and clean the vegetables. Cut into bite-size pieces. If you prefer some vegetables lightly cooked, such as broccoli or green beans, blanch them in a large saucepan of boiling water for about 1 minute, or until they've lost their raw taste. Drain in a colander. Immediately rinse under cold water to stop the cooking and set the color. Wrap the vegetables separately in paper toweling and seal them in plastic bags. Refrigerate until ready to serve.
2. Prepare the Tomato Cream Cheese Dip: Beat the heavy cream in a small bowl with an electric mixer until stiff. Mash the cream cheese in a second small bowl. Whisk the sour cream into the cream cheese with a small whisk or fork until smooth and creamy. Whisk in the whipped cream until light and smooth. Whisk in the tomato paste, garlic and herbs. (You should have about 2 cups of dip.) Cover and refrigerate for 1 to 2 hours for the flavors to develop. The dip will keep refrigerated for up to 3 days.
3. To serve, spoon the dip into a small serving bowl. Arrange the vegetables in bundles on a large platter or in a wicker basket or tray. Serve with the dip.

## Chick Pea Spread

Makes about 1⅔ cups.

*Nutrient Value Per Tablespoon: 42 calories, 1 g protein, 2 g fat, 5 g carbohydrate, 60 mg sodium, 0 mg cholesterol.*

1 **can (19 ounces) chick peas**
1 **small onion, chopped (¼ cup)**
¼ **cup olive oil**
2 **tablespoons lemon juice**
½ **cup watercress**
¼ **teaspoon pepper**
 **Assorted fresh vegetables, cut into bite-size pieces (optional)**

Drain the chick peas in a colander, rinse them with cold water and drain the chick peas well. Place the chick peas, onion, oil, lemon juice, watercress and pepper in the container of a food processor or, working in batches, of an electric blender. Cover and whirl until the mixture is puréed. Transfer the purée to a small bowl. Refrigerate the purée, covered, until chilled. Serve with assorted fresh vegetables, if you wish.

## Cucumber Mustard Dip

Makes 1½ cups.

*Nutrient Value Per Tablespoon: 19 calories, 0 g protein, 2 g fat, 1 g carbohydrate, 48 mg sodium, 2 mg cholesterol.*

|   |   |
|---|---|
| 1 | medium-size cucumber, peeled, halved, seeded and coarsely chopped |
| ½ | cup plain nonfat yogurt |
| ½ | cup reduced-calorie mayonnaise |
| 1 | tablespoon grainy coarse mustard |
| 1 | tablespoon snipped fresh dill OR: 1 teaspoon dillweed |
| 1½ | teaspoons lemon juice |
| ⅛ | teaspoon black pepper Assorted fresh vegetables, cut into bite-size pieces |

1. Place the cucumber pieces in the container of a food processor. Cover and whirl until finely chopped. Add ¼ cup of the yogurt, cover and whirl until smooth. Turn the cucumber mixture into a small bowl.
2. Stir in the remaining ¼ cup of yogurt, the mayonnaise, mustard, dill, lemon juice and black pepper. Serve with the assorted fresh vegetable dippers.

---

### Food for Thought . . .

**Chick Peas** *Widely used in the Mediterranean, chick peas are ivory-hued beans packed with nutrition. They are known as **garbanzo beans** in Spanish-speaking countries, referred to as **hommos** or **hummus** in the Middle East and Italians call them **ceci**.*

*Chick peas are the seeds of a bush-like plant that grows in dry regions. Although three varieties are grown, only one is widely used.*

*Chick peas are available dried in one-pound packages or sold in bulk by the pound. They also are available cooked and canned.*

## Pizza Snacks

Bake in a toaster oven for 3 to 5 minutes. Makes 12 "snacks" (4 servings).

*Nutrient Value Per Serving: 72 calories, 3 g protein, 3 g fat, 8 g carbohydrate, 82 mg sodium, 7 mg cholesterol.*

|   |   |
|---|---|
| 1 | tablespoon tomato paste |
| 12 | melba toast rounds |
| ⅓ | cup thinly sliced yellow squash |
| ½ | teaspoon olive oil |
| ¼ | cup shredded mozzarella cheese |
| 1 | tablespoon grated Parmesan cheese |
| ⅛ | teaspoon leaf basil, crumbled Pitted black olives, sliced, for garnish (optional) |

1. Lightly spread the tomato paste on the melba rounds. Top the rounds with the squash slices. Brush the tops with the oil. Combine the mozzarella and Parmesan cheeses and the basil in a small bowl. Sprinkle the cheese mixture over the squash. Place the rounds on a toaster oven tray.
2. Bake the rounds in the toaster oven set at 350° for 3 to 5 minutes, or until the cheese melts. Garnish the snacks with slices of black olives, if you wish.

### Microwave Instructions
*(for a 650-watt variable power microwave oven)*

**Directions:** Place the "snacks" on a microwave-safe plate. Microwave, uncovered, at full power for 45 seconds, or until the cheese melts, rotating the plate one quarter turn once.

## Food for Thought . . .

**Radish** *A pungent-tasting root vegetable usually served raw in salads. The small, bright red variety is the most common type, but radishes are grown in many shapes and colors.*

*Small, slender, white radishes are called **icicles**. There also is a round white and a round black radish. The largest radish is the Oriental radish called **daikon**. It is white, about 12 inches long and has a flavor similar to the common red radish but a bit hotter. It is pickled, whole or shredded, as a relish, thinly sliced into soups or cut into thin strips for vegetable platters. Do not confuse daikon with another large, white root vegetable called **low bok or Chinese turnip**.*

*Radishes are one of the oldest vegetables cultivated, believed to be native to middle Asia and China. They are available year-round, but the peak season is during the summer. Radishes should be crisp and smooth, never soft or spongy. Store them in the refrigerator vegetable compartment and use within one week.*

*Red and icicle radishes are ideal as garnishes. They can be cut into a variety of shapes to add visual interest (and taste) to a dish: fans, flowers, roses or pompons. Place the cut radishes in ice water and chill them until they open. Drain them thoroughly and use them to garnish any appetizer tray, main-dish platter or salad.*

## Sweet 'n Sour Radishes

*An unusual hors d'oeuvre/condiment, this dish makes an excellent adjunct to grilled meat. Or intersperse the radishes with other raw vegetables to make a salad. To turn these radishes into a relish, thinly slice and mix with thin rounds of carrots and pearl onions.*

Makes 6 servings.

*Nutrient Value Per Serving: 34 calories, 1 g protein, 2 g fat, 5 g carbohydrate, 181 mg sodium, 0 mg cholesterol.*

1 **bunch red radishes, with leaves**
1 **bunch white radishes, without leaves (or, if unavailable, use another bunch of red)**
4 **green onions, white parts only, thinly sliced (⅓ cup)**
6 **tablespoons tarragon white wine vinegar**
2 **tablespoons soy sauce**
2 **tablespoons sugar**
4 **teaspoons Oriental sesame oil***

1. Trim the leaves from one bunch of red radishes. Wash the leaves well, dry and chop; you should have about ¼ cup of chopped leaves. Set aside.
2. Trim the white radishes, and cut in half if large. With the flat side of a heavy knife, lightly crack the red and white radishes. Combine the radishes, radish leaves and green onion in a medium-size bowl.
3. Combine the vinegar, soy sauce, sugar and Oriental sesame oil in a small bowl. Stir to mix all the ingredients well and pour over the radish mixture. Cover and let stand at room temperature for 3 hours, no longer, or the radishes will become too soft. Drain and serve at room temperature or chilled.

***Note:** Oriental sesame oil has more flavor and is darker in color than regular sesame oil. It can be found in the Oriental food section of many supermarkets or in Oriental specialty food stores.*

# Salsa California

Makes 6 cups.

*Nutrient Value Per ¼ Cup: 19 calories, 1 g protein, 0 g fat, 5 g carbohydrate, 98 mg sodium, 0 mg cholesterol.*

3  **pounds ripe tomatoes, peeled, seeded and chopped**
¾  **pound fresh Anaheim chili peppers, seeded and chopped OR: 3 cans (4 ounces each) green chili peppers, chopped**
¼  **pound fresh poblano chili peppers, seeded and chopped OR: ½ teaspoon crushed red pepper flakes, or to taste**
½  **pound medium-size white onions, chopped (1½ cups)**
2  **tablespoons chopped fresh cilantro (coriander)**
1  **teaspoon salt**
1  **teaspoon pepper**
¼  **cup lemon juice**

Combine the tomatoes, chili peppers, onion, cilantro, salt, pepper and lemon juice in a large bowl. Stir to mix all the ingredients well. Chill overnight for maximum flavor, or refrigerate in a tightly sealed jar for up to 2 weeks.

*Note: When working with fresh chilies, wear rubber gloves and avoid touching the eyes or any exposed skin areas. Work in a well-ventilated area.*

# Cheesy Herb Popcorn

Makes about 2 quarts.

*Nutrient Value Per ½ Cup: 30 calories, 1 g protein, 2 g fat, 2 g carbohydrate, 20 mg sodium, 3 mg cholesterol.*

1  **tablespoon olive oil**
1  **tablespoon grated Parmesan cheese**
¼  **teaspoon leaf basil, crumbled**
¼  **teaspoon leaf thyme, crumbled**
2  **quarts freshly popped popcorn**
⅓  **cup finely shredded Cheddar cheese**

Stir together the oil, Parmesan cheese, basil and thyme in a cup. Combine the hot popcorn and the Cheddar cheese in a large bowl. Drizzle the oil mixture over the popcorn. Stir gently to mix all the ingredients well.

## Microwave Instructions
*(for a 650-watt variable power microwave oven)*

**Ingredient Changes:** Use two 3½-ounce bags of microwave popping corn, which each yield 1 quart.

**Directions:** Pop the corn in the microwave oven, following the package directions. Meanwhile, combine the oil, Parmesan cheese, basil, thyme and Cheddar cheese in a cup. Empty the hot popcorn into a large bowl and add the oil mixture. Mix the popcorn gently with a spoon to combine all the ingredients well, and serve.

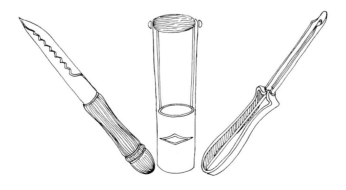

# Soups: Hot & Cold

◪ ◧ $

## Spicy Tomato Vegetable Soup

Makes 6 servings.

*Nutrient Value Per Serving: 47 calories, 2 g protein, 0 g fat, 11 g carbohydrate, 565 mg sodium, 0 mg cholesterol.*

1   can (16 ounces) whole tomatoes, undrained
2   cans (12 ounces each) tomato juice
1   medium-size sweet green pepper, halved, cored, seeded and finely chopped
½   cup finely chopped, unpeeled zucchini (1 small)
¼   cup finely chopped onion
¼   cup finely chopped cilantro (coriander) OR: parsley
3   tablespoons fresh lemon juice
1   tablespoon vinegar
2   cloves garlic, finely chopped
½   fresh jalapeño pepper, seeded and finely chopped

1. Drain the liquid from the tomatoes into a soup tureen. Transfer the tomatoes to a cutting board and coarsely chop, discarding as many of the seeds as possible. Add the tomatoes to the liquid in the tureen.
2. Stir the tomato juice, green pepper, zucchini, onion, cilantro or parsley, lemon juice, vinegar, garlic and jalapeño pepper into the soup tureen. Cover the tureen and refrigerate the soup for several hours, or overnight, to chill and blend the flavors. Serve the soup cold.

◧ ◪ $

## Cold Plum Soup

*Serve at the beginning of a warm-weather meal, or at the end for a fruity dessert.*

Makes 6 servings.

*Nutrient Value Per Serving: 198 calories, 2 g protein, 8 g fat, 32 g carbohydrate, 9 mg sodium, 27 mg cholesterol.*

1   piece (1 inch) stick cinnamon
1   whole clove
2   pounds plums, such as Laroda, Simka or Friar, cut in half and pitted
1   can (5½ ounces) apple juice
⅓   cup water
1   tablespoon lemon juice
¼   cup sugar
½   cup heavy cream whipped with 1 tablespoon 10X (confectioners' powdered) sugar
    Ground cinnamon

1. Tie the cinnamon stick and the whole clove in a small piece of cheesecloth. Place in a saucepan with the plums, apple juice, water, lemon juice and sugar. Bring to boiling. Lower the heat and simmer, covered, for 15 minutes, or until the plums are soft.
2. Remove and discard the spices. Purée the plum mixture in batches in the container of an electric blender or a food processor. Pour into a heatproof glass bowl. Refrigerate, covered, until well chilled, for 3 hours or overnight.
3. Serve with the whipped cream and a sprinkle of the ground cinnamon.

## Pimiento Basil Soup

*Canned pimientos are the base of this soup.*

Makes 4 servings.

---

*Nutrient Value Per Serving: 93 calories, 3 g protein, 0 g fat, 22 g carbohydrate, 663 mg sodium, 0 mg cholesterol.*

---

1   **can (28 ounces) whole tomatoes in thick purée**
1½  **cups tomato juice**
2   **jars (4⅔ ounces each) whole sweet pimientos, drained**
2   **tablespoons finely chopped onion**
1   **clove garlic, finely chopped**
2   **tablespoons chopped fresh basil OR: 1½ tablespoons leaf basil, soaked in 1 tablespoon water**
    **Salt and pepper, to taste**
    **Dairy sour cream OR: plain lowfat yogurt, for garnish (optional)**

1. Drain the tomatoes, reserving the purée separately. Place the tomatoes in the container of a food processor. Cover and pulse on and off until the tomatoes are coarsely chopped. Transfer the tomatoes to a medium-size bowl.
2. Combine the reserved purée, the tomato juice, pimientos, onion, garlic and basil in the food processor container. Cover and whirl on high speed until the mixture is a smooth purée. Add the puréed mixture to the chopped tomatoes in the bowl. Stir to blend all the ingredients well. Taste and add the salt and pepper.
3. Cover the soup and refrigerate until chilled. Taste the soup once more and adjust the seasonings, if necessary.
4. At serving time, garnish the soup with dollops of the sour cream or plain yogurt.

## Cold Spinach Soup

*The butter in this soup is used to form a thin white sauce base, so it won't solidify too much when the soup is chilled.*

Makes 2 servings.

---

*Nutrient Value Per Serving: 303 calories, 14 g protein, 17 g fat, 27 g carbohydrate, 349 mg sodium, 57 mg cholesterol.*

---

2   **tablespoons butter or margarine**
1   **cup chopped green onion**
2   **tablespoons all-purpose flour**
2   **cups lowfat milk**
1   **package (10 ounces) chopped spinach**
    **Salt and pepper, to taste**
¼   **cup snipped fresh dill**
    **Dairy sour cream or plain lowfat yogurt**
    **Dill sprigs, for garnish (optional)**

1. Melt the butter or margarine in a medium-size saucepan over medium heat. Stir in the green onion and sauté until tender but not brown.
2. Stir in the flour. Cook, stirring constantly, for 1 minute. Gradually stir in the milk. Lower the heat.
3. Cook, stirring constantly, until the mixture thickens.
4. Add the spinach and cover the saucepan. Cook, stirring several times with a fork to break up the spinach, for 10 minutes, or until the spinach is cooked. Taste and season with the salt and pepper. Stir in the dill. Cover and refrigerate for at least two hours, or until cold.
5. At serving time, top the soup with dollops of the sour cream or plain yogurt, and garnish with dill sprigs, if you wish.

## SOME LIKE IT COLD

*Most hot soup recipes can be served chilled. To convert a hot soup recipe: Avoid using butter, because it will solidify when the soup is refrigerated. Taste the soup after it is cold; it probably will need a bit more flavoring, since chilling a soup often diminishes its flavor.*

## Quick Tomato Broth

**Add cooked chopped vegetables to this refreshing soup.**

Makes 4 servings.

*Nutrient Value Per Serving: 61 calories, 5 g protein, 1 g fat, 8 g carbohydrate, 848 mg sodium, 2 mg cholesterol.*

2   **cups tomato juice**
2   **cups chicken broth**
½   **cup plain lowfat yogurt**
¼   **cup sliced fresh basil**

1. Combine the tomato juice and the broth in a medium-size bowl. Cover and refrigerate until serving time, removing any fat that floats to the surface.
2. At serving time, garnish each serving with a dollop of the plain yogurt and a sprinkling of the fresh basil.

***Note:*** *Tiny garden peas, sliced celery or carrot, sautéed mushroom slices and chopped blanched green beans all are nice additions to this soup. In winter, the soup can be served hot.*

## Creamy Avocado Soup

**Lemon adds a sprightly touch to avocado.**

Makes 8 servings.

*Nutrient Value Per Serving: 248 calories, 6 g protein, 15 g fat, 27 g carbohydrate, 552 mg sodium, 1 mg cholesterol.*

1   **medium-size onion, chopped (½ cup)**
2   **leeks, trimmed, halved, washed well and chopped (white part only)**
1   **tablespoon vegetable oil**
1   **quart chicken broth**
4   **boiling potatoes (about 2 pounds), peeled and diced**
½   **cup plain lowfat yogurt**
½   **cup buttermilk**
2   **ripe avocados, peeled, seeded and sliced**
    **Juice of 2 lemons**
½   **teaspoon liquid red pepper seasoning**
    **Salt and pepper, to taste**
    **Lemon slices, for garnish (optional)**

1. Sauté the onion and the leeks in the oil in a medium-size stockpot over medium heat until soft but not brown. Add the broth and bring to boiling. Add the potatoes. Lower the heat and simmer, stirring occasionally, for 20 to 30 minutes, or until the potatoes are very tender. Let the potato mixture cool.
2. Place part of the potato mixture in the container of an electric blender or a food processor. Add part of the yogurt, buttermilk, avocado and lemon juice. Cover and whirl until the mixture is puréed. Transfer the purée to a large bowl. Repeat the puréeing with the remaining potato mixture, yogurt, buttermilk, avocado and lemon juice and transfer to the bowl. Stir in the liquid red pepper seasoning and the salt and pepper.
3. Cover the bowl and refrigerate the soup until well chilled. Taste and adjust the seasonings, if necessary. Garnish each serving with a lemon slice, if you wish.

## *Burgundy Tomato Soup*

Makes 8 servings (about 7 cups).

*Nutrient Value Per Serving: 161 calories, 3 g protein, 12 g fat, 12 g carbohydrate, 340 mg sodium, 36 mg cholesterol.*

***2¼ pounds tomatoes (7 medium-size)***
***1 cup coarsely chopped celery***
***1 large onion, coarsely chopped (1 cup)***
***1 tablespoon chopped fresh basil***
***OR: 1 teaspoon leaf basil, crumbled***
***¼ cup (½ stick) butter***
***¼ cup all-purpose flour***
***2 cups chicken broth***
***½ cup red Burgundy wine***
***½ cup heavy cream***
***Salt and pepper, to taste***
***Chopped parsley, for garnish***

1. Bring a large pot of water to boiling. Drop in the tomatoes. When the skins begin to split, immediately remove the tomatoes with a slotted spoon, plunge them into cold water and drain them. Peel, core and halve the tomatoes. Seed them, if you wish. Cut the tomatoes into small pieces and set aside.
2. Sauté the celery, onion and basil in the butter in a large saucepan over medium-low heat until the vegetables are tender, stirring occasionally. Sprinkle the flour over all; cook and stir for 1 minute. Add the tomatoes, broth and wine. Cook over medium heat, stirring constantly, until the mixture thickens and boils.
3. Lower the heat, cover and simmer for 8 minutes. Uncover and simmer for 2 minutes more. Cool slightly. Pour the soup into the container of an electric

blender or a food processor, cover and whirl until the soup is puréed.

4. Return the soup to the saucepan. Stir in the cream. Heat to serving temperature; *do not* boil. Season with the salt and pepper, and garnish with chopped parsley, if you wish.

## *French Onion Soup with Cheese Croutons*

Toast croutons at 325° for 15 minutes; melt cheese at 375°.
Makes 4 servings (4 generous cups).

*Nutrient Value Per Serving: 418 calories, 15 g protein, 22 g fat, 41 g carbohydrate, 1,065 mg sodium, 41 mg cholesterol.*

|   |   |
|---|---|
| 2 | to 3 Spanish onions (about 2 pounds) |
| 2 | tablespoons vegetable oil |
| 2 | tablespoons butter |
| 1 | clove garlic, finely chopped |
| 2 | tablespoons all-purpose flour |
| 2 | cans (13¾ ounces each) beef broth |
| 1 | bay leaf |
| ¼ | to ½ teaspoon leaf thyme, crumbled |
| ¼ | to ½ teaspoon salt (optional) |
| 4 | slices French bread, diagonally sliced, ¾ inch thick |
| 1 | clove garlic, crushed |
| 4 | thin slices Gruyère cheese, or as needed |
| 2 | teaspoons grated Parmesan cheese |
| 2 | teaspoons lemon juice |
|   | Freshly ground pepper, to taste |

1. Peel the onions and trim the ends. Cut the onions in half lengthwise, then cut them crosswise into thin slices. When slicing, anchor the end of each onion with your knuckles, curving your fingers in toward the palm to avoid cuts.

2. Heat together the oil and the butter in a large, heavy-bottomed wide kettle or Dutch oven. Add the onion and stir to coat well. Reduce the heat to medium-low. Cover and cook, stirring occasionally, until the onion is very limp and just beginning to color, for about 20 minutes.

3. Stir in the chopped garlic. Increase the heat to medium. Cook, uncovered, stirring frequently, until the onion is amber or caramel colored, for about 30 minutes. Stir more frequently toward the end of the cooking time to prevent sticking.

4. Sprinkle the onion with the flour. Stir to thoroughly combine the flour with the onion. Cook over medium heat for 2 to 3 minutes, stirring the mixture frequently.

5. Stir in 1 cup of the broth, scraping up the browned bits from the bottom of the kettle. Bring to a gentle boil and cook for 1 minute. Stir in the bay leaf, thyme, the remaining broth and the salt, if you wish. Simmer, partially covered, for 20 to 30 minutes.

6. Preheat the oven to slow (325°).

7. Place the bread slices on a cookie sheet. (Trim, if necessary, so the slices fit into the soup bowls.) Place in the preheated slow oven (325°) until golden brown and crispy, for about 15 minutes. Increase the oven temperature to moderate (375°).

8. Remove the cookie sheet with the toasted slices (croutons) from the oven. Rub each of the croutons on both sides with the crushed garlic clove.

9. Place the Gruyère cheese on each crouton so the top is covered. Sprinkle each with ½ teaspoon of the Parmesan cheese. Return the croutons to the preheated moderate oven (375°) until the cheese is melted and golden brown.

10. Flavor the soup with the lemon juice and the pepper. Discard the bay leaf. Ladle the soup into 4 soup crocks or bowls. With a spatula, transfer one crouton to each bowl of onion soup. Serve immediately.

# Salads

## Cauliflower and Artichoke Heart Salad

*Use the marinade from prepared artichoke hearts to dress the cauliflower.*

Makes 6 servings.

*Nutrient Value Per Serving: 173 calories, 3 g protein, 14 g fat, 10 g carbohydrate, 110 mg sodium, 0 mg cholesterol.*

1   **head cauliflower, trimmed and cut into 1-inch pieces OR: 2 packages (10 ounces each) frozen cauliflower**
2   **jars (6 ounces each) marinated artichoke hearts**
1   **cup thinly sliced sweet red pepper strips, cut in half**

1. Cook the cauliflower pieces in boiling water to cover in a large saucepan over medium heat until tender but still crisp. Or prepare the frozen cauliflower, following the package directions. Drain the cooked cauliflower and immediately place under cold running water to stop the cooking. Drain the cauliflower well, then place in a large serving bowl.
2. Drain the artichoke hearts, reserving the marinade.
3. Toss the cauliflower with the artichoke hearts and the red pepper. Add the reserved marinade to taste and toss the salad to mix all the ingredients well.

## Two-Bean Salad with Dill and Lemon

*The combination of green and wax beans is colorful and tasty. But you can use just one kind of bean if you wish.*

Makes 2 servings.

*Nutrient Value Per Serving: 278 calories, 2 g protein, 27 g fat, 9 g carbohydrate, 44 mg sodium, 0 mg cholesterol.*

½   **pound green and/or wax beans, trimmed and cut into 3-inch pieces**
2   **tablespoons freshly squeezed lemon juice**
½   **teaspoon Dijon-style mustard**
¼   **cup vegetable oil**
1   **tablespoon snipped fresh dill
    Salt and pepper, to taste
    Dill sprigs, for garnish (optional)**

1. Steam or boil the beans in water for 5 minutes, or until crisp-tender. Immediately place the beans under cold running water and drain very well. Place the beans in a medium-size bowl.
2. Beat together the lemon juice and the mustard until well blended. Slowly beat in the oil in a thin stream until the mixture is emulsified. Stir in the dill. Taste and add the salt and pepper.
3. Pour the dressing over the beans. Let stand for at least 30 minutes to blend the flavors. Garnish with additional dill sprigs, if you wish.

## Food for Thought . . .

**Wax Beans** *A yellow or golden variety of snap beans. Wax beans are grown, selected, stored and cooked in a similar way to green beans, but are not as readily available. Wax beans are in season from April to October. Look for fresh, crisp pods that will snap easily and are free of blemishes. Allow 1 pound for 4 servings. Store wax beans, unwashed, in a plastic bag in the refrigerator, and use them within 4 days. When you're ready to cook the beans, snap off the stem ends and rinse the beans in cold water. Cut them up or leave them whole. Steam the beans, or cook them in a small amount of boiling water, until crisp-tender. Wax beans also are available canned.*

# Radish and Cucumber Salad

*Minted yogurt dressing adds a refreshing accent to this crisp combination.*

Makes 2 servings.

*Nutrient Value Per Serving: 178 calories, 4 g protein, 15 g fat, 9 g carbohydrate, 327 mg sodium, 3 mg cholesterol.*

- 1   **small cucumber**
    **Salt**
- 1   **cup sliced radishes**
- ½   **cup plain lowfat yogurt**
- 2   **tablespoons vegetable oil**
- 1   **tablespoon freshly squeezed lemon juice**
- 1   **tablespoon finely chopped fresh mint**
    **OR: 1 teaspoon dried mint, crumbled**

1. Trim and slice the cucumber in half lengthwise. Seed the cucumber halves with a small spoon. Peel one of the cucumber halves; leave the remaining half unpeeled. Slice both halves into ½-inch-thick crescents.

2. Place the cucumber pieces in a colander and sprinkle them lightly with the salt. Place the colander over a bowl, and let the cucumber drain for 30 minutes.

3. Pat the cucumber pieces with paper toweling. Place in a small bowl and add the radish.

4. Stir together the yogurt, oil, lemon juice and mint in a small bowl until well blended. Pour over the cucumber and radish mixture. Toss gently to coat evenly.

# Mushroom and Asparagus Salad

*Raw mushrooms have a special texture all their own.*

Makes 6 servings.

*Nutrient Value Per Serving: 181 calories, 2 g protein, 18 g fat, 4 g carbohydrate, 3 mg sodium, 0 mg cholesterol.*

- ¼   **cup freshly squeezed lemon juice**
- ¼   **teaspoon dry mustard powder**
- ½   **cup olive oil**
- 1   **large clove garlic, peeled and quartered**
    **Salt and pepper, to taste**
- ½   **pound thin asparagus spears, trimmed and cut into 2-inch lengths**
- ½   **pound medium-size fresh mushrooms, trimmed**
- 4   **green onions, trimmed and chopped**

1. Beat together the lemon juice and the mustard powder in a small bowl. Slowly whisk in the oil in a steady stream. Add the garlic and the salt and pepper. Let the dressing stand for 30 minutes.

2. Meanwhile, blanch the asparagus in boiling water for 4 to 5 minutes, or until barely tender. Immediately rinse under cold running water and drain well. Place in a medium-size bowl.

3. Slice the mushrooms and add to the bowl along with the green onion. Pour the dressing over and toss to coat evenly.

# KNOW YOUR SALAD GREENS

*There's more than one way to make a salad! By mixing and matching different types of greens, you can create a wonderful variety of tastes, textures and colors.*

**Arugula** *(rocket, rugala):* Spicy, bright green leaves that resemble watercress. Snip the stems and use the leaves in salads with an oil and vinegar dressing, or try arugula with an herb butter on bread. It's also wonderful with brie as a sandwich filling.

**Belgian Endive** *(witloof):* Small, compact head with greenish-white leaves. Has a pleasant bitter taste and crisp texture. It also is one of the most expensive greens on

the market today (less expensive domestic varieties now are being produced). The leaves can be cut or eaten whole, or try filling them with a spread or dip.

**Bibb Lettuce** *(limestone lettuce):* Small, curly head with tender, butter-textured green leaves, white near the

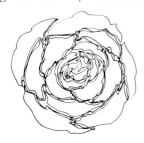

core. Delicate flavor. It usually is sandy, so Bibb lettuce must be washed thoroughly. Rinse under cool water and wash away all traces of dirt. Then pat dry rather than spin dry, because the leaves bruise easily. Use it, alone or mixed with other greens, with a light dressing.

**Boston Lettuce** *(butterhead):* Larger and looser than Bibb lettuce,

with a similar soft, tender leaf and buttery texture. Sweet flavor.

**Chicory** *(curly endive):* Lacy, fringed leaves with a bitter taste. The outer leaves

are darker with a stronger flavor than the inner leaves.

**Chinese Cabbage** *(celery cabbage):* Tightly closed head with wide, tapered

leaves and crinkly edges. Has a celery-like color with

white ribbing. Good eaten raw or added to stir-fried dishes.

**Cress:** Tiny green leaves with a peppery bite similar to radish. Used often in many European countries as a flavoring or as a garnish.

**Dandelion Greens:** Dark green leaves with a slightly bitter taste. Choose the youngest leaves for the freshest flavor.

**Escarole:** Wide, flat leaves with slightly curly edges. Outer leaves are green and inner ones are yellow to

cream color. Slightly bitter taste combines well with other greens. Escarole also is good braised and served with a cheese topping.

*Fennel (finocchio):* Feathery leaves on a stalk with a bulb. Has a pronounced anise flavor and should be used sparingly with mixed greens. Thinly slice the bulb for salads. Or braise by topping with grated Parmesan cheese and broiling until bubbly.

*Fiddleheads:* A coiled edible fern usually grown on stream banks. Available in early spring. The flavor is a cross between asparagus and mushrooms. Best sautéed or lightly steamed.

*Field Salad (lamb's quarter):* Dark green, small, spoonlike leaves with a

radish-sharp flavor. Available in the fall and winter.

*Iceberg Lettuce (crisphead lettuce):* Large, compact head. Crisp leaves are darker green on the outside, lighter in color closer to the core.

Heads should be heavy for their size. Its mild flavor makes it especially suitable for mixing with other greens that are sharper in taste.

*Leaf Lettuce (garden lettuce):* Loose, ruffled, pale green

leaves with a delicate flavor.

*Mache (lamb's lettuce, corn salad):* A spring and early summer green that grows from a short center stem. Has a delicate flavor similar to arugula.

*Napa:* Similar to a Chinese cabbage in shape and flavor, but napa heads are stronger and broader.

*Nasturtium Leaves:* Pungent, peppery leaves from the garden plant. Use the stem or flower in salads.

*Radicchio:* Small, firm head with ruby red leaves. Has a slightly bitter taste similar to endive, so a little goes a long way. Radicchio is more expensive than most greens.

*Radish Sprouts:* Clover-like, tiny, dark leaves with a peppery taste and a slight radish flavor. Discard the roots and use only the leaves and stems in salads or to garnish hors d'oeuvres.

*Romaine (cos):* Long heads of loose, firm, crisp leaves

with a nutty flavor. The standard lettuce used in Caesar salad. Try it as wilted salad by sautéeing it quickly in a little oil and garlic, then sprinkling it with balsamic vinegar and chopped fresh herbs.

*Sorrel (sour grass):* Long, arrow-shaped leaves with a sour flavor. Pick young,

crisp, bright leaves. Sorrel may be served raw, or cooked in soups and sauces.

*Spinach:* Dark, crisp, green leaves. Wash or soak the leaves in several changes of cool water to remove all traces of sand and dirt. Trim the coarse stems and wilted or yellowed leaves. Add spinach to mixed greens, or serve with raw enoki mushrooms and bacon in a curried dressing.

*Watercress:* Crisp, green leaves with a peppery taste. Combine it with other greens, or use it as a

sandwich filling with an herb butter. Watercress also is good tossed with orange and red onion slices.

# Eggplant and Feta Cheese Salad

*Leave the skin on the grilled eggplant, so it retains its "blue" color.*

Grill or broil for 6 to 10 minutes.
Makes 8 servings.

*Nutrient Value Per Serving: 288 calories, 4 g protein, 26 g fat, 13 g carbohydrate, 204 mg sodium, 12 mg cholesterol.*

| | |
|---|---|
| 4 | **Italian eggplants** |
| ⅓ | **cup olive oil** |
| | **Salt and freshly ground pepper, to taste** |
| 1 | **teaspoon leaf oregano, crumbled** |
| 4 | **ripe plum tomatoes** |
| ¼ | **pound mild feta cheese, crumbled** |
| 2 | **teaspoons Dijon-style mustard** |
| 3 | **tablespoons balsamic vinegar** |
| ¼ | **teaspoon leaf oregano** |
| ½ | **cup olive oil** |
| ¼ | **cup chopped red onion** |

1. Slice the eggplants lengthwise and score the flesh in diagonal directions to create a diamond pattern. Brush all over with the ⅓ cup of oil, then sprinkle with the salt and pepper and the 1 teaspoon of oregano.
2. Grill or broil the eggplants 4 inches from the source of the heat, cut sides down, for 3 to 5 minutes, or until golden brown. Turn the eggplants. Grill or broil for 3 to 5 minutes more, or until the eggplants are tender. Remove from the grill or broiler pan.
3. Slice the tomatoes crosswise and arrange them around the edge of a serving dish. Fill the center with the eggplant halves. Sprinkle the feta cheese over.
4. Blend the mustard, vinegar and the ¼ teaspoon of oregano in a small bowl. Slowly add the ½ cup of oil in a steady stream. Drizzle the dressing over the salad and sprinkle the onion on top.

## Food for Thought . . .

***Italian or Plum Tomatoes*** *The names "plum" and "Italian" tomatoes are used interchangeably. These tomatoes are small to medium in size and egg-shaped. They have a meaty texture and a less watery pulp than round tomatoes, which makes them ideal for use in sauces and for eating raw.*

## Food for Thought . . .

***Feta*** *A Greek cheese made from sheep's milk, feta is semisoft and highly salted. It originated around Athens and was called pickled cheese because it was stored in brine. Feta can be eaten with Greek olives as an appetizer, or crumbled into salads. In supermarkets, chunks of feta are available refrigerated in jars, or packaged in brine or vacuum-sealed packages.*

# Orange and Onion Salad

Makes 4 servings.

*Nutrient Value Per Serving: 170 calories, 2 g protein, 14 g fat, 12 g carbohydrate, 25 mg sodium, 0 mg cholesterol.*

| | |
|---|---|
| 1 | **medium-size head Boston lettuce** |
| 2 | **navel oranges** |
| 1 | **medium-size red onion** |
| 1 | **tablespoon balsamic vinegar** |
| ½ | **teaspoon Dijon-style mustard** |
| ⅛ | **teaspoon sugar** |
| | **Salt and freshly ground pepper, to taste** |
| ¼ | **cup fruity olive oil** |
| 1 | **tablespoon finely chopped fresh watercress (optional)** |

1. Separate the lettuce into leaves and wash the leaves well. Dry the leaves and tear them into a large bowl.
2. Cut the peel and the white pith from the oranges. Working over a bowl to catch the juice, section the oranges; reserve the orange juice. Peel and slice the onion. Arrange the orange sections and the onion slices over the lettuce in the bowl. Cover the salad with damp paper toweling. Chill the salad.
3. Combine 2 tablespoons of the reserved orange juice, the vinegar, mustard, sugar, salt and pepper in a small bowl. Slowly beat in the oil. Stir in fresh watercress, if you wish.
4. Pour the dressing over the salad and toss gently to coat evenly.

## Avocado and Mandarin Orange Salad

Makes 4 servings.

*Nutrient Value Per Serving: 299 calories, 5 g protein, 24 g fat, 22 g carbohydrate, 40 mg sodium, 0 mg cholesterol.*

2   *heads bibb lettuce*
1   *can (11 ounces) mandarin oranges, drained*
1   *small avocado, halved, seeded and diced (about 1 cup)*
¼   *cup pine nuts or walnuts*
¼   *cup white wine vinegar*
¼   *cup sesame oil*
¼   *teaspoon soy sauce*
¼   *teaspoon honey*
     *Dash dry white wine*

1. Trim, rinse and dry the lettuce leaves very well. Tear the leaves into small pieces and arrange in a salad bowl. Add the mandarin oranges, avocado and the pine nuts or walnuts, and toss gently.
2. Combine the vinegar, oil, soy sauce, honey and wine in a screw-top jar. Shake until all the ingredients are combined.
3. Pour the dressing over the salad to serve.

## Spinach and Orange Salad

Makes 4 servings.

*Nutrient Value Per Serving: 37 calories, 2 g protein, 0 g fat, 8 g carbohydrate, 290 mg sodium, 0 mg cholesterol.*

1   *navel orange*
1   *tablespoon soy sauce*
2   *tablespoons water*
1   *tablespoon grated onion*
½   *pound fresh spinach, washed well and stems removed*
½   *large red onion, thinly sliced into rings*
¼   *large sweet red pepper, cut lengthwise into very thin strips*

1. Cut the peel from the orange, holding the orange over a pie plate to catch the juice. Section the orange, again catching the juice, and set aside the sections in a small bowl. Set aside about 2 tablespoons of the orange juice.
2. Combine the orange juice, soy sauce, water and grated onion in a small bowl.
3. Toss together the orange sections, spinach, onion rings and red pepper in a salad bowl. Briskly whisk the dressing. Pour the dressing over the salad and toss gently to combine.

### RUB-A-DUB-DUB

*To insure that all sand is removed from fresh spinach leaves, wash them several times in a basin filled with cool water. Gently lift the leaves from the water; the sand will fall to the bottom of the basin. Change the water each time the spinach is washed.*

# SALAD DAYS

Everyone has his or her own vision of "the perfect salad." Purists insist that a true salad should contain only mixed greens tossed with a simple vinaigrette. The adventurous salad-eater sees just about anything as a potential salad ingredient, from grilled chicken to sliced mango to taco filling. Healthful, tasty and filling, salads can be served as side dishes, appetizers or entrées. There's more to a salad than you think!

**Lettuce Talk** Until recently, most people thought that "lettuce" meant *iceberg* lettuce. Actually, lettuce comes in two categories: head lettuce and leaf lettuce.

Head lettuce furls its leaves like a cabbage. This category includes iceberg, Bibb and Boston lettuces.

Leaf lettuce doesn't form a head. Included in this category are red leaf, green leaf, Ruby and Romaine lettuces. *(For a complete listing of the different greens available, see pages 56-57.)*

**Picking Perfect Lettuce** Most lettuce is available year round, but there is a decline in supply as winter sets in.

When buying head lettuce, look for firm leaves that show no signs of browning. Iceberg lettuce should be compact and feel heavy for its size, although a very heavy weight may indicate that the lettuce is so tightly packed the leaves will be hard to separate.

**The Greens Store** Before storing lettuce, it's a good idea to separate it into leaves. Rinse the leaves under cool water and transfer them to paper toweling or an absorbent kitchen towel. Pat the leaves dry and place them in a plastic bag. Iceberg lettuce will stay fresh in the refrigerator for up to seven days. Leaf lettuce will start to deteriorate after three days, so use it promptly.

**The Herb Garden** Fresh or dried, herbs add a subtle flavor to salad dressings. In general, 1 part dried herbs is equal to 3 parts fresh herbs. In other words, 1 teaspoon of dried herbs is equal in strength of flavor to 1 tablespoon of fresh herbs.

Try some of these herbs in your salad dressing: basil, bay leaves, borage, chervil, cilantro (coriander), dill, lemon balm, marjoram, mint, oregano, parsley, sage, rosemary, savory, tarragon and thyme.

**Measure For Measure** A dressed salad doesn't keep very well, so it's better to prepare just enough for your guests than to have leftovers. With green salads, estimate about 1 cup per person, if the salad will be served with other dishes; for salad lovers, plan on 2 cups. By dressing salad a part at a time, you'll be able to refrigerate leftover, *undressed* salad in plastic bags and serve it the following day. Remember to remove tomatoes from a salad before storing it to avoid wilting the lettuce.

**Salad Savvy**
• Lettuce and greens should be torn into bite-size pieces. It should not be necessary to cut salad greens after they are served.
• To avoid soggy salads, toss the salad with the dressing at the table just before serving.
• Make the dressing ahead of time to insure a good blending of the flavors, and to save you time in the kitchen before a meal.

**Prepare To Tear** Gently tear leaves into bite-size pieces. It's not a good idea to cut leaves with a knife, because the edges will bruise and turn brown faster. You may, however, use a knife to shred iceberg lettuce.

**What Goes In . . .** A little imagination can turn a salad from ho-hum to wow! Raid your refrigerator for likely leftovers: cheese, cooked rice, steamed vegetables, cold pasta, meats, chicken or fish. Search your cupboard for inventive add-ins: sesame, poppy or sunflower seeds, raisins, nuts, croutons, bacon bits, olives or canned peppers.

**Dressed For Success** You can add a personal touch to bottled or homemade dressing to make a memorable "house dressing". Fresh or dried herbs, onion and grated Parmesan cheese are just a few of the "secret ingredients" that can liven up a vinaigrette or creamy dressing.

Vinaigrette is just a fancy way of saying vinegar and oil. A simple vinaigrette of two parts oil to one part vinegar is equally delicious on a green or a mixed salad.

**Viva La Vinegar!** Vinegar varieties include: white distilled, red distilled, white wine, red wine, raspberry and other fruit-flavored, tarragon and other herb-flavored, apple cider and balsamic vinegars.

**Oil You Need To Know** The perfect dressing calls for the perfect oil. Here, too, there are many kinds to choose from: all-purpose vegetable, sesame, olive, corn, sunflower, saffron, peanut, safflower, almond, hazelnut, walnut or avocado.

---

## Food for Thought . . .

**Gorgonzola** *A blue cheese made in, and named for, a village near Milan, Italy. Gorgonzola is a semisoft, creamy and delicately flavored cheese.*

---

# Five Greens Salad with Walnut Vinaigrette

Makes 20 servings.

*Nutrient Value Per Serving: 207 calories, 3 g protein, 21 g fat, 5 g carbohydrate, 160 mg sodium, 1 mg cholesterol.*

1 **cup walnuts, toasted\* and coarsely chopped**
2 **heads Boston lettuce**
2 **heads red-leaf lettuce**
2 **heads radicchio**
1 **head curly endive**
2 **bunches watercress, stems removed**
  **Walnut Vinaigrette (recipe follows)**
1 **cup Gorgonzola cheese, crumbled (optional)**

1. Place the walnuts in a large salad bowl.
2. Tear the Boston lettuce, leaf lettuce, radicchio, endive and watercress into bite-size pieces and add them to the walnuts in the salad bowl.
3. To serve, pour the Walnut Vinaigrette over the salad. Sprinkle with the Gorgonzola cheese, if you wish. Toss the salad to mix all the ingredients well.

**Walnut Vinaigrette:** Combine ¼ cup of red wine vinegar, 1 tablespoon of Dijon-style mustard, 1 tablespoon of heavy cream, 1 teaspoon of salt and 1 teaspoon of pepper in the container of an electric blender or a food processor. Combine ¾ cup of walnut oil and ¾ cup of safflower oil in a measuring cup. With the motor running, slowly pour in the oil in a steady stream until well blended and smooth.

**\*Note:** *To toast the walnuts, spread them in an even layer in a jelly-roll pan. Toast in a slow oven (325°), stirring often, until browned, for about 20 minutes. Also, the salad dressing may be made ahead and refrigerated for up to 4 days.*

## Food for Thought . . .

**Mandarin Oranges** *Loose-skinned, easily peeled and sectioned, Mandarin oranges are subdivided into three categories: tangerines, satsumas and miscellaneous hybrids, which include tangelo and temple oranges. Florida and Mexico are the largest producers of Mandarin oranges, which are most readily available from October to May.*

## Tangy Tangerine Salad

Makes 4 servings.

*Nutrient Value Per Serving: 76 calories, 3 g protein, 3 g fat, 11 g carbohydrate, 41 mg sodium, 2 mg cholesterol.*

- 1 piece fresh gingerroot, peeled (about 3 inches x 1 inch)
- 4 teaspoons wine vinegar
- 1 tablespoon frozen undiluted tangerine juice concentrate
- 2 teaspoons olive oil
  Pinch dry mustard
- ½ cup plain lowfat yogurt
- 2 large tangerines, peeled and sliced crosswise into 6 rounds
- 12 spinach leaves
- ¼ cup sliced red onion, for garnish

1. Grate the gingerroot onto wax paper. Squeeze the ginger over a 2-cup glass measure. Set aside about 2 teaspoons of the ginger juice. Whisk the vinegar, tangerine juice concentrate, oil and mustard into the 2 teaspoons of ginger juice. Gradually whisk in the yogurt. Cover the dressing and refrigerate for at least 2 hours. For a very intense ginger flavor, chill the dressing overnight.
2. To serve the salad, arrange the tangerine slices and the spinach leaves on 4 individual salad plates. Stir the dressing and drizzle over the top. Garnish the salad with the onion slices.

## Snow Peas and Sprout Salad

*All the ingredients for this delicious mix of crisp pods and curly shoots once were found only in Chinese groceries. Today, they are available in supermarkets all over the country. Make the dressing in advance, but spoon over the salad just before tossing.*

Makes 6 servings.

*Nutrient Value Per Serving: 153 calories, 3 g protein, 13 g fat, 7 g carbohydrate, 188 mg sodium, 0 mg cholesterol.*

- 1 clove garlic, finely chopped
- ½ teaspoon salt
- 1½ tablespoons lemon juice
- 1½ teaspoons dry mustard
- 2 tablespoons dry sherry
- ⅓ cup peanut, corn or olive oil
- ⅛ teaspoon crushed dried hot red peppers
- ½ pound snow peas, trimmed
- ½ pound Chinese (mung bean) sprouts (3 cups)
- 2 green onions, white bulbs and green tops, finely chopped
- 2 tablespoons finely diced sweet red pepper
- 1 tablespoon toasted* sesame seeds

1. With the back of a spoon, mash the garlic with the salt in a small bowl to form a paste. Stir in the lemon juice, mustard and sherry. Whisk in the peanut, corn or olive oil and the hot red pepper. Set aside.
2. Cook the snow peas in a large pot of boiling salted water for 30 seconds. Drain the snowpeas, rinse them under cold running water and drain again.
3. Arrange the sprouts in the bottom of a large serving bowl. Place the snow peas in the center. Sprinkle with the green onion, sweet red pepper and sesame seeds. Pour on the dressing and toss to mix all the ingredients well.

*Note: To toast the sesame seeds, heat a small, heavy skillet over medium-high heat. Add the sesame seeds and cook, shaking the pan constantly, until the seeds are a light amber color, for about 1 minute.*

## Food for Thought . . .

**Chinese Snow Peas** *Also called mange-tout, which means "eat it all" in French, snow peas have crisp, flat pods that are about 3 inches long and contain immature peas. Allow 1 pound for 3 servings.*

*Tangy Tomato Sorbet*

⟨⟨ 🍸 💲

# Tangy Tomato Sorbet

*The combination of tomato, avocado and seasonings makes this delicious sorbet a refreshing appetizer or salad.*

Makes 8 servings (1 quart).

*Nutrient Value Per ½ Cup Serving: 90 calories, 2 g protein, 3 g fat, 15 g carbohydrate, 122 mg sodium, 0 mg cholesterol.*

⅓   **cup sugar**
⅓   **cup water**
2   **pounds very ripe tomatoes (about 6 medium-size), coarsely chopped**
1   **ripe avocado (8 ounces), peeled, seeded and coarsely chopped**
1   **tablespoon Worcestershire sauce***
1   **tablespoon lime juice**
½   **teaspoon celery salt**
½   **teaspoon ground coriander**
¼   **teaspoon ground hot red pepper Tomato wedges, lime slices and parsley, for garnish (optional)**

1. Heat together the sugar and the water in a small saucepan over medium heat until the sugar dissolves. Set aside and cool the sugar syrup.
2. Place the tomatoes and the avocado in the container of an electric blender or a food processor, cover and whirl until the mixture is a smooth purée. Strain the purée, forcing it gently through a sieve with the back of a spoon. Discard the solids in the sieve. Stir in the Worcestershire sauce, lime juice, celery salt, coriander, ground hot red pepper and sugar syrup.
3. Freeze the tomato mixture in an ice cream maker** following the manufacturer's directions. Serve immediately, or cover and freeze for no more than 2 hours. Garnish with tomato wedges, lime slices and parsley, if you wish.

**Notes:** *\*For a redder sorbet, substitute 4 tablespoons of white wine Worcestershire sauce for the regular Worcestershire. \*\*If you do not have an ice cream maker, freeze the sorbet in a 9-inch-square pan, covered with plastic wrap, until firm, for 3 to 6 hours. Break the mixture into small pieces, place them in the container of a food processor or an electric mixer bowl and beat just until fluffy. Serve immediately, or return to the freezer for no more than 2 hours.*

## TOMATO TIDBIT

*To ripen tomatoes, keep them at room temperature and out of direct sunlight.*

# CHAPTER 3

# The Main Event

*Coming soon to a kitchen near you: delicious dinners your family will flip over!*

*Piquant Baby Back Ribs (recipe, page 108); Barbequed Frank Kebabs (recipe, page 109); Veal Kebabs (recipe, page 108); Butterflied Cornish Hens (recipe, page 110); Key West Burgers (recipe, page 109)*

**G**ood food, good meat, good grief, let's eat!

That irreverent but apt blessing does make its point: the "meat" of the meal is considered the most important part, whether it's beef, poultry or seafood. That's why we're presenting over 50 recipes—enough to try a new entrée a week for a year!

Beef still ranks as America's favorite, and its versatility is renowned. We take advantage of that with recipes such as Mexican Crêpes *(recipe, page 70)*, Marinated Meatball Kebabs *(recipe, page 69)* and Key West Burgers *(recipe, page 109)*.

Poultry and seafood lovers will enjoy these new twists on classics: Honey Mustard Chicken *(recipe, page 92)*, Jamaican Chicken Calypso *(recipe, page 86)*, Flounder Fillets with Chick Pea Relish *(recipe, page 104)*.

Pork, lamb and veal are offered in a delicious new array of recipes, from spicy and satisfying California Burritos *(recipe, page 74)*, to elegant Spinach Veal Roll with Mushroom Sauce *(recipe, page 80)*.

Wrapping it up is a section on barbecues. You'll find a slew of marinades and sauces, and of course, main dishes: Grilled Thai Chicken *(recipe, page 111)*, Honolulu Spareribs *(recipe, page 107)*, Seasoned Sirloin Tri-Tips *(recipe, page 105)*.

For more entrées, flip to the next chapter—Other Main Events—to find great recipes on pasta, beans and main-dish salads. ■

# Beef

## Stir-Fried Steak, Tofu and Vegetables

Makes 6 servings.

*Nutrient Value Per Serving: 269 calories, 20 g protein, 17 g fat, 10 g carbohydrate, 757 mg sodium, 30 mg cholesterol.*

- ¼ **cup soy sauce**
- ¼ **cup dry sherry**
- 1 **tablespoon cornstarch**
- 1 **teaspoon white vinegar**
- 1 **teaspoon sugar**
- 3 **tablespoons peanut or vegetable oil**
- ¾ **pound flank steak, thinly sliced on the diagonal**
- 2 **squares (8 ounces) firm tofu (bean curd), cubed**
- ½ **pound spinach, stemmed, torn in bite-size pieces**
- ¼ **pound mushrooms, sliced**
- ¼ **pound snow peas**
- 3 **green onions, cut into ½-inch slices**
- 1 **can (8 ounces) sliced bamboo shoots, drained**

1. Combine the soy sauce, sherry, cornstarch, vinegar and sugar in a small bowl. Mix well and set aside.
2. Heat the peanut or vegetable oil in a wok or large skillet. Add the steak and stir-fry for 3 minutes. Add the tofu, spinach, mushrooms, snow peas, green onion and bamboo shoots. Stir-fry for 1 minute, or until the spinach wilts. Stir the sauce into the wok and cook for 1 minute more.

## Corned Beef

Makes 8 to 10 servings.

*Nutrient Value Per Serving: 324 calories, 23 g protein, 24 g fat, 1 g carbohydrate, 1,452 mg sodium, 125 mg cholesterol.*

- 4 **pounds corned beef**
- 2 **tablespoons pickling spice**
- 3 **cloves garlic**
- 1 **small onion, cut in half**

1. Rinse the corned beef. Place it in a large pot, cover with cold water and bring to a boil.
2. Meanwhile, tie the pickling spice and the garlic in a cheesecloth bag.
3. After the water boils, lower the heat to simmer. Add the cheesecloth bag and the onion. Cook for 3½ to 4 hours, or until the corned beef is fork-tender, adding water as necessary. Remove to a cutting board.
4. To serve, cut across the grain into thin diagonal slices. Serve with mustard.

**To Reheat:** Wrap the corned beef in aluminum foil. Place in a slow oven (325°) for 45 minutes, or until heated through.

### Food for Thought . . .

**Corned Beef** *The term "corned beef" is derived from an old English word meaning "cured," or preserving with salt—the word "corn" referred to any small particle, which is how salt was described. Today beef is preserved by curing in a brine made of salt, sugar, spices and saltpeter. The salt preserves the meat, the sugar inhibits the salt from hardening the meat and the saltpeter provides the red coloring.*

*Corned Beef, Potato Apple Pancakes (recipe, page 159) and Irish Coffee Mousse with Praline (recipe, page 193)*

## Speedy Shepherd's Pie

*A vegetable pie with a zesty ground meat crust and mashed potato cheese topping. Serve with cinnamon-flavored applesauce (from the cupboard) and whole wheat Italian bread.*

Bake crust at 375° for 15 minutes, bake whole pie at 375° for 15 minutes.
Makes 6 servings.

*Nutrient Value Per Serving: 388 calories, 24 g protein, 23 g fat, 19 g carbohydrate, 693 mg sodium, 130 mg cholesterol.*

**Meat Crust:**
- ½ **cup fresh bread crumbs**
- 1 **tablespoon grated onion**
- 1 **egg, slightly beaten**
- 2 **tablespoons catsup**
- 2 **tablespoons milk**
- 1½ **teaspoons Dijon-style mustard**
- ½ **teaspoon leaf thyme, crumbled**
- ¼ **teaspoon salt**
- ¼ **teaspoon pepper**
- 1½ **pounds ground beef**

**Vegetable Filling:**
- 1 **package (16 ounces) frozen mixed vegetables in small pieces**
- 1 **tablespoon butter or margarine**
- 1 **tablespoon all-purpose flour**
- 1 **cup beef broth**
- ¼ **cup fresh bread crumbs**
- ½ **teaspoon leaf thyme, crumbled**
  **Pinch pepper**

**Potato Topping:**
- 4 **servings mashed potatoes made from instant mashed potato flakes**
- 2 **tablespoons grated Parmesan cheese, plus 1 tablespoon, for garnish (optional)**

1. Preheat the oven to moderate (375°).
2. Prepare the Meat Crust: Combine the bread crumbs, onion, egg, catsup, milk, mustard, thyme, salt, pepper and beef in a 9-inch pie plate. Pat the meat mixture around the bottom and up the sides of the plate in a uniform layer, keeping the meat inside the pie plate rim.

3. With aluminum foil under the pie plate to catch any fat drippings, bake the "crust" in the preheated moderate oven (375°) for 15 minutes, or until the meat juices run clear when the meat is pierced with a fork. Using pot holders to hold the plate, carefully drain off the excess fat. Leave the oven temperature at 375°.
4. Meanwhile, prepare the Vegetable Filling: Cook the vegetables in a saucepan following the package directions. Drain in a colander and set aside.
5. In the saucepan used to cook the vegetables, melt the butter or margarine over low heat. Stir in the flour until smooth. Stir in the broth until smooth. Bring to boiling over medium heat, stirring, until thick and bubbly. Stir in the vegetables, bread crumbs, thyme and pepper. Pour the mixture into the baked meat crust.
6. Prepare the Potato Topping: Make mashed potatoes for 4 servings from instant mashed potato flakes, following the package directions and using water, milk and butter. Stir in the 2 tablespoons of Parmesan cheese. Spoon the mixture into a pastry bag fitted with a large star tip. Pipe a lattice design on the pie. (If the pastry bag filled with mashed potatoes is too hot to hold, let it cool slightly or wrap a kitchen towel around the bag to protect your hands.) Garnish the top with an additional 1 tablespoon of Parmesan cheese, if you wish.
7. Bake in the preheated moderate oven (375°) for 15 minutes, or until the topping is golden and the filling is hot.

### FRESH FROM THE SOURCE

*To make your own bread crumbs, tear slices of bread into small pieces with your fingers. Or place one slice at a time, quartered, in the container of a blender or a food processor, cover and whirl at high speed for 15 seconds.*

## Microwave Instructions
*(for a 650-watt variable power microwave oven)*

*For this microwave oven adaptation, we've changed the layering from the original recipe in order to produce a moister dish, and we've used instant mashed potato granules rather than flakes.*

*Nutrient Value Per Serving: 435 calories, 25 g protein, 25 g fat, 27 g carbohydrate, 733 mg sodium, 132 mg cholesterol.*

**Ingredient Changes:** Increase the salt in the meat crust mixture to ¾ teaspoon. In the vegetable filling, reduce the beef broth to ½ cup and eliminate the bread crumbs. Use instant mashed potato granules instead of flakes. Omit the optional 1 tablespoon of Parmesan cheese garnish.

**Directions:** For the Vegetable Mixture: Place the frozen vegetables in an 8-inch-square microwave-safe baking dish and pour in ¼ cup of water. Cover with pleated plastic wrap. Microwave at full power for 7 minutes, stirring once. Drain the vegetables in a colander. Place the butter or margarine in a 4-cup microwave-safe measure. Microwave, uncovered, for 45 seconds to melt. Stir in the flour until smooth. Mix in ½ cup of beef broth, the thyme and pepper. Microwave, uncovered, for 2 to 2½ minutes to boiling. Whisk well until smooth. Combine with the vegetables in a small bowl. For the Meat Mixture: Combine the bread crumbs, onion, egg, catsup, milk, mustard, thyme, ¾ teaspoon of salt, the pepper and meat in the same 8-inch-square dish; mix well. Pat into an even layer on the bottom of the dish, but *not* up the sides of the dish. Cover with wax paper. Microwave at full power for 8 minutes. Carefully drain off the liquid. For the Potato Mixture: Combine 1 cup of water, ½ cup of milk and 1 tablespoon of butter in the same 4-cup measure. Microwave, uncovered, at full power for 4 to 4½ minutes just to boiling. Mix in 6 tablespoons of instant mashed potato granules and the 2 tablespoons of Parmesan cheese. To assemble: Spread the potatoes in an even layer over the meat. Top with the vegetable mixture. Cover with wax paper. Microwave at full power for 2 minutes to heat through. Let the pie stand for 5 minutes before serving.

## Marinated Meatball Kebabs

*These savory meatballs can be broiled or barbecued.*

Broil for 12 to 14 minutes.
Makes 4 servings.

*Nutrient Value Per Serving: 253 calories, 22 g protein, 15 g fat, 7 g carbohydrate, 1,014 mg sodium, 70 mg cholesterol.*

**Marinade:**
3   tablespoons soy sauce
1   tablespoon grated sweet onion

**Meatballs:**
1   pound lean ground beef
2   teaspoons soy sauce
1   tablespoon grated sweet onion
    Pinch pepper

1   large sweet green pepper
1   pint cherry tomatoes, washed

1. Prepare the Marinade: Combine the soy sauce and the onion in a pie plate.
2. Prepare the Meatballs: Gently break apart the beef, using 2 forks, in a medium-size bowl. Sprinkle the soy sauce, onion and pepper over the meat. Gently toss to combine.
3. Shape the mixture into twelve 1¼-inch meatballs. Place in the marinade, turning to coat evenly. Let stand for 10 minutes. Turn and let stand for 10 minutes longer.

4. Cut the green pepper into 1-inch pieces. Thread the cherry tomatoes alternately with the green pepper and the meatballs onto 4 large skewers. Be careful not to break the meatballs. Brush the marinade over the green pepper and the tomatoes.

5. Broil the skewers 4 to 5 inches from the source of the heat for 6 to 8 minutes, or until the meatballs are browned on one side. Turn carefully. Brush with the marinade. Broil for 6 minutes longer, or until the meatballs are browned and cooked through.

## Mexican Crêpes

Bake at 375° for 10 minutes.
Makes 8 crêpes.

*Nutrient Value Per Crêpe: 320 calories, 15 g protein, 20 g fat, 20 g carbohydrate, 619 mg sodium, 121 mg cholesterol.*

1   **cup buttermilk baking mix**
1   **cup milk**
2   **eggs, slightly beaten**
1   **package (1¼ ounces) taco seasoning mix**
1   **pound ground beef**
1   **medium-size sweet green pepper, cored, seeded and chopped**
1   **medium-size onion, chopped**
½   **cup water**
½   **cup canned refried beans**
    **Shredded lettuce, chopped tomato, shredded Cheddar cheese, dairy sour cream, sliced ripe olives**

1. Preheat the oven to moderate (375°). Grease a large baking sheet.

2. Whisk together the buttermilk baking mix, milk, eggs and 3 tablespoons of the taco seasoning mix in a medium-size bowl until smooth.

3. For each crêpe, pour ¼ cup of batter into a hot, lightly greased nonstick skillet with an 8-inch bottom and rotate the skillet until the batter covers the bottom. Cook until golden brown, for about 1 minute. Flip and cook the other side until golden brown. You should have 8 crêpes, measuring 7½ to 8 inches. Stack the crêpes between pieces of wax paper.

4. Brown the beef in the skillet. Drain the excess fat. Stir in the remaining taco seasoning mix, the green pepper, onion and water. Bring to boiling. Lower the heat and simmer, uncovered, stirring frequently, until the beef mixture is very thick, for about 2 minutes.

5. Divide the beef mixture and the refried beans evenly among the crêpes, spooning down the center of each crêpe. Fold the sides and ends of the crêpes over the filling. Place the crêpes, seam side down, on the prepared baking sheet.

6. Bake in the preheated moderate oven (375°) until heated through, for about 10 minutes. Serve with the lettuce, tomato, Cheddar cheese, sour cream and olives.

### Food for Thought . . .

**Ground Beef** *Ground beef, or hamburger, contains at least 70% lean meat. Use it for burgers, chili, Sloppy Joes and casseroles. Lean ground beef, or ground chuck, has at least 77% lean meat. Use it for meatloaf, meatballs and chopped steaks. Extra-lean ground beef, or ground round or sirloin, has at least 85% lean meat. Use it as you would ground chuck or when you're watching calorie and fat consumption.*

# Aztec Pie

*For this hearty casserole, layers of tortilla chips, chili sauce and cheese are baked in a cast iron skillet.*

Bake at 400° for 20 minutes.
Makes 6 servings.

*Nutrient Value Per Serving: 667 calories, 28 g protein, 47 g fat, 36 g carbohydrate, 852 mg sodium, 93 mg cholesterol.*

| | |
|---|---|
| 2 | **cups chopped onion (2 large)** |
| 1 | **tablespoon vegetable oil** |
| 2 | **cloves garlic, finely chopped** |
| 1 | **pound lean ground beef** |
| 2 | **tablespoons chili powder** |
| 1 | **tablespoon sugar** |
| 1 | **teaspoon ground cumin** |
| 1 | **teaspoon leaf oregano, crumbled** |
| 1/4 | **teaspoon salt** |
| 1/4 | **teaspoon pepper** |
| 1/8 | **teaspoon ground cinnamon** |
| 1 | **can (16 ounces) whole tomatoes, undrained** |
| 1 | **can (4 ounces) chopped mild green chili peppers** |
| 1 | **bag (8 ounces) unsalted tortilla chips** |
| 1 | **cup thinly sliced green onion (1 bunch)** |
| 1 | **cup (6 ounces) pitted black olives, drained** |
| 1 | **cup shredded mild Cheddar cheese (4 ounces)** |
| 1 | **cup shredded Monterey Jack cheese (4 ounces)** |
| | **Avocado, lime and green onion, for garnish (optional)** |

1. Sauté the onion in the oil in a 9- or 10-inch well-seasoned cast iron skillet over medium-low heat until soft, for 5 minutes. Add the garlic and cook for 1 minute more. Transfer to a small bowl.
2. Crumble the beef into the skillet. Cook without stirring over medium-high heat until well browned on the bottom. Stir and cook until the meat no longer is pink, for about 8 minutes. Return the onion and garlic mixture to the skillet. Stir in the chili powder, sugar, cumin, oregano, salt, pepper and cinnamon. Cook for 2 to 3 minutes more, stirring, to blend the flavors. Stir in the tomatoes with their liquid and the green chili peppers; break up the tomatoes. Reduce the heat to medium-low and simmer gently for 10 minutes, stirring occasionally. Transfer the mixture to a bowl and set aside.
3. Preheat the oven to hot (400°). Wipe the skillet clean with paper toweling.
4. Place half the tortilla chips in an even layer on the bottom of the skillet. Spoon half the meat sauce over them. Sprinkle with the green onion. Remove and reserve 6 olives; scatter the remainder over the green onion. Sprinkle with half the Cheddar and Monterey Jack cheeses. Press down with a spatula to compress slightly. Top with the remaining chips and press down. Spread the remaining meat sauce over the top and sprinkle with the remaining Cheddar and Monterey Jack cheeses.
5. Bake in the preheated hot oven (400°) for 20 minutes, or until hot and bubbly. Using a pot holder, remove the skillet from the oven and let stand for 10 minutes before serving. Garnish the top with the reserved olives, and with avocado, lime and additional green onion, if you wish.

## Food for Thought . . .

***Monterey Jack*** *Named for David Jacks, a Scotsman whose dairies first produced this cheese, Monterey Jack was first made in Monterey County, California in 1892. The cheese may be a soft, creamy white or a firm, zesty, pale yellow. Fresh Jack is soft and somewhat porous, with a delicate flavor. Dry Jack is firm and aged much longer than fresh Jack; it has a pleasant flavor, is semidry and can be easily sliced or shredded. Dry Jack makes an excellent table cheese, and it is ideal for cooking because it melts smoothly with little stringing. It's a popular ingredient in Mexican dishes.*

# Pork

## Miniature Sausage Meatballs

Makes 24 meatballs (4 to 6 per serving).

*Nutrient Value Per Meatball: 59 calories, 4 g protein, 4 g fat, 1 g carbohydrate, 130 mg sodium, 23 mg cholesterol.*

- ½ **pound sweet Italian sausage**
- ½ **pound ground beef**
- 1 **clove garlic, finely chopped**
- ½ **cup finely chopped parsley**
- 1 **egg, slightly beaten**
- 1 **cup fresh bread crumbs**
- ½ **teaspoon salt**
- ¼ **teaspoon pepper**
- ½ **cup milk**
- 1 **tablespoon oil, or more as needed**
  **Easy Spaghetti Sauce**
  **(recipe, page 212)**

1. Remove the casings from the sausage and crumble the meat. Combine with the beef, garlic, parsley, egg, bread crumbs, salt and pepper in a large bowl. Pour the milk over. Toss lightly with a wooden spoon or clean hands until thoroughly mixed. Do not overmix or the meatballs will become "tough."
2. Break off walnut-size pieces of the meat mixture and roll between the palms of your hands to form 24 small meatballs. Place the meatballs on a platter or baking sheet lined with a piece of wax paper.
3. Heat the oil in a large, nonstick skillet. Working in 2 batches, brown the meatballs in the oil for about 10 minutes per batch. (Be careful not to crowd the skillet or the meatballs will steam rather than brown.) Remove to paper toweling to drain.

4. Add the meatballs to the Easy Spaghetti Sauce in a large skillet and simmer for 10 minutes to blend the flavors. The meatballs can be made ahead, then simmered with the sauce before serving.

# Jiffy Jambalaya

*A quick version of the traditional Creole dish.*

Makes 6 servings.

*Nutrient Value Per Serving: 324 calories, 28 g protein, 8 g fat, 34 g carbohydrate, 1,289 mg sodium, 124 mg cholesterol.*

- 1   *medium-size onion, chopped*
- 1   *sweet green pepper, chopped*
- 1   *tablespoon butter*
- 1   *clove garlic, finely chopped*
- 1   *tablespoon all-purpose flour*
- 1   *can (16 ounces) whole tomatoes, undrained*
- 1   *cup tomato juice*
- 1/2   *cup bottled clam juice*
- 1   *tablespoon chopped fresh parsley*
- 1   *tablespoon Worcestershire sauce*
- 1/4   *teaspoon leaf thyme, crumbled*
- 1/8   *teaspoon liquid red pepper seasoning*
- 1/2   *teaspoon salt*
    *Pinch pepper*
- 2   *cups diced cooked ham (2/3 pound)*
- 3   *cups cooked white rice*
- 1   *pound medium-size shrimp, shelled and deveined*

1. Sauté the onion and the green pepper in the butter in a Dutch oven until softened, for about 5 minutes. Add the garlic and cook for 30 seconds. Add the flour and cook, stirring, for 1 minute.
2. Pour in the tomatoes with their liquid, the tomato juice, clam juice, parsley, Worcestershire sauce, thyme, liquid red pepper seasoning, salt and pepper. Bring to boiling. Lower the heat to simmer. Add the ham and the rice. Cook, covered, for 15 minutes. Add the shrimp and cook, covered, for 5 minutes more, or until the shrimp are cooked through.

# Pork Kebabs with Vegetables

Broil for 2 to 4 minutes.
Makes 4 servings.

*Nutrient Value Per Serving: 259 calories, 23 g protein, 8 g fat, 24 g carbohydrate, 80 mg sodium, 59 mg cholesterol.*

- 1   *pound boneless pork loin, fat trimmed*
- 2   *tablespoons dry mustard*
- 2   *tablespoons water*
- 2   *tablespoons honey*
- 1/8   *teaspoon leaf marjoram, crumbled*
- 1   *can (10 ounces) low-sodium beef broth, refrigerated and then fat removed from top*
- 1   *cup potato sticks, 3 x 1/4 inch (6 ounces)*
- 1   *cup yellow squash sticks, 3 x 1/4 inch (2 small)*
- 1   *cup carrot sticks, 3 x 1/4 inch (2 medium-size)*

1. Cut the pork loin crosswise into 8 equal slices. Divide each slice into 4 equal pieces to yield 32 pieces, each about 3/4 to 1 inch. Set aside.
2. Stir together the mustard and the water in a 11¾ x 7½ x 1¾-inch glass baking dish until smooth. Stir in the honey and the marjoram. Add the pork and toss well to coat with the marinade. Cover and refrigerate for at least 4 hours, turning once.
3. Bring the broth to boiling in a medium-size saucepan.
4. Meanwhile, thread 8 pork pieces on each of 4 skewers. Broil 5 inches from the source of the heat, turning often and brushing with the marinade, for 2 to 4 minutes, or until the center no longer is pink. Arrange one skewer on each of 4 individual plates and keep warm.
5. Add the potatoes to the boiling broth and cook for 2 minutes. Add the yellow squash and the carrots; cook for 2 to 3 minutes more, or until the potatoes are tender. Remove the vegetables with a slotted spoon and divide among the 4 plates.

## *California Burritos*

Makes 8 large burritos.

*Nutrient Value Per Serving: 515 calories, 25 g protein, 28 g fat, 40 g carbohydrate, 998 mg sodium, 71 mg cholesterol.*

**Chili Sauce:**
- 2    cloves garlic, finely chopped
- 2    teaspoons vegetable oil
- 2    teaspoons chili powder
- ¼    teaspoon ground cumin
- 2    teaspoons all-purpose flour
- ½    teaspoon salt
- 1    can (16 ounces) stewed tomatoes, undrained

**Filling:**
- 1    cup chopped onion (1 large)
- 1    tablespoon vegetable oil
- 1    clove garlic, finely chopped
- 1    pound lean ground pork OR: beef
- 1    teaspoon chili powder
- ½    teaspoon ground cumin
- ½    teaspoon leaf oregano, crumbled
- ½    teaspoon salt
- ¼    teaspoon pepper
- 1    teaspoon all-purpose flour
- ¼    cup water

- 2⅔   cups refried beans (about one and a half 16-ounce cans)
- 8    flour tortillas (10-inch)
- 2    cups shredded mild Cheddar cheese (8 ounces)

---

### ▄▄▄ WHAT IS A BURRITO?

*A rolled flour tortilla usually filled with meat and/or beans and cheese.*

---

1. Prepare the Chili Sauce: Sauté the garlic in the oil in a small saucepan over low heat for 30 seconds. Add the chili powder, cumin, flour and salt. Cook, stirring, for 30 seconds more. Add the tomatoes with their liquid and stir over medium heat, mashing with a spoon to break up the tomatoes, until thick, for 10 minutes. You should have about 1 cup. Set aside.

2. Prepare the Filling: Sauté the onion in the oil in a medium-size, heavy skillet over medium heat until soft, for about 5 minutes. Add the garlic and cook for 1 minute. Crumble in the pork or beef and sauté until half-cooked. Add the chili powder, cumin, oregano, salt and pepper. Cook, stirring, until the meat is cooked through. Stir in the flour and cook for 1 minute. Add the water and cook until thickened, stirring occasionally, for 3 to 5 minutes. Keep the filling hot, or reheat when ready to assemble the burritos.

3. To assemble the burritos, heat the refried beans in a saucepan until very hot and a good spreading consistency; add a few drops of water if the beans are too thick. The meat filling should be hot. The chili sauce can be hot or at room temperature.

4. Heat a griddle or large skillet over very low heat. Warm 1 tortilla on it until soft, pliable and just hot, turning to heat both sides evenly, for 10 to 15 seconds. Spread the tortilla evenly with about ⅓ cup of the beans. Place a scant ⅓ cup of the meat filling in a line along the lower third of the tortilla. Top the meat with ¼ cup of the Cheddar cheese and ⅛ cup of the chili sauce. Fold the right and left sides of the tortilla over the ends of the filling and roll up to enclose the filling. Repeat with the remaining ingredients. (If the griddle becomes too hot, remove from the heat and cool slightly.) Let the burritos rest for a minute or two to melt the Cheddar cheese before serving.

## TEMPERATURE AND TIME FOR ROASTING HAM AND SMOKED PORK

| Cut | Approx. Pound Weight | Oven Temperature | Internal Meat Temperature When Done | Roasting Time (min. per pound) |
|---|---|---|---|---|
| **Cook-before-eating Ham** | | | | |
| Whole | 10 to 14 | 300° to 325° | 160° | 18 to 20 |
| Half | 5 to 7 | 300° to 325° | 160° | 22 to 25 |
| Shank or Butt portion | 3 to 4 | 300° to 325° | 160° | 35 to 40 |
| **Fully Cooked Ham** | | | | |
| Whole | 12 to 14 | 325° | 130° | 15 |
| Half | 5 to 7 | 325° | 130° | 18 to 24 |
| **Picnic Shoulder** | 5 to 8 | 300° to 325° | 170° | 35 |
| **Shoulder Roll** | 2 to 3 | 300° to 325° | 170° | 35 to 40 |

# Stir-Fried Ham and Peanuts

Makes 4 servings.

*Nutrient Value Per Serving: 609 calories, 37 g protein, 44 g fat, 20 g carbohydrate, 2,313 mg sodium, 67 mg cholesterol.*

¼ cup light soy sauce
⅓ cup dry sherry
1 tablespoon rice wine vinegar
2 teaspoons Oriental sesame oil*
1 teaspoon sugar
2 leeks, cut diagonally into 1-inch slices and rinsed well
2 medium-size zucchini, peeled, quartered, and cut diagonally into 1-inch slices
1 tablespoon finely chopped, peeled fresh gingerroot
2 cloves garlic, finely chopped
4 teaspoons cornstarch
⅓ cup water
¼ cup peanut oil
1 cup dry-roasted unsalted peanuts
3 cups diced cooked ham (1 pound)

1. Combine the soy sauce, sherry, vinegar, Oriental sesame oil and sugar in a small bowl. Set aside.
2. Prepare the leeks, zucchini, ginger and garlic. Stir together the cornstarch and the water in a small cup. Arrange the ingredients near the stove top.
3. Heat the peanut oil in a large skillet. Add the peanuts and stir-fry until golden brown, for about 1 minute. Remove with a slotted spoon to paper toweling, leaving the oil in the skillet.
4. Add the leeks, zucchini, ginger and garlic to the skillet with the oil and stir-fry for 2 minutes. Add the soy sauce mixture and stir-fry for 1 minute. Quickly restir the cornstarch mixture and add to the skillet. Cook until the sauce thickens, for about 1 minute.
5. Add the ham and the peanuts and stir-fry for 2 to 3 minutes, or until heated through. Serve over hot cooked rice.

*__Note:__ Oriental sesame oil has more flavor and is darker in color than regular sesame oil. It can be found in the Oriental food section of many supermarkets or in Oriental specialty food stores.*

## *Chicago Deep-Dish Pizza*

Bake at 425° for 15 to 20 minutes.
Makes 6 servings (9- or 10-inch pie).

*Nutrient Value Per Serving: 435 calories, 19 g protein, 26 g fat, 29 g carbohydrate, 828 mg sodium, 61 mg cholesterol.*

½    **pound sweet Italian sausage**
1    **large sweet green or red pepper,
        cored, seeded and cut into strips,
        2 x ¼ inch**
1    **medium-size onion, thinly sliced
        (½ cup)**
1    **tablespoon olive oil**
1    **clove garlic, finely chopped**
¼    **pound mushrooms, sliced**
2    **tablespoons thinly sliced pepperoni,
        cut into thin strips**
1    **teaspoon leaf basil, crumbled**
1    **teaspoon leaf oregano, crumbled**
¼    **teaspoon black pepper**
1    **tube (10 ounces) refrigerated pizza-
        crust dough**
½    **cup bottled or canned pizza or
        spaghetti sauce**
2    **tablespoons grated Parmesan cheese**
1    **package (8 ounces) mozzarella cheese,
        coarsely shredded (2 cups)**

1. Preheat the oven to hot (425°).
2. Remove the casings from the sausage and crumble the meat into a large, heavy skillet. Cook over medium heat, stirring often, for 5 minutes, or until the sausage no longer is pink. Transfer the meat with a slotted spoon to a plate lined with paper toweling. Discard the fat from the skillet.
3. Sauté the green or red pepper and the onion in the oil in the same skillet over medium heat for 5 minutes, stirring occasionally. Add the garlic and cook for 1 minute more. Add the mushrooms, pepperoni, basil, oregano and black pepper and cook for 2 to 3 minutes, stirring occasionally. If the mixture becomes too dry, add 1 to 2 tablespoons of water.
4. Unroll the pizza dough. Place in a 9- or 10-inch well-seasoned cast iron skillet, stretching the dough slightly to fit up the sides about 1 inch. Roll the 4 pointed corners inward slightly. Spread the dough with 2 tablespoons of the pizza or spaghetti sauce. Spread half the vegetable mixture evenly over the sauce and top with half the sausage. Sprinkle with 1 tablespoon of the Parmesan cheese. Dot with 3 tablespoons of the pizza sauce. Top with half the mozzarella cheese. Repeat the layering.
5. Bake in the preheated hot oven (425°) for 15 to 20 minutes, or until the mozzarella cheese is melted and the crust is golden brown. Let stand for 5 minutes. Slide the pizza onto a plate, using a metal spatula.

---

### *WHY CHOOSE CAST IRON?*

• *Cast iron heats up and cooks evenly.*
• *Cast iron pans are thick and heavy so food doesn't burn as easily.*
• *Everything prepared in a cast iron pan retains some of the iron from the skillet, giving you a free mineral supplement.*
• *You can use cast iron pans on the stove, in the oven and even on an outdoor grill.*

# Lamb & Veal

## Lamb à la Française

*The lamb is marinated overnight before being roasted, then chilled again for easy slicing and serving.*

Bake at 350° for 1½ to 2½ hours.
Makes 8 servings.

*Nutrient Value Per Serving: 336 calories, 32 g protein, 22 g fat, 1 g carbohydrate, 303 mg sodium, 113 mg cholesterol.*

- 1  **boneless rolled leg of lamb (about 4 pounds)**
  **Salt and pepper, to taste**
- ½  **cup French olive oil**
- ¼  **cup French red wine vinegar**
- 2  **cloves garlic, finely chopped**
- ¼  **cup Dijon-style mustard**
- 1  **tablespoon Herbes de Provence (French dried herb blend, available in specialty food stores)**

1. Preheat the oven to moderate (350°).
2. Sprinkle the lamb on all sides with the salt and pepper. Place in a shallow glass or enamel dish.
3. Beat together the oil, vinegar, garlic, mustard and herbs in a small bowl until well blended; pour over the lamb. Cover and refrigerate overnight.
4. Drain the lamb, reserving the marinade. Place the lamb in a shallow roasting pan.
5. Bake in the preheated moderate oven (350°), spooning the reserved marinade over the lamb every 15 minutes, for 1½ hours for rare to medium-rare (pink) lamb, 2½ hours for well-done lamb, or until done as you prefer. Cool to room temperature.
6. Refrigerate the lamb, then slice it. Serve with French cornichon pickles (midget gherkins), if you wish.

## Potato Moussaka

Bake potatoes at 400° for 15 minutes; bake moussaka at 375° for 35 to 40 minutes.
Makes 6 servings.

*Nutrient Value Per Serving: 585 calories, 29 g protein, 34 g fat, 43 g carbohydrate, 1,112 mg sodium, 156 mg cholesterol.*

- 2  **pounds red-skinned potatoes with skins (7 or 8 medium-size), washed**
- 2  **tablespoons olive oil**

**Meat Filling:**
- 2  **cups chopped onion (2 large)**
- 1  **tablespoon olive oil**
- 2  **cloves garlic, finely chopped**
- 1½ **pounds lean ground lamb OR: beef**
- ½  **teaspoon ground cinnamon**
- ½  **teaspoon leaf oregano, crumbled**
- ½  **teaspoon leaf thyme, crumbled**
- 1  **teaspoon salt**
- ¼  **teaspoon pepper**
- ½  **cup dry white wine**
- 1  **can (35 ounces) tomatoes, drained and chopped**

- 4  **cups White Sauce (see recipe, page 99)**
- 2  **egg yolks**
- 1  **cup grated Parmesan cheese (about 3 ounces)**
- 2  **tablespoons dry bread crumbs**

1. Preheat the oven to hot (400°). Generously grease 2 or 3 jelly-roll pans.
2. Cut the potatoes into ¼-inch-thick slices. Brush both sides of the potato slices using 1 tablespoon of the oil. Place on the prepared pans.
3. Bake in the preheated hot oven (400°) for 7 minutes. Remove from the oven and turn the slices over. Brush with the remaining 1 tablespoon of oil. Bake for 8

## Food for Thought . . .

**Parmesan Cheese** *An excellent and well-known cheese originating in Italy in the 1200's, Parmesan is named for a small region in Italy called Parma. It is made from whole cow's milk. When fresh, Parmesan can be sliced for eating, but it is best known as a hard, aged cheese that must be grated before being used. When aged, it has a sharp, pungent flavor.*

minutes more, or just until tender. Set aside. Lower the oven temperature to moderate (375°).

4. Prepare the Meat Filling: Sauté the onion in the oil in a medium-size skillet over medium heat just until soft, for about 5 minutes. Add the garlic and cook for 1 minute. Crumble in the lamb or beef and sauté until half-cooked. Add the cinnamon, oregano, thyme, salt, pepper and wine. Cook, stirring occasionally, until the wine evaporates, for about 5 minutes. Add the tomatoes and cook for 5 minutes to blend the flavors. Set aside.
5. Prepare the White Sauce.
6. Whisk the egg yolks in a medium-size bowl. Slowly whisk in about 1 cup of the hot White Sauce. Whisk back into the remaining White Sauce in the saucepan. Reserve 2 tablespoons of the Parmesan cheese for the top and stir the remaining cheese into the sauce.
7. Grease a 13 x 9 x 2-inch baking pan. Sprinkle the bottom with the bread crumbs. Arrange the potato slices in the pan, placing large slices in first; there will be about 2 layers. Spoon the meat filling over the potatoes. Pour the White Sauce over the top. Sprinkle with the reserved 2 tablespoons of Parmesan cheese.
8. Bake in the preheated moderate oven (375°) until hot, puffed and golden brown, for 35 to 40 minutes. Let cool for 10 to 15 minutes before serving.

## Baked Samosas

*This traditional Indian hors d'oeuvre or snack usually is fried. We've made the procedure simpler and less messy by baking. Prepare the samosas ahead and bake when ready to serve, or bake ahead and then reheat. Unbaked samosas freeze well. The filling is a bit dry, so try a little plain yogurt an accompaniment. The pastry and the filling can be made a day ahead.*

Bake at 425° for 15 to 18 minutes.
Makes 3 dozen.

*Nutrient Value Per Samosa: 144 calories, 4 g protein, 9 g fat, 11 g carbohydrate, 209 mg sodium, 25 mg cholesterol.*

**Pastry:**
3¾ cups unsifted all-purpose flour
1¼ teaspoons salt
10 tablespoons (1 stick plus 2 tablespoons) butter, chilled and sliced
½ cup plus 2 tablespoons vegetable shortening, chilled
9 to 10 tablespoons ice water

**Meat Filling (about 2½ cups):**
1 cup chopped onion (1 large)
1 tablespoon vegetable oil
1 tablespoon finely chopped fresh gingerroot
1 tablespoon finely chopped garlic
1 to 2 fresh hot green chili peppers, such as jalapeño or serrano, seeded and finely chopped OR: pickled jalapeño peppers, seeded and finely chopped
1 pound lean ground lamb OR: beef
2 teaspoons ground coriander
1½ teaspoons curry powder
¼ teaspoon ground cinnamon
1½ teaspoons salt
½ teaspoon pepper
2 teaspoons all-purpose flour
¾ cup water
¼ cup fresh lemon juice
¼ cup chopped fresh parsley
1 teaspoon dried mint

**Glaze:**
1 egg yolk
½ teaspoon water
⅛ teaspoon curry powder

## TEMPERATURE AND TIME FOR ROASTING LAMB

| Cut | Approx. Pound Weight | Oven Temperature | Internal Meat Temperature When Done | Roasting Time (min. per pound) |
|---|---|---|---|---|
| **Leg** | 5 to 9 | 300° to 325° | 140° (rare) | 20 to 25 |
| | | | 160° (medium) | 25 to 30 |
| | | | 170° to 180° (well) | 30 to 35 |
| **Leg, Shank** | 3 to 4 | 300° to 325° | 140° (rare) | 25 to 30 |
| | | | 160° (medium) | 30 to 35 |
| **Half** | | | 170° to 180° (well) | 35 to 40 |
| **Rib** | 2 to 3 | 375° | 140° (rare) | 25 to 30 |
| | | | 160° (medium) | 30 to 35 |
| | | | 170° to 180° (well) | 35 to 40 |

1. Prepare the Pastry: Combine the flour and the salt in a large bowl. Cut in the butter and the shortening with a pastry blender until the mixture resembles coarse meal. Drizzle about 5 tablespoons of the ice water over the top, lightly stirring with a fork. Sprinkle with enough of the remaining ice water, stirring, just until the dough can be gathered together. Divide the dough into thirds and shape each into flat rounds. Wrap and chill for at least 1 hour, or overnight.
2. Prepare the Meat Filling: Sauté the onion in the oil in a medium-size, heavy skillet over medium heat, stirring frequently, until deep golden brown, for about 8 to 10 minutes. Add the ginger, garlic and chili peppers; cook for 2 to 3 minutes. Crumble in the ground lamb and sauté until half-cooked; drain off any fat. Add the coriander, curry powder, cinnamon, salt and pepper. Sauté until the meat is fully cooked. Add the flour and cook for 1 or 2 minutes. Add the water and simmer until the mixture is thick and dry, for about 5 minutes. Transfer to a bowl. Stir in the lemon juice, parsley and mint. Cool to room temperature.
3. Preheat the oven to hot (425°).
4. Roll out one third of the dough on a lightly floured surface to about an ⅛-inch thickness or slightly less. Cut out six 6-inch rounds, using a 6-inch pot lid or dish as a guide. Gather any scraps and reroll, if necessary. Cut the circles in half to make 12 half circles.
5. Brush water in a 1-inch band along half the flat side of a half circle, starting in the center and brushing to the edge. Shape the dough into a cone, overlapping to make a seam. Press the overlap together to seal, and pinch the point. Fill the cone with 1 tablespoon of the meat mixture. Moisten the top half of the cone with water and pinch closed, crimping the edge with a fork, if you wish. Place on an ungreased baking sheet. Repeat with the remaining half circles.
6. Prepare the Glaze: Stir together the egg yolk, water and curry powder in a small bowl. Brush the glaze over the tops of the samosas. Prick each with a fork once, making sure the tines go halfway down into the filling.
7. Bake in the preheated hot oven (425°) for 15 to 18 minutes, or until crisp and golden brown.
8. Remove to a wire rack. Repeat with the remaining dough and filling. Serve hot or warm.

*Note: Any leftover filling may be used as omelet filling, or mixed with hot cooked rice for a quick main course.*

# Spinach Veal Roll with Mushroom Sauce

*An elegant and easy main course.*

Bake at 350° for 1 hour.
Makes 6 servings.

*Nutrient Value Per Serving: 392 calories, 23 g protein, 26 g fat, 17 g carbohydrate, 996 mg sodium, 156 mg cholesterol.*

**Veal Roll:**

| | |
|---|---|
| 1½ | pounds fresh spinach |
| 1 | cup finely chopped onion (1 large) |
| 2 | tablespoons butter |
| 1 | clove garlic, finely chopped |
| ½ | pound finely chopped mushrooms (3 cups) |
| ½ | teaspoon leaf thyme, crumbled |
| 1 | pound ground veal |
| 1 | cup fresh bread crumbs (2 slices) |
| 1 | egg |
| ½ | cup milk |
| ½ | teaspoon grated lemon rind |
| 1 | tablespoon lemon juice |
| 1 | teaspoon salt |
| ¼ | teaspoon pepper |
| ¼ | cup chopped parsley |

**Mushroom Sauce:**

| | |
|---|---|
| 3 | tablespoons butter |
| 3 | tablespoons all-purpose flour |
| 1¼ | cups chicken broth |
| ¼ | pound finely chopped mushrooms (1½ cups) |
| | Pinch leaf thyme |
| ¼ | cup dry white wine |
| ½ | cup heavy cream OR: half-and-half |
| ½ | teaspoon salt |
| ¼ | teaspoon pepper |

Chopped parsley, for garnish

1. Preheat the oven to moderate (350°).
2. Prepare the Veal Roll: Wash the spinach well and remove any tough stems. Do not pat the spinach dry. Place the spinach in a heavy pot. Cover and cook over medium-high heat until wilted, for 2 to 3 minutes, stirring occasionally. Drain in a colander. Squeeze the spinach between pieces of paper toweling to press out excess moisture. Cool slightly and finely chop; you should have 1½ cups. Set aside.
3. Sauté the onion in the butter in a large, heavy skillet over medium heat until soft, for about 5 minutes. Add the garlic and cook for 1 minute. Add the mushrooms and the thyme; sauté until the mushrooms become juicy, for 2 to 3 minutes. Cool slightly.
4. Combine the veal, bread crumbs, egg, milk, lemon rind and juice, salt, pepper and parsley in a large bowl. Mix just until evenly blended. Mix in the mushroom mixture.
5. Place a 12-inch square of wax paper on the work surface. Place the veal mixture on the wax paper and pat into a 10-inch square. Spread the spinach evenly over the veal square. Starting at one side, fold over the veal by about 2 inches, using the wax paper as a guide. Then roll up tightly, jelly-roll fashion, removing the paper as you roll. Carefully transfer the roll to a jelly-roll pan. Cover tightly with aluminum foil.
6. Bake in the preheated moderate oven (350°) for 1 hour.
7. Meanwhile, prepare the Mushroom Sauce: Melt 2 tablespoons of the butter in a small, heavy-bottomed saucepan. Add the flour and cook over medium heat, stirring, for 1 or 2 minutes. Add the broth and cook, whisking until smooth and thick, for 3 to 5 minutes.
8. Melt the remaining 1 tablespoon of butter in a medium-size skillet over medium heat. Add the mushrooms and the thyme and cook until the mushrooms become juicy, for 2 to 3 minutes. Add the wine and boil until the liquid completely evaporates, for 3 to 4 minutes. Add the cream, salt and pepper. Bring to boiling. Stir the mushroom mixture into the broth mixture. Simmer for 2 to 3 minutes to blend the flavors.
9. Serve the veal roll, hot and garnished with the chopped parsley, together with the hot mushroom sauce.

*Clockwise from top: Baked Samosas (recipe, page 79), Spinach Veal Roll with Mushroom Sauce (recipe, page 80) and Turkey Lasagna (recipe, page 98)*

## COOKING CASSEROLES

*1. When buying a casserole dish, choose one decorative enough to be used as a serving dish as well as a container for cooking.*

*2. Check to make sure the casserole dish cover fits tightly. If it does not, place a layer of aluminum foil over the open casserole before putting on the cover.*

*3. Most casseroles should be baked at moderate oven temperatures (350° to 375°) so that the meats do not toughen and the flavors of the ingredients have time to blend well.*

*4. When adding any extra liquid to a cooking casserole, be sure to heat the liquid first so that the mixture continues to cook.*

*5. If you are planning to freeze a casserole, line the casserole dish with aluminum foil before pouring in the cooked casserole. Cool, then freeze. When the casserole is solid, remove the contents in the foil and overwrap with more foil—you'll still have the use of your casserole dish. Store the wrapped casserole in the freezer for 2 to 3 months*

## Vegetable Beef Casserole

Bake at 375° for 40 minutes.
Makes 4 servings.

*Nutrient Value Per Serving: 439 calories, 15 g protein, 29 g fat, 32 g carbohydrate, 336 mg sodium, 61 mg cholesterol.*

2  **tomatoes (about 12 ounces)**
2  **small yellow squash (about 1 pound)**
1  **medium-size onion, finely chopped**
½  **pound ground beef**
  **Salt and pepper**
½  **cup long-grain rice**
2  **tablespoons olive oil**
1  **cup beef broth**
2  **tablespoons tomato paste**
½  **cup dairy sour cream**
2  **tablespoons chopped fresh dill**

1. Preheat the oven to moderate (375°).
2. Thinly slice the tomatoes. Cut the squash into ¼-inch-thick slices. Spread one of the sliced tomatoes over the bottom of a 2-quart flameproof casserole dish. Top with half the squash slices and sprinkle with half the onion. Crumble the beef over the top and sprinkle with ¼ teaspoon of salt and ¼ teaspoon of pepper. Sprinkle the rice evenly over the top. Add the remaining onion. Overlap the remaining tomato and squash slices over the top. Sprinkle lightly with a little additional salt and pepper. Drizzle with the oil. Combine the broth and the tomato paste and pour into the casserole dish.
3. Bring to a full boil on top of the stove. Cover tightly and bake in the preheated moderate oven (375°) for 40 minutes, or until the rice is cooked.
4. Stir together the sour cream and the dill. Serve with the casserole.

# Poultry

## Chicken Morocco

*Spiced with the exotic flavors of Africa, couscous becomes a delicious stuffing for roast chicken.*

Bake at 375° for 1½ to 2 hours.
Makes 4 servings.

*Nutrient Value Per Serving: 791 calories, 56 g protein, 40 g fat, 51 g carbohydrate, 420 mg sodium, 154 mg cholesterol.*

| | |
|---|---|
| 1 | **cup couscous\*, prepared according to package directions** |
| ½ | **cup chopped walnuts** |
| ¼ | **cup raisins** |
| 2 | **tablespoons honey** |
| ½ | **teaspoon ground cinnamon** |
| ¼ | **teaspoon ground ginger** |
| ¼ | **teaspoon ground cumin** |
| ¼ | **teaspoon ground coriander** |
| ¼ | **teaspoon ground turmeric** |
| 1 | **roasting chicken (3 to 4 pounds)** |
| 2 | **tablespoons corn oil** |
| ½ | **teaspoon salt** |
| ⅛ | **teaspoon pepper** |
| ⅛ | **teaspoon paprika** |
| | **Additional salt and pepper** |

1. Stir together the couscous, walnuts, raisins, honey, cinnamon, ginger, cumin, coriander and turmeric in a large bowl until well mixed.
2. Remove the liver and gizzards from the chicken; reserve for another use. Rub the chicken all over with the oil and sprinkle with the ½ teaspoon of salt, the ⅛ teaspoon of pepper and the paprika.
3. Preheat the oven to moderate (375°).
4. Season the inside of the chicken with additional salt and pepper. Spoon the couscous mixture lightly into the cavity. Skewer the opening closed. (Spoon any remaining couscous mixture into a shallow casserole dish. Cover and bake for the last 20 minutes of roasting.)

Place the chicken on a rack in a shallow roasting pan.
5. Roast in the preheated moderate oven (375°), basting occasionally with the pan juices, for 1½ to 2 hours, or until the bird tests done and the juices run clear. Cover the chicken loosely with aluminum foil if it is browning too quickly.
6. To serve, spoon the stuffing into a serving bowl and pass with the carved chicken.

*\*Note: Couscous, also known as "Moroccan pasta," is coarsely ground wheat granules and can be found in the rice and grain section of many supermarkets.*

---

### A CHICKEN FOR THE ROASTING

*A "roaster" is a young chicken, about 3 to 5 months old. It weighs 4½ to 6 pounds and, as its name implies, is best when roasted.*

---

### PICKIN' CHICKEN

**For Frying:** *Allow ¾ to 1 pound per serving.*
**For Roasting:** *Allow ¾ to 1 pound per serving.*
**For Broiling or Barbecuing:** *Allow ½ a chicken or 1 pound per serving.*
**For Stewing:** *Allow ½ to 1 pound per serving.*
**Chicken Livers:** *Allow ¼ pound per serving.*
**Rock Cornish Game Hen:** *Allow 1 game hen per person.*

## Chicken, Ham and Sausage Skillet Dinner

Makes 8 servings.

*Nutrient Value Per Serving: 416 calories, 40 g protein, 24 g fat, 9 g carbohydrate, 1,096 mg sodium, 120 mg cholesterol.*

1 broiler-fryer (3½ pounds), cut into 8 serving pieces
1 tablespoon olive oil
2 hot Italian sausages, sliced into fourths (5 ounces)
2 sweet Italian sausages, sliced into fourths (5 ounces)
1 large onion, chopped (1 cup)
1 medium-size sweet green pepper, coarsely chopped (⅔ cup)
1 medium-size sweet red pepper, coarsely chopped (⅔ cup)
1 clove garlic, finely chopped
12 large mushrooms, halved (10 ounces)
2 cups cubed cooked ham (⅔ pound)
1 can (14 ounces) Italian plum tomatoes, undrained and chopped
½ cup dry vermouth
½ cup chicken broth
1 teaspoon leaf oregano, crumbled
1 teaspoon leaf thyme, crumbled
¼ teaspoon salt
¼ teaspoon pepper
Chopped parsley, for garnish

1. Brown the chicken in batches in the oil in a large, heavy skillet for about 15 minutes per batch. Transfer to a plate.
2. Brown the sausages in the fat remaining in the skillet. Transfer to the plate.
3. Pour off all but 1 tablespoon of the fat from the skillet. Add the onion, green and red peppers and garlic. Sauté until tender, for about 5 minutes. Add the mushrooms and sauté for 3 minutes.
4. Return the chicken and sausages to the skillet. Add the vegetables, ham, tomatoes with their liquid, vermouth, broth, oregano, thyme, salt and pepper; stir to mix. Cover the skillet and simmer for 20 minutes, or until the chicken is thoroughly cooked. Garnish with parsley.

## Skillet Chicken Medley

*Be sure you have good ventilation above the stove.*

Makes 4 servings.

*Nutrient Value Per Serving: 476 calories, 42 g protein, 22 g fat, 26 g carbohydrate, 473 mg sodium, 106 mg cholesterol.*

¼ cup milk
¼ teaspoon ground nutmeg
¼ teaspoon black pepper
1 clove garlic, finely chopped
4 skinless, boned chicken breast halves (4 to 6 ounces each), split in half lengthwise
4 ounces mozzarella cheese, cut into 8 logs
3 tablespoons red wine vinegar OR: cider vinegar
1 tablespoon sugar
1 tablespoon soy sauce
1 tablespoon water
4 red-skinned potatoes (about 12 ounces)
8 large romaine lettuce leaves
2 medium-size yellow squash OR: zucchini (about 1 pound)
About ¼ cup olive oil
Green onion brushes, for garnish (optional)

1. Combine the milk, nutmeg, black pepper and garlic in a bowl. Add the chicken, turn to coat and set aside to marinate. Place the mozzarella cheese in a small bowl, pour the vinegar over and set aside. Stir together the sugar, soy sauce and water in a small cup and set aside.
2. Boil the potatoes until tender. Drain and cut in half. Cover with aluminum foil and keep warm.
3. Bring a medium-size pot of water to boiling. Dip the romaine leaves, one at a time, into the water for 5 seconds to soften. Diagonally slice off the thick part of the center vein. Place one piece of mozzarella cheese across the wide end of each leaf and roll up the leaf, folding in the ends to make a little parcel.
4. Cut the squash or zucchini diagonally

*Skillet Chicken Medley*

into ¾-inch-thick slices. Score each side in a ½-inch diamond pattern, if you wish. Place the potatoes, romaine parcels and squash on a baking sheet or jelly-roll pan. Brush with the oil on all sides.

5. Heat one 10-inch or two 9-inch well-seasoned cast iron skillets over medium heat until hot, for about 5 minutes; drops of water sprinkled on the skillets should sizzle and bead. Drain the chicken. Working in batches and keeping the foods in a single layer, char all the ingredients until speckled black on one side. Turn and char the other side. Cook the foods in the following order: the squash for about 7 minutes, the romaine parcels for about 3 minutes, the potatoes for about 6 minutes and the chicken for about 10 minutes. As the foods are cooked, place them on a hot serving platter to keep warm. Brush with the soy sauce mixture. Garnish with green onion brushes, if you wish.

# *Jamaican Chicken Calypso*

*This lively dish is seasoned with spices often used by Jamaican cooks. Serve with buttered sweet potatoes or yams.*

Bake at 375° for 40 to 45 minutes.
Makes 4 servings.

*Nutrient Value Per Serving: 506 calories, 49 g protein, 21 g fat, 30 g carbohydrate, 816 mg sodium, 145 mg cholesterol.*

| | |
|---|---|
| 1 | **can (8 ounces) pineapple chunks, undrained** |
| 1/2 | **cup rum** |
| 3 | **tablespoons lime juice** |
| 2 | **tablespoons soy sauce** |
| 1 | **tablespoon dark brown sugar** |
| 2 | **teaspoons curry powder** |
| 2 | **cloves garlic, finely chopped** |
| 1/2 | **teaspoon ground ginger** |
| 1/4 | **teaspoon ground cloves** |
| 1/4 | **teaspoon crushed red pepper flakes** |
| 4 | **chicken breast halves on bone (about 2 pounds)** |
| 1 | **can (11 ounces) mandarin oranges, drained** |
| 1 | **lime, cut into wedges, for garnish (optional)** |

1. Drain the juice from the pineapple chunks into a shallow, nonmetal dish large enough to hold the chicken. Reserve the pineapple chunks, covered and refrigerated. To the pineapple juice, add the rum, lime juice, soy sauce, brown sugar, curry powder, garlic, ginger, cloves and red pepper flakes. Stir to blend.
2. Add the chicken to the marinade, turning to coat well. Leave the chicken skin side down. Cover and marinate in the refrigerator for 3 to 6 hours.
3. Preheat the oven to moderate (375°).
4. Drain the marinade from the chicken and reserve. Place the chicken, skin side up, in a shallow roasting pan.
5. Bake, uncovered, in the preheated moderate oven (375°), basting often with the pan juices and the reserved marinade, for 35 minutes. Add the mandarin oranges and the reserved pineapple chunks to the pan. Bake for 5 to 10 minutes longer, or until the chicken no longer is pink near the bone.
6. To serve, arrange the chicken with the pineapple chunks and the mandarin oranges on a platter. Skim the fat from the pan juices and pour the juices over the chicken. Garnish with lime slices.

## *Microwave Instructions*
*(for a 650-watt variable power microwave oven)*

***Ingredient Changes:*** Use only 1/4 cup of the juice drained from the pineapple. Reduce the rum to 2 tablespoons, reduce the lime juice to 2 tablespoons, reduce the curry powder to 1 teaspoon, reduce the ginger to 1/4 teaspoon and reduce the cloves to 1/8 teaspoon.

***Directions:*** Combine the pineapple juice, rum, lime juice, soy sauce, brown sugar, curry powder, garlic, ginger, cloves and red pepper flakes in a medium-size bowl. Place the chicken in the marinade, turning to coat all sides. Cover and marinate for 3 hours, turning the chicken once. Arrange the chicken in a 10-inch microwave-safe pie plate, placing the thicker parts toward the outside of the plate. Pour on half the marinade. Cover with wax paper. Microwave at full power for 6 minutes. Add the remaining marinade, the pineapple chunks and mandarin oranges. Microwave, uncovered, at full power for 3 to 5 minutes longer, or until the chicken is tender.

## Tomato Cilantro Chicken

Bake at 400° for 20 to 25 minutes.
Makes 4 servings.

*Nutrient Value Per Serving: 357 calories, 34 g protein, 20 g fat, 9 g carbohydrate, 511 mg sodium, 89 mg cholesterol.*

1    **tablespoon lime juice**
½    **teaspoon salt**
⅛    **teaspoon ground hot red pepper**
4    **skinless, boned chicken breast halves (about 1 pound), slightly flattened**
3    **tablespoons olive oil**
1    **medium-size onion, chopped (½ cup)**
½    **cup chopped sweet green pepper**
1    **clove garlic, finely chopped**
¼    **cup chopped fresh cilantro (coriander) OR: 2 teaspoons dried cilantro and 3 tablespoons chopped fresh parsley**
1¼  **pounds ripe tomatoes, sliced (about 4 medium-size)**
4    **ounces shredded Monterey Jack cheese (1 cup)**
     **Parsley or cilantro (coriander) leaves and lime slices, for garnish (optional)**

1. Preheat the oven to hot (400°). Combine the lime juice, ¼ teaspoon of the salt and the ground hot red pepper in a small bowl. Add the chicken and turn to coat. Let stand for 10 minutes.
2. Heat 2 tablespoons of the oil in a large skillet over medium heat. Add the chicken and sauté until lightly browned on both sides. Remove to paper toweling to drain. Add the remaining 1 tablespoon of oil to the skillet. Add the onion, green pepper and garlic and sauté until tender but not browned, stirring often. Remove from the heat and stir in the cilantro.
3. Place about two thirds of the tomato slices on the bottom of a 9-inch-square baking dish, or divide among 4 individual 2-cup baking dishes. Sprinkle with two thirds of the onion mixture and the remaining ¼ teaspoon of salt. Sprinkle with about two thirds of the Monterey Jack cheese. Layer on the chicken. Top with the remaining tomato slices and onion mixture.
4. Bake in the preheated hot oven (400°) for 15 to 20 minutes, or for 10 to 15 minutes for individual dishes, or until the chicken

is tender. Sprinkle with the remaining Monterey Jack cheese. Bake for 5 minutes longer, or until the cheese is melted. Garnish with parsley or cilantro leaves and lime slices, if you wish.

---

## CALORIE-WISE COOKING WITH FOIL

*Calories say "Foiled again!" when you cook foods in packets of aluminum foil—no fattening oil or butter is needed. Just spray a bit of nonstick vegetable cooking spray on the foil, add the meat, fish or poultry and/or vegetables, and bake. Because the foil packet holds in moisture, this method works especially well for lean cuts of meat such as chicken, pork or turkey cutlets, for boneless pork loin and for fish. The results are moist and juicy. And putting one serving in each foil packet is an easy way to control your portion size. Take a look at Oriental Chicken (recipe, page 90) as an example of smart foil cooking.*
*• Measure carefully and use only the amount of foil you need per portion.*
*• Marinate food for at least 20 minutes before cooking, discard the marinade, wrap the food in foil and bake. For a simple marinade, try lime juice mixed with spicy taco sauce; or lowfat buttermilk with slivered garlic and sprigs of fresh rosemary.*
*• Score the top of the meat, fish or poultry with a knife. Make three diagonal slices 1/8 to 1/4 inch deep, about 1 inch apart. Brush the cut areas with a flavorful liquid, such as a mixture of lemon juice, salt, sage, paprika and cayenne, a tangy fresh herb vinaigrette or a store-bought, light salad dressing. Then wrap the food in foil and bake.*

# Bavarian Chicken Schnitzel

*Germans and Austrians make this simple dish from veal, pork and beef as well as from chicken.*

Makes 4 servings.

*Nutrient Value Per Serving: 525 calories, 46 g protein, 25 g fat, 26 g carbohydrate, 645 mg sodium, 260 mg cholesterol.*

4   **skinless, boned chicken breast halves (about 1½ pounds)**
½   **teaspoon salt**
¼   **teaspoon pepper**
¾   **cup unseasoned fine dry bread crumbs**
1   **tablespoon chopped parsley**
    **Grated rind of 1 lemon**
2   **eggs**
2   **tablespoons water**
½   **cup unsifted all-purpose flour**
3   **tablespoons butter**
3   **tablespoons corn oil**
1   **lemon, thinly sliced, for garnish**

1. Place the chicken between pieces of wax paper and pound with the smooth side of a meat mallet or a skillet bottom to a ¼-inch thickness. Sprinkle with the salt and the pepper. Cut each flattened breast crosswise into 2 or 3 pieces.
2. Stir together the bread crumbs, parsley and lemon rind in a shallow dish. In a separate dish, lightly beat the eggs and the water. Place the flour in a third dish.
3. Coat each piece of chicken lightly with the flour, shaking off the excess. Dip into the egg mixture to coat, then the bread crumb mixture to coat well, shaking off the excess. Place on a tray or between pieces of wax paper. Chill for at least 15 minutes, or for up to 2 hours to set the coating.
4. Heat 1½ tablespoons of the butter and 1½ tablespoons of the oil in a large skillet. Cook the chicken over medium-high heat, a few pieces at a time, for 2 to 3 minutes per side, or until browned. Add more butter and oil as needed. As the pieces brown, remove to a serving platter and keep warm. Garnish with lemon slices.

# Chicken Rolls Hollandaise

Bake at 450° for 15 minutes.
Makes 4 servings.

*Nutrient Value Per Serving: 508 calories, 27 g protein, 28 g fat, 37 g carbohydrate, 812 mg sodium, 121 mg cholesterol.*

**Nonstick vegetable cooking spray**
**4   small skinless, boned chicken breast halves (about 3 ounces each), pounded very thin**
**¼   to ½ teaspoon bottled chopped garlic-in-oil**
**½   teaspoon salt**
**⅛   teaspoon pepper**
**12   to 16 very thin fresh asparagus spears, trimmed to 5- to 6-inch lengths**
**8   to 12 small frozen whole baby carrots (from 16-ounce package), thawed and drained**
**1   teaspoon olive oil**
**2   tablespoons loose-crumb herb-seasoned stuffing mix**
**2   teaspoons grated Parmesan cheese**
**1⅓  cups water**
**⅛   teaspoon ground turmeric**
**1⅓  cups quick-cooking rice**
**1   package (0.9 ounce) hollandaise sauce mix**
**1   to 2 tablespoons chopped fresh basil OR: 1 teaspoon leaf basil, crumbled Cherry tomatoes, for garnish (optional)**

1. Place the oven rack in the upper third of the oven. Preheat the oven to very hot (450°). Lightly spray a 12 x 8 x 2-inch (2-quart capacity) shallow baking dish with nonstick vegetable cooking spray. Set aside.
2. Brush one side of each chicken breast with the garlic-in-oil. Sprinkle the same sides equally with the salt and the pepper.
3. Place 3 to 4 asparagus spears and 2 to 3 baby carrots onto the seasoned side of each chicken breast and roll up, using your fingers to hold the vegetables inside. Place, seam side down, in the prepared dish. Lightly brush each roll with the olive oil. Sprinkle equal amounts of the stuffing mix and the Parmesan cheese onto each roll.
4. Bake in the preheated very hot oven (450°) for 15 minutes. Remove from the oven and let stand for 5 minutes before slicing.
5. Meanwhile, bring the water and the turmeric to boiling in a medium-size saucepan. Stir in the rice. Remove from the heat, cover and let stand until ready to serve.
6. Meanwhile, prepare the hollandaise sauce following the package directions. When cooked, lay a piece of plastic wrap directly on the surface to prevent a skin from forming.
7. Just before serving, stir the basil into the rice. Divide the rice equally among 4 individual plates. Cut the chicken rolls into ½-inch-thick slices and serve over the rice. Top with the hollandaise sauce. Garnish with cherry tomatoes.

## Microwave Instructions
*(for a 650-watt variable power microwave oven)*

**Ingredient Changes:** Add ¼ teaspoon of paprika.

**Directions:** Assemble the chicken rolls as in the above recipe. Place the rolls, seam side down, in a microwave-safe 10-inch pie plate. Brush the rolls with the olive oil. Combine the stuffing mix, Parmesan cheese and ¼ teaspoon of paprika; sprinkle the mixture over the chicken rolls. Cover the pie plate with microwave-safe plastic wrap, turned back slightly on one side to vent. Microwave at full power for 8 minutes, rotating the pie plate one quarter turn after 4 minutes. Let stand, covered, for 2 minutes.

**Note:** *Check the back of the hollandaise sauce mix package for microwave directions.*

*Oriental Chicken*

# Oriental Chicken

Bake at 500° for 12 minutes.
Makes 4 servings.

*Nutrient Value Per Serving: 262 calories, 41 g protein, 6 g fat, 9 g carbohydrate, 887 mg sodium, 99 mg cholesterol.*

**Vegetable oil**
**1   large sweet red pepper, cored, seeded and cut into thin slices**
**¼   pound snow peas, cleaned and strings removed**
**½   cup water chestnuts, sliced**
**⅓   cup chopped green onion**
**4   skinless, boned chicken breast halves (6 ounces each)**
**3   tablespoons soy sauce**
**1   tablespoon Oriental sesame oil***
**½   teaspoon grated, peeled fresh gingerroot**
**1   clove garlic, finely chopped**

1. Preheat the oven to very hot (500°).
2. Tear off four 14 x 12-inch sheets of regular weight aluminum foil. Lightly oil the center of the lower half of each sheet with vegetable oil.
3. Place one eighth of the red pepper, snow peas, water chestnuts and green onion on the oiled portion of each foil sheet. Place a chicken breast over the vegetables on each sheet. Sprinkle the remaining vegetables over the chicken breasts.
4. Stir together the soy sauce, Oriental sesame oil, ginger and garlic in a small bowl. Spoon the mixture evenly over the chicken and vegetables.
5. Fold the upper half of the foil over the ingredients, matching the upper and lower edges evenly to enclose the filling. Turn up the long double edge of foil to create a ½-inch double fold; fold over again. Fold the two shorter sides in the same way, completely sealing the packet.
6. Place 2 baking sheets in the preheated very hot oven (500°) for about 2 minutes. Place the aluminum foil packets in a single layer on the hot baking sheets.
7. Bake the packets in the preheated very hot oven (500°) for 12 minutes. Place each packet on a dinner plate. Cut an X from corner to corner in the top of each packet. Fold back the edges and serve right away, with hot cooked rice, if you wish.

***Note:** Oriental sesame oil has more flavor and is darker in color than regular sesame oil. It can be found in the Oriental food section of many supermarkets or in Oriental specialty food stores.*

# Chicken with Ginger Sauce

Makes 4 servings.

*Nutrient Value Per Serving: 274 calories, 24 g protein, 16 g fat, 7 g carbohydrate, 237 mg sodium, 106 mg cholesterol.*

**1   small onion, quartered**
**2   large cloves garlic, coarsely chopped**
**1   piece (1-inch cube) fresh gingerroot, peeled and coarsely chopped**
**¼   cup plus 2 teaspoons water**
**1½  pounds chicken drumsticks**
**1   large onion, sliced ½ inch thick and separated into rings**
**½   cup chicken broth**
**1   teaspoon cornstarch**
**½   cup dairy sour cream**
**Sweet red pepper strips, for garnish (optional)**

1. Purée the small onion, the garlic, ginger and ¼ cup of the water in the container of a food processor or an electric blender until smooth. Set aside.
2. Fry the chicken, skin side down, without oil in a large, nonstick saucepan or Dutch oven. Cook over medium-high heat for about 3 to 5 minutes, or until crusty and very golden brown. Shake the pan back and forth to prevent sticking. Turn the chicken over and fry for 1 to 2 minutes more, or until the underside is brown. Push the chicken to one side of the pan.
3. Add the onion rings and cook, stirring constantly, until the edges are coated

with the browned bits from the bottom of the pan, for 2 minutes.

4. Stir in the broth. Lower the heat to very low. Cover the pan and simmer for 15 minutes, or until the chicken no longer is pink. Transfer the chicken to a warm serving platter.

5. Remove the pan from the heat. Stir together the cornstarch and the remaining 2 teaspoons of water in a small cup. Add to the saucepan along with the ginger purée. Stir in the sour cream, 1 tablespoon at a time.

6. Bring to boiling. Boil for 1 minute, or just to thicken; do not overboil. Spoon the sauce over the chicken. Garnish with red pepper strips and serve with hot cooked rice, if you wish.

## Honey Mustard Chicken

*Cook and serve these chicken thighs on skewers for easy eating.*

Broil for 18 minutes.
Makes 4 servings.

*Nutrient Value Per Serving: 385 calories, 29 g protein, 26 g fat, 6 g carbohydrate, 634 mg sodium, 143 mg cholesterol.*

> Nonstick vegetable cooking spray
> 8 boned chicken thighs (about 1½ pounds)
> 2 tablespoons Dijon-style mustard
> 1 tablespoon lemon juice
> 1 tablespoon honey
> ½ teaspoon salt
> ¼ teaspoon liquid red pepper seasoning

1. Spray the broiler pan with nonstick vegetable cooking spray.

2. Cut 3 slits in each thigh on the skin side, perpendicular to the bone. The cuts should be about ¼ inch deep. Thread 2 chicken thighs on each of 4 skewers. Place the skewered chicken, skin side up, on a rack in the broiling pan.

3. Broil about 3 inches from the source of the heat for 8 minutes; the skin should just begin to brown.

4. Meanwhile, stir together the mustard, lemon juice, honey, salt and liquid red pepper seasoning in a small bowl.

5. Turn over the skewers. Brush the tops generously with the mustard glaze. Continue broiling, skin side down, for 6 minutes. Turn again so that the skin side is up and brush with the glaze. Broil for 4 minutes more, or until the skins are a rich brown. Serve with hot cooked noodles or rice, if you wish.

## Chunky Chicken with Tomatoes and Olives

Makes 4 servings.

*Nutrient Value Per Serving: 226 calories, 24 g protein, 12 g fat, 6 g carbohydrate, 765 mg sodium, 94 mg cholesterol.*

> 1 pound skinless, boned chicken thighs, cut into 1½-inch chunks
> ½ teaspoon black pepper
> ¼ teaspoon salt
> 1 tablespoon olive oil
> 1 clove garlic, finely chopped
> ½ teaspoon leaf thyme, crumbled
> ½ teaspoon leaf marjoram, crumbled
> ½ teaspoon leaf basil, crumbled
> 1 can (14 ounces) Italian tomatoes, undrained
> ¼ cup dry white wine
> ⅓ cup oil-cured black olives, pitted

1. Sprinkle the chicken with the black pepper and the salt.

2. Heat the oil in a large, nonstick skillet over medium-high heat until hot. Add the chicken to the hot oil. Sauté, stirring constantly, until the chicken is browned on all sides, for about 5 minutes. Add the garlic, thyme, marjoram and basil; sauté, stirring, for 30 seconds more.

3. Pour the tomatoes with their liquid and the wine into the skillet. Bring the mixture to boiling over medium-high heat. Boil rapidly, stirring occasionally, for about 5 minutes, or until the sauce is thickened. Stir in the olives and cook the mixture for 1 minute more.

4. Toss the chicken mixture with hot cooked pasta, if you wish, and serve right away.

# Bow Ties with Chicken and Spinach

*This creamy pasta dish will please the crowd — and the cook — with its great taste and easy preparation.*

Makes 4 servings.

*Nutrient Value Per Serving: 608 calories, 37 g protein, 20 g fat, 68 g carbohydrate, 846 mg sodium, 103 mg cholesterol.*

1½   teaspoons salt
¾   pound bow tie pasta
3   quarts boiling water
2   teaspoons olive oil
2   teaspoons unsalted butter
1   small onion, chopped
¾   pound skinless, boned chicken breasts, cut into 1-inch chunks
½   teaspoon pepper
1   bag (10 ounces) cleaned spinach, stemmed and coarsely chopped
½   cup heavy cream
½   cup grated Parmesan cheese

1. Add 1 teaspoon of the salt and the bow ties to the boiling water in a large pot. Cook following the package directions. Drain the bow ties in a colander.
2. Meanwhile, heat together the oil and the butter in a large skillet over medium-high heat until the butter melts. Add the onion and sauté, stirring often, until the onion is tender, for about 3 minutes. Add the chicken and sprinkle with the remaining ½ teaspoon of salt and the pepper. Sauté, stirring constantly, until the chicken is lightly browned.
3. Add the spinach to the skillet, continue cooking and stirring until the spinach is wilted. Add the cream and bring to a rapid boil. Boil gently until the mixture is slightly thickened.
4. Combine the bow ties, chicken mixture and Parmesan cheese in a large bowl and toss gently to mix well. Serve immediately, and pass more Parmesan cheese, if you wish.

# Southern Fried Chicken Strips

Makes 4 servings.

*Nutrient Value Per Serving: 360 calories, 31 g protein, 16 g fat, 21 g carbohydrate, 375 mg sodium, 70 mg cholesterol.*

¼   cup milk
½   cup plain lowfat yogurt
1   pound skinless, boned chicken breasts, cut into strips about 3 x ½ x ½ inches
¾   cup all-purpose flour
¾   teaspoon leaf thyme, crumbled
½   teaspoon salt
½   teaspoon black pepper
¼   teaspoon ground hot red pepper
    Vegetable oil

1. Combine the milk and the yogurt in a medium-size bowl. Add the chicken strips and toss to mix well.
2. Combine the flour, thyme, salt, black pepper and ground hot red pepper on a piece of wax paper; stir to mix.
3. Pour about ¼ inch of the oil into a cast iron skillet. Heat over medium-high heat.
4. Lift the chicken strips out of the yogurt mixture; they should be thinly but evenly coated. Toss the strips, a few pieces at a time, in the flour mixture.
5. When the oil is hot (about 325°), add the coated strips, being careful not to crowd the skillet. Work in 2 batches, if necessary, allowing the oil to heat up before adding the second batch. Fry until the chicken is browned on the bottom, then turn to brown the other side. Remove from the oil with a slotted spoon and drain on paper toweling.
6. Serve the chicken strips immediately, with oven-fried shoe-string potatoes, if you wish.

*Chicken Rolls with Mandarin Sauce*

## Chicken Rolls with Mandarin Sauce

Bake at 450° for 15 minutes.
Makes 4 servings.

*Nutrient Value Per Serving: 340 calories, 24 g protein, 4 g fat, 53 g carbohydrate, 630 mg sodium, 49 mg cholsterol.*

|   |   |
|---|---|
| | **Nonstick vegetable cooking spray** |
| 4 | **small skinless, boned chicken breast halves (about 3 ounces each), pounded very thin** |
| 1½ | **teaspoons Oriental sesame oil\*** |
| ¾ | **teaspoon leaf rosemary, crumbled** |
| ½ | **teaspoon salt** |
| ⅛ | **teaspoon pepper** |
| 1 | **package (9 ounces) frozen whole green beans, thawed and drained** |
| ¼ | **cup fresh whole wheat bread crumbs (½ to ¾ slice bread)** |
| 1⅓ | **cups water** |
| ½ | **teaspoon salt** |
| ⅛ | **teaspoon ground turmeric** |
| 1⅓ | **cups quick-cooking rice** |
| 1 | **cup orange juice** |
| 1 | **tablespoon cornstarch** |
| 1 | **can (11 ounces) mandarin oranges, drained** |
| ¼ | **teaspoon lemon juice** |
| 2 | **tablespoons chopped parsley** |
| | **Boston lettuce leaves, for garnish (optional)** |
| | **Cherry tomatoes, for garnish (optional)** |

1. Place the oven rack in the upper third of the oven. Preheat the oven to very hot (450°). Lightly spray a 12 x 8 x 2-inch (2-quart) baking dish with nonstick vegetable cooking spray.
2. Using ½ teaspoon of the Oriental sesame oil, equally brush one side of each chicken breast with oil. Sprinkle the same sides equally with ½ teaspoon of the rosemary, the salt and pepper.
3. Place one fourth of the green beans on each cutlet and roll up, using your fingers to hold the green beans inside. Place the rolls, seam side down, in the prepared dish. Lightly brush the rolls with the remaining 1 teaspoon of Oriental sesame oil. Sprinkle with the bread crumbs and the remaining ¼ teaspoon of rosemary.
4. Bake in the preheated very hot oven (450°) for 15 minutes. Remove the rolls from the oven and let them stand for 5 minutes before slicing.
5. Bring the water, salt and turmeric to boiling in a medium-size saucepan. Stir in the rice. Remove from the heat, cover and let stand until ready to serve.
6. Meanwhile, combine the orange juice and the cornstarch in a small saucepan and mix until well blended. Bring to boiling over medium heat and cook, stirring, for 2 to 3 minutes, or until thickened. Stir in the mandarin oranges and heat through. Stir in the lemon juice.
7. Just before serving, stir the parsley into the rice. Divide the rice equally among 4 individual plates. Cut the rolls into ½-inch-thick pieces. Serve over the rice and top with the mandarin sauce. Garnish with Boston lettuce and cherry tomatoes.

**\*Note:** *Oriental sesame oil has more flavor and is darker in color than regular sesame oil. It can be found in the Oriental food section of many supermarkets or in Oriental specialty food stores.*

## Microwave Instructions
*(for a 650-watt variable power microwave oven)*

**Directions:** Assemble the chicken rolls as in the above recipe. Place the rolls, seam side down, in a microwave-safe 10-inch pie plate. Brush with the Oriental sesame oil and sprinkle with the bread crumbs and the rosemary as directed in Step 3 of the above recipe. Cover the plate with microwave-safe plastic wrap, turned back slightly on one side to vent. Microwave at full power for 8 minutes, rotating the plate one quarter turn after 4 minutes. Let stand, covered, for 2 minutes. To make the mandarin sauce, combine the orange juice and the cornstarch in a microwave-safe 4-cup measure; whisk until well blended. Microwave, uncovered, at full power for 4 minutes to a full boil, whisking well after 2 minutes and after removing from the microwave oven. Stir in the mandarin oranges. Microwave, uncovered, at full power for 1 minute, or until the sauce is hot. Stir in the lemon juice.

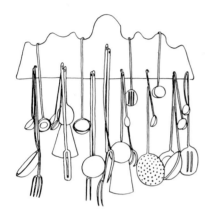

## TEMPERATURE AND TIME FOR COOKING CHICKEN PARTS

| Part | Oven Temperature | Cooking Time (minutes) |
|---|---|---|
| 4 Chicken Wings | 350° | 20 |
| 1 Half Breast | 350° | 25 to 27 |
| 2 Chicken Thighs | 375° | 22 |
| 1 Leg-Thigh Combination | 375° | 35 |

# Chicken with Peanut Sauce

*This is a colorful stir-fried combination of chicken and vegetables with a subtly flavored peanut sauce.*

Makes 4 servings.

*Nutrient Value Per Serving: 272 calories, 31 g protein, 13 g fat, 7 g carbohydrate, 684 mg sodium, 66 mg cholesterol.*

- 3 **tablespoons peanut butter**
- 2 **tablespoons soy sauce**
- 2 **tablespoons water**
- 2 **teaspoons brown sugar**
- 2 **teaspoons Oriental sesame oil***
- 1 **canned flat anchovy**
- ½ **teaspoon crushed red pepper flakes**
- 1 **tablespoon peanut oil**
- 1 **pound skinless, boned chicken breasts, cut into strips about 3 x ½ inches**
- 1 **clove garlic, finely chopped**
- 1 **teaspoon finely chopped, peeled fresh gingerroot**
- 4 **green onions (first 5 inches from root end), cut into 1-inch pieces**
- 1 **medium-size sweet red pepper, cored, seeded and cut into ¼-inch-wide strips**

1. Combine the peanut butter, soy sauce, water, brown sugar, Oriental sesame oil, anchovy and red pepper flakes in the container of an electric blender or a food processor. Whirl to mix.
2. Heat the peanut oil in a large wok or nonstick skillet over high heat until hot. Add the chicken strips and stir-fry until browned, for about 4 minutes. Add the garlic, ginger, green onion and red pepper. Reduce the heat to medium-high and stir-fry for 3 minutes.
3. Add the peanut butter mixture to the wok and cook for 1 minute, stirring to coat the chicken strips. Serve immediately, over hot cooked rice.

*__Note:__ Oriental sesame oil has more flavor and is darker in color than regular sesame oil. It can be found in the Oriental food section of many supermarkets or in Oriental specialty food stores.*

*Chicken with Peanut Sauce*

# Turkey Lasagna

*A new version of an old favorite — the sauce for this rich lasagna is made with ground turkey instead of beef. The flavor improves if you make it the day before.*

Bake at 400° for 1 hour.
Makes 12 servings.

---

*Nutrient Value Per Serving: 572 calories, 30 g protein, 23 g fat, 62 g carbohydrate, 1,109 mg sodium, 82 mg cholesterol.*

### Turkey Sauce:
- 1 cup finely chopped onion (1 large)
- 1 tablespoon butter
- 1 tablespoon olive oil
- ½ cup finely chopped carrot (1 carrot)
- ½ cup finely chopped celery (1 stalk)
- 1 tablespoon finely chopped garlic
- 2 pounds uncooked ground turkey
  OR: chicken
- 2 teaspoons salt
- 2 cups dry white wine
- 1 tablespoon leaf basil, crumbled
- 2 teaspoons leaf oregano, crumbled
- 1 teaspoon whole fennel seeds
- ½ teaspoon leaf rosemary, crumbled
- 1 cup milk
- ¼ teaspoon ground nutmeg
- ¼ teaspoon pepper
- 1 can (6 ounces) tomato paste
- 1 cup water
- 1 can (28 ounces) whole tomatoes, undrained

- 4 cups White Sauce
  (recipe, page 99)
- 2 teaspoons olive oil
- 1½ pounds lasagna noodles
- 1 cup finely chopped parsley
- 1⅓ cups grated Parmesan cheese

1. Prepare the Turkey Sauce: Sauté the onion in the butter and the oil in a large, heavy saucepan over medium heat until soft, for about 5 minutes. Add the carrot, celery and garlic; sauté for 2 to 3 minutes. Crumble in the turkey or chicken and sprinkle with the salt. Cook over low heat, stirring to break up the turkey, until half-cooked, for 3 to 4 minutes. Add 1½ cups of the wine, the basil, oregano, fennel and rosemary. Cook over medium-high heat until the wine has evaporated, for about 15 minutes. Add the milk, nutmeg and pepper. Cook over medium heat, stirring frequently, until the milk has evaporated, for 10 to 15 minutes. Stir in the tomato paste and the water. Add the tomatoes with their liquid, breaking them up with a spoon. Bring to boiling. Lower the heat and simmer, stirring occasionally, for 1 hour, or until the sauce is thick.
2. Add the remaining ½ cup of wine. Simmer for 5 to 10 minutes to blend the flavors. You'll have 7 cups of sauce.
3. Use the sauce right away, or cool to room temperature and refrigerate, covered, overnight.
4. Prepare the White Sauce and have it hot.
5. Preheat the oven to hot (400°). Lightly grease a deep lasagna pan, about 14 x 10 x 3 inches with a 4- to 5-quart capacity, with the 2 teaspoons of oil.
6. Bring a large pot of lightly salted water to boiling. Add the noodles, one piece at a time. Return to boiling, stirring. Boil just until firm-tender, for about 10 minutes. Drain the noodles in a colander. Return them to the pot and fill the pot with cold water.
7. Spread 1 cup of the Turkey Sauce in the prepared pan. Remove one quarter of the noodles from the cold water and pat dry with paper toweling. Arrange in a layer in the pan, slightly overlapping. Spread with 1½ cups of the Turkey Sauce. Spoon 1 cup of the White Sauce in small spoonfuls evenly spaced over the Turkey Sauce; do not spread out. Sprinkle with ⅓ cup of the parsley and ⅓ cup of the

Parmesan cheese. Repeat three more times (there will be no parsley for the top layer). Cover with aluminum foil.

8. Bake in the preheated hot oven (400°) for 45 minutes. Uncover and bake for 15 minutes more, or until lightly browned. Let stand for 15 minutes before cutting.

# White Sauce

Makes 4 cups.

*Nutrient Value Per ¼ Cup: 86 calories, 2 g protein, 6 g fat, 6 g carbohydrate, 189 mg sodium, 14 mg cholesterol.*

| | |
|---|---|
| *1* | *quart milk* |
| *3* | *tablespoons butter* |
| *2* | *tablespoons olive oil* |
| *½* | *cup all-purpose flour* |
| *1* | *teaspoon salt* |
| *¼* | *teaspoon pepper* |
| *¼* | *teaspoon grated nutmeg* |

1. Heat the milk in a medium-size, heavy saucepan over low heat just until bubbles appear around the edge. Remove from the heat.
2. Combine the butter and the oil in a clean medium-size, heavy saucepan over medium heat. When the butter has melted, add the flour. Stir until bubbly and cook for 1 minute more. Add the milk all at once, whisking or stirring constantly. Add the salt, pepper and nutmeg. Stir over low heat until the sauce is thick, then simmer for 2 to 3 minutes more.

# Sloppy Joes Olé!

*A great American sandwich — South-of-the-Border style. You can make the ground turkey filling a day or two ahead for ease at serving time.*

Makes 8 servings.

*Nutrient Value Per Serving: 266 calories, 15 g protein, 10 g fat, 30 g carbohydrate, 948 mg sodium, 40 mg cholesterol.*

| | |
|---|---|
| *1* | *cup chopped onion (1 large)* |
| *1* | *cup finely diced celery (2 large stalks)* |
| *1* | *cup finely diced sweet green pepper (1 large)* |
| *1* | *tablespoon vegetable oil* |
| *1* | *large clove garlic, finely chopped* |
| *1* | *pound uncooked ground turkey* |
| *2* | *tablespoons chili powder* |
| *½* | *teaspoon ground cumin* |
| *½* | *teaspoon leaf oregano, crumbled* |
| *½* | *teaspoon leaf basil, crumbled* |
| *¼* | *teaspoon leaf thyme, crumbled* |
| *1* | *teaspoon salt* |
| *¼* | *teaspoon pepper* |
| *2* | *tablespoons Worcestershire sauce* |
| *1* | *can (16 ounces) tomato sauce* |
| *¾* | *cup water* |
| *8* | *hamburger buns, lightly toasted* |

1. Sauté the onion, celery and green pepper in the oil in a medium-size, heavy skillet until soft, for about 5 minutes. Add the garlic and cook for 1 minute. Crumble in the turkey and sauté until half-cooked, for about 2 minutes. Add the chili powder, cumin, oregano, basil, thyme, salt and pepper. Cook just until the meat is cooked through, for 3 minutes.
2. Stir in the Worcestershire sauce, tomato sauce and water. Bring to boiling over medium heat. Lower the heat and simmer, stirring occasionally, until thick, for about 30 minutes.
3. Spoon ½ cup of the filling into each bun. Serve hot.

# Fish & Shellfish

## Penne with Mussels and Shrimp

Makes 6 servings.

*Nutrient Value Per Serving: 395 calories, 23 g protein, 5 g fat, 64 g carbohydrate, 165 mg sodium, 76 mg cholesterol.*

1     tablespoon extra-virgin olive oil
2     to 3 cloves garlic, finely chopped
⅛    teaspoon crushed red pepper flakes
2     cups chopped, peeled and seeded
        tomatoes (about 1¾ pounds)
2     tablespoons finely chopped flat-leaf
        Italian parsley
1     teaspoon leaf basil, crumbled
1     teaspoon leaf mint, crumbled
¼    cup bottled clam juice
¾    pound medium-size shrimp (about 18),
        shelled and deveined
1     pound mussels in shells, scrubbed and
        beards removed*
1     tablespoon brandy
1     box (16 ounces) penne
        Finely chopped flat-leaf Italian
        parsley and grated lemon rind

### STORING FRESH FISH

*Fresh fish is highly perishable so use it within 1 day and always keep it refrigerated. To freeze fresh fish, wrap it in moisture-proof paper and store it for up to 6 months at 0° F. Your store-bought frozen fish should be frozen solid when purchased. If even partially thawed, use it immediately—do not refreeze.*

### SHOPPING FOR SHRIMP

*Raw shrimp is sold unshelled (fresh), shelled (fresh or frozen) or breaded and uncooked (frozen). Jumbo or extra large shrimp have up to 20 per pound; large shrimp have 21 to 30 per pound; medium have 31 to 40 per pound; small shrimp have over 40 per pound. One pound of unshelled shrimp yields ½ pound of cooked, shelled meat, or about 2 servings. One pound of shelled shrimp yields about 3 servings.*

1. Heat the oil in a large, nonstick saucepan. Add the garlic and red pepper flakes and sauté until the garlic just begins to color, for 2 to 3 minutes.
2. Stir in the tomatoes, parsley, basil and mint. Bring to boiling, lower the heat, cover and simmer 10 minutes. Add the clam juice and shrimp. Cover; cook over low heat for 2 minutes, stirring once.
3. Add the mussels and brandy. Cover and cook for 2 to 3 minutes more, or until the shrimp are pink and the mussels open. Remove the mussels from the sauce.
4. Meanwhile, cook the penne following the package directions. Drain the penne in a colander. Transfer them to a warm serving bowl and top with the hot sauce. Stir to mix well. Place the mussels on top. Garnish with chopped parsley and grated lemon rind, if you wish.

***Note:** This dish can be made entirely with shrimp. Replace the 1 pound of mussels with an additional ¼ of pound shrimp.*

*Savory Green Sauce (recipe, page 161) on barbecued chicken, Penne with Mussels and Shrimp*

## Microwave Instructions
*(for a 650-watt variable power microwave oven)*

***Ingredient Changes:*** Eliminate the clam juice. Reduce the basil and the mint *each* to ½ teaspoon. Add ½ teaspoon of grated lemon rind.

***Directions:*** Combine the oil, garlic and red pepper flakes in a microwave-safe 13 x 9-inch baking dish. Microwave, uncovered, at full power for 3 minutes. Stir in the tomatoes, brandy, parsley, basil and mint. Microwave, uncovered, at full power for 4 minutes. Arrange mussels in a single layer around edges of the dish and place shrimp in the center. Cover with microwave-safe plastic wrap, turned back at one corner to vent. Microwave at full power for 5 minutes, or until mussels open. Sprinkle with lemon rind. Serve over hot penne.

### Food for Thought . . .

***Mussels*** *The best time to eat mussels is from fall to early spring. The summer months are the "off" season, when mussels spawn and are lean and watery. Compared to oysters and clams, mussels are inexpensive. They usually are served cooked and in their shells as an appetizer or main dish. They also can be cooked, removed from their shells and used in appetizers, soups, salads or main dishes. Allow 12 large, 18 medium or 24 small mussels per serving as a main dish.*

**Salmon** *The Romans are credited with naming this fish "salmo," meaning "the leaper," around 56 B.C. Known to man for 10 to 15 thousand years, salmon has always been a prized food.*

*The Atlantic Ocean produces only one species of salmon: the Atlantic or Kennebec salmon. Five species of salmon are found in the Pacific Ocean: sockeye, chinook, coho, pink and chum.*

*Salmon is a "fat" fish containing large amounts of natural oil. It is a high quality protein food, rich in phosphorus, potassium, niacin, riboflavin and some vitamin A.*

*Fresh salmon is sold whole, as steaks and fillets or in large pieces. Salmon also is available smoked, canned and frozen.*

*Store fresh salmon in the coldest part of the refrigerator and use it within 2 days. For longer storage, wrap salmon carefully and freeze it.*

## Herb Baked Salmon

Bake at 400° for about 40 minutes.
Makes 6 servings.

*Nutrient Value Per Serving: 161 calories, 21 g protein, 7 g fat, 3 g carbohydrate, 55 mg sodium, 58 mg cholesterol.*

| | |
|---|---|
| *1* | *whole salmon (about 4 pounds), cleaned, with head and tail left on* |
| | *Salt and pepper, to taste* |
| *1* | *medium-size onion, sliced* |
| *1* | *lemon, sliced* |
| *1* | *stalk celery, sliced* |
| *⅓* | *cup mixed chopped fresh herbs such as parsley, dill, chives, basil* |
| | *Vegetable oil* |
| | *Sliced cucumbers and additional chopped fresh herbs, for garnish (optional)* |

1. Preheat the oven to hot (400°).
2. Clean the salmon inside and out and pat dry with paper toweling. Season the cavity with the salt and pepper. Fill with half the onion, lemon and celery slices, and all the herbs.
3. Place the salmon in an aluminum foil-lined baking dish. Rub with the oil, season with the salt and pepper, and top with the remaining onion, lemon and celery slices. Cover tightly with aluminum foil.
4. Bake in the preheated hot oven (400°) for 40 minutes, or until the salmon flakes with a fork. Carefully skin the salmon, if you wish. Place on a serving platter. Garnish with sliced cucumbers and more fresh herbs, if you wish.
5. Serve the salmon in slices at room temperature, or chilled.

## Creole Fillets

*Frozen fish at its best — simmered in an easy Creole sauce. Round out this zesty meal with hot cooked rice, okra and corn muffins.*

Makes 4 servings.

*Nutrient Value Per Serving of Fish with Sauce: 172 calories, 23 g protein, 5 g fat, 10 g carbohydrate, 581 mg sodium, 54 mg cholesterol.*

| | |
|---|---|
| *1* | *cup chopped onion, fresh or frozen* |
| *2* | *cloves garlic, chopped* |
| *1* | *tablespoon olive oil* |
| *1* | *can (14 ounces) Italian-style plum tomatoes, undrained* |
| *½* | *cup white wine* |
| *½* | *teaspoon leaf oregano, crumbled* |
| *½* | *teaspoon leaf basil, crumbled* |
| *¼* | *teaspoon salt* |
| *⅛* | *teaspoon ground black pepper* |
| *½* | *teaspoon liquid red pepper seasoning* |
| *1* | *can (4 ounces) chopped green chili peppers, drained* |
| *1* | *package (1 pound) flounder or sole fillets, from the freezer, slightly thawed, about 30 minutes* |

1. Sauté the onion and the garlic in the oil in a large skillet over medium-high heat until soft, for 5 minutes.
2. Stir in the tomatoes with their liquid, the wine, oregano, basil, salt, black pepper, liquid red pepper seasoning and green chili peppers. Bring to boiling, breaking up the tomatoes with a wooden spoon. Lower the heat and simmer over medium heat, uncovered, for 10 minutes to reduce the sauce.
3. Slice the slightly thawed fish into 4 equal pieces. Add to the skillet, spooning a little sauce over the pieces. Simmer, covered, for 10 minutes. Gently turn the fish. Simmer, covered, for 10 minutes more, or until the fish just begins to flake when touched with a fork.

## Microwave Instructions
*(for a 650-watt variable power microwave oven)*

*Nutrient Value Per Serving: 162 calories, 21 g protein, 5 g fat, 9 g carbohydrate, 530 mg sodium, 57 mg cholesterol.*

**Ingredient Changes:** Drain off ⅓ cup of the liquid from the tomatoes and reserve for another recipe. Reduce the wine to ¼ cup.

**Directions:** Combine the onion, garlic and oil in a microwave-safe, shallow 1½-quart casserole dish. Microwave, uncovered, at full power for 3 minutes, stirring once. Add the tomatoes with their liquid, the wine, oregano, basil, salt, black pepper, liquid red pepper seasoning and green chili peppers. Microwave, uncovered, at full power for 4 to 5 minutes until boiling. Slice the slightly thawed fish into 4 equal pieces, place the pieces in the sauce and spoon some sauce over. Cover with the casserole lid or pleated plastic wrap. Microwave at full power for 4 to 5 minutes, or until the fish just begins to flake when touched with a fork. Turn the fish over after 2 minutes. Let stand for 3 minutes before serving.

# Tuna, Rice and Cheese
Makes 6 servings.

*Nutrient Value Per Serving: 357 calories, 22 g protein, 10 g fat, 44 g carbohydrate, 696 mg sodium, 31 mg cholesterol.*

| | |
|---|---|
| 2 | tablespoons olive oil |
| ¾ | cup chopped onion |
| ½ | cup chopped sweet red pepper |
| ½ | cup chopped celery |
| 1½ | teaspoons bottled finely chopped garlic-in-oil |
| 1½ | cups long grain white rice |
| 1 | bottle (8 ounces) clam juice |
| ½ | cup dry white wine |
| ¾ | cup water |
| 1 | cup canned crushed tomatoes, undrained |
| ⅓ | cup pimiento-stuffed green olives (about 2 ounces), cut in half |
| ½ | cup grated Romano cheese OR: Parmesan cheese |
| 2 | cans (6½ ounces each) solid white tuna packed in oil, undrained and flaked |
| 1 | lemon, cut into 6 wedges |

1. Heat the oil in a 10-inch skillet. Add the onion, red pepper, celery, garlic-in-oil, rice, clam juice, wine, water, tomatoes with their liquid and olives. Bring the mixture to a rolling boil. Reduce the heat to low, cover the skillet and simmer for 20 to 25 minutes, or until the rice is tender.
2. Stir ¼ cup of the Romano or Parmesan cheese and all the tuna into the rice with a fork. Sprinkle with the remaining ¼ cup of Romano or Parmesan cheese. Serve with the lemon wedges.

# Flounder Fillets with Chick Pea Relish

Bake at 400° for 7 to 10 minutes.
Makes 6 servings.

*Nutrient Value Per Serving: 258 calories, 28 g protein, 8 g fat, 18 g carbohydrate, 119 mg sodium, 109 mg cholesterol.*

**Chick Pea Relish:**
½  cup chopped tomato
¼  cup chopped onion
1  teaspoon finely chopped, seeded fresh jalapeño pepper
1  small clove garlic, finely chopped
1  tablespoon wine vinegar
2  cups cooked dried chick peas (garbanzo beans), no salt added (do not use canned)
   Lettuce cups (optional)

**Flounder Fillets:**
½  cup dairy sour cream
1  egg, slightly beaten
1  tablespoon all-purpose flour
   Pinch ground hot red pepper
6  flounder fillets (about 1½ pounds)
   Additional ground hot red pepper
   OR: paprika (optional)

1. Prepare the Chick Pea Relish: Combine the tomato, onion, jalapeño pepper, garlic and vinegar in a small bowl. Add the chick peas and mix. Set aside.
2. Preheat the oven to hot (400°).
3. Prepare the Flounder Fillets: Whisk together the sour cream and the egg in a small saucepan. Whisk in the flour and the ground hot red pepper until smooth. Cook the sauce, stirring constantly, over very low heat for 3 to 4 minutes, or until thickened slightly; do not boil. Remove the saucepan from the heat.
4. Fold the flounder fillets in half crosswise. Arrange the fish in a single layer on an aluminum foil-lined broiler pan.
5. Bake the fish in the preheated hot oven (400°) for 7 to 10 minutes, or until the center of the fish just begins to flake when touched with a fork. Carefully transfer the fillets with a spatula to individual plates. Spoon about 2 tablespoons of the sour cream sauce over each fillet. Sprinkle the tops of the fillets with ground hot red pepper or paprika, if you wish. Serve the relish in lettuce cups, if you wish.

## IN THE MARKET FOR FISH

*When you buy fresh fish, choose those that are clear eyed, red gilled, bright skinned and sweet smelling.*
***Whole Fish:*** *This is, of course, the entire fish, exactly as if you'd just pulled it from the water. Fish in this form takes the most amount of work to prepare before it can be cooked. It must be cleaned, dressed, scaled and finned.*
***Drawn Fish:*** *This form of fish already has been eviscerated (gutted), but it still must be scaled and finned before cooking.*
***Pan-dressed Fish:*** *In this form, the fish is completely cleaned and dressed—all you have to do is cook it.*
***Fish Fillets:*** *These are the sides of fish, skinned and boned, that are ready to cook.*
***Fish Steaks:*** *Crosscut slices of large fish containing the backbone and vertebrae, fish steaks come ready to cook.*
***Amount to Buy:*** *As a general rule, allow 1 pound of whole or drawn fish per serving, or ½ pound of pan-dressed fish, fillets or steaks per serving.*

# Barbecue

## Seasoned Sirloin Tri-Tips

Grill over medium-high heat for 40 minutes. Makes 20 to 24 servings.

*Nutrient Value Per Serving: 583 calories, 57 g protein, 34 g fat, 9 g carbohydrate, 1,698 mg sodium, 174 mg cholesterol.*

- **4  tri-tip OR: sirloin tip roasts (3½ pounds each), trimmed**
- **1  cup Seasoning Salt (recipe follows)**

1. Rub each roast with ¼ cup of the Seasoning Salt. Place the roasts in a large glass baking dish. Cover and refrigerate for at least 8 hours, or overnight.
2. Bring the roasts to room temperature.
3. Heat the grill to medium-high.
4. Grill the roasts over medium-high heat, turning frequently, until an instant-reading meat thermometer inserted in the thickest part of one roast registers 130° for rare, for about 40 minutes. (Do not leave the thermometer in the meat.)
5. Loosely cover the roasts with aluminum foil and let stand for 15 minutes. Carve against the grain into ¼-inch-thick slices.

**Seasoning Salt:** Place 2 cups of kosher (coarse) salt in the container of an electric blender or a food processor. Cover and whirl until finely granulated. Separate 1 head of garlic into cloves and peel the cloves. Add to the blender, cover and whirl for 10 seconds, or until finely chopped. Add ¼ cup of chili powder, 2 tablespoons of white pepper, 1½ tablespoons of poultry seasoning, and 1 tablespoon *each* of celery seeds, leaf oregano (crumbled), dry mustard, ground ginger and paprika. Cover and whirl until the mixture is the consistency of salt. Store in an airtight glass container for up to 2 weeks. *Makes 2¾ to 3 cups.*

## Barbecue Melted Cheese Dip

Makes 20 servings (5½ cups).

*Nutrient Value Per Serving: 338 calories, 14 g protein, 24 g fat, 17 g carbohydrate, 593 mg sodium, 69 mg cholesterol.*

- **1  large loaf sourdough, French or Italian bread, cut into bite-size cubes**
- **1  pound Cheddar cheese, shredded**
- **1  pound Monterey Jack cheese, shredded**
- **1  cup (2 sticks) butter or margarine**
- **1  jar (8 ounces) chili salsa**

1. Place the bread cubes in a napkin-lined basket. Place near the grill.
2. Combine the Cheddar and Monterey Jack cheeses and the butter or margarine in a 10-inch cast iron skillet. Place on the grill rack over medium-hot coals or over medium-low heat on the stove top. Stir constantly with a wire whisk until the cheeses melt and the mixture is smooth. Stir in the chili salsa.
3. Keep the cheese dip hot on top of the grill, stirring occasionally. Have guests dip the bread cubes into the cheese mixture.

## Microwave Instructions
*(for a 650-watt variable power microwave oven)*

**Directions:** Combine the Cheddar and Monterey Jack cheeses in a microwave-safe 2-quart casserole dish. Cut each stick of butter or margarine into 4 pieces and add to the casserole dish with the chili salsa. Cover with the casserole lid. Microwave at full power for about 5½ to 6 minutes, stirring well every 2 minutes. Keep warm.

# Malaysian Scallops and Shrimp

Grill over high heat for 5 to 8 minutes.
Makes 6 servings.

*Nutrient Value Per Serving: 324 calories, 27 g protein, 120 g fat, 8 g carbohydrate, 2,204 mg sodium, 118 mg cholesterol.*

| | |
|---|---|
| 1 | **pound medium-size sea scallops** |
| 1 | **pound large shrimp, shelled, deveined and tails left intact** |
| ²⁄₃ | **cup soy sauce** |
| 4 | **teaspoons finely slivered lime peel** |
| ½ | **cup lime juice** |
| 3 | **cloves garlic, finely chopped** |
| 2 | **tablespoons Dijon-style mustard** |
| ½ | **cup peanut oil** |
| ½ | **cup finely chopped green onion** |
| ½ | **teaspoon black pepper** |
| | **Vegetable oil** |

1. Place the scallops and the shrimp in a large bowl. Combine the soy sauce, lime peel and juice, garlic, mustard, oil, green onion and black pepper in a bowl and mix well. Pour over the scallops and the shrimp. Refrigerate, covered, for 30 minutes, stirring often.
2. Prepare the grill so the coals are hot.
3. Thread 6 large skewers, alternating the scallops and the shrimp. Brush with the marinade.
4. Brush the grill rack with the vegetable oil. Grill the skewers, uncovered, over high heat, turning once, for 5 to 8 minutes, or until the scallops are springy to the touch and the shrimp are pink.

---

## Food for Thought . . .

**Scallops** *There are two varieties of scallops: tiny bay scallops, usually ½ inch in diameter, and larger, less expensive sea scallops, which measure up to 2 inches across. Bay scallops, which have a more delicate flavor and a tender texture, are not as readily available as sea scallops. The larger sea scallops, which are best for broiling, have a somewhat stronger flavor and firmer texture. There are natural color differences among scallops harvested from different waters. The color of the flesh can range from white to cream to yellow-orange.*

*Low in calories (81 calories for 3½ ounces of meat), scallops are rich in protein, phosphorous and iodine.*

*Fresh scallops should have a sweet aroma. They should be moist and shiny but they should not be swimming in liquid. Fresh scallops should be stored in the coldest part of the refrigerator and used within 2 days.*

---

## TEMPERATURE GUIDE FOR GRILLING

**Testing by Thermometer**
**Low:** *about 300°*
**Medium:** *about 350°*
**Hot:** *about 400°*

**Testing by Hand***
**Low:** *4 to 5 seconds*
**Medium:** *3 to 4 seconds*
**Hot:** *less than 3 seconds*

*\*The length of time you can hold your hand over the coals before you have to remove it can determine the distance the grill rack should be from the coals.*

# Honolulu Spareribs

*The best and easiest spareribs are parboiled first to remove excess fat and assure a tender bite after a stay on the grill. These are savory, rather than sweet.*

Grill, covered, over medium heat for
12 minutes.
Makes 6 servings.

*Nutrient Value Per Serving: 599 calories, 36 g protein, 46 g fat, 8 g carbohydrate, 608 mg sodium, 147 mg cholesterol.*

| | |
|---|---|
| 4 | **pounds meaty pork ribs, in 1 or 2 pieces** |
| 1 | **lemon, sliced** |
| 4 | **sprigs parsley** |
| 1 | **sprig fresh oregano OR: ¼ teaspoon leaf oregano, crumbled** |
| 2 | **tablespoons soy sauce** |
| 2 | **tablespoons dry sherry** |
| 1½ | **tablespoons honey** |
| 1 | **teaspoon finely chopped fresh gingerroot** |
| 1 | **clove garlic, finely chopped** |
| ½ | **teaspoon five-spice powder\*** |
| ¼ | **teaspoon pepper** |
| ¼ | **cup chili sauce** |
| ¼ | **cup peanut oil** |
| | **Additional peanut oil** |

1. Place the ribs in a large pot and add enough water to cover them. Add the lemon slices, parsley and oregano. Bring to boiling. Lower the heat and simmer, partially covered, for 45 minutes. Drain. Place the ribs in a shallow, nonaluminum dish.
2. Combine the soy sauce, sherry, honey, ginger, garlic, five-spice powder, pepper, chili sauce and the ¼ cup of oil in a small bowl and mix well. Pour the mixture over the ribs and turn to coat. Cover the ribs and refrigerate for 1 hour.
3. Prepare the grill so the heat is medium.
4. Brush the grill rack with the additional oil. Grill the ribs, covered, with the vents open, over medium heat, basting the ribs often with any remaining marinade, until the ribs are crisp, for about 6 minutes per side.

## Food for Thought . . .

**Sparerib** *The cut of pork consisting of long rib bones with a thin covering of meat on the outside and between the ribs. This cut is obtained from the lower portion of the rib cage. The upper portion is where pork chops are cut from. Country-style ribs are meatier than spareribs. They are made by splitting the blade end pork loin into halves lengthwise. Country-style ribs contain part of the loin eye bones. Pork back ribs are cut from the blade and center section of the loin. They contain the upper rib bones and a layer of meat from the loin eye muscle. Pork back ribs usually are obtained when pork loins are boned for roasts.*

*Because of the amount of bone, allow ¾ to 1 pound of spareribs per serving.*

**\*Note:** *Five-spice powder is available in the gourmet section of many supermarkets, or make your own: Combine 1 teaspoon of ground cinnamon, 1 teaspoon of crushed anise seed, ¼ teaspoon of crushed fennel seed, ¼ teaspoon of pepper and ⅛ teaspoon of ground cloves. Store in an airtight container. Makes about 2½ teaspoons.*

## Piquant Baby Back Ribs

*A barbecue sauce with ingredients low in sodium imparts special flavor to spareribs.*

Grill over high heat for 40 to 50 minutes.
Makes 4 servings.

*Nutrient Value Per Serving: 808 calories, 53 g protein, 54 g fat, 25 g carbohydrate, 216 mg sodium, 214 mg cholesterol.*

¾ **cup no-salt-added catsup**
⅔ **cup salt-free steak sauce**
2 **tablespoons cider vinegar**
1 **tablespoon finely chopped fresh gingerroot**
1 **tablespoon salt-free 14 herb and spice seasoning blend**
3 **cloves garlic, finely chopped**
¼ **teaspoon liquid red pepper seasoning**
⅛ **teaspoon ground hot red pepper**
4 **pounds baby back spareribs, halved crosswise**

1. Combine the catsup, steak sauce, cider vinegar, ginger, seasoning blend, garlic, liquid red pepper seasoning and ground hot red pepper in a small bowl. Blend well with a spoon.
2. Place the ribs in a large, shallow roasting pan. Brush the barbecue sauce over and let stand for 2 hours. (Cover the ribs and place in the refrigerator if marinating for longer than 2 hours.)
3. Build a hot fire, or set a gas or electric grill to high, following the manufacturer's directions.
4. Place the ribs on a double thickness of heavy-duty aluminum foil and brush with part of the sauce. Wrap the ribs in the foil, completely enclosing them.
5. Grill the ribs over high heat, turning the foil packet once, for 30 to 40 minutes. Unwrap, brush with more barbecue sauce and grill for 10 minutes more, or until the ribs are brown and crisp. Serve with cole slaw made with plain lowfat yogurt mixed with additional salt-free 14 herb and spice seasoning blend.

## Veal Kebabs

*Enjoy these kebabs year-round! For a tasty winter treat, broil them in an aluminum foil-lined pan for 6 to 8 minutes.*

Grill over high heat for 4 to 5 minutes.
Makes 12 appetizers.

*Nutrient Value Per Serving: 47 calories, 4 g protein, 3 g fat, 1 g carbohydrate, 14 mg sodium, 16 mg cholesterol.*

½ **pound boneless loin of veal, cut into ½-inch cubes**
3 **tablespoons salt-free steak sauce**
1 **tablespoon unsalted butter**
1 **teaspoon grated lemon rind**
1 **teaspoon lemon juice**

1. Build a hot fire, or set a gas or electric grill to high, following the manufacturer's directions.
2. Thread four cubes of veal on each of 12 bamboo skewers.
3. Combine the steak sauce, butter and lemon rind in a small saucepan. Cook over medium heat just until well blended. Add the lemon juice. Brush the kebabs with the sauce.
4. Grill the kebabs for 4 to 5 minutes, turning them once and coating with the remaining sauce; don't overcook.

**Note:** *To minimize burning, soak the bamboo skewers in water for 30 minutes before using.*

# Barbecued Frank Kebabs

*A spicy sauce turns ordinary hot dogs into an extraordinary treat.*

Makes 8 servings.

*Nutrient Value Per Serving: 147 calories, 6 g protein, 11 g fat, 6 g carbohydrate, 301 mg sodium, 22 mg cholesterol.*

6   **lower-salt jumbo all beef hot dogs, each cut into 4 pieces**
16  **one-inch chunks red onion**
16  **one-inch pieces sweet yellow or green pepper**
½   **cup Spicy Barbecue Sauce (recipe, page 114)**

1. Soak 8 eight-inch bamboo skewers in cold water for several hours, or overnight.
2. Build a hot fire, or set a gas or electric grill to high, following the manufacturer's directions.
3. Alternately thread 3 pieces of hot dog, 2 red onion chunks and 2 pieces of yellow or green pepper on each skewer. Brush the skewers with some of the Spicy Barbecue Sauce.
4. Grill the kebabs over high heat for 5 minutes, turning them once or twice and brushing with the remaining sauce.

### ▬ HAMBURGERS ON HAND

*To freeze a large number of ground beef patties: Shape the patties, place them on wax paper on a baking sheet, cover them with more wax paper and place them in the freezer. When the patties are frozen, remove them from the baking sheet, place them in a freezer-proof plastic bag, or wrap them in aluminum foil with 2 pieces of wax paper between each patty and refreeze.*

# Key West Burgers

*Delicately seasoned meat patties cook along with grilled onions and toasted pita breads.*

Grill over high heat for 30 minutes.
Makes 4 servings.

*Nutrient Value Per Serving: 571 calories, 27 g protein, 30 g fat, 49 g carbohydrate, 487 mg sodium, 70 mg cholesterol.*

1   **pound lean ground beef**
1   **medium-size carrot, trimmed and grated**
1   **small onion, finely chopped (¼ cup)**
1   **tablespoon salt-free 14 herb and spice seasoning blend**
2   **large onions**
½   **cup Key West Marinade (recipe, page 110)**
4   **medium-size pita breads**

1. Gently toss the beef, carrot, chopped onion and seasoning blend in a large bowl. Shape into 4 patties about 3 inches wide and 2 inches high. Refrigerate, loosely covered, until ready to grill.
2. Build a hot fire, or set a gas or electric grill to high, following the manufacturer's directions.
3. Cut the large onions crosswise into ½-inch slices. Carefully run a metal skewer through each onion slice to hold its shape while grilling. Brush each onion slice lightly with the Key West Marinade.
4. Grill the onion slices over high heat, turning and brushing frequently with additional marinade, for 30 minutes, or until lightly charred and tender when pierced with a knife. Remove from the grill.
5. Halfway through grilling the onions, place the burgers on the grill and cook for 7 minutes on each side for medium rare, brushing with the Key West Marinade.
6. During the last 4 minutes of grilling time, grill the pita breads for 2 minutes on each side, just to toast lightly.
7. Serve the burgers in the pitas with the onion slices on the side.

# Key West Marinade

*This rich marinade can double as a piquant salad dressing.*

Makes about 1 cup.

*Nutrient Value Per Serving: 65 calories, 0 g protein, 7 g fat, 1 g carbohydrate, 26 mg sodium, 0 mg cholesterol.*

- ½ **cup vegetable oil**
- ¼ **cup lime juice**
- 2 **tablespoons prepared mustard**
- 1 **tablespoon salt-free 14 herb and spice seasoning blend**
- 1 **teaspoon fennel seeds**

1. Place the oil in the container of an electric blender. Add the lime juice, mustard, seasoning blend and fennel seeds.
2. Cover and whirl until thick and creamy. Store the unused marinade in a covered container in the refrigerator. Stir thoroughly before using.

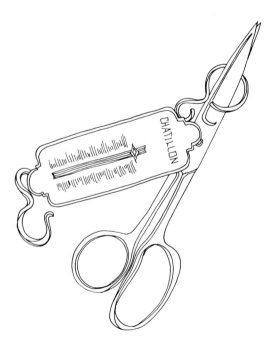

## Food for Thought . . .

***Rock Cornish Game Hen*** *A special breed developed by crossing a Cornish game cock with a white Rock hen. It is marketed at 4 to 6 weeks old and weighs 1½ pounds or less. It's popular with white-meat lovers.*

# Butterflied Cornish Hens

*The French marinade adds a pungent flavor to Cornish hens; however, most of the alcohol burns off during the grilling, leaving a crisp skin with just a taste of vermouth.*

Grill over medium heat for 40 minutes.
Makes 4 servings.

*Nutrient Value Per Serving: 610 calories, 57 g protein, 31 g fat, 22 g carbohydrate, 1,191 mg sodium, 176 mg cholesterol.*

- 4 **small Cornish hens (about 1 pound each), butterflied or split**
- 1 **cup French Marinade (recipe follows)**

1. Place the hens in a large, shallow container. Rub the halves on all sides with the French Marinade.
2. Cover loosely and refrigerate for 6 hours or overnight, turning several times.
3. Build a medium fire, or set a gas or electric grill to medium, following the manufacturer's directions.
4. Grill the hens, cut side down, on the edge of the grill over medium heat, turning every 10 minutes, for 40 minutes, or until crisp and cooked through. Serve immediately.

***French Marinade:*** Place ½ cup of dry vermouth and ½ cup of finely chopped shallots or green onions in a medium-size bowl. Add ½ cup of salt-free 14 herb and spice seasoning blend. Stir in 1 tablespoon of olive oil until the mixture is thick and smooth. Stir to blend just before using. *Makes 1 cup.*

# Grilled Thai Chicken

*This dish can be enhanced further by adding fruit wood chips, such as apple or cherry wood, to the hot coals.*

Grill, over high heat for 30 to 35 minutes. Makes 8 servings.

*Nutrient Value Per Serving: 304 calories, 34 g protein, 17 g fat, 1 g carbohydrate, 241 mg sodium, 110 mg cholesterol.*

| | |
|---|---|
| 2 | **chickens (2½ pounds each), each cut into 8 serving pieces** |
| 1 | **teaspoon salt** |
| 2 | **tablespoons black peppercorns** |
| 6 | **cloves garlic, peeled** |
| 4 | **whole sprigs cilantro (coriander), chopped** |
| 1 | **small hot green chili pepper, seeded, deveined and coarsely chopped** |
| ¼ | **cup lemon juice** |
| ¼ | **cup vodka** |
| | **Vegetable oil** |
| 2 | **tablespoons chopped fresh parsley** |

1. Set the chicken in a large, shallow glass dish.
2. Blend the salt, peppercorns, garlic, cilantro, green chili pepper, lemon juice and vodka in the container of an electric blender or a food processor. Pour the cilantro mixture over the chicken and coat well. Refrigerate the chicken, covered, for 1 hour, turning often.
3. Prepare the grill so the coals are hot. Brush the grill rack with the oil. If using presoaked wood chips, sprinkle them over the hot coals.
4. Grill the dark chicken meat (legs and thighs), covered, with the vents open, over high heat for 15 minutes, turning once.
5. Add the white chicken meat (breasts and wings). Grill, covered, turning once, for 15 to 20 minutes more, or until the skin is crisp and the meat is no longer pink near the bone. Remove the grill cover if the chicken is not crispy enough. Sprinkle with the parsley.

## THE VEGETABLE GRILL

### Direct Grilling

*Grilling vegetables directly imparts that wonderful barbecue flavor, though it is a bit trickier than foil-grilling. Zucchini, yellow squash, eggplant and onion should be sliced 1 inch thick and brushed with a basting sauce, melted butter or margarine, or oil. Vegetables prepared for kebabs should be cut into equal sizes so that they cook evenly. Lightly grease the grill rack and turn the vegetables occasionally to prevent sticking.*

### Foil Grilling

*Rinse the vegetables thoroughly and do not dry them—the water that clings will help steam-cook the vegetables in their packets. Place no more than four servings of vegetables on a single sheet of heavy-duty aluminum foil. When combining vegetables in foil packets or on kebabs, cut them into similar sizes to insure even cooking; corn on the cob should be wrapped separately. Evenly dot the vegetables with butter or margarine, or sprinkle them with vegetable oil, olive oil or salad dressing before sealing the foil. Most vegetables are done when just fork-tender.*

### Coal Roasting

*Hearty root vegetables, such as potatoes, carrots and onions, may be wrapped whole in aluminum foil and cooked in the coals—a great method for campfire cooking. Place the foil-wrapped vegetables on the edge of the fire or place them directly into a low, low flame. The cooking time varies greatly, depending on the intensity of the heat.*

## *HOW TO CUT AND BONE A CHICKEN*

**1.** Place the chicken breast-side up. Using a sharp knife, make a lengthwise slit through the skin and flesh from the neck to the cavity. Turn the bird over and repeat the cut.

**2.** Using poultry shears (a) or kitchen shears (b), cut right through the bones (ribs). Cutting to one side of the breast bone is easier than cutting directly through it.

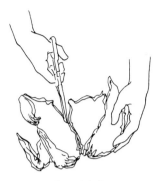

**3.** Turn the chicken over. Cut through the bones, cutting to one side of the backbone. You may remove the backbone. A small bird is cut this way for serving.

**4.** For quartering chicken, continue using the shears. Cut across half the bird, following the natural division just below the rib cage and the breastbone.

**5.** The thigh may be left attached to the leg for broiling. For frying, bend the leg joint and cut through the joint with a sharp knife, separating the leg from the thigh.

**6.** To separate the wing from the breast, bend the joint and cut through the joint with a sharp knife. The chicken now will be in eight pieces and ready for frying.

**7.** If the recipe calls for skinless chicken breasts, use a small, sharp paring knife to start separating the skin from the flesh, then slip your fingers between the skin and flesh and peel off the skin.

**8.** To bone a chicken breast, use a small paring knife. Cut the meat away from the rib bones with little, quick strokes, feeling the way with your fingers.

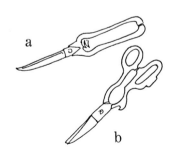

a

b

# A GUIDE TO GREAT GRILLING

Proper grilling techniques must be used to produce succulent, crusty, charcoal-flavored (not smothered) barbecued food. Use the following guide for a no-fail, no-burn barbecue.

• Store the charcoal in a cool, dry place, tightly closed in its original package. Charcoal is difficult to light if it gets wet or absorbs a lot of moisture from the air.

• If the firebox is not adjustable, cook food on a hinged grill rack that you can raise and lower manually.

• For easy cleanup, line the fire pan with heavy-duty aluminum foil.

• Heap the charcoal in the center of the grill, or around the drip pan if you're using one, and set aflame.

• To start the fire, use charcoal starter or an electric starter. Chemical charcoal starter may cause "off" flavors in food; the electric starter imparts no odor. If you're using liquid starter, wait for 2 minutes before igniting so the starter can soak in properly.

• Start a charcoal fire at least 30 to 40 minutes before you want to begin cooking, to allow the coals to burn and become covered with a gray ash. The heat then will be radiant and cook the food gradually without burning.

• Once the coals are hot, separate them into an even layer on the bottom of the grill. To add coals, start them burning in another pan and transfer them to the grill when they are gray.

• Sprinkle the charcoal with fresh herbs, such as marjoram, rosemary, thyme or mint, or dried herbs that have been soaked in water, such as bay leaf or fennel, to give the grilled meat a subtle flavor. Additional flavorings, such as hickory, apple, cherry, alder and mesquite, may be obtained in the form of soaked aromatic wood chips. Sprinkle the chips over the glowing coals before grilling.

• Brush the grill rack with fat or oil or use nonstick vegetable cooking spray on the grill rack just before cooking to prevent the food from sticking.

• When grilling fatty foods, make a drip pan of aluminum foil and place it directly under the food to prevent flare-ups from dripping fat.

• To maintain an even temperature, place the grill in a sheltered place, away from drafts. On windy days, cover the grill with a hood or a tent of aluminum foil.

• When grilling foods that require slow cooking, set the grill rack at its highest position and lower it as the coals cool.

• When using a gas grill, the same basic principles apply. Preheat the grill to allow the ceramic element to become radiantly hot. Use marinades and barbecue sauces that contain as little sugar as possible; if you have a favorite sweet sauce, keep the grill rack as high as possible and turn the food every five minutes, brushing with sauce every time the food is turned. Use tongs for turning to avoid piercing the food and releasing the juices.

• If any marinade or basting sauce remains, heat it in a saucepan on the grill rack and serve it on the side.

• The last glowing embers can be used to keep coffee hot, toast marshmallows or pound cake, heat fudge or sauce for ice cream, warm cookies, rolls and pie, or grill orange or pineapple slices.

## Food for Thought . . .

**Pineapple** *A tropical fruit, pineapple was so named because it resembled a pine cone. A pineapple which weighs about 4 pounds takes almost 2 years to grow. The pineapple plant is grown from slips or crowns, not seeds. It is a good source of vitamin C with only 52 calories per 3½-ounce serving.*

*Pineapple is available fresh or canned. Fresh pineapples are marketed year-round with peak supplies between April and June. A pineapple does not ripen after it is harvested.*

*Select a pineapple that is firm with fresh-looking, green crown leaves. The larger the fruit, the greater the proportion of edible flesh—it's also a better buy because a pineapple is usually sold by the piece rate rather than weight. A very slight separation of the eyes and a pleasant pineapple fragrance are the signs of a ripe fruit. Store pineapple at room temperature, away from heat or sun and use within 3 days. Refrigerate until chilled just before serving.*

## Spicy Pineapple Grill

*Pineapple, native to our 50th State, is a classic adjunct to pork, particularly when brushed with a tangy sauce and then lightly grilled.*

Grill over high heat 3 to 4 minutes.
Makes 6 servings.

*Nutrient Value Per Serving: 48 calories, 0 g protein, 0 g fat, 12 g carbohydrate, 190 mg sodium, 0 mg cholesterol.*

- 3 **tablespoons chili sauce**
- 1 **tablespoon Dijon-style mustard**
- 2 **tablespoons sweetened lime juice**
- 6 **fresh pineapple slices (about ½ inch thick), trimmed (about ½ pineapple)**
  **Vegetable oil**

1. Prepare the grill so the coals are hot.
2. Combine the chili sauce, mustard and lime juice in a small bowl and mix well. Brush the mixture over both sides of the pineapple slices. Let stand for 15 minutes at room temperature.
3. Brush the grill rack of the barbecue with the oil. Grill the pineapple slices over high heat, for 1½ to 2 minutes per side, or until golden brown. Cut each slice in half to serve, if you wish.

## Spicy Barbecue Sauce

*Relatively low in sodium, this homemade blend boasts no-salt-added tomato sauce, salt-free steak sauce and an herb and spice seasoning blend.*

Makes 1¾ cups.

*Nutrient Value Per Tablespoon: 12 calories, 1 g protein, 13 g fat, 3 g carbohydrate, 8 mg sodium, 0 mg cholesterol.*

- 2 **cans (8 ounces each) no-salt-added tomato sauce**
- ⅓ **cup chopped onion**
- 2 **tablespoons salt-free steak sauce**
- ¼ **cup salt-free 14 herb and spice seasoning blend**
- 1 **tablespoon chili powder**

1. Place the tomato sauce in a small saucepan. Add the onion, steak sauce, seasoning blend and chili powder.
2. Bring to boiling, cover and simmer for 15 minutes.
3. Store the unused portion of the sauce in an airtight container in the refrigerator for up to 1 week.

# Special Barbecue Sauce

Makes 2 cups.

*Nutrient Value Per Tablespoon: 21 calories, 0 g protein, 0 g fat, 5 g carbohydrate, 182 mg sodium, 0 mg cholesterol.*

- 2 **cups catsup**
- 2 **teaspoons dry mustard**
- 2 **teaspoons garlic powder**
- 2 **teaspoons light corn syrup**
- 2 **teaspoons Worcestershire sauce**

Combine the catsup, mustard, garlic powder, corn syrup and Worcestershire sauce. Brush the sauce on the franks or burgers during the last 10 minutes of grilling.

# Tomato Beer Baste

*A tangy sauce to use with sausages or any cut of beef.*

Makes 3½ cups.

*Nutrient Value Per Tablespoon: 12 calories, 0 g protein, 0 g fat, 3 g carbohydrate, 119 mg sodium, 0 mg cholesterol.*

- 1 **bottle (16 ounces) barbecue sauce**
- 1 **can (12 ounces) beer**
- 2 **tablespoons Worcestershire sauce**
  **Few drops liquid red pepper seasoning**

Combine the barbecue sauce, beer, Worcestershire sauce and liquid red pepper seasoning in a 4-cup screw-top glass jar. Store for at least 1 day. Brush the baste on the meat, for the last 15 minutes of grilling.

---

> ## Food for Thought . . .
>
> ***Chutney*** *This sweet accompaniment to spicy curry dishes is made from a mixture of fresh fruit (usually mango), dried fruit (such as raisins) and spices. Chutney, which is of Indian origin, also can be served as a relish with poultry, pork or ham.*

# Plum Chutney Glaze

*Pungent and spicy, this baste makes lamb riblets, spareribs or pork chops taste extra-special.*

Makes 4 cups.

*Nutrient Value Per Tablespoon: 23 calories, 0 g protein, 0 g fat, 6 g carbohydrate, 2 mg sodium, 0 mg cholesterol.*

- 1 **large red onion, chopped (1 cup)**
- 1 **large sweet green pepper, halved, seeded and chopped**
- 1 **California orange, peeled, sectioned and chopped**
- 1 **large tomato, cored and chopped**
- 1 **clove garlic, finely chopped**
- ½ **cup lime juice**
- 1 **jar (1 pound) plum jam**
- 1 **tablespoon pumpkin pie spice**

1. Combine the onion, green pepper, orange and tomato in a large, heavy saucepan. Add the garlic and the lime juice and stir with a wooden spoon.
2. Bring slowly to boiling, stirring often. Lower the heat and simmer for 45 minutes. Stir in the plum jam and the pumpkin pie spice; simmer for 15 minutes more, stirring often.
3. Pour into a glass bowl to cool completely. Store in a glass decanter or a 4-cup screw-top glass jar.

## Chutney Barbecue Glaze

*Your blender does the work in seconds.*

Makes about 2 cups.

*Nutrient Value Per Tablespoon: 27 calories, 0 g protein, 0 g fat, 7 g carbohydrate, 67 mg sodium, 0 mg cholesterol.*

1   **cup mango chutney**
½   **cup catsup**
½   **cup lemon juice**
1   **tablespoon Worcestershire sauce**

Combine the chutney, catsup, lemon juice and Worcestershire sauce in the container of an electric blender. Cover and whirl on high speed for 30 seconds, or until the mixture is smooth. Store in a 2-cup screw-top glass jar. Brush the glaze on chicken, burgers or pork chops.

## Tangy Molasses Sauce

*Split chicken and grill it with this Southern-style barbecue sauce.*

Makes 1½ cups.

*Nutrient Value Per Tablespoon: 24 calories, 0 g protein, 0 g fat, 6 g carbohydrate, 99 mg sodium, 0 mg cholesterol.*

½   **cup light molasses**
½   **cup cider vinegar**
½   **cup prepared mustard**
¼   **cup Worcestershire sauce**
1   **teaspoon liquid red pepper seasoning**

Combine the molasses, vinegar, mustard, Worcestershire sauce and liquid red pepper seasoning in a small bowl; stir to blend. Spoon into a 2-cup screw-top jar.

## Sweet 'n Sour Baste

*A classic of great taste — your food never had it so good!*

Makes 1¾ cups.

*Nutrient Value Per Tablespoon: 14 calories, 2 g protein, 0 g fat, 4 g carbohydrate, 250 mg sodium, 0 mg cholesterol.*

1   **can (8 ounces) tomato sauce**
¼   **cup honey**
¼   **cup freshly squeezed lemon juice**
1   **tablespoon soy sauce**
1   **tablespoon Worcestershire sauce**
1   **clove garlic, finely chopped**
2   **teaspoons salt**
1   **teaspoon leaf basil, crumbled**
1   **teaspoon dry mustard**
¼   **teaspoon liquid red pepper seasoning**

1. Combine the tomato sauce, honey, lemon juice, soy sauce, Worcestershire sauce, garlic, salt, basil, mustard and liquid red pepper seasoning in a large screw-top jar. Cover and shake vigorously to blend well.
2. Refrigerate the baste for at least 2 hours to allow the flavors to blend.
3. Brush the baste on ribs, chops or chicken breasts during the last 20 minutes of grilling.

## Lemon Pineapple Glaze

*Sweet and tangy — just great for chicken, fish or hot dogs.*

Makes 3 cups.

*Nutrient Value Per Tablespoon: 29 calories, 0 g protein, 0 g fat, 79 g carbohydrate, 2 mg sodium, 0 mg cholesterol.*

1   **jar (1 pound) pineapple jam**
1   **can (6 ounces) apricot nectar**
½   **cup lemon juice**
2   **teaspoons ground ginger**

Combine the pineapple jam, apricot nectar, lemon juice and ginger in a medium-size bowl until the mixture is smooth. Pour into a decanter or 4-cup screw-top glass jar. Chill for at least 2 days.

## Lemon Herb Marinade

*Rosemary and lemon juice deliciously compliment chicken, beef or lamb.*

Makes ¾ cup.

*Nutrient Value Per Tablespoon: 60 calories, 2 g protein, 6 g fat, 1 g carbohydrate, 226 mg sodium, 0 mg cholesterol.*

| | |
|---|---|
| ⅓ | **cup vegetable oil** |
| ⅓ | **cup lemon juice** |
| 1 | **teaspoon grated lemon rind** |
| 3 | **tablespoons Worcestershire sauce** |
| 1 | **clove garlic, finely chopped** |
| 1 | **teaspoon salt** |
| 1 | **teaspoon leaf rosemary, crumbled** |
| ¼ | **teaspoon freshly ground pepper** |

1. Combine the oil, lemon juice and rind, Worcestershire sauce, garlic, salt, rosemary and pepper in a 1-cup screw-top jar.
2. Cover the jar and shake to blend well. Chill for at least 1 hour to blend the flavors.
3. Marinate chicken, beef or lamb for at least 2 hours before grilling time.

## Lemon Butter Baste

*Here's the perfect baste to use with fish.*

Makes 1¾ cups.

*Nutrient Value Per Tablespoon: 62 calories, 0 g protein, 7 g fat, 1 g carbohydrate, 237 mg sodium, 18 mg cholesterol.*

| | |
|---|---|
| 1 | **cup (2 sticks) butter or margarine** |
| 1 | **medium-size onion, chopped (½ cup)** |
| ⅔ | **cup lemon juice** |
| 2 | **tablespoons Worcestershire sauce** |
| 2 | **teaspoons salt** |
| 1 | **teaspoon paprika** |

1. Melt the butter over the grill in a saucepan with a flameproof handle. Stir in the onion and sauté until soft.
2. Stir in the lemon juice, Worcestershire sauce, salt, paprika; simmer 10 minutes.

## Peachy Barbecue Sauce

*Try this savory sauce on your next roast pork loin.*

Makes ¾ cup.

*Nutrient Value Per Tablespoon: 38 calories, 0 g protein, 0 g fat, 10 g carbohydrate, 25 mg sodium, 0 mg cholesterol.*

| | |
|---|---|
| ½ | **cup peach preserves** |
| 2 | **tablespoons cider vinegar** |
| 1 | **tablespoon bottled steak sauce** |

Combine the peach preserves, vinegar and steak sauce in a small metal saucepan with a flameproof handle. Heat on the grill, stirring often, until the sauce bubbles. Push the saucepan to the side of the grill and keep the sauce warm. Brush the sauce on the pork loin, to coat evenly, for the last 30 minutes of grilling.

# CHAPTER 4

## Other Main Events

*Delicious pastas, meltingly good cheese dishes, main-dish salads and more!*

*Peppery Bean Soup (recipe, page 132) and White Bean Tuna Salad (recipe, page 137)*

nce upon a time, pasta was looked on as a side dish. Beans were something to be served with a "real" meal. And who ever heard of a main-dish salad? But today, these dishes are as much a part of our diet as burgers and chicken.

Let's start with main-dish salads. They often combine small quantities of meat, poultry or fish with a grain, cheese or pasta. Dilled Salmon Pasta Salad *(recipe, page 126)* is one example that meets all the nutritional needs for a complete meal in one dish.

Next time you're in the supermarket, take a look at the variety of pasta shapes, sizes— and flavors! From convenient Saucy Stuffed Shells *(recipe, page 128)* to colorful Pasta with Sweet Pepper Sauce *(recipe, page 127)*, the choices are limitless for pasta lovers.

Dried beans, peas and legumes have finally achieved recognition as an economical and nutritious mainstay. An excellent way to stretch recipes, they also provide the base for many soups, salads and baked dishes, such as Slow-Cooked Beans with Lamb *(recipe, page 130)*, and Peppery Bean Soup *(recipe, page 132)*.

Try these entrée alternatives— nutritionally sound and very adaptable, they offer terrific mealtime variety. ∎

# Main Dish Salads

## Turkey Rice Salad

Makes 4 servings.

*Nutrient Value Per Serving: 503 calories, 31 g protein, 21 g fat, 46 g carbohydrate, 412 mg sodium, 59 mg cholesterol.*

| | |
|---|---|
| 4 | ounces brown rice (about ½ cup) |
| 1½ | cups water |
| ½ | teaspoon salt |
| ⅓ | cup white rice |

*Tarragon Mustard Vinaigrette:*

| | |
|---|---|
| ⅓ | cup vegetable oil |
| ¼ | cup red wine vinegar |
| 1½ | teaspoons Dijon-style mustard |
| ½ | teaspoon leaf tarragon, crumbled |
| 1 | clove garlic, crushed |
| ¼ | teaspoon pepper |

| | |
|---|---|
| ¾ | pound green beans, trimmed |
| ¾ | pound cooked turkey breast, cut into ½-inch pieces |
| ¼ | pound mushrooms, sliced thin |
| 1 | cup thinly sliced carrots |
| ¼ | cup chopped parsley |
| 8 | leaves red-tipped leaf lettuce Parsley sprigs, for garnish |

1. Combine the brown rice with the water and the salt in a medium-size saucepan. Bring to boiling. Lower the heat, cover and simmer the brown rice for 25 minutes. Add the white rice. Simmer the rice, covered, for 20 minutes, or until all the water is absorbed. Spoon into a large bowl. Let the rice stand for 30 minutes.
2. Prepare the Tarragon Mustard Vinaigrette: In a jar with a tight-fitting lid, combine the oil, vinegar, mustard, tarragon, garlic and pepper. Cover and shake to mix the vinaigrette. Set aside.
3. Cook the green beans in enough boiling water to cover the beans in a large pot for 3 to 5 minutes, or until crisp-tender. Drain the beans in a colander. Run the beans under cold running water and drain the beans well. Place in a medium-size bowl. Add 2 tablespoons of the dressing and toss to coat the beans. (If preparing the salad ahead, don't dress the beans until just before serving.) Set aside.
4. Combine the rice, turkey, mushrooms, carrot, chopped parsley and the remaining dressing in a large bowl.
5. Arrange the lettuce leaves on a serving platter and spoon the salad on top. Garnish with the green beans and the parsley sprigs.

***Tarragon Mustard Vinaigrette Serving Suggestions:*** Use it to dress most rice, pasta or green salads. This vinaigrette also is good with lightly cooked green beans, broccoli or other vegetables for a summer side dish.

## Food for Thought . . .

**Wild Rice** *This is not actually a rice but the seed of a water grass native to some of our northern states. Wild rice is harvested by hand from small boats, which accounts for its high price.*

*Wild rice varies in length. The longer the grain, the longer the cooking time and the higher the price. When cooked, these long, slender, brownish grains have a sweet, nutty flavor. Wild rice is available by itself or mixed with long-grain white rice.*

# Oriental Turkey Salad

Makes 6 servings.

*Nutrient Value Per Serving: 196 calories, 21 g protein, 8 g fat, 10 g carbohydrate, 912 mg sodium, 47 mg cholesterol.*

| | |
|---|---|
| 1 | **pound boneless turkey cutlets** |
| 2 | **cups chicken broth** |
| 1 | **small onion, quartered** |
| 1 | **small celery stalk, chopped** |
| 1 | **slice fresh gingerroot** |
| 4 | **green onions, trimmed and halved** |
| 1 | **small carrot, trimmed and halved** |
| 6 | **sprigs fresh coriander OR: parsley** |
| 6 | **peppercorns** |
| 1/2 | **pound snow peas** |
| 1 1/2 | **cups bean sprouts, rinsed and well drained** |
| 1 | **large sweet green pepper, halved, seeded and cut into thin strips** |
| | **Oriental Vinaigrette (recipe follows)** |

1. Combine the turkey cutlets, broth, onion, celery, ginger, green onion, carrot, coriander or parsley and the peppercorns in a large saucepan. Bring to boiling over medium heat. Lower the heat.
2. Poach the turkey cutlets for 5 minutes. Turn off the heat and let the cutlets cool in the liquid. Remove the cutlets from the poaching liquid and cut into chunks.
3. Tip and string the snow peas, if necessary. Return the poaching liquid to boiling. Plunge the snow peas into the liquid and blanch for 5 seconds. Immediately place the snow peas under cold running water, then drain well.
4. Combine the turkey, snow peas, bean sprouts and green pepper strips in a large bowl. Drizzle the Oriental Vinaigrette over and toss to coat ingredients evenly.
5. Transfer the salad to a portable container, cover and refrigerate until serving time. Let the salad come to room temperature and toss before serving.

**Oriental Vinaigrette:** Combine 1/4 cup of freshly squeezed lemon juice, 3 tablespoons of soy sauce, 2 tablespoons of peanut or vegetable oil and 2 teaspoons of Oriental sesame oil* in a small bowl. Beat until well blended and add salt and pepper to taste. *Makes about 1/2 cup.*

***Note:** Oriental sesame oil has more flavor and is darker in color than regular sesame oil. It can be found in the Oriental food section of many supermarkets or in Oriental specialty food stores.*

# South-of-the-Border Salad

*A hearty salad that's easy to assemble. Serve the Jalapeño Dressing (recipe, page 122) on the side.*

Makes 4 servings.

*Nutrient Value Per Serving: 443 calories, 16 g protein, 32 g fat, 30 g carbohydrate, 291 mg sodium, 44 mg cholesterol.*

| | |
|---|---|
| 2 | **cups cooked whole-kernel corn** |
| 3 | **small or 2 medium-size ripe avocados, pitted, peeled and cut into 1/2-inch cubes (about 3 cups)** |
| 1 1/2 | **cups Cheddar cheese OR: Monterey Jack cheese, cut into 1/2-inch cubes (about 6 ounces)** |
| 2 | **tablespoons lemon juice** |
| 1 | **to 2 tablespoons chopped fresh coriander OR: parsley** |
| | **Romaine lettuce** |
| | **Jalapeño Dressing (recipe, page 122)** |

1. Gently toss together the corn, avocado, Cheddar or Monterey Jack cheese, lemon juice and coriander or parsley in a large salad bowl. Chill slightly, if you wish.
2. Arrange the salad on the romaine leaves, or in a tortilla basket, if you wish. Spoon the Jalapeño Dressing on the side.

## Jalapeño Dressing

*Also delicious as a dip. To insure its fresh flavor, make the dressing no more than an hour before serving.*

Makes 1½ cups.

*Nutrient Value Per Serving: 4 calories, 0 g protein, 0 g fat, 1 g carbohydrate, 62 mg sodium, 0 mg cholesterol.*

| | |
|---|---|
| 2 | medium-size ripe tomatoes, cored, seeded and chopped (about 2 cups) |
| 1 | clove garlic, finely chopped |
| 2 | green onions, finely chopped (2 tablespoons) |
| 1 | can (4 ounces) chopped green chili peppers |
| 1 | pickled jalapeño pepper, cored, seeded and chopped |
| 1 | tablespoon lemon juice |
| ¼ | teaspoon salt |
| 1 | tablespoon chopped fresh coriander OR: parsley Tomato juice (optional) |

1. Combine the tomatoes, garlic, green onion, green chili peppers, jalapeño pepper, lemon juice, salt and coriander or parsley in the container of an electric blender or a food processor.
2. Cover and process until coarsely chopped. For a thinner dressing, add a little tomato juice, if you wish.

### THE JALAPEÑO HOTLINE

*Avoid touching your face, eyes, nose, mouth or other sensitive areas when you're handling jalapeño peppers. The juice from these peppers will burn and sting, even several hours later.*

### DON'T WAIT UNTIL DARK!

*To prevent an avocado from turning dark after cutting, brush it with lemon juice as soon as it's peeled or, if you're using a recipe that includes lemon or lime juice, mash the avocado with the juice first, then proceed with the recipe.*

## Chicken Salad with Cilantro Dressing

Makes 4 servings.

*Nutrient Value Per Serving: 556 calories, 35 g protein, 27 g fat, 45 g carbohydrate, 325 mg sodium, 70 mg cholesterol.*

**Cilantro Dressing:**

| | |
|---|---|
| 1 | ripe tomato, peeled, seeded and chopped |
| ¼ | cup chopped fresh cilantro (coriander) |
| 2 | tablespoons olive oil |
| 1 | tablespoon lime juice |
| 1 | tablespoon lemon juice |
| 1 | tablespoon chopped pickled jalapeño pepper* |
| ¼ | teaspoon salt |
| ⅛ | teaspoon pepper |
| 2 | cups shredded cooked chicken (about 14 ounces uncooked boneless breasts) |
| 6 | cups shredded lettuce (romaine or iceberg) |
| 1 | ripe avocado (about 14 ounces), halved, pitted, peeled and sliced lengthwise |
| 2 | ounces shredded Monterey Jack cheese (about ½ cup) |
| ⅓ | cup small red onion rings (½ small onion) |
| 8 | warm flour tortillas |

1. Prepare the Cilantro Dressing: Combine the tomato, cilantro, oil, lime juice, lemon juice, jalapeño pepper, salt and pepper in a medium-size bowl.

2. Add the chicken to the dressing and toss to mix well.
3. Arrange the lettuce on a serving platter. Spoon the chicken over the lettuce. Arrange the avocado slices around the chicken. Sprinkle the salad with the Monterey Jack cheese and the red onion rings. Serve the salad with the warm tortillas.

*Note: Pickled or marinated jalapeño peppers can be found in the Mexican food section of many supermarkets.*

## Warm Turkey Salad with Peanuts

Makes 4 servings.

*Nutrient Value Per Serving: 573 calories, 56 g protein, 32 g fat, 16 g carbohydrate, 697 mg sodium, 123 mg cholesterol.*

2  **tablespoons dry sherry**
2  **tablespoons soy sauce**
2  **tablespoons water**
4  **tablespoons corn oil**
1  **tablespoon light brown sugar**
1  **tablespoon creamy-style peanut butter**
1/4  **to 3/4 teaspoon crushed red pepper flakes**
1  **cup shredded carrot**
1  **cup shredded, peeled, seeded cucumber**
2  **tablespoons vinegar, preferably rice wine vinegar**
1 3/4  **pounds turkey cutlets, cut crosswise into strips**
1/2  **cup thinly sliced celery**
2  **green onions, sliced**
2  **cloves garlic, finely chopped**
3/4  **cup dry-roasted unsalted peanut halves**
8  **to 12 lettuce leaves**

1. Stir together the sherry, soy sauce, water, 1 tablespoon of the oil, the brown sugar, peanut butter and red pepper

flakes in a small bowl. Blend the mixture well and set aside.
2. In a separate bowl, toss together the carrot, cucumber and vinegar. Cover the bowl and refrigerate until serving time.
3. Heat the remaining 3 tablespoons of oil in a wok or large skillet over medium-high heat. Add the turkey strips, celery, green onion and garlic, half at a time, to the wok and stir-fry for about 3 minutes, or until the turkey is cooked through. Remove the turkey mixture from the wok. Add the peanuts and stir-fry for 1 minute. Add the soy sauce mixture to the wok along with the turkey mixture. Stir-fry for 1 minute, or until the mixture is heated through. Remove the wok from the heat.
4. Arrange the lettuce leaves on 4 individual plates. Top with the carrot-cucumber mixture, dividing equally. Spoon the turkey mixture over each salad. Serve immediately.

## Roast Beef Summer Salad

Makes 4 servings.

*Nutrient Value Per Serving: 497 calories, 30 g protein, 26 g fat, 39 g carbohydrate, 350 mg sodium, 69 mg cholesterol.*

1 1/4  **pounds all-purpose potatoes**
1  **tablespoon red wine vinegar**
2  **medium-size ears corn OR: 1 1/2 cups cooked corn kernels**

**Mustard Dressing:**
1/3  **cup vegetable oil**
3  **tablespoons red wine vinegar**
1  **tablespoon Dijon-style mustard**
1  **clove garlic, crushed**
1/4  **teaspoon salt**
1/4  **teaspoon pepper**
1  **cup sliced green onions**

6  **cups spinach leaves (about 5 ounces), washed**
3/4  **pound thinly sliced roast beef (leftover or deli)**
1/3  **cup sliced red radish (about 4 or 5), for garnish**

1. Cover the potatoes with cold water in a pan big enough to hold them in one layer. Bring to boiling and cook until tender, for about 20 minutes. Remove from the water and cool for 30 minutes. Peel and cut into ½-inch pieces. Place in a medium-size bowl and sprinkle the 1 tablespoon of vinegar over the potatoes while still warm. Cover and refrigerate until well chilled.
2. Bring 2 quarts of water to boiling in a Dutch oven. Add the ears of corn and boil for 2 to 4 minutes until tender. Remove from the water. Set aside until cool. Scrape the kernels off with a sharp knife and set aside.
3. Prepare the Mustard Dressing: Combine the oil, vinegar, mustard, garlic, salt and pepper in a small bowl; mix all the ingredients well. Stir in the green onion and the corn. Reserve ½ cup of the dressing for the beef. Toss the remaining dressing with the potatoes.
4. Arrange the spinach leaves on a serving platter. Fan the sliced roast beef down the middle of the plate. Arrange the potato salad around the beef. Spoon the reserved dressing over the beef slices. Garnish with the radish.

***Mustard Dressing Serving Suggestions:***
Use it to dress potato, chicken or green salads for extra zip. Mix it with cold cooked vegetables, such as broccoli, carrots or cauliflower.

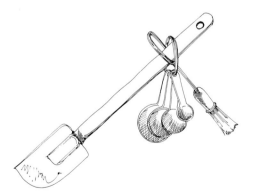

## Cheese and Broccoli Salad with Basil Dressing

Makes 4 servings.

*Nutrient Value Per Serving: 496 calories, 20 g protein, 43 g fat, 10 g carbohydrate, 464 mg sodium, 60 mg cholesterol.*

***Basil Dressing:***
- ¼ **cup olive oil**
- ¼ **cup chopped fresh basil**
- 2 **tablespoons red wine vinegar**
- 1 **clove garlic, crushed**
- ⅛ **teaspoon pepper**

- 8 **ounces mild Cheddar cheese, cut into 1 x ¼-inch sticks**
- 2 **cups broccoli flowerets (4 ounces), blanched**
- ½ **cup slivered toasted almonds**
- ⅓ **cup chopped ripe olives in brine\* (12 large black olives)**
- 8 **leaves romaine lettuce**
- 1 **bunch arugula OR: watercress, trimmed of large stems**
- 2 **roasted sweet red peppers, cut into strips\*\* OR: 1 jar (7 ounces) pimiento, drained and cut into strips, for garnish**

1. Prepare the Basil Dressing: Whisk together the oil, basil, vinegar, garlic and pepper in a large bowl until all the ingredients are well mixed.
2. Add the Cheddar cheese, broccoli, almonds and olives to the dressing and toss to coat all the ingredients well.
3. For each serving, arrange 2 romaine leaves and some of the watercress or arugula on a plate. Spoon one quarter of the cheese salad over the lettuce. Garnish with the roasted red pepper strips.

*Notes:* *For the best flavor, use black Italian or Greek olives packed in brine. \*\*To roast sweet peppers, rub the outside skin with vegetable oil. Roast the peppers in a pan in a preheated hot oven (450°), turning once, for about 30 minutes, or until the skin is blackened all over. Cool the peppers in the pan. Gently peel the blackened skin off the peppers with your fingers. Remove the stems and seeds.*

*Basil Dressing Serving Suggestions:* Use it to dress salad greens or tomatoes when fresh basil is plentiful.

◄◄◄ ☖

# Lobster Salad with Chive Dressing

Makes 4 servings.

*Nutrient Value Per Serving: 362 calories, 19 g protein, 27 g fat, 15 g carbohydrate, 418 mg sodium, 60 mg cholesterol.*

2  **live lobsters (about 1½ pounds each) OR: 12 ounces imitation lobster, thawed if frozen**

**Chive Dressing:**
3  **tablespoons mayonnaise**
2  **tablespoons plain yogurt**
4  **tablespoons chopped chives**
4  **teaspoons fresh lemon juice**
   **Pinch white pepper**

⅓  **cup finely chopped celery**
¼  **cup chopped sweet green pepper**
2  **medium-size ripe avocados\***
1  **pint cherry tomatoes, halved**
2  **tablespoons chopped parsley**
2  **teaspoons red wine vinegar**
2  **teaspoons vegetable oil**
⅛  **teaspoon pepper**
   **Pinch salt**
8  **leaves of leaf lettuce**
1  **small bunch flat-leaf Italian parsley, trimmed, for garnish (optional)**
   **Lemon twists, for garnish (optional)**

1. If using imitation lobster meat, proceed to Step 3 below. If using live lobsters, pour water into a large pot to a depth of 2 to 4 inches and bring to a boil. Add the lobsters and cook, covered, for 12 minutes. Remove the lobsters from the pot with tongs and cool for 30 minutes at room temperature. Refrigerate until well chilled, for 2 to 4 hours.
2. Pull off the claws at the joint to the main body. Leave the small legs attached. Cut the lobsters in half lengthwise with a sharp knife or poultry shears. Remove the meat from the tail and the lower body. Discard the sac with the stomach and the intestine. Remove the tomalley and the coral, if any, and reserve the coral, if you wish. Rinse the shell halves with cold water and drain on paper toweling. Crack the claws and the claw joints with a nutcracker or the back of a heavy knife or meat mallet. Remove the meat. Cut the lobster meat into ½-inch pieces; add the coral, if you wish.
3. Prepare the Chive Dressing: Combine the mayonnaise, yogurt, chives, lemon juice and white pepper in a medium-size bowl. Add the lobster meat, celery and green pepper to the dressing and toss to mix all the ingredients well.
4. Spoon the lobster salad back into the shells or, if using imitation lobster meat, into 4 avocado halves. (Remove the pits and peels; rub the cut surfaces with lemon juice to prevent discoloration.)
5. Toss the cherry tomatoes with the chopped parsley, vinegar, oil, pepper and salt in a medium-size bowl.
6. For each serving, place 2 lettuce leaves on a plate. Place half a lobster shell, or half an avocado, filled with the salad on the leaves. Spoon the cherry tomatoes on the side. Garnish with the flat-leaf parsley, and a lemon twist, if you wish.

*\*Note: Use the avocado only if using imitation lobster meat instead of live lobsters.*

# Dilled Salmon Pasta Salad

*Cook the fresh salmon ahead of time, or use canned salmon. Then assemble and dress the salad early in the day.*

Bake fresh salmon at 350° for 12 to 15 minutes.
Makes 4 servings.

*Nutrient Value Per Serving: 503 calories, 27 g protein, 21 g fat, 50 g carbohydrate, 353 mg sodium, 64 mg cholesterol.*

¾  **pound fresh salmon fillet OR: 1 pound canned salmon (pink or red)**
1  **teaspoon lime juice***
⅛  **teaspoon salt***

**Cucumber Dressing:**
2  **medium-size cucumbers, peeled and seeded**
⅓  **cup dairy sour cream**
⅓  **cup plain yogurt**
¼  **cup mayonnaise**
2  **tablespoons chopped fresh dill OR: 1 teaspoon dillweed, crumbled**
1  **tablespoon finely chopped shallots OR: finely chopped green onion, white part only**
1  **tablespoon distilled white vinegar**
¼  **teaspoon salt**
⅛  **teaspoon white pepper**

8  **ounces elbow twist pasta**
8  **leaves Boston lettuce**
   **Cucumber slices, for garnish (optional)**
   **Dill sprigs, for garnish (optional)**

1. If using fresh salmon, preheat the oven to moderate (350°). If using canned salmon, proceed to Step 5 below.
2. If using fresh salmon, place the fillet, skin side down, in a small baking pan about 10 x 6¼ inches. Sprinkle the salmon with the lime juice and the ⅛ teaspoon of salt. Cover the salmon with a buttered piece of wax paper, buttered side down.
3. Bake the salmon in the preheated moderate oven (350°) for 12 to 15 minutes, or until the fish flakes easily

when tested with a fork. Cool the salmon in the pan at room temperature for 20 to 30 minutes without removing the buttered wax paper. Refrigerate the salmon, covered, until well chilled, for about 2 hours.

4. Remove the skin and bones, if any, from the salmon. Break the fish into ½-inch pieces and refrigerate.
5. If using canned salmon, drain the salmon and remove all the skin and bones. Break the salmon into ½-inch pieces and set aside in the refrigerator.
6. Prepare the Cucumber Dressing: Grate the cucumbers, place them in a fine sieve and drain for at least 30 minutes at room temperature.
7. Combine the drained cucumber with the sour cream, yogurt, mayonnaise, dill, shallots or green onion, vinegar, salt and white pepper in a small bowl.
8. Cook the pasta following the package directions until *al dente*, firm but tender. Drain the pasta in a colander and rinse briefly under cold running water. Drain the pasta well.
9. Place the pasta in a large bowl and add the dressing. Toss until the pasta is well coated. Gently fold in the salmon.
10. Arrange the lettuce leaves on a serving platter. Spoon the salad over the leaves. Garnish the salad with cucumber slices and dill sprigs, if you wish. Serve the salad immediately.

***Note:** Use the lime juice and the ⅛ teaspoon of salt only if using fresh salmon instead of canned salmon.*

**Cucumber Dressing Serving Suggestions:**
Mix it with cooked pasta, ham or any fish, including canned tuna.

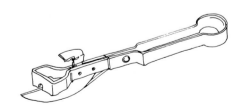

# Pasta

## Spinach Fettuccine Primavera

Makes 4 to 6 servings.

*Nutrient Value Per Serving: 800 calories, 35 g protein, 48 g fat, 60 g carbohydrate, 1,358 mg sodium, 229 mg cholesterol.*

- 1 **medium-size onion, finely chopped**
- 3 **tablespoons butter**
- 2 **cups thinly sliced mushrooms (about 8 ounces)**
- 1½ **cups heavy cream**
- 2 **cups 3 x ¼-inch strips cooked ham (about ⅔ pound)**
- 1 **package (10 ounces) frozen peas and carrots, thawed and drained**
- 1 **box (12 ounces) spinach fettuccine**
- 1 **cup grated Parmesan cheese**
- ½ **teaspoon black pepper**

1. Bring a large pot of water to boiling for the fettuccine.
2. Meanwhile, sauté the onion in the butter in a large skillet until the onion is softened but not browned, for about 5 minutes. Add the mushrooms and brown slightly, for about 4 minutes. Stir in the cream and simmer for 2 minutes.
3. Add the ham and the peas and carrots. Cook the mixture until heated through, stirring, for about 3 minutes.
4. Meanwhile, add the fettuccine to the boiling water and cook until *al dente*, firm but tender. Drain the fettuccine in a colander. Place the pasta in a large serving bowl.
5. Stir the Parmesan cheese into the sauce in the skillet. Add the sauce to the fettuccine along with the black pepper. Toss the pasta mixture gently to mix thoroughly. Serve immediately.

## Pasta with Sweet Pepper Sauce

Makes 6 servings.

*Nutrient Value Per Serving: 422 calories, 12 g protein, 11 g fat, 69 g carbohydrate, 399 mg sodium, 0 mg cholesterol.*

- ¼ **cup good-quality olive oil**
- 2 **medium-size onions, halved and thinly sliced**
- 3 **pounds sweet red peppers, halved, cored, seeded and cut into ½-inch-thick strips**
- 1 **clove garlic, finely chopped**
- 2 **tablespoons chopped fresh mint OR: 1 teaspoon dried mint**
- ½ **teaspoon salt**
- ¼ **teaspoon pepper**
- 1 **to 1½ cups chicken broth**
- 1 **pound bow tie pasta, penne or ziti**
- 2 **tablespoons chopped parsley, for garnish Parmesan cheese (optional)**

1. Heat the oil in a large skillet or Dutch oven over high heat. Add the onion, red peppers and garlic and cook, stirring often, until the edges of the onion begin to brown, for about 15 minutes. Lower the heat to medium. Add the mint, salt and pepper to the skillet. Cook until the red peppers are tender, for about 15 minutes. Add 1 cup of the broth to the skillet. Cover the skillet and cook for 5 minutes more.
2. Remove 12 slices of the cooked red peppers and reserve. Place the remaining pepper mixture in the container of a food processor or, working in batches, of an electric blender. Cover and whirl until the mixture is the consistency of a thick tomato sauce. If the sauce is too thick,

add some of the remaining ½ cup of broth.

3. While the sauce is cooking, cook the pasta in a large pot of boiling salted water until *al dente*, firm but tender. Drain the pasta in a colander. Add the pasta to the sauce in the skillet. Toss to mix well. Serve the pasta garnished with the reserved slices of red pepper and the parsley. Serve with Parmesan cheese, if you wish.

# Saucy Stuffed Shells

Bake at 375° for 45 minutes.
Makes 4 servings.

*Nutrient Value Per Serving: 522 calories, 25 g protein, 20 g fat, 62 g carbohydrate, 1,402 mg sodium, 64 mg cholesterol.*

 1   *teaspoon leaf oregano, crumbled*
 1   *jar (15½ ounces) plain spaghetti sauce*
 2   *packages (12½ ounces each) frozen cheese-stuffed large macaroni shells*
 2   *teaspoons olive oil*
 2   *teaspoons grated Parmesan cheese*

1. Preheat the oven to moderate (375°).
2. Gently stir the oregano into the jar of spaghetti sauce. Spoon 1 cup of the sauce over the bottom of a 13 x 9 x 2-inch baking pan.
3. Place the stuffed shells, stuffed side up, on the sauce. Brush the shells with the oil. Spoon the remaining sauce over the shells. Cover the baking pan with aluminum foil.
4. Bake in the preheated moderate oven (375°) for 40 minutes, or until the sauce is bubbly and the shells are heated through.
5. Remove the foil from the pan. Sprinkle the shells with the Parmesan cheese. Return to the oven and bake until the cheese is golden, for about 5 minutes.

# Ziti with Plum Tomatoes

Makes 6 servings.

*Nutrient Value Per Serving: 393 calories, 11 g protein, 10 g fat, 65 g carbohydrate, 104 mg sodium, 0 mg cholesterol.*

10   *ripe plum tomatoes (2 pounds)*
 ¼   *cup good-quality olive oil*
 1   *small onion, chopped*
 1   *clove garlic, finely chopped*
 ¼   *cup coarsely chopped fresh basil*
 ¼   *teaspoon leaf oregano, crumbled*
 ¼   *teaspoon salt*
 ⅛   *teaspoon pepper*
 1   *pound ziti*
     *Whole fresh basil leaves, for garnish (optional)*

1. Blanch the tomatoes in a large pot of boiling water for 10 seconds. Drain the tomatoes in a colander and run under cold water. Peel the tomatoes, cut them in half lengthwise and remove the seeds. Slice each tomato into wedges lengthwise and set aside. (If ripe tomatoes are not available, use 4 cups of sliced canned tomatoes.)
2. Heat the oil in a large skillet or Dutch oven over medium heat. Add the onion and the garlic. Cook, stirring. When the garlic begins to color, after about 1 minute, add the tomatoes, basil, oregano, salt and pepper. Cover the skillet, lower the heat and simmer until the tomatoes are tender but not falling apart, for about 8 minutes.
3. While the sauce is cooking, cook the ziti in a large pot of boiling water until *al dente*, firm but tender. Drain the ziti in a colander.
4. Add the ziti to the tomato sauce in the skillet and cook over high heat for 1 minute, stirring constantly. Garnish each portion with several whole fresh basil leaves, if you wish. Serve immediately.

# Pasta Pesto Salad

Makes 6 servings.

*Nutrient Value Per Serving: 804 calories, 23 g protein, 58 g fat, 55 g carbohydrate, 401 mg sodium, 23 mg cholesterol.*

¾ **pound rigatoni pasta**
⅓ **cup olive oil**
3 **ripe plum tomatoes, cut into sixths lengthwise**
¼ **pound imported Provolone cheese, cut into small pieces**
1½ **cups Pasta Pesto Dressing (recipe follows)**
½ **cup fresh basil leaves**

1. Cook the rigatoni in a large pot of boiling water for 7 minutes, or until *al dente,* firm but tender. Drain the pasta and rinse immediately with cold water. Drain the rigatoni well. Toss with the oil in a large bowl.
2. Add the tomato pieces and the Provolone cheese. Drizzle the Pasta Pesto Dressing over the salad. Toss very gently with two spoons to coat all the ingredients evenly. Cover the salad and refrigerate for at least 1 hour, to blend the flavors.
3. Bring the salad to room temperature to serve. Sprinkle with the basil leaves.

*Pasta Pesto Dressing:* Combine 5 cups of chopped fresh basil, 1 cup of pine nuts (pignoli), 1 cup of olive oil and 3 cloves of garlic in the container of an electric blender or a food processor fitted with a metal blade. Cover and process at high speed until the mixture is smooth. Turn off the motor and add 1 cup of freshly grated Parmesan cheese. Cover and process until blended. Taste and season with salt and pepper. To freeze, prepare the pesto omitting the Parmesan cheese. Freeze in an ice cube tray. Thaw as needed, then add the cheese. *Makes about 2 cups.*

*Nutrient Value Per Tablespoon: 104 calories, 3 g protein, 10 g fat, 2 g carbohydrate, 58 mg sodium, 2 mg cholesterol.*

# Rotelle with Tuna Sauce

Makes 6 servings.

*Nutrient Value Per Serving: 437 calories, 19 g protein, 13 g fat, 61 g carbohydrate, 337 mg sodium, 5 mg cholesterol.*

1 **medium-size onion, finely chopped (½ cup)**
¼ **cup good-quality olive oil**
1 **clove garlic, finely chopped**
2 **cups coarsely chopped fresh tomatoes OR: canned tomatoes if ripe are unavailable**
2 **tablespoons chopped parsley**
¼ **teaspoon salt**
⅛ **teaspoon pepper**
1 **can (6½ ounces) Italian-style tuna fish, packed in olive oil, undrained**
¾ **to 1 cup chicken broth**
1 **pound rotelle**

1. Cook the onion in the oil in a medium-size skillet over medium heat until the onion is very soft, for about 6 minutes. Add the garlic and cook for about 2 minutes more.
2. Add the tomatoes, parsley, salt and pepper. Cover the skillet, lower the heat and simmer for 10 minutes. Transfer the mixture to the container of an electric blender or a food processor. Cover and whirl until the mixture is puréed. Add the tuna with its oil to the blender and purée until smooth. Add enough of the broth to make the sauce the consistency of heavy cream.
3. While the sauce is cooking, cook the rotelle in a large pot of boiling water until *al dente,* firm but tender. Drain the rotelle in a colander. Toss the rotelle with the sauce in a large serving bowl. Serve immediately.

# Beans & Peas

## Slow-Cooked Beans with Lamb

*Whether you remove the bones from the lamb before serving is up to you.*

Makes 8 servings (about 9 cups).

*Nutrient Value Per Serving: 664 calories, 34 g protein, 30 g fat, 66 g carbohydrate, 877 mg sodium, 84 mg cholesterol.*

| | |
|---|---|
| 1 | **pound dried kidney beans, soaked** |
| 1 | **quart cold water** |
| 6 | **slices bacon (about 4 ounces), diced** |
| 2 | **pounds lamb neck pieces** |
| 3 | **cups chopped yellow onions (3 large onions)** |
| 3 | **large cloves garlic, finely chopped** |
| 1 | **can (1 pound) whole-berry cranberry sauce** |
| 2 | **to 2½ cups dry red wine** |
| 1 | **can (6 ounces) tomato paste** |
| 1 | **teaspoon ground ginger** |
| 1 | **teaspoon leaf oregano, crumbled** |
| 2 | **teaspoons salt** |
| ½ | **teaspoon pepper** |

1. Drain the kidney beans, place them in a large saucepan and add the water. Bring to boiling over medium heat. Lower the heat, cover and simmer for 1 hour, or until almost tender.
2. Meanwhile, sauté the bacon in a very large, heavy skillet over medium heat until crisp. Remove with a slotted spoon to paper toweling to drain.
3. Brown the lamb on all sides in the bacon drippings in the skillet. Remove the lamb with a slotted spoon. Pour off all but 2 tablespoons of the drippings from the skillet.
4. Sauté the onion and the garlic in the drippings until softened, for about 5 minutes.
5. Drain the kidney beans, reserving 1 cup of their cooking liquid. Return the kidney beans and the reserved liquid to the saucepan. Add the cranberry sauce, 2 cups of the wine, the tomato paste, ginger, oregano, salt, pepper and the onion mixture. Bring to boiling. Add the lamb and the bacon. Lower the heat, cover and simmer for about 2½ hours, stirring occasionally, or until the beans are tender. Uncover and simmer for 20 to 30 minutes more, or until the kidney beans and the lamb are tender and the sauce thickens; add the remaining ½ cup of wine if the mixture gets too dry.
6. Serve with egg noodles, if you wish.

# Black Bean Chili

*. . . Or pinto beans or red beans, but black beans are most dramatic. This chili is mildly hot. For those who like it fiery, pass extra salsa jalapeño.*

Warm chips at 300° for 3 to 5 minutes.
Makes 4 servings.

*Nutrient Value Per Serving: 535 calories, 27 g protein, 16 g fat, 75 g carbohydrate, 663 mg sodium, 28 mg cholesterol.*

- **2 cans (16 ounces each) black beans, undrained**
- **1 can (8 ounces) tomato sauce**
- **1 cup frozen chopped sweet green pepper**
- **1 medium-size onion, chopped (½ cup)**
- **1 clove garlic, finely chopped**
- **2 tablespoons bottled salsa jalapeño OR: ¼ cup salsa picante**
- **1 tablespoon chili powder**
- **½ teaspoon ground cumin**
- **1 cup crushed tortilla chips (2 ounces)**
- **½ cup dairy sour cream, for garnish**
- **½ cup shredded Cheddar cheese, for garnish**
- **2 cups shredded iceberg lettuce (about ½ head), for garnish**
  **Additional salsa, for garnish**

1. Combine the black beans with their liquid, the tomato sauce, green pepper, onion, garlic, salsa, chili powder and cumin in a 2-quart saucepan. Bring to a boil. Lower the heat to medium and cook for 15 minutes, or until the flavors are well blended.
2. Preheat the oven to slow (300°).
3. Place the tortilla chips on a baking sheet and warm the chips in the preheated slow oven (300°) for 3 to 5 minutes, or until the chips are crisped and fragrant.
4. To serve, divide the chips evenly among 4 bowls. Spoon the chili over the chips. Garnish the chili with the sour cream, Cheddar cheese, lettuce and additional salsa, if you wish.

*(From top) chick peas, kidney beans, lima beans, pinto beans, black beans, lentils, pea (navy) beans, pink beans*

## *Peppery Bean Soup*

*Without the addition of the final cup of water, these beans also are wonderful served over steamed rice.*

Makes 6 generous servings
(about 2½ quarts).

*Nutrient Value Per Serving: 386 calories, 18 g protein, 10 g fat, 58 g carbohydrate, 741 mg sodium, 0 mg cholesterol.*

| | |
|---|---|
| 1 | *pound dried black beans, soaked* |
| 2 | *quarts water* |
| 1 | *medium-size onion, coarsely chopped* |
| 2 | *large cloves garlic, smashed but left whole* |
| 3 | *cups chopped onion (3 large onions)* |
| 4 | *large cloves garlic, finely chopped* |
| 1 | *sweet green pepper, halved, cored, seeded and chopped* |
| ¼ | *cup olive or vegetable oil* |
| 2 | *teaspoons salt* |
| ¾ | *teaspoon pepper* |
| ½ | *teaspoon leaf oregano, crumbled* |
| 2 | *sweet red peppers* |
| 2 | *to 3 tablespoons red wine vinegar* |
| 1 | *cup water* |
| | *Dairy sour cream OR: plain yogurt (optional)* |

1. Drain the black beans and place them in a large saucepan. Add the 2 quarts of water, the coarsely chopped onion and smashed garlic cloves. Bring to boiling over medium heat. Lower the heat, cover and simmer for 1½ hours, or until almost tender.
2. Meanwhile, sauté the chopped onion, chopped garlic and green pepper in the oil in a large skillet, stirring often, until the mixture is soft, for about 10 minutes.
3. Stir the green pepper mixture into the black beans with the salt, pepper and oregano. Cover and simmer for 1 hour more, or until the beans are very tender.
4. Char the red peppers on all sides over a gas flame or under the broiler. Place them in a paper bag for 5 minutes to loosen the skin. Peel and seed the red peppers. Reserve about half a red pepper for garnish; coarsely chop the remainder.
5. Add the chopped red peppers to the black beans with the 2 to 3 tablespoons of vinegar, and if necessary, up to 1 cup additional water to make a good soup consistency. Simmer for 15 minutes more. Taste and adjust the seasonings, if necessary.
6. Garnish the soup with the reserved red pepper, and serve with dollops of sour cream or yogurt, if you wish.

---

## *Food for Thought . . .*

***Black Beans** Also called turtle beans, these small, oval beans have a purplish-black skin and a creamy white interior. Traditionally, they are served with rice, but also are delicious in soup. They are widely used in the southeastern United States, South America, the Caribbean Islands and Puerto Rico.*

# THE BEAN BAG

Cooking beans from scratch is relatively easy, but it helps to have some bean-smarts.

### Shopping
Look for beans that are bright in color (this indicates freshness) and uniform in size and shape (they'll cook more evenly). Avoid beans with cracks or pinhole marks. Store them in a cool, dry place.

### Soaking
To prepare beans for cooking, rinse them well and sort through them to remove misshapen or discolored beans and any foreign matter, such as pebbles or twigs. Except for split peas and lentils, all dried beans need to be soaked before cooking. There are two basic methods:
• If you want beans to retain their shape, place them in at least twice their volume of cold water in a large bowl, cover the bowl and let the beans soak overnight. This method allows the beans to swell slowly, which is preferable for black-eyed pea and chick pea side dishes.
• If you're making a dish (a soup, or baked or refried beans) in which the consistency of the beans doesn't matter, use the quick-soak method: Add enough water to the beans in a saucepan to cover by 2 inches. Bring to boiling over medium heat and simmer for 2 minutes. Turn off the heat and let the beans stand, covered, for 1 to 2 hours. This method is harder on the beans causing them to break up and lose their shape.

### Cooking
• Generally speaking, beans should be cooked before being combined with other ingredients. To prepare beans for cooking, drain the soaking water (this eliminates some of the gas-forming ingredients), refill the saucepan with fresh water and simmer gently until the beans are tender.
• Salt should not be added to the beans until at least halfway through the cooking time because it tends to toughen the skins making tenderizing difficult. As the beans simmer, remove any residue that floats to the top of the water. Be prepared to add water, as necessary, so the beans always are covered. This is particularly true for long-simmering beans.
• Most beans are cooked fully when the skin cracks as you blow on one. But the best way to determine doneness is the taste test: Bite into one. As with pasta, the bean should be *al dente*, tender but still firm enough to retain its shape. (When making soups or purées, however, a firm texture is unnecessary.)

### Serving
Beans are adaptable. Once cooked, beans will keep for a week in the refrigerator and 4 to 6 months in the freezer, so you can make a large batch to last several meals. Reheat the beans gently to retain their shape.

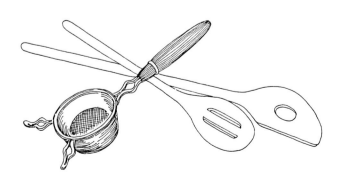

# Pink Bean Picadillo

*Usually made with ground beef, this version of the classic Mexican dish combines pink beans with raisins, olives and capers in a piquant tomato sauce. Wear rubber gloves when chopping the jalapeño pepper.*

Makes 8 servings (about 9 cups).

*Nutrient Value Per Serving: 334 calories, 14 g protein, 9 g fat, 52 g carbohydrate, 761 mg sodium, 0 mg cholesterol.*

- 1 **pound small dried pink beans, soaked**
- 7 **cloves garlic, peeled**
- 1 **medium-size carrot**
- 5 **cups chopped onion (5 large onions)**
- 1 **quart water**
- 1 **large sweet green pepper, halved, seeded and chopped**
- 1 **jalapeño pepper, halved, seeded and finely chopped**
- 1/4 **cup olive oil**
- 1 **tablespoon ground cumin**
- 1/2 **teaspoon leaf thyme, crumbled**
- 1/4 **teaspoon ground hot red pepper**
- 1 **teaspoon salt**
- 1 **can (8 ounces) stewed tomatoes**
- 1/2 **cup stuffed green olives, sliced**
- 1/3 **cup cider vinegar**
- 1 **jar (3½ ounces) capers, drained**
- 1/4 **cup raisins**

1. Drain the pink beans and place them in a large saucepan. Slice 4 of the garlic cloves. Halve the carrot lengthwise and slice crosswise. Add the sliced garlic and carrot, 2 cups of the onion and the water to the pink beans. Bring to boiling over medium heat. Lower the heat, cover and simmer for 1 hour.
2. Meanwhile, finely chop the remaining 3 garlic cloves. Sauté the remaining 3 cups of onion, the chopped garlic, green pepper and jalapeño pepper in the oil in a large skillet, stirring often, until the onion is wilted and golden.
3. Add the pepper mixture to the pink beans with the cumin, thyme, ground hot red pepper, salt and tomatoes. Cover and simmer for 30 minutes.
4. Add the olives, vinegar, capers and raisins. Simmer, uncovered, for 30 minutes more, until the pink beans are tender and the mixture thickens. Serve the picadillo over cooked rice, if you wish.

# Pinto Bean and Sausage Bake

*Use hot sausage and hot chili powder for a dish that's extra-spicy.*

Bake at 350° for 30 minutes.
Makes 10 servings.

*Nutrient Value Per Serving: 503 calories, 25 g protein, 24 g fat, 50 g carbohydrate, 773 mg sodium, 47 mg cholesterol.*

- 1 **pound dried pinto beans, soaked Cold water**
- 1 **pound sweet or hot Italian sausage, casings removed**
- 4 **cups chopped onion (4 large onions)**
- 3 **large cloves garlic, finely chopped**
- 2 **tablespoons chili powder**
- 2½ **cups canned crushed tomatoes**
- 1 **teaspoon salt**
- 1 **package (7½ ounces) unsalted tortilla chips, crushed**
- 8 **ounces Monterey Jack cheese, shredded (2 cups)**

1. Drain the pinto beans, place them in a large saucepan and add the cold water to cover by 2 inches. Bring to boiling over medium heat. Lower the heat, cover and simmer for 1 hour, or until almost tender. Drain the pinto beans, reserving 1 cup of the cooking liquid. Return the pinto beans to the saucepan.
2. Meanwhile, brown the sausage in a large nonstick skillet, breaking it up with a wooden spoon into small pieces. Remove the sausage with a slotted spoon to paper toweling to drain. Pour off all but 1 tablespoon of the drippings.
3. Add the onion to the skillet. Sauté over medium heat until softened, for about 10 minutes. Add the garlic and the chili powder; sauté for 1 minute more.
4. Stir the sausage, onion mixture, tomatoes, salt and reserved cooking liquid into the pinto beans. Cover and simmer for 1 hour, or until the pinto beans are tender and the mixture is slightly thickened.
5. Preheat the oven to moderate (350°).
6. Divide one third of the crushed tortilla chips between two 9 x 5 x 3-inch loaf pans. Divide half the pinto bean mixture between the pans to cover the chips. Top with the second third of the chips and half the Monterey Jack cheese. Cover with the remaining pinto bean mixture, chips and cheese.
7. Bake in the preheated moderate oven (350°) for 30 minutes, or until hot. Let stand for 5 minutes in the pans. Unmold onto a serving platter. If some crust sticks to the pans, remove with a spoon and place on top of the loaves. Cut into slices to serve.

**Note:** *This recipe can be assembled ahead of time and refrigerated or frozen before baking. To serve, cover the pans with aluminum foil. Bake the loaves, thawed if frozen, in a preheated moderate oven (350°) for 45 to 60 minutes, or until hot. Remove the foil during the last 15 minutes of baking time.*

## Curried Apple and Lima Bean Soup

Makes 6 servings (about 8 cups).

*Nutrient Value Per Serving: 232 calories, 10 g protein, 6 g fat, 37 g carbohydrate, 665 mg sodium, 0 mg cholesterol.*

8   ounces dried lima beans, soaked
1   quart water
1½  cups chopped onion (3 medium-size onions)
1   medium-size tart apple, peeled, cored and chopped
1   large clove garlic, finely chopped
1   tablespoon finely chopped fresh, peeled gingerroot
2   tablespoons vegetable oil
2   to 3 teaspoons curry powder
¼   teaspoon ground cumin
1   teaspoon salt
¼   teaspoon pepper
1   can (13¾ ounces) chicken broth
1   large potato, peeled and diced
1   teaspoon cider vinegar
⅓   cup chopped green onion

1. Drain the lima beans and place them in a large saucepan. Add the water and bring to boiling over medium heat. Lower the heat, cover and simmer for 45 minutes, or until the lima beans are almost tender.
2. Meanwhile, sauté the onion, apple, garlic and ginger in the oil in a large skillet over medium heat, stirring often, until softened, for about 5 minutes. Add the curry powder, cumin, salt and pepper; sauté for 1 minute more.
3. Add the onion mixture, broth and potato to the lima beans. Cover and simmer for 30 minutes more, or until the potato is soft. Let cool slightly.
4. Working in batches, remove the solids with a slotted spoon to the container of an electric blender or a food processor; add a little of the cooking liquid. Cover and whirl until smooth. Return the purée to the saucepan with any remaining cooking liquid. Stir in the vinegar and the green onion. Heat gently to serve.

# Chick Peas and Rice

Makes 4 main-dish or 6 side-dish servings (about 8 cups).

*Nutrient Value Per Main-Dish Serving: 541 calories, 18 g protein, 18 g fat, 78 g carbohydrate, 1,126 mg sodium, 0 mg cholesterol.*

| | |
|---|---|
| 1½ | **cups dried chick peas, soaked** |
| 1 | **quart water** |
| 1 | **large onion, halved and thinly sliced** |
| ¼ | **cup olive oil** |
| 3 | **large cloves garlic, finely chopped** |
| 2 | **teaspoons salt** |
| ¾ | **cup long-grain rice** |
| ⅔ | **cup chopped fresh parsley** |
| ⅔ | **cup chopped fresh cilantro*** |
| ½ | **teaspoon pepper** |

1. Drain the chick peas. Place them in a medium-size saucepan, add the water and bring to boiling over medium heat. Lower the heat, cover and simmer for 2 hours, or until the chick peas are almost tender.
2. Meanwhile, sauté the onion in the oil until golden, for 10 to 15 minutes. Add the garlic and sauté for 1 minute more.
3. Add the onion mixture and the salt to the chick peas. Cover and continue cooking, adding water, if necesary, until the chick peas are tender, for about 30 minutes.
4. Drain the chick peas in a colander, reserving the cooking liquid. Measure the liquid and add water, if necessary, to make 2 cups. Return the liquid and the chick peas to the saucepan. Bring to boiling.
5. Stir the rice into the chick peas and bring to boiling. Lower the heat, cover and simmer for 20 to 25 minutes, or until the rice is tender and most of the cooking liquid is absorbed. Turn off the heat and let stand for 5 minutes.
6. Stir in the parsley, cilantro and pepper.

***Note:** Cilantro, also called Chinese parsley or coriander, is a pungent herb used in Southwestern, Mexican and Middle Eastern cuisines.*

## Food for Thought . . .

**White Rice** *Dubbed "regular" because it is the best known and most popular rice in the United States. The hull, bran and polishings have been removed from the rice, leaving a snow white grain. The size of the grain regulates the price: short-grain and medium-grain rice are less expensive. These are moist and tender when cooked—perfect for casseroles, puddings and croquettes. Long-grain rice, at a few pennies more a pound, cooks fluffier and flakier; it is prefered for serving with vegetables and curries. Most white rice is enriched, but check the label to be sure.*

**Processed White Rice** *The term "parboiled" or "converted" on a package of rice simply means that the grains have been partly cooked before milling, with special care taken to protect the vitamins and minerals in the outer layer. This is a long-grain rice with a light golden color and is prepared in the same way as regular white rice.*

**Precooked White Rice** *This is known as "instant" rice because it needs only a very short cooking time. It is milled from special long-grain rice, is enriched and comes plain or seasoned.*

**Brown Rice** *This is whole-grain rice with only the outer hull removed. The cooking time for brown rice is longer than for regular white rice. Its savory, nutlike flavor makes it a perfect partner for meat and game.*

# White Bean Tuna Salad

Makes 4 servings.

*Nutrient Value Per Serving: 446 calories, 25 g protein, 22 g fat, 38 g carbohydrate, 986 mg sodium, 8 mg cholesterol.*

- 8 ounces small dried white pea beans, soaked
  Cold water
- 1½ teaspoons salt
- 1 jar (2 ounces) sliced pimiento, drained
- 1 small red onion, quartered and thinly sliced
- 1 can (7 ounces) tuna, drained and coarsely flaked
- ¼ to ⅓ cup red wine vinegar
- 2 tablespoons lemon juice (1 lemon)
- ½ teaspoon finely chopped garlic
- ⅓ cup olive oil
- ¼ teaspoon pepper
- 2 tablespoons finely chopped parsley
  Lettuce leaves
  Lemon wedges, for garnish (optional)

1. Drain the white pea beans, place them in a medium-size saucepan and add the cold water to cover by 2 inches. Bring to boiling over medium heat. Lower the heat, cover and simmer for 1 hour. Add 1 teaspoon of the salt. Cover and simmer for 30 minutes more, or until the white pea beans are tender but still hold their shape. Drain the white pea beans and place them in a bowl.
2. Gently stir the pimiento, onion and tuna into the white pea beans.
3. Combine ¼ cup of the vinegar, the lemon juice, garlic, oil, pepper and the remaining ½ teaspoon of salt in a small bowl. Stir in the parsley. Pour the dressing over the white pea bean mixture and toss gently to mix. Taste and add the remaining vinegar, if you wish. Cover and refrigerate for at least 2 hours, or overnight, to blend the flavors.
4. Serve the salad on the lettuce leaves. Garnish with lemon wedges, if you wish.

## SO LONG, SODIUM!

*If you're using canned vegetables or beans, rinse them first to eliminate some of the sodium. You can add a little water for cooking, if necessary.*

# Cheese

## Cheese-Topped Macaroni

Bake at 350° for 40 minutes.
Makes 16 servings (2 casseroles).

*Nutrient Value Per Serving: 223 calories, 11 g protein, 10 g fat, 23 g carbohydrate, 186 mg sodium, 30 mg cholesterol.*

1   **package (16 ounces) elbow macaroni**
1   **large white onion, coarsely chopped (1 cup)**
1   **pound Cheddar cheese, coarsely shredded (4 cups)**
    **Salt and pepper, to taste**

1. Preheat the oven to moderate (350°).
2. Cook the macaroni in a large pot of boiling water just until almost tender. Drain the macaroni in a colander.
3. Divide the macaroni between two 13 x 9 x 2-inch baking dishes.
4. Sprinkle the onion and Cheddar cheese over the macaroni. Season with the salt and pepper.
5. Bake in the preheated moderate oven (350°) for about 40 minutes, or until the Cheddar cheese is completely melted and the top is slightly crusty. Let stand for 15 minutes before serving.

**Note:** *This dish may be prepared through Step 3, covered and refrigerated for up to 24 hours.*

### Food for Thought . . .

**Macaroni** *The word macaroni comes from the phrase "ma caroni," meaning "the little dears." According to legend, the phrase was coined by an Italian clergyman when he was first presented with the tubular-shaped pasta.*

## Bacon Cheese Strata

Bake at 350° for 1 hour.
Makes 4 servings.

*Nutrient Value Per Serving: 477 calories, 25 g protein, 31 g fat, 24 g carbohydrate, 698 mg sodium, 472 mg cholesterol.*

3   **tablespoons butter or margarine, softened**
6   **slices day-old bread**
1   **cup shredded Cheddar cheese (4 ounces)**
4   **slices bacon, crisply fried, drained and crumbled**
6   **eggs, slightly beaten**
1½  **cups skim milk**
1   **teaspoon dry mustard**
⅛   **teaspoon pepper**
    **Watercress, for garnish (optional)**
    **Cherry tomatoes, for garnish (optional)**

1. Butter the slices of bread and cut them into small cubes. Alternate layers of the bread cubes, Cheddar cheese and bacon in a buttered 8-cup casserole dish.
2. Blend the eggs, milk, dry mustard and pepper in a medium-size bowl and pour over the bread-cheese mixture. Cover the casserole dish with plastic wrap.
3. Refrigerate for up to 24 hours. One hour before serving, remove the casserole dish from the refrigerator.
4. Preheat the oven to moderate (350°).
5. Bake in the preheated moderate oven (350°) for 1 hour, or until the casserole is puffed and golden. Garnish with watercress and cherry tomatoes, if you wish.

# Two Crust Pizza Pie

Bake at 375° for 45 to 50 minutes.
Makes 6 servings.

*Nutrient Value Per Serving: 539 calories, 20 g protein, 34 g fat, 34 g carbohydrate, 1,029 mg sodium, 183 mg cholesterol.*

**Pastry dough for two-crust 9-inch pie**
3 **eggs, slightly beaten**
1 **cup pizza or spaghetti sauce, homemade or store-bought**
1 **teaspoon leaf basil, crumbled**
1½ **cups ricotta cheese**
¼ **cup coarsely shredded Provolone**
¼ **cup grated Romano or Parmesan cheese**
2 **ounces prosciutto, thinly sliced and shredded**
2 **ounces mortadella, thinly sliced and shredded**

1. Preheat the oven to moderate (375°).
2. Roll out half the pastry dough to fit into a 9-inch pie plate and fit the pastry into the plate. Roll out the remaining pastry dough to make a top crust and set aside.
3. Reserve 1 tablespoon of the eggs to glaze the pie. Combine the pizza or spaghetti sauce and the basil in a large bowl. Stir in about half the remaining eggs. Place the ricotta cheese in another bowl and stir in the remaining eggs, the Provolone, the Romano or Parmesan cheese, prosciutto and mortadella. Pour the sauce mixture over the ricotta and marbelize with a few strokes of a rubber spatula.
4. Spoon the filling into the pastry-lined pie plate, spreading into an even layer. Cover the pie with the top crust. Brush the edges of the bottom crust with a little water to seal the edges together. Flute the pastry edges or press them together with the tines of a fork. Brush the top with the reserved 1 tablespoon of egg.
5. Bake the pie in the preheated moderate oven (375°) for 45 to 50 minutes, or until the top crust is puffed and browned.

## Food for Thought . . .

**Cheese** *Cheese is divided into two categories: natural cheese, and cheese blends, in which natural cheeses are used to make new products.*

*Natural cheeses can be subdivided by texture or consistency, and by degree or method of ripening. The amount of whey drained from the curd determines the consistency.*
• *Very hard—Parmesan, Romano*
• *Hard—Cheddar, Swiss*
• *Semi-soft to hard—Colby, Gouda*
• *Semi-soft—Blue, Brick, Muenster, Roquefort*
• *Soft—Brie, Camembert, cottage cheese, cream cheese, Limburger, Neufchâtel, ricotta.*

*Cheese blends can be subdivided into three products:*
• *Pasteurized process cheese—a blend of shredded fresh and aged natural cheeses heated with water and an emulsifier to an homogeneous mixture. It is shaped into loaves and wheels, and can be bought by the piece, sliced or cut up and packaged. Usually inexpensive, it is used in cooking or in sandwiches. American cheese is an example of process cheese.*
• *Pasteurized process cheese food—made the same way as process cheese, but with nonfat dry milk added. The moisture content is higher, so it is softer and spreads more easily; it also melts faster than process cheese. It is packaged as loaves, rolls and links.*
• *Pasteurized process cheese spread—similar to process cheese food but spreads even more easily because it has an even higher moisture content (although the milk fat content is lower). It's packaged in jars, tubes and cans. Some spreads are flavored with pimiento, olives or onions.*

## POPULAR CHEESES

| Kind | Description | Flavor | Uses |
| --- | --- | --- | --- |
| **American** | Process cheese of uniform texture made from domestic Cheddar. Sold as slices and loaves. | Mild. Very popular with children. | A favorite for sandwiches and casseroles. |
| **Bel Paese** | Mellow, semi-soft Italian cheese. | Mildly nutty. | Superb teamed with fresh fruit as dessert. Also good with cocktails. |
| **Blue, Gorgonzola, Roquefort, Stilton** | Medium-soft with blue to blue-green veins; crumbles easily. | Mild to tangy, slightly peppery. | These give a gourmet touch to appetizers, salads, dressings, desserts. |
| **Brie, Camembert** | Rounds and wedges with an edible gray-white crust; soft inside. | Mild to pungent, depending on age. | Favorites for desserts and appetizers. Serve at room temperature. |
| **Cheddar** | Semi-hard, cream to orange color. Sold as wedges, blocks, cubes, slices; also sold shredded. | Mild to very sharp, depending on age; always clearly marked on the package. | America's choice for sandwiches, cooked dishes, salads, snacks, desserts. |
| **Cottage, Ricotta, Cream** | Cottage and ricotta are creamy-white, curd-like, low-calorie. Cream cheese is smooth and calorie-rich. | All are delicately mild, easily spoonable and spreadable. | Perfect for appetizers, sandwiches, cooked dishes, desserts, cake fillings or frostings. |
| **Edam, Gouda** | Creamy orange with red-wax coat. Edam is round, Gouda is flattish. | Mellow, slightly salty, with a nut-like taste. | Excellent for appetizer and dessert trays. Good snack cheeses, too. |

| Kind | Description | Flavor | Uses |
|------|-------------|--------|------|
| *Gruyère* | Smooth, firm, pale, cream-colored cheese; process Gruyère often is sold in foil-wrapped triangles. | Nut-like, faintly caramel. | An all-purpose cheese, excellent for sauces, toppings. Also good in salads, soufflés, omelets. Delicious eaten out-of-hand. |
| *Liederkranz, Limburger* | Soft, bacteria-ripened cheese. | Strong to overpowering; acquired tastes. | Best eaten out-of-hand or on crackers. |
| *Mozzarella* | Soft, white, with a ball-like shape; also sold shredded. | Mild and a bit chewy to eat, especially when heated. | Known as the pizza-lasagna cheese. Use in salads or on appetizer platters. |
| *Muenster, Brick* | Semi-soft, tiny holes, creamy-yellow to white color. | Muenster is mild, Brick is mild to sharp. | Appetizers, sandwiches, salads, desserts. |
| *Parmesan, Romano, Sapsago* | The grating cheeses—very hard. White to light green color. Sold in blocks, as well as grated. | Parmesan is pungent, but milder than Romano. Sapsago has an herb-like flavor. | Topper for casserole dishes and spaghetti. Also popular for sauces and vegetable seasoners. |
| *Port du Salut* | Firm, smooth French cheese, the color of cream. | Fairly sharp. | A good cocktail or dessert cheese. |
| *Provolone* | Light brown outside, light yellow inside. Sometimes lined with rope marks. | Mellow to sharp, smoky and salty. | Try it in macaroni or spaghetti dishes, for sandwiches, snacks or appetizer trays. |
| *Swiss* | Light to creamy-yellow color, large uneven holes. Sold sliced or in cuts. | Mild, with nut-like sweetness. One of our most popular cheeses. | Same as Cheddar, but in cooked dishes it may string somewhat. |

# CHAPTER 5

## Side Shows

*Good-bye, boring vegetables!
These recipes will make a
veggie lover out of anyone.*

*California Home Fries (recipe, page 156)*

"Eat your vegetables!" That admonition, whether spoken by us or by our mothers, seems to stay with us all our lives. We *know* vegetables are good for us, but quite frankly, they can also be the most boring thing on the plate.

Not any more. Vegetables have finally gotten their fair share of innovative recipes. Interesting combinations, such as Red Cabbage Pineapple Slaw *(recipe, page 144)* and Chèvre-Filled Tomatoes *(recipe, page 153)* give veggies new life. There are new twists on old favorites, too, such as Asparagus with Orange Hollandaise *(recipe, page 148)*. As for dynamic duos, rice and vegetables are a natural together: witness Mushroom Rice Pilaf *(recipe, page 159)*.

And don't forget: the potato is a vegetable too! Mashed or baked is wonderful, but also try Potatoes Olé! *(recipe, page 155)* with picante sauce and Monterey Jack cheese, or Potato Apple Pancakes *(recipe, page 159)*. The point we're making: vegetables and side dishes can be fun, flavorful and downright delicious. And you just might make some fussy eaters love their vegetables to boot! ∎

# Vegetables

## Red Cabbage Pineapple Slaw

Makes 6 servings.

*Nutrient Value Per Serving: 313 calories, 4 g protein, 24 g fat, 23 g carbohydrate, 193 mg sodium, 21 mg cholesterol.*

1  small red cabbage (2 pounds),
    coarsely shredded (about
    12 cups)
½  cup grated carrot (1 large, peeled)
½  cup finely chopped onion
    (1 medium-size onion)
¼  cup finely chopped sweet green pepper
¼  cup finely chopped sweet red pepper
1  can (8 ounces) pineapple chunks
    packed in juice, drained and
    ¼ cup juice reserved
¾  cup mayonnaise OR: salad dressing
¼  cup plain lowfat yogurt
¼  cup dairy sour cream
1½ teaspoons tarragon vinegar
¼  teaspoon crushed red pepper flakes
1  slice dried pineapple, slivered
    (about ⅓ cup)
    Sweet green or red pepper rings, for
    garnish (optional)

1. Combine the cabbage, carrot, onion and
   green and red peppers in a large bowl.
2. Chop the pineapple chunks and add to the
   cabbage mixture.
3. Mix together the mayonnaise or salad
   dressing, the yogurt, sour cream, vinegar
   and red pepper flakes in a bowl. Whisk in
   the reserved pineapple juice. Pour over
   the cabbage mixture and mix thoroughly.
   Garnish with the dried pineapple and, if
   you wish, green or red pepper rings.

## Dilled Carrot Coins

Makes 12 servings.

*Nutrient Value Per Serving: 221 calories, 2 g protein, 10 g fat, 34 g carbohydrate, 403 mg sodium, 0 mg cholesterol.*

3  pounds carrots, peeled and cut into
    ½-inch-thick slices
1  large sweet green pepper, halved,
    seeded and cut into ¼-inch-wide
    strips
1  large sweet red pepper, halved, seeded
    and cut into ¼-inch-wide strips
2  large red onions, thinly sliced
    into rings
1  can (10¾ ounces) tomato soup
1  cup sugar
½  cup vegetable oil
½  cup wine vinegar
1  teaspoon Worcestershire sauce
1  teaspoon salt
½  teaspoon pepper
¼  cup snipped fresh dill
    OR: 4 teaspoons dried dillweed

1. Cook the carrots in boiling water to cover
   in a large saucepan until crisp-tender, for
   about 5 minutes. Drain and cool.
2. Combine the carrot, green and red
   peppers and the onion in a large bowl.
   Divide the vegetables between two
   13½ x 8½ x 2-inch glass baking dishes.
3. Stir together the soup, sugar, oil,
   vinegar, Worcestershire sauce, salt and
   pepper in a 4-cup glass measure. Pour
   half the marinade over the vegetables in
   each dish. Stir gently to combine. Cover
   and refrigerate for 24 hours. Just before
   serving, drain the excess marinade, if you
   wish. Stir in the dill.

## Food for Thought . . .

**Carrots** *A produce counter staple, carrots are a thrifty and versatile vegetable. A plant with a pale yellow root probably was the predecessor of today's large, fleshy, orange-rooted plant; it grew some 2,000 years ago in south central Asia and the Near East. Europeans found carrots easy to cultivate and very nourishing. One carrot has only 20 calories and is an excellent source of vitamin A.*

*The cultivation of many varieties of carrots in different regions of the world keeps the supply constant year-round. In most supermarkets, you'll find carrots trimmed of their tops, washed and bagged in 1- or 3-pound sizes. Carrots sold with their tops intact have a shorter shelf life (they must be sold before the tops wilt or die), and so may be fresher than bagged carrots; they're also more expensive.*

## Italian Green Beans

Makes 4 servings.

*Nutrient Value Per Serving: 37 calories, 2 g protein, 1 g fat, 6 g carbohydrate, 3 mg sodium, 0 mg cholesterol.*

| | |
|---|---|
| 1 | **package (10 ounces) frozen Italian green beans** |
| 1 | **teaspoon olive oil** |
| ½ | **teaspoon leaf oregano, crumbled** |

Cook the green beans following the package directions. Drain the green beans in a colander and return them to the saucepan. Add the oil and the oregano. Toss to mix all the ingredients well. Serve immediately.

## Ratatouille Niçoise

**One of the nicest ways to use up summer's abundant vegetable crop.**

Bake at 350° for 30 minutes.
Makes 6 servings.

*Nutrient Value Per Serving: 324 calories, 6 g protein, 24 g fat, 24 g carbohydrate, 538 mg sodium, 3 mg cholesterol.*

| | |
|---|---|
| 1 | **medium-size eggplant, cut into strips (about 1 pound)** |
| 2 | **medium-size zucchini, sliced** |
| 1 | **teaspoon salt** |
| 6 | **tablespoons all-purpose flour** |
| ½ | **to ¾ cup imported Italian olive oil** |
| 1 | **large onion, chopped (1 cup)** |
| 2 | **sweet green peppers, cut into strips** |
| 2 | **large cloves garlic, finely chopped** |
| 4 | **tomatoes, cut into wedges** |
| 1 | **package (10 ounces) frozen artichoke hearts, thawed** |
| ¼ | **cup grated Parmesan cheese** |
| ¼ | **cup chopped fresh parsley** |
| 2 | **tablespoons drained capers** |
| 1 | **tablespoon fresh basil** |

1. Combine the eggplant, zucchini and salt in a large bowl and let stand for 30 minutes. Drain and dry the vegetables on paper toweling. Toss with the flour on a piece of wax paper.
2. Preheat the oven to moderate (350°).
3. Heat 3 tablespoons of the oil in a large skillet over medium heat. Add half the eggplant-zucchini mixture and sauté until golden. Transfer to a medium-size bowl. Repeat with the remaining mixture.
4. Sauté the onion and the green peppers with the garlic in 2 tablespoons of the oil. Add the tomatoes and the artichokes. Cook for several minutes.
5. Layer the zucchini mixture, tomato mixture, Parmesan cheese, parsley, capers and basil in a 1½-quart baking dish.
6. Bake in the preheated moderate oven (350°) for 30 minutes, or until the vegetables are tender. Serve warm, at room temperature or chilled.

# *AVAILABILITY OF FRESH FRUIT AND VEGETABLES*

The following fruits and vegetables usually are available all year, thanks to refrigeration and efficient transportation:

Apples
Artichokes
Avocados
Bananas
Beans, green
Beets
Broccoli
Brussels Sprouts
Cabbage
Carrots
Cauliflower
Celery
Chinese Cabbage
Coconuts
Corn, sweet
Cucumbers
Eggplant
Escarole
Garlic
Grapefruit
Grapes
Greens
Lemons
Lettuce
Limes
Mushrooms
Onions
Onions, green
Oranges
Papayas
Parsley
Parsnips
Pears
Peas, green
Peppers, sweet
Pineapples
Plantains
Potatoes
Radishes
Spinach
Squash
Strawberries
Sweet Potatoes
Tomatoes
Turnips, Rutabagas

The following are widely available in markets during the months indicated:

Apricots—June to August
Asparagus—March to July
Blueberries—June to August
Cantaloupes—April to October
Cherries—May to August
Cranberries—September to December
Honeydews—February to October
Mangoes—March to August
Nectarines—January and February, June to September
Okra—April to November
Peaches—May to September
Persimmons—October to February
Plums and Prunes—June to October
Pomegranates—September to December
Pumpkins—September to December
Tangelos—October to February
Tangerines—November to March
Watermelons—April to September

Fruits and vegetables may be stored in the refrigerator for several days. The longer they are refrigerated, the greater the vitamin loss, so it is best to eat them as soon after purchase as possible.

Asparagus, broccoli, cabbage, cauliflower, celery, cucumbers, green beans, green onions, sweet green and red peppers, radishes and greens (kale, spinach, turnip greens, chard and salad greens) should be refrigerated promptly in a covered container, moisture-proof bag or vegetable crisper.

Apples, apricots, berries, cherries, corn (in husks), grapes, nectarines, peaches, pears, peas (in shell) and plums should be refrigerated loosely covered or in a ventilated plastic produce bag.

# *VARIATIONS ON A THEME: COOKING VEGETABLES*

*Don't overcook!* Vegetables should be cooked only until firm-tender.

• *To Boil:* Use a small amount of water, cover the pan with a tight-fitting lid and cook over low heat to minimize loss of vitamins and minerals. Cook until just tender.

• *To Blanch:* Bring a large pot of water to a rolling boil, immerse the vegetables and bring the water back to a boil for 2 to 4 minutes. Refresh the vegetables in ice cold water and use them in salads.

• *To Steam:* Place a steaming basket, colander or bamboo steamer over 1½ to 2 inches of boiling water and place the vegetables in the steamer. Cover the pan and reduce the heat, but keep the water boiling. Cook until just tender.

• *To Stir-fry:* Place a wok or large skillet over high heat. When it's hot, add oil and cut-up vegetables. Cook uncovered, stirring constantly, just until the vegetables have been lightly coated and slightly cooked (for approximately 1 to 2 minutes). Add approximately ¼ cup of broth to 4 cups of vegetables, cover and cook, stirring occasionally, until just tender. Add more broth, if necessary.

• *To Microwave:* Microwave all vegetables at full power, following the manufacturer's directions. Cover the cooking dish with a lid or microwave-safe plastic wrap. The cooking time depends on the freshness, moisture content and maturity of the vegetables. Remove the vegetables from the microwave after the shortest recommended cooking time and let stand. Then test for doneness. If the vegetables still are too crisp, microwave further in one-minute segments.

• *To Sauté:* Melt butter, margarine or oil in a large skillet; you also can try a combination of butter and corn oil or olive oil and corn oil (butter and olive oil impart flavor, while corn oil allows for cooking over high heat). Add the vegetables and cook, stirring constantly, until the vegetables are coated lightly. Cover the skillet, reduce the heat and cook until just tender.

• *To Bake:* Cut the vegetables into thick slices and arrange them in a single layer in a baking pan or casserole dish, or place them directly on aluminum foil. Dot the vegetables with butter or oil and bake, uncovered, until just tender.

Try tucking in vegetables (onions, squash and any of the root vegetables) with a roast and increase the cooking time accordingly.

• *Testing for Doneness:* Cooking time depends on the freshness or maturity of the vegetables. They should be cooked until just tender, that is, until they give slightly, but remain firm when pierced. The color of vegetables becomes intense when they are cooked until just tender.

• *Serving Suggestions:* Season vegetables after they have been cooked; do not salt the water!

Try snipping fresh garden herbs over vegetables before serving, or sprinkle the vegetables with fresh lemon or lime juice.

# Asparagus with Orange Hollandaise

*Cook the spears loose in a skillet, stir-fry them, or cook them in bundles standing up so the stems boil and the tips steam for uniform tenderness.*

Makes 6 servings.

*Nutrient Value Per Serving: 191 calories, 4 g protein, 18 g fat, 4 g carbohydrate, 214 mg sodium, 178 mg cholesterol.*

**2  pounds asparagus of uniform diameter**

**Orange Hollandaise:**
**3  egg yolks**
**1  teaspoon Dijon-style mustard**
**¼  teaspoon salt**
   **Dash liquid red pepper seasoning**
**1  teaspoon grated orange rind**
**2  tablespoons orange juice**
**½  cup (1 stick) unsalted butter**

1. Gently bend each asparagus spear near the stem end until the spear snaps (the spear will break where the tender part ends). Remove the scales with a small knife. Wash the asparagus gently to remove any sand from the tips.
2. If the thick ends of the spears are tough and woody, peel off their outer layer with a swivel-bladed vegetable peeler or small paring knife. Peel just to the point where the outer flesh becomes tender. Save the peelings for the soup pot.
3. To cook the spears loose, fill a skillet with water and bring to boiling. Add the asparagus and return to boiling. Cook, uncovered, until the spears are done, for 5 to 8 minutes for medium-thick spears, 8 to 10 minutes for large spears.
4. To cook the spears in bundles, gather together one quarter of the trimmed asparagus spears. Place them in the center of a length of kitchen twine. Wind the twine around the bundle a few times and tie. Repeat with the remaining asparagus.
5. Pour water into the bottom of a double boiler or tall, narrow pot to a depth of 2 inches. Bring to boiling. Carefully stand the bundles upright in the pot. Cover with an inverted double-boiler top or pot lid, or make a dome cover with aluminum foil. Cook until done, for about 10 to 12 minutes; the bottoms will boil while the tops steam.
6. To test the bundles for doneness, lift them with a large fork; the stalks should bend slightly. For either the bundle or the loose method, you should be able to insert the tip of a small sharp knife easily into the thick ends.
7. To stir-fry the asparagus, diagonally cut the trimmed asparagus into ¾- to 1-inch lengths. Sauté in 2 to 3 tablespoons of oil in a large wok or skillet for about 1 minute. Add ½ cup of water or chicken broth. Cover, reduce the heat to low and steam until just tender, for 3 to 6 minutes.
8. To drain if the asparagus was cooked upright, lay each bundle on a clean kitchen towel or paper toweling and cut the string. If cooked in a skillet or stir-fried, remove the spears with a skimmer, tongs or a pancake spatula and place on the paper toweling.
9. Prepare the Orange Hollandaise: Place the egg yolks, mustard, salt, liquid red pepper seasoning, orange rind and orange juice in the container of an electric blender. Cover and whirl for 4 to 5 seconds to combine. Melt the butter just until bubbly; do not let it brown. With the blender running, remove the cover and slowly add the hot butter. Whirl for 10 to 15 seconds, or until thickened. Spoon the hollandaise over the warm asparagus.

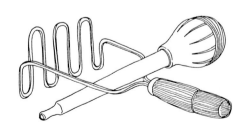

*Asparagus with Orange Hollandaise*

## STALKING THE ASPARAGUS

• Domestic asparagus from California, Washington and New Jersey is most plentiful from February through June.
• Select straight, firm stalks with closed, compact tips. Open tips mean old stalks.
• Stalks should not appear dry or wrinkled.
• The diameter of the stalks is not related to the tenderness of the asparagus. Select spears of the same thickness, however, so they will cook at the same rate.
• About two thirds of the stalk should be green.
• Store asparagus in a plastic bag in the refrigerator at about 36°. Do not wash before storing. Or stand the spears upright with the stems in a pan of water, cover with plastic wrap and store in the refrigerator.
• Try to use asparagus within 2 to 3 days of purchase because it ages rapidly.
• One pound of fresh asparagus yields ½ to ¾ pound of trimmed asparagus, or about 3 servings.
• Asparagus is a good source of vitamins A and C, potassium and dietary fiber, and it is low in sodium. Four spears contain only about 15 calories.

## Gingered Green Beans

Makes 4 servings.

*Nutrient Value Per Serving: 123 calories, 2 g protein, 10 g fat, 8 g carbohydrate, 7 mg sodium, 0 mg cholesterol.*

- 1 **pound green beans, trimmed**
- 2 **tablespoons olive oil**
- 2 **green onions, chopped (2 tablespoons)**
- 2 **teaspoons chopped, peeled fresh gingerroot**
- 1 **tablespoon lemon juice**
- 1 **tablespoon Oriental sesame oil***

1. Blanch the green beans in a large saucepan of boiling water for about 2 minutes, or until just tender. Drain and rinse under cold water. Drain well.
2. Heat a wok or large skillet. Add the olive oil and swirl to coat the pan. When hot, add the green onion and the ginger. Stir-fry for about 10 seconds, or until fragrant.
3. Add the green beans and stir-fry for 4 to 5 minutes, or until heated through. Add olive oil as necessary, to prevent sticking.
4. Remove from the heat; drizzle the lemon juice and the Oriental sesame oil over the green beans and toss. Serve immediately.

***Note:** Oriental sesame oil has more flavor and is darker in color than regular sesame oil. It can be found in the Oriental food section of many supermarkets or in Oriental specialty food stores.*

---

### Food for Thought . . .

**Mushrooms** *A simple plant with no roots, stems or leaves, mushrooms rely on non-living organic matter for food because they cannot produce their own. There are thousands of wild mushrooms, but only a few species are cultivated. Mushrooms are grown commercially in natural caves, or in specially designed buildings where the temperature, humidity, ventilation and light can be controlled.*

---

## Cherry Tomatoes with Basil

*Fresh basil enhances the delicate flavor of ripe cherry tomatoes.*

Makes 4 servings.

*Nutrient Value Per Serving: 66 calories, 1 g protein, 6 g fat, 3 g carbohydrate, 168 mg sodium, 8 mg cholesterol.*

- 1 **tablespoon butter**
- 1 **tablespoon olive oil**
- 1 **pint cherry tomatoes, stems removed and tomatoes rinsed**
- ¼ **teaspoon salt**
- ¼ **teaspoon pepper**
- 2 **tablespoons chopped fresh basil OR: 2 teaspoons leaf basil, crumbled**

1. Heat the butter and the oil in a large skillet.
2. Add the tomatoes, salt and pepper. Gently sauté the tomatoes over medium heat for 3 to 4 minutes, or until the tomatoes are heated through and slightly softened. Be careful not to break the tomato skins. Remove the skillet from the heat.
3. Sprinkle the tomatoes with the basil. Serve the tomatoes immediately.

## Marinated Stuffed Mushrooms

*Zucchini-stuffed mushrooms with a lemon and garlic marinade.*

Bake at 350° for 20 minutes.
Makes 6 servings.

*Nutrient Value Per Serving: 147 calories, 2 g protein, 14 g fat, 6 g carbohydrate, 190 mg sodium, 0 mg cholesterol.*

- 24 **medium-size mushrooms**
- ¼ **cup chopped onion**
- 2 **tablespoons imported Italian olive oil**
- 1 **cup shredded zucchini**
- ½ **cup finely chopped carrot**
- ¼ **cup chopped fresh parsley**
  **Italian Marinade (recipe, page 151)**

1. Preheat the oven to moderate (350°).
2. Remove the stems from the mushrooms and set the caps aside. Chop the stems.
3. Sauté the stems with the onion in the oil in a small skillet over medium heat until the onion is tender. Add the zucchini and the carrot. Continue sautéing for 3 minutes more, stirring often. Remove from the heat. Stir in the parsley.
4. Fill the mushroom caps with the vegetable mixture. Place the caps, stuffing side up, in a shallow baking dish.
5. Bake in the preheated moderate oven (350°) for 20 minutes.
6. Pour the Italian Marinade over the baked mushrooms. Cover and refrigerate for at least 4 hours, or overnight.

## Italian Marinade

Makes about ⅓ cup.

*Nutrient Value Per ⅓ Cup: 493 calories, 0 g protein, 54 g fat, 4 g carbohydrate, 1,095 mg sodium, 0 mg cholesterol.*

- 2  **tablespoons freshly squeezed lemon juice**
- 1  **medium-size clove garlic, finely chopped**
- ½  **teaspoon leaf thyme, crumbled**
- ½  **teaspoon salt**
- ¼  **teaspoon paprika**
- ¼  **cup imported Italian olive oil**

Combine the lemon juice, garlic, thyme, salt and paprika in a small bowl. Using a wire whisk, slowly beat in the oil in a stream until the mixture is emulsified. Beat again just before using.

## Mauna Kea Roasted Tomatoes

*A splash of coconut cream and a pinch of red pepper turn spinach into an exotic filling for tomatoes.*

Bake at 400° for 15 minutes.
Makes 6 servings.

*Nutrient Value Per Serving: 89 calories, 3 g protein, 5 g fat, 10 g carbohydrate, 117 mg sodium, 46 mg cholesterol.*

- 6  **medium-size firm, ripe tomatoes**
- ¼  **teaspoon salt**
- 8  **ounces fresh spinach, trimmed and washed**
- 2  **shallots, finely chopped OR: 2 green onions, white part only, finely chopped**
- 6  **tablespoons canned cream of coconut**
- ¼  **cup dry unseasoned bread crumbs**
- 1  **teaspoon crushed red pepper flakes**
- 1  **hard-cooked egg yolk, crumbled**

1. Slice off the upper third of each tomato. Scoop out the insides with a spoon, leaving a ¼-inch-thick shell. Lightly sprinkle the insides of the tomatoes with the salt, dividing equally. Place the tomatoes upside down on paper toweling to drain.
2. Preheat the oven to hot (400°).
3. Cook the spinach in a large pot of boiling water until wilted, for about 1 minute. Drain. When cool enough to handle, squeeze out all the excess liquid with your hands. Chop the spinach; you should have ½ cup. Combine the spinach, the shallots or green onion, the cream of coconut, bread crumbs and red pepper flakes in a medium-size bowl.
4. Wipe out the inside of each tomato with paper toweling. Fill with the spinach mixture. Arrange snugly in a shallow 8 x 8- or 9 x 9-inch square baking pan.
5. Bake in the preheated hot oven (400°) for 15 minutes, or until heated through. Sprinkle the tomato tops with the egg yolk and serve.

## *Tomato Corn Popover*

Bake at 400° for 40 to 50 minutes.
Makes 6 servings.

*Nutrient Value Per Serving: 430 calories, 18 g protein, 22 g fat, 42 g carbohydrate, 477 mg sodium, 186 mg cholesterol.*

| | |
|---|---|
| 1¼ | **pounds ripe tomatoes, sliced (about 4 medium-size tomatoes)** |
| 1 | **can (15 or 16 ounces) whole kernel corn, drained** |
| ¼ | **cup (½ stick) unsalted butter or margarine, melted** |
| 8 | **ounces bacon, cooked and crumbled** |
| 3 | **eggs** |
| 2½ | **cups milk** |
| 1½ | **cups unsifted all-purpose flour** |
| ¼ | **teaspoon salt** |
| ¼ | **teaspoon chili powder** |
| ½ | **cup grated Parmesan cheese** |

1. Preheat the oven to hot (400°). Lightly grease a 13 x 9 x 2-inch baking dish.
2. Drain the tomato slices on paper toweling for 10 minutes. Spread the corn evenly over the bottom of the prepared baking dish. Arrange the tomato slices over the corn. Pour the butter or margarine over the vegetables. Sprinkle three quarters of the bacon over all.
3. Combine the eggs, milk, flour, salt, chili powder and about three quarters of the Parmesan cheese in the container of an electric blender. Cover and whirl until smooth and well combined, scraping down the sides of the container as necessary. Pour the batter over the mixture in the baking dish. Sprinkle with the remaining Parmesan cheese and bacon.
4. Bake in the preheated hot oven (400°) for 40 to 50 minutes, or until puffed and browned on top. Serve immediately.

# Chèvre-Filled Tomatoes

*These are wonderful served with cold roast chicken or beef.*

Makes 6 servings.

*Nutrient Value Per Serving: 183 calories, 10 g protein, 12 g fat, 10 g carbohydrate, 389 mg sodium, 122 mg cholesterol.*

6  **large, ripe tomatoes**
  **Salt and pepper, to taste**
2  **hard-cooked eggs, chopped**
1  **log (about 7 ounces) French chèvre, crumbled**
2  **tablespoons imported Dijon-style mustard**
2  **shallots, finely chopped**
3  **tablespoons finely chopped celery leaves**
  **Heavy or whipping cream (optional)**
  **Curly lettuce leaves**

1. Slice off the tops of the tomatoes and set aside. Scoop out the seeds and some pulp; save them for another use. Sprinkle the insides of the tomatoes with salt, invert the tomatoes onto paper toweling and let stand for 30 minutes.
2. Combine the eggs, chèvre, mustard, shallots and celery leaves in a medium-size bowl. If the mixture is too thick, add a little heavy or whipping cream, if you wish, until you reach the desired consistency. Taste and add the salt and pepper.
3. Fill the tomato cups with the chèvre mixture. Replace the tops.
4. Line a serving platter with the lettuce. Place the tomatoes on the lettuce. Chill until ready to serve.

## Food for Thought . . .

**Kosher Salt** *A fine-grained sea salt, kosher salt also is called flake, dairy or cheese salt.*

# Oven-Dried Tomatoes

*Use these in salads, pasta sauce, soups or any dish that would benefit from a sharp tomato flavor. Use sparingly, since the flavor is very concentrated.*

Bake at 150° for 14 to 17 hours.
Makes 4 half pints.

*Nutrient Value Per Dried Tomato Half: 19 calories, 0 g protein, 2 g fat, 100 mg sodium, 0 mg cholesterol.*

6  **pounds large, uniform-size ripe plum tomatoes, halved lengthwise**
2  **tablespoons coarse kosher salt**
4  **sprigs fresh herbs, such as basil, thyme or oregano**
4  **cloves garlic, split**
16  **whole black peppercorns**
  **Olive and vegetable oils**

1. Preheat the oven to very slow (150°).
2. Arrange the tomatoes, cut side up, on 2 wire racks set over jelly-roll pans. Sprinkle with the salt.
3. Bake in the preheated very slow oven (150°) for 14 to 17 hours, or until the tomatoes are very wrinkled, deep red and without signs of moisture. Begin checking the tomatoes every hour after 14 hours. (The size of the tomatoes will determine how long they will take to dry out completely.)
4. When ready to can, wash 4 half-pint canning jars, lids and bands in hot soapy water. Rinse. Leave the jars in hot water until needed. Place the lids and bands in a saucepan of simmering water until ready to use.
5. Pack the tomatoes into the clean, hot canning jars. Place 1 herb sprig, 2 pieces of garlic and 4 peppercorns in each jar. Cover with the olive and vegetable oils. Seal and refrigerate for up to 3 months.

## ◄◄◄ Tangy Vegetable Medley

Makes 10 servings.

*Nutrient Value Per Serving: 249 calories, 5 g protein, 17 g fat, 23 g carbohydrate, 259 mg sodium, 0 mg cholesterol.*

- 2 pounds fresh green beans OR: 2 packages (10 ounces each) frozen whole green beans
- 1 package (10 ounces) frozen baby lima beans
- 2 cups cooked fresh corn (2 medium-size corn on cob) OR: 1 package (10 ounces) frozen kernel corn, thawed
- 1 cup thinly sliced celery (2 large stalks)
- 1 medium-size red onion, chopped (½ cup)
- 1 sweet red pepper, halved, seeded and diced
- 1 jar (4 ounces) pimiento, sliced
- ¾ cup distilled white vinegar
- ¾ cup vegetable oil
- 2 tablespoons water
- 1 teaspoon salt
- ½ teaspoon pepper
- ½ teaspoon paprika

1. Cook the fresh green beans in boiling water to cover in a large pot for 7 minutes, or until crisp-tender. Or cook the frozen green beans following the package directions. Drain and rinse under cold water. Cut into 2-inch lengths.
2. Cook the frozen lima beans following the package directions.
3. Combine the green beans, lima beans, corn, celery, onion, red pepper and pimiento in a large, shallow, glass baking dish.
4. Combine the vinegar, oil, water, salt, pepper and paprika in a screw-top jar and shake until all the ingredients are well blended. Pour over the vegetables and stir to coat all the ingredients well. Marinate, covered, in the refrigerator overnight. Drain the marinade before serving, if you wish.

### Food for Thought . . .

***Pimiento*** *Pimiento is the Spanish name for a sweet red pepper. When fresh, pimiento looks like a small, heart-shaped, fleshy red pepper.*

## ◄◄◄ Marinated Vegetables

Makes 6 servings.

*Nutrient Value Per Serving: 160 calories, 3 g protein, 12 g fat, 12 g carbohydrate, 273 mg sodium, 0 mg cholesterol.*

- ⅓ cup olive or vegetable oil
- ¼ cup wine vinegar
- ¼ cup chopped parsley
- ¼ cup chopped sweet green pepper
- 1 tablespoon chopped sweet pickle
- 2 teaspoons Dijon-style mustard
- ½ teaspoon salt
- ¼ teaspoon pepper
- 3 medium-size carrots, sliced crosswise
- 1 cup cauliflower flowerets
- 1 medium-size yellow squash (about 1 cup), cut into ½-inch sticks
- 1 cup onion rings
- ½ pound small or button mushrooms

1. Combine the olive or vegetable oil, the vinegar, parsley, green pepper, sweet pickle, mustard, salt and pepper in a screw-top jar. Cover and shake until all the ingredients are well blended. Set aside.
2. Cook the carrot and the cauliflower in boiling water to cover in a saucepan for 3 minutes, or just until the carrot brightens in color. Drain and place under cold running water to stop the cooking.
3. Combine the carrot, cauliflower, yellow squash, onion and mushrooms in a bowl. Shake the dressing and pour over the vegetables. Toss to coat all the ingredients well. Marinate, covered, in the refrigerator overnight.

## Food for Thought . . .

**Pine Nuts** *The edible seeds from the cones of a variety of pine tree that grows in the mountainous states of the Southwest, pine nuts also are called Indian nuts, pignons or piñons. In Italy and France, pine nuts are called pinoleas or pignoli. American-grown pine nuts are smaller than the European variety.*

*Pine nuts are ivory colored and have sweet-tasting kernels. They are sold unshelled or shelled and always are raw or unroasted.*

*One ounce of pine nuts contains 158 calories and 8 grams of protein.*

## Red Potatoes with Basil Dressing

Makes 8 servings.

*Nutrient Value Per Serving: 184 calories, 5 g protein, 3 g fat, 35 g carbohydrate, 79 mg sodium, 0 mg cholesterol.*

**Basil Dressing:**
½ cup chicken broth
1 tablespoon olive oil
2 teaspoons fresh lemon juice
2 tablespoons pine nuts (pignoli)
2 to 3 large cloves garlic
2 cups well-packed fresh basil leaves
¼ cup parsley leaves
¼ teaspoon pepper

3 pounds unpeeled red-skinned potatoes
1 tablespoon distilled white vinegar

1. Prepare the Basil Dressing: Combine the broth, oil, lemon juice, pine nuts, garlic, basil, parsley and pepper in the container of an electric blender or a food processor. Cover and whirl until the pine nuts and the garlic are finely chopped. Transfer

the dressing to a bowl. Cover the bowl and refrigerate until the dressing is needed.
2. Cook the potatoes in boiling unsalted water to cover in a large saucepan for 15 to 20 minutes, or just until the potatoes are tender. Drain the potatoes. When the potatoes are cool enough to handle, cut them crosswise into ½-inch-thick slices. Place the potatoes in a large serving bowl. Sprinkle with the vinegar and toss gently to coat the potatoes.
3. Spoon the dressing over the potatoes. Toss the potatoes carefully to coat well.

## Potatoes Olé!

Bake crust at 375° for 15 minutes, then bake mixture for 20 to 25 minutes.
Makes 4 to 6 servings.

*Nutrient Value Per Serving: 438 calories, 18 g protein, 26 g fat, 33 g carbohydrate, 899 mg sodium, 100 mg cholesterol.*

2 cups hot mashed potatoes*
1 egg
½ cup all-purpose unbleached flour
¼ cup yellow cornmeal
½ teaspoon garlic salt
½ teaspoon black pepper
4 to 5 tablespoons olive oil
1 cup bottled mild Picante sauce (or thick and chunky salsa)
1 cup shredded cooked chicken
1 cup Monterey Jack cheese with jalapeño peppers, shredded (4 ounces)
1 tablespoon chopped fresh parsley
Dairy sour cream and/or guacamole (optional)

1. Preheat the oven to moderate (375°). Grease an 11-inch tart pan with a removable bottom.
2. Mix together the mashed potatoes and the egg in a large bowl until smooth. Add the flour, cornmeal, garlic salt, black pepper and 2 to 3 tablespoons of the oil. Stir until all the ingredients are well

mixed. Press evenly into the bottom and up the sides of the prepared tart pan.

3. Bake the crust in the preheated moderate oven (375°) for 15 minutes.
4. Spread the sauce or salsa over the bottom of the crust. Arrange the chicken over the sauce. Sprinkle the Monterey Jack cheese and the parsley over the top. Drizzle the remaining oil over the top.
5. Bake in the preheated moderate oven (375°) for about 20 to 25 minutes, or until the Monterey Jack cheese is melted and lightly browned. Cut into wedges and serve hot, with sour cream and/or guacamole, if you wish.

*Note: One and one-quarter pounds of raw potatoes will make about 2 cups mashed. You also may use packaged instant mashed potatoes.*

## California Home Fries

Makes 6 servings.

Nutrient Value Per Serving: 210 calories, 6 g protein, 7 g fat, 33 g carbohydrate, 527 mg sodium, 8 mg cholesterol.

| | |
|---|---|
| 1/4 | pound sliced bacon, cut into 1/2-inch pieces |
| 2 | large onions, chopped (2 cups) |
| 1 | medium-size sweet green pepper, cored, seeded and chopped |
| 1 | medium-size sweet red pepper, cored, seeded and chopped |
| 1/2 | pound mushrooms, sliced |
| 2 | pounds medium-size red-skinned potatoes, peeled and cut into 3/4-inch cubes |
| 1/4 | cup chicken broth |
| 1 1/2 | teaspoons sweet paprika |
| 1 | teaspoon salt |
| 1/4 | teaspoon leaf basil, crumbled |
| 1/4 | teaspoon leaf oregano, crumbled |
| 1/4 | teaspoon black pepper |
| 1 | tablespoon cider vinegar |
| 1 | tablespoon chopped parsley, for garnish |

1. Cook the bacon in a 10-inch well-seasoned cast iron skillet over medium heat until crisp, stirring occasionally. Transfer the bacon with a slotted spoon to a small plate lined with paper toweling and set aside. Pour off the drippings from the skillet and reserve 5 tablespoons (if necessary, add vegetable oil to make 5 tablespoons).
2. Sauté the onion and the green and red peppers in 1 tablespoon of the reserved drippings for 5 minutes, or until almost tender. Remove the vegetables to a plate lined with paper toweling. Sauté the mushrooms in 2 tablespoons of the reserved drippings for 3 minutes, or until almost tender. Remove to the plate with the other vegetables. Sauté the potatoes in the remaining 2 tablespoons of the reserved drippings for 10 minutes, or until almost tender, stirring occasionally. Return the vegetables to the skillet with the broth, paprika, salt, basil, oregano and black pepper. Carefully toss to mix all the ingredients. Cover and cook until the potatoes are tender, for about 15 minutes, turning with a spatula every 2 to 3 minutes.
3. Stir in the vinegar and the bacon. Garnish with the parsley.

---

### Food for Thought . . .

*Gruyère* Gruyère cheese was named after a valley in Switzerland where it was first produced centuries ago. It is a firm, buttery but piquant cheese. It has a higher butterfat content and smaller holes than Emmenthaler (which is more commonly known as Swiss cheese).

# Potato Onion Au Gratin

*Using lowfat milk and less cheese in a traditional au gratin recipe really can alter the calorie count.*

Bake at 300° for 45 to 50 minutes, then at 400° for 1 to 3 minutes.
Makes 6 servings.

*Nutrient Value Per Serving: 196 calories, 9 g protein, 3 g fat, 33 g carbohydrate, 355 mg sodium, 11 mg cholesterol.*

2¼  **pounds all-purpose potatoes, peeled and thinly sliced crosswise**
2   **onions, halved lengthwise, thinly sliced crosswise, slices separated**
2   **large cloves garlic, finely chopped**
2½  **cups lowfat milk**
¾   **teaspoon salt**
½   **teaspoon pepper**
3   **tablespoons all-purpose flour**
⅓   **cup shredded Gruyère cheese**

1. Preheat the oven to slow (300°).
2. Combine the potatoes, onion, garlic, milk, salt and pepper in a large, heavy saucepan. Sprinkle with the flour and stir gently to combine the ingredients. Bring to boiling, then lower the heat. Simmer, stirring occasionally, over low heat for 2 to 3 minutes, or until the liquid begins to thicken.
3. Turn the mixture into an 11¾ x 7½ x 1¾-inch glass casserole dish. Sprinkle with the Gruyère cheese.
4. Bake in the preheated very slow oven (300°) until the potatoes are tender and the sauce is bubbly, for 45 to 50 minutes. Increase the heat to 400° and bake for 1 to 3 minutes more, or until the Gruyère cheese melts and the top is golden. Let stand for 5 minutes before serving.

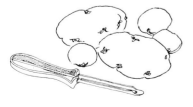

## Food for Thought . . .

*Potatoes There are four types of potatoes available in the United States, with many varieties therein. The types are Russet Burbank, long white, round red and round white.*
• ***Russet Burbank potatoes** may be long or round, and are characterized by their russetted, heavy-netted skin — the familiar Idaho potato is a russet. Russets are suited especially to baking, so use them in recipes calling for baking potatoes. They also can be deep-fat fried or boiled.*
• ***Long white potatoes** are elliptical and flattened in shape, with a thin, tan skin; White Rose is a well-known variety. They're ideal for boiling and pan frying.*
• ***Round red potatoes** are best when boiled whole and in their skins; Pontiac is a variety of red potato.*
• ***Round white potatoes** are the all-purpose potato. They often are called Maine or Eastern potatoes. They boil well, mash into fluffy creaminess and are good in soups, stews and casseroles.*
*When buying potatoes, choose firm, relatively smooth, clean and reasonably well-shaped ones (to avoid waste in peeling). Store potatoes in a cool, dark, well-ventilated place; they should keep for several weeks. (Warm temperatures cause potatoes to sprout and shrivel.) Avoid prolonged exposure to light—it causes potatoes to turn green. This greening causes a bitter flavor, so it should be peeled off before the potato is used. Don't refrigerate potatoes: When stored in temperatures below 40°, potatoes develop a sweet taste, the result of starch changing to sugar. The sugar will cause the potato to darken when it is cooked.*

## THE PERFECT POTATO

- *Potatoes are high in complex carbohydrates, rich in protein and vitamin C; they contain some B vitamins, potassium, fiber and iron. One 5-ounce potato has 105 calories.*
- *Potatoes are low in sodium and almost fat-free.*
- *The potato skin is full of dietary fiber.*
- *Satisfy a yen for fatty French fries with homemade shoestring potato fries. (A 2½-ounce serving has only 145 calories, compared to 217 calories for the average packet [2½ ounces] of fast-food fries.) To make shoestrings, spray a nonstick baking sheet with nonstick vegetable cooking spray. Slice an unpeeled potato into ¼-inch-wide sticks, coat the sticks with nonstick spray and toss them in paprika. Spread the sticks on the baking sheet and bake at 475° for 10 to 15 minutes, or until crisp.*
- *Make great low-cal mashed potatoes: Use skim instead of whole milk, serve without butter, and mix in a cooked, peeled Granny Smith apple for a deliciously different taste.*
- *Try these tempting toppings for your baked potato: 2 teaspoons of caraway, fennel or celery seeds or toasted sesame seeds; or plain yogurt, chopped tomatoes, onions and green chili peppers for a Tex-Mex touch.*
- *How about some lowfat potato salad? Drizzle chicken broth or vinegar over warm, cooked potato slices. Let them stand until the liquid is absorbed. Then, if you wish, coat the slices lightly with a lowfat salad dressing or vinaigrette.*

# Home-Style Potatoes Anna

Makes 6 servings.

*Nutrient Value Per Serving: 171 calories, 2 g protein, 12 g fat, 16 g carbohydrate, 122 mg sodium, 31 mg cholesterol.*

**3    large baking potatoes (about 1½ pounds)**
**6    tablespoons butter**
**2    cloves garlic, finely chopped**
       **Salt and pepper, to taste**

1. Peel the potatoes and drop them into a large bowl of cold water. Slice 2 potatoes crosswise as thinly as possible and pat dry with paper toweling.
2. Melt 3 tablespoons of the butter in a 12-inch heavy skillet. Arrange the potato slices in the bottom of the skillet in a spiral pattern, overlapping the slices, until the bottom is completely covered. Sprinkle with the garlic, salt and pepper. Slice the remaining potato and pat dry. Continue arranging slices in a spiral pattern on top of the first layer. Sprinkle with the salt and pepper. Dot with the remaining 3 tablespoons of butter.
3. Cover the skillet and cook over medium heat until the bottom is brown and crusty, for about 8 minutes. Peek occasionally to make sure the heat is not too high and the potatoes are browning, not burning.
4. With a sharp knife, cut the potato circle in half. Lift one half with a pancake turner and return to the skillet, crusty side up. Repeat with the other half. Or carefully place a large, oiled baking sheet or pizza pan over the skillet and invert both. Return the skillet to the heat. Slide the potato circle back into the skillet, crusty side up. Lower the heat. Cook, uncovered, until brown and crusty on the bottom, for about 8 minutes. Cut each half into 3 equal wedges and serve.

## Potato Apple Pancakes

Makes 6 servings.

*Nutrient Value Per Serving: 278 calories, 4 g protein, 13 g fat, 38 g carbohydrate, 823 mg sodium, 77 mg cholesterol.*

1½  **pounds Granny Smith apples, cored, peeled and coarsely chopped**
2  **tablespoons water**
1½  **pounds potatoes, peeled, boiled until tender, and mashed**
6  **tablespoons unsalted butter**
2  **teaspoons salt**
¾  **teaspoon pepper**
½  **cup all-purpose flour**
1  **teaspoon baking soda**
1  **large egg**
2  **large green onions, finely chopped (¼ cup)**

1. Combine the apples and the water in a medium-size saucepan. Cook, covered, over medium heat until the apples are soft and fall apart when stirred, for about 20 minutes. Raise the heat to medium-high. Remove the cover and cook for another 4 to 5 minutes, stirring constantly, until the excess liquid has evaporated.
2. Combine the apples, potatoes, 1½ tablespoons of the butter, the salt and pepper in a large bowl and stir until the butter melts. Refrigerate until cold, for at least 2 hours.
3. Stir in the flour, baking soda, egg and green onion into the potato mixture.
4. Heat 1 tablespoon of the remaining butter in a nonstick skillet over medium heat. Drop the pancake mixture by spoonfuls (2 rounded tablespoons per pancake) into the skillet, being careful not to overcrowd the pan. Cook until the undersides are golden brown. Carefully turn over, flattening the pancakes to a ¼-inch thickness. Cook for 4 minutes more, or until golden brown.
5. Transfer the pancakes to paper toweling to drain. Keep the cooked pancakes warm in the oven while you finish the recipe.

## Mushroom Rice Pilaf

Makes 4 servings.

*Nutrient Value Per Serving: 275 calories, 8 g protein, 4 g fat, 49 g carbohydrate, 493 mg sodium, 0 mg cholesterol.*

½  **cup chopped onions, frozen or fresh**
1  **tablespoon olive oil**
1  **can (13¾ ounces) chicken broth**
1  **cup uncooked long grain converted white rice**
¼  **cup freeze-dried mushrooms**
1  **package (10 ounces) frozen peas**
   **Pinch white pepper**
2  **tablespoons chopped parsley**

1. Sauté the onion in the oil in a medium-size saucepan until tender, for 5 minutes.
2. Pour the broth into a 4-cup liquid measure. Add enough water to make 2½ cups of liquid. Add to the onion along with the rice and the mushrooms. Bring to boiling over high heat. Lower the heat and simmer, covered, stirring occasionally, for 15 minutes.
3. Add the frozen peas and the white pepper. Simmer for 10 minutes more, or until the liquid is absorbed and the rice is tender. Stir in the parsley.

### REVVED-UP RICE

*Add pizzazz—but almost no calories!—to rice by mixing in vegetables and/or herbs. Chopped mushrooms, celery, onion and green or red pepper can be added to rice at the start of cooking. (For a splurge, sauté the vegetables and the rice in 2 teaspoons of butter before adding the liquid.) You can also replace part of the water with dry white wine or tart fruit juice. Just before removing the rice from the saucepan, toss in some freshly chopped herbs.*

# Savories & Sauces

## ◀◀ Tomato Chutney

Makes about 2 quarts.

*Nutrient Value Per 2 Tablespoons: 27 calories, 0 g protein, 0 g fat, 7 g carbohydrate, 47 mg sodium, 0 mg cholesterol.*

2¼ **pounds ripe tomatoes, cored and diced (about 5 cups)**
2 **cups peeled, cored and diced tart apples (about 2 medium-size apples)**
2 **cups diced onions (about 2 large onions)**
1 **package (8 ounces) pitted dates, cut into thirds**
4 **large cloves garlic, finely chopped**
1 **lemon, sliced paper-thin and slices quartered**
  **Juice of 1 lemon**
¾ **cup tomato juice**
¾ **cup apple juice**
¾ **cup cider vinegar**
½ **cup honey**
2 **teaspoons ground coriander**
1½ **teaspoons black pepper**
1 **teaspoon salt**
  **Pinch ground hot red pepper**

1. Place the tomatoes, apples, onion, dates, garlic, lemon slices, lemon juice, tomato juice, apple juice, vinegar, honey, coriander, black pepper, salt and ground hot red pepper in a large, heavy nonaluminum pot (at least 6 quarts). Mix to combine all the ingredients well. Bring the mixture to boiling, stirring occasionally. Reduce the heat to low. Simmer gently for 30 to 45 minutes, or until the mixture is a good chutney consistency, stirring occasionally. Let the mixture cool slightly.
2. Ladle the chutney into clean jars or other containers. Refrigerate until serving.

### TOMATO TIPS

*Florida tomato growers recommend that consumers purchase winter and spring tomatoes several days before using them, and store the tomatoes at room temperature (tomatoes should not be refrigerated). After a few days of ripening, the tomatoes will be deep red with a delicious taste and excellent texture.*

# Red Pepper Sauce

*Serve chilled as a dip or warm as a sauce.*

Makes about 1 cup.

*Nutrient Value Per Tablespoon: 13 calories, 2 g protein, 1 g fat, 1 g carbohydrate, 93 mg sodium, 0 mg cholesterol.*

2   **green onions, chopped (2 tablespoons)**
1   **tablespoon olive oil**
2   **medium-size sweet red peppers, halved, seeded and cut into ½-inch pieces**
1   **cup drained, canned whole tomatoes, chopped**
½   **teaspoon salt**
2   **teaspoons chopped fresh basil OR: ½ teaspoon leaf basil, crumbled**
½   **teaspoon lemon juice**

1. Sauté the green onion in the oil in a medium-size skillet for 2 minutes, or until softened. Add the red peppers and sauté over low heat for 3 minutes, or until the red peppers are slightly wrinkled.
2. Add the tomatoes and the salt. Simmer, covered, for 10 to 15 minutes, or until the red peppers are very soft. Add the basil and the lemon juice and cook for 1 minute.
3. Scrape the pepper mixture into the container of an electric blender or a food processor. Cover and whirl until the mixture is a coarse purée. To serve, heat the sauce in a small saucepan over low heat until warm.

# Savory Green Sauce

*This no-cook sauce is excellent served with broiled, barbecued or boiled meats, poultry and fish.\**

Makes about 1⅔ cups.

*Nutrient Value Per Tablespoon: 16 calories, 0 g protein, 1 g fat, 1 g carbohydrate, 12 mg sodium, 0 mg cholesterol.*

1   **bunch green onions, coarsely chopped (1 cup)**
2   **large stalks celery, coarsely chopped (1 cup)**
1   **ripe tomato, peeled and coarsely chopped**
1   **small white onion (not pearl onion), coarsely chopped**
2   **tablespoons chopped flat-leaf Italian parsley**
2   **cloves garlic, chopped**
2½  **tablespoons red wine vinegar**
2½  **tablespoons extra-virgin olive oil**
1   **tablespoon prepared mustard**
⅛   **teaspoon crushed red pepper flakes**

Combine the green onion, celery, tomato, white onion, parsley, garlic, vinegar, oil, mustard and red pepper flakes in the container of an electric blender or a food processor. Cover and whirl until all the vegetables are finely chopped.

*\*Note: To barbecue chicken breasts (skinless and on the bone): Spray a barbecue grill and both sides of the chicken breasts with nonstick vegetable cooking spray. For a 7-ounce chicken breast half, grill over medium coals, bone side down, for 30 minutes. Turn over and grill for 5 to 10 minutes more, or until the chicken no longer is pink near the bone.*
*To barbecue whole fish: Spray a grill basket with nonstick vegetable cooking spray. Preheat the grill basket over the barbecue or in the fireplace. Add the fish. Set the basket with the fish on top of the barbecue or in the fireplace. Barbecue the fish for 10 minutes per inch of thickness, measured at its thickest part. Turn over the fish halfway through the cooking time.*

# Toute Sweet

*Scrumptious treats for your sweet tooth: cakes, cookies, pies, tarts and frozen delights.*

*Strawberry Kropsua (recipe, page 186)*

**P**iña Colada Cheesecake. Orange Soufflé. Decadent Chocolate Mousse. Whether you're a confirmed dessert-alcoholic or just an occasional indulger, these sweets are bound to entice you. And while we'd never advocate a steady diet of desserts, there are days when nothing but a little "heaven on earth" will do.

You've heard the expression, "pie in the sky". That's where we think these pies came from—so good, they *had* to be heaven sent. There's classic Strawberry Rhubarb *(recipe, page 186)*, airy, light and luscious Lime Chiffon *(recipe, page 187)*, Lattice Cherry Pie *(recipe, page 180)* and many others. We even give you pointers on perfect edging and handling pie dough for a tender, flaky crust.

Nature's bounty—fresh fruit—is delicious by itself, but sometimes you *can* improve on Mother Nature. Case in point: Tulip Cups with Strawberries and Zabaglione *(recipe, page 191)* or refreshing Blueberry Lemon Swirl *(recipe, page 194)*.

Can we discuss desserts without talking about America's favorite—ice cream? We've got exotic Mango Ice Cream *(recipe, page 198)*, an outrageous Ice Cream Bombe *(recipe, page 199)* and even Old-Fashioned French Vanilla *(recipe, page 198)* when you have a yearning for a classic.

Counting calories? You still don't have to miss dessert! Check out Chapter 7, *On The Light Side*, for some guilt-free treats. ∎

# Cakes

## Applesauce Cake

*A delicious old-fashioned cake flecked with raisins and walnuts.*

Bake at 350° for 1 hour and 10 minutes.
Makes 16 servings.

*Nutrient Value Per Serving: 418 calories, 5 g protein, 14 g fat, 71 g carbohydrate, 298 mg sodium, 58 mg cholesterol.*

|   |   |
|---|---|
| 3 | **cups** unsifted **all-purpose flour** |
| 2 | **teaspoons baking soda** |
| 1 | **teaspoon baking powder** |
| 3 | **teaspoons ground cinnamon** |
| 1½ | **teaspoons ground nutmeg** |
| 1 | **teaspoon ground cloves** |
| ½ | **teaspoon salt** |
| ¾ | **cup (1½ sticks) butter or margarine, at room temperature** |
| 2 | **cups sugar** |
| 2 | **eggs** |
| 2 | **cups** unsweetened **applesauce** |
| 1 | **cup walnuts, chopped** |
| 1 | **cup raisins** |
|   | **Apple Glaze (recipe follows)** |

1. Preheat the oven to moderate (350°). Grease and flour the bottom and sides of a 10-inch tube pan.
2. Stir together the flour, baking soda, baking powder, cinnamon, nutmeg, cloves and salt in a medium-size bowl. Set aside.
3. Beat together the butter or margarine, the sugar and eggs in a large bowl until light and fluffy. Stir in the flour mixture alternately with the applesauce, beginning and ending with the flour mixture. Fold in the walnuts and the raisins. Turn the batter evenly into the prepared pan, smoothing the top with a rubber spatula to make it level.
4. Bake in the preheated moderate oven (350°) for 1 hour and 10 minutes, or until a cake tester inserted in the center of the cake comes out clean. Cool the cake in the pan on a wire rack for 10 minutes. Remove from the pan and cool on the rack to room temperature.
5. Spoon the Apple Glaze over the top of the cake so it drizzles down the sides.

**Apple Glaze:** Place 2 cups of *un*sifted 10X (confectioners' powdered) sugar in a small bowl. Gradually stir in 3 to 4 tablespoons of apple juice until the glaze is smooth and a good spreading consistency.

### THE FRUIT FLOAT

*To prevent fruits and nuts from sinking to the bottom of a cake, reserve a small portion of the cake flour and toss the fruits and nuts together with the flour until they're lightly coated. This method only works with thicker cake batters. If the batter is thin, fruits and nuts always will sink and should be left out altogether.*

## Food for Thought . . .

**Cinnamon** *Cinnamon is the bark of several varieties of an evergreen tree native to Southeast Asia. True cinnamon is the Ceylon variety; others are from cassia trees.*

*Ceylon cinnamon is native to Ceylon and India. It has the mildest tasting bark and, for that reason, is not popular in this country. It is used extensively in Mexico. Americans tend to prefer the stronger taste of the bark from the cassia trees. One variety, the Saigon cassia, originated in China but now is grown extensively in Vietnam; this variety is ground. Another variety, the Batavia cassia, is rolled into sticks.*

*Cinnamon or cassia bark is harvested by cutting the young shoots off the tree. The bark is stripped from the shoots and scraped. The inner bark, which is the fragrant layer, folds into itself when it starts to dry out and looks like a roll of paper. It is rolled until it is about ½ inch in diameter, and it can be up to 3 feet long.*

*Oil of cinnamon is extracted from the berries of the tree and also from the residue of the bark.*

### THE SOFT TOUCH

*The best way to soften butter is to let it stand at room temperature. For faster softening, slice the butter into a bowl. Then, for no more than 2 seconds at a time and stirring constantly, place the bowl of butter over a bowl of hot water; the butter should soften, not melt.*

# Best Butter Cake

Bake at 350° for 1 hour.
Makes 16 servings.

*Nutrient Value Per Serving: 300 calories, 4 g protein, 14 g fat, 41 g carbohydrate, 230 mg sodium, 102 mg cholesterol.*

2½ **cups all-purpose flour**
2 **teaspoons baking powder**
¼ **teaspoon salt**
1 **cup (2 sticks) butter, softened**
2 **cups sugar**
4 **eggs**
2 **teaspoons vanilla**
1 **cup milk**

1. Preheat the oven to moderate (350°). Grease and flour a 12-cup fluted tube pan. Stir together the flour, baking powder and salt on a piece of wax paper.
2. Beat together the butter and the sugar in a large bowl with an electric mixer at high speed until light. Lower the mixer speed to medium.
3. Add the eggs, one at a time, beating well after each addition. Beat in the vanilla. Lower the mixer speed to low.
4. Add the flour mixture alternately with the milk, beginning and ending with the flour mixture.
5. Spoon the batter into the prepared pan.
6. Bake in the preheated moderate oven (350°) for 1 hour, or until a toothpick inserted in the center of the cake comes out clean. Cool the cake in the pan on a wire rack for 10 minutes. Loosen the cake around the edges with a knife and invert onto the rack to cool completely.

## Fresh Tomato Cake

Bake at 350° for 40 to 45 minutes.
Makes 9 servings.

*Nutrient Value Per Serving: 410 calories, 7 g protein, 19 g fat, 57 g carbohydrate, 332 mg sodium, 58 mg cholesterol.*

**10** ounces tomatoes
  (2 medium-size tomatoes)
**¼** cup white rum
**1** cup raisins
**1** cup slivered almonds
**1¾** cups sifted all-purpose flour
**1** teaspoon baking soda
**½** teaspoon salt
**2** teaspoons ground cinnamon
**½** teaspoon ground cloves
**½** cup (1 stick) butter or margarine,
  softened
**1** cup sugar
**1** egg
  10X (confectioners' powdered) sugar,
  optional

1. Preheat the oven to moderate (350°). Grease and flour an 8-inch square baking pan.
2. Core and coarsely chop the tomatoes. Place in the container of an electric blender or a food processor, cover and whirl until puréed. Pour into a 2-cup measure; you should have 1 cup. Stir in the rum and set aside.
3. Combine the raisins and the almonds in a small bowl. Stir about 1 tablespoon of the flour into the mixture and set aside. Combine the remaining flour, the baking soda, salt, cinnamon and cloves in a second small bowl, mix well and set aside.
4. Beat together the butter or margarine and the sugar in a large bowl with an electric mixer until light and fluffy. Beat in the egg until well mixed. Gradually beat in the puréed tomato mixture until smooth. Fold in the flour and the almond mixtures until blended. Pour the batter into the prepared pan.

5. Bake in the preheated moderate oven (350°) for 40 to 45 minutes, or until a cake tester inserted in the center of the cake comes out clean. Cool the cake in the pan on a wire rack for 10 minutes. Remove the cake from the pan to the rack and cool to room temperature. Slide the cake onto a serving plate. If you wish, sprinkle the top of the cake with 10X (confectioners' powdered) sugar, using a doily to create a pattern.

## Apricot Upside-Down Cake

*A cast iron skillet helps to make the caramel good and crunchy.*

Bake at 350° for 40 minutes for 9-inch skillet, or 30 minutes for 10-inch.
Makes 8 servings.

*Nutrient Value Per Serving: 383 calories, 5 g protein, 18 g fat, 53 g carbohydrate, 201 mg sodium, 68 mg cholesterol.*

- 1¼ cups unsifted all-purpose flour
- 2 teaspoons baking powder
- ¾ cup sugar
- ¼ teaspoon salt
- ½ cup (1 stick) unsalted butter or margarine, softened
- ¼ cup firmly packed light brown sugar
- 1 can (17 ounces) apricot halves, drained
- ½ cup chopped walnuts
- ¾ cup milk
- 1 egg
- 1 teaspoon vanilla

1. Preheat the oven to moderate (350°). Sift together the flour, baking powder, sugar and salt into a large bowl. Set aside.
2. Melt ¼ cup of the butter or margarine in a 9- or 10-inch well-seasoned cast iron skillet over low heat. Sprinkle the brown sugar over the melted butter. Continue to heat, stirring occasionally, until the sugar is melted. Remove from the heat. Arrange the apricot halves, cut side up,

### CAST IRON CARE

*If your cast iron pan or skillet is new, wash it with soap and water, rinse it well and wipe dry. Then put it in a preheated slow oven (200°) for 5 minutes to dry completely. Pour 1 to 2 inches of cooking oil into the pan or skillet. Place it over very low heat until the oil shimmers and is very hot. Turn off the heat and allow the oil to cool down to room temperature. Repeat the heating and cooling twice more. Discard the oil and wipe the pan clean with paper toweling. After each use, wash the pan if necessary, but do not use abrasive cleansers (use salt on stubborn stains, and scrub lightly with a sponge). Dry the pan thoroughly, wipe it out with lightly oiled paper toweling and store it in an airy, dry place. An oven with a pilot light or a pot rack in an airy kitchen both are ideal storage spaces. For pans that have been neglected and are rusty, scour with salt and reseason.*

over the top of the butter-sugar mixture. Sprinkle with the walnuts and set aside.
3. Add the remaining butter or margarine and the milk to the dry ingredients. Beat for 2 minutes with an electric mixer at medium speed. Add the egg and the vanilla and beat for 2 minutes more. Spoon over the fruit and nuts.
4. Bake in the preheated moderate oven (350°) for 40 minutes for a 9-inch skillet, or 30 minutes for a 10-inch skillet, or until the center of the cake springs back when lightly pressed with your fingertip and a wooden pick inserted in the center comes out clean.
5. Using a pot holder, remove the skillet from the oven and invert the cake onto a serving plate. Rearrange any loosened walnuts. Serve warm or at room temperature.

## Pineapple Coconut Ribbon Cake

Bake at 325° for 35 to 40 minutes.
Makes 20 servings.

*Nutrient Value Per Serving: 242 calories, 2 g protein, 9 g fat, 39 g carbohydrate, 175 mg sodium, 62 mg cholesterol.*

| | |
|---|---|
| 1 | **can (20 ounces) crushed pineapple, un*drained*** |
| 2¼ | **cups sifted cake flour** |
| 2½ | **teaspoons baking powder** |
| ¼ | **teaspoon salt** |
| ½ | **cup (1 stick) butter or margarine, softened** |
| 1¼ | **cups sugar** |
| 3 | **eggs** |
| | **Pineapple Frosting (recipe follows)** |
| ⅔ | **cup flaked coconut, for garnish** |

1. Preheat the oven to slow (325°). Grease a 13 x 9 x 2-inch baking pan.
2. Drain the crushed pineapple well, reserving the juice. Set the crushed pineapple aside.
3. Stir together the flour, baking powder and salt on a piece of wax paper until well mixed. Set aside.
4. Beat together the butter or margarine and the sugar in a large bowl until light and fluffy. Add the eggs, one at a time, beating well after each addition. Add the flour mixture alternately with ⅔ cup of the reserved pineapple juice and mix until well blended. Spread the batter in the prepared pan.
5. Bake in the preheated slow oven (325°) for 35 to 40 minutes, or until a cake tester inserted in the center of the cake comes out clean. Cool the cake in the pan on a wire rack for 5 minutes. Turn the cake out onto the rack and invert onto another wire rack. Cool to room temperature.
6. Spread the Pineapple Frosting over the top of the cake. Garnish the top with alternating diagonal stripes of the crushed pineapple and the coconut.

**Pineapple Frosting:** Beat ⅓ cup of softened butter or margarine in a small bowl until smooth and creamy. Alternately mix in 2 cups of *un*sifted 10X (confectioners' powdered) sugar with 3 to 4 tablespoons of the reserved pineapple juice from Step 2 of the above recipe, until the frosting is smooth and a good spreading consistency.

## Maple Walnut Banana Squares

Bake at 350° for 30 to 35 minutes.
Makes 24 squares.

*Nutrient Value Per Square: 223 calories, 2 g protein, 10 g fat, 33 g carbohydrate, 125 mg sodium, 40 mg cholesterol.*

- 2 **cups unsifted all-purpose flour**
- 1 **teaspoon baking powder**
- ½ **teaspoon baking soda**
- ¼ **teaspoon salt**
- ½ **cup (1 stick) butter or margarine, softened**
- 1¼ **cups sugar**
- 2 **eggs**
- 2 **large, fully ripe bananas, mashed (1 cup)**
- ½ **cup dairy sour cream**
    **Maple Butter Cream (recipe follows)**
- ¾ **cup walnuts, chopped**

1. Preheat the oven to moderate (350°). Grease and flour a 13 x 9 x 2-inch baking pan.
2. Stir together the flour, baking powder, baking soda and salt on a piece of wax paper until well mixed. Set aside.
3. Beat together the butter or margarine and the sugar in a large mixing bowl until light and fluffy. Add the eggs, one at a time, beating well after each addition.
4. Combine the banana and the sour cream in a small bowl. Stir the flour mixture and the banana mixture alternately into the butter mixture, beginning and ending with the flour. Spread the batter evenly in the prepared pan.
5. Bake in the preheated moderate oven (350°) for 30 to 35 minutes, or until a cake tester inserted in the center of the cake comes out clean. Cool the cake in the pan on a wire rack for 5 minutes. Loosen the sides, turn the cake out onto the rack and invert onto another wire rack. Cool to room temperature.
6. Frost the top of the cake with the Maple Butter Cream. Sprinkle the walnuts over the top. Cut into 24 squares.

*Maple Butter Cream:* Beat ¼ cup (½ stick) of softened butter in a small bowl until smooth and creamy. Alternately beat in 2 cups of *un*sifted 10X (confectioners' powdered) sugar and 4 to 5 tablespoons of maple syrup until the frosting is smooth and a good spreading consistency.

## Banana Mocha Muffins

Bake at 400° for 25 to 30 minutes.
Makes 2 dozen muffins.

*Nutrient Value Per Muffin: 208 calories, 2 g protein, 11 g fat, 28 g carbohydrate, 162 mg sodium, 32 mg cholesterol.*

- 2½ **cups unsifted all-purpose flour**
- 1 **teaspoon baking powder**
- ½ **teaspoon baking soda**
- ½ **teaspoon salt**
- 1 **tablespoon instant coffee granules**
- 1 **tablespoon hot water**
- 1⅓ **cups mashed fully ripe banana (about 3 bananas)**
- 1 **cup (2 sticks) butter or margarine, softened**
- 1¼ **cups sugar**
- 1 **egg**
- 1 **cup semisweet chocolate pieces**

1. Preheat the oven to hot (400°). Grease 2½-inch muffin-pan cups.
2. Stir together the flour, baking powder, baking soda and salt in a small bowl. Set aside.
3. Dissolve the instant coffee in the hot water. Stir into the banana and set aside.
4. Beat together the butter or margarine and the sugar until light and fluffy. Beat in the egg. Mix in the banana mixture. Stir in the flour mixture until well blended. Fold in the chocolate pieces. Spoon the batter into the prepared cups.
5. Bake in the preheated hot oven (400°) for 25 to 30 minutes, or until a wooden pick inserted in the center of the muffins comes out clean. Remove the muffins from the cups to a wire rack to cool.

# Petits Fours

Bake at 325° for 30 to 35 minutes.
Makes about 40 petits fours.

*Nutrient Value Per Petit Four: 145 calories, 1 g protein,
8 g fat, 18 g carbohydrate, 85 mg sodium, 38 mg cholesterol.*

## Cake:
- ¾   **cup (1½ sticks) butter, softened**
- 3   **ounces cream cheese, softened**
- 1½  **cups sugar**
- 1   **teaspoon vanilla**
- ¼   **teaspoon salt**
- 1½  **cups sifted cake flour**
- 3   **eggs**

## Chocolate Frosting:
- 4   **ounces semisweet chocolate, melted
  and cooled**
- ½   **cup (1 stick) butter, softened**
- 2   **teaspoons amaretto liqueur**

  ***Decorative Icing (recipe follows)***

1. Preheat the oven to slow (325°). Grease a
   15½ x 10½ x 1-inch jelly-roll pan. Line
   with wax paper and grease the paper.
2. Prepare the Cake: Beat together the
   butter and the cream cheese in a large
   bowl with an electric mixer at high speed
   until light and fluffy, for about 2 minutes.
   Add the sugar, vanilla and salt. Beat until
   all the ingredients are well mixed. With
   the mixer at low speed, add the flour
   alternately with the eggs, beginning and
   ending with the flour, just until mixed.
   Spread evenly in the prepared pan.
3. Bake in the preheated slow oven (325°)
   for 30 to 35 minutes, or until a wooden
   pick inserted in the center of the cake
   comes out clean. Cool the cake in the pan
   for 10 minutes; invert onto a wire rack,
   peel off the paper and cool completely.
4. Prepare the Chocolate Frosting: Combine
   the chocolate, butter and amaretto in a
   small bowl. Beat until smooth.
5. Trim the edges of the cake. Cut the cake
   in half crosswise to form two 10 x 7-inch
   rectangles. Spread half the frosting on
   one rectangle. Place the second rectangle

on top. Spread the remaining frosting on
top. Cut the cake into 7 strips, each 10
inches long and 1 inch wide. Cut the
strips diagonally to form 40 diamond-
shaped petits fours.
6. Decorate the tops of the petits fours with
   flowers and leaves or the design of your
   choice using the Decorative Icing.

**Decorative Icing:** Mix together 1 egg white
and 1 cup of *unsifted* 10X (confectioners'
powdered) sugar in a bowl with an electric
mixer. Add 1 teaspoon of lemon juice; mix
well. Gradually beat in 1 more cup of 10X
sugar until smooth. Add lemon juice to
reach a good consistency. Divide the icing
depending on the number of colors you plan
to use. Add food coloring, a drop at a time
per portion, to create the shades desired.
Use a pastry bag fitted with decorative tips
to form flowers and leaves.

# Chocolate Cheesecake

Makes 12 servings.

*Nutrient Value Per Serving: 285 calories, 5 g protein, 20 g
fat, 24 g carbohydrate, 172 mg sodium, 80 mg cholesterol.*

- 1   **package (11¾ ounces) frozen
  chocolate-swirl pound cake**
- 1   **package (8 ounces) cream cheese,
  softened**
- 1¾  **cups cold milk**
- 1   **package (4-serving size) instant
  chocolate pudding**
- ½   **cup heavy cream, whipped
  Whole strawberries, chocolate curls
  and additional whipped cream, for
  garnish (optional)**

1. Cut the pound cake into ½-inch-thick
   slices. Cut enough slices into triangles to
   stand up around the sides of an 8-inch
   springform pan. (Use the bottom of each
   cake slice as the triangle base, and cut the
   two angled sides to a point midway on the
   opposite side.) Line the bottom of the pan
   with slices of cake. Stand the triangles,
   base down, around the sides of the pan.

*Chocolate Cheesecake, No-Cook Cheesecake (recipe, page 172), Piña Colada Cheesecake (recipe, page 172)*

**2.** Combine the cream cheese and ½ cup of the milk in the container of an electric blender* and whirl until smooth. Add the remaining milk and the instant pudding; whirl until smooth. Pour the mixture into a bowl. Fold in the whipped cream. Spoon the mixture into the prepared pan. Cover and chill until firm, for about 3 hours.

**3.** To serve, remove the sides of the pan. Place the cake on a serving plate. Garnish the top with additional whipped cream, whole strawberries and chocolate curls, if you wish.

***Note:** You also may use an electric mixer, but the blender produces a smoother filling.*

## No-Cook Cheesecake

Makes 12 servings.

*Nutrient Value Per Serving: 285 calories, 5 g protein, 18 g fat, 27 g carbohydrate, 230 mg sodium, 71 mg cholesterol.*

1 package (11¾ ounces) frozen chocolate-swirl pound cake
1 package (8 ounces) cream cheese, softened
1¾ cups cold milk
1 package (4-serving size) instant vanilla pudding
½ cup dairy sour cream
½ teaspoon vanilla
½ cup strawberries, halved
2 tablespoons raspberry preserves
   Whipped cream, whole strawberries and mint leaves, for garnish (optional)

1. Cut the pound cake into ½-inch-thick slices and cut each slice into thirds. Line the bottom and sides of an 8-inch springform pan with the cake.
2. Combine the cream cheese and ½ cup of the milk in the container of an electric blender* and whirl until smooth. Add the remaining milk, the instant pudding, sour cream and vanilla; whirl until smooth. Spoon the mixture into the prepared pan. Cover and chill until firm, for about 3 hours.
3. To serve, remove the sides of the pan. Place the cake on a serving plate. Arrange the halved strawberries on top. Spoon the raspberry preserves over the berries. Garnish with whipped cream, whole strawberries and mint leaves, if you wish.

*Note: You also may use an electric mixer, but the blender produces a smoother filling.*

## Piña Colada Cheesecake

Makes 12 servings.

*Nutrient Value Per Serving: 289 calories, 4 g protein, 16 g fat, 31 g carbohydrate, 224 mg sodium, 66 mg cholesterol.*

1 package (11¾ ounces) frozen pound cake
1 can (20 ounces) pineapple slices
1 package (8 ounces) cream cheese, softened
1⅔ cups cold milk
1 package (4-serving size) instant vanilla pudding
3 tablespoons dark rum
   Toasted fresh or canned coconut
   Whipped cream, for garnish (optional)

1. Cut the pound cake into ½-inch-thick slices. Cut enough slices into triangles to stand up around the sides of an 8-inch springform pan. (Use the bottom of each cake slice as the triangle base and cut the two angled sides to a point midway on the opposite side.) Line the bottom of the pan with slices of cake. Stand the triangles, base down, around the sides of the pan.
2. Drain the pineapple slices well. Cut half the slices into bite-size pieces. Halve the remaining slices and reserve. Combine the cream cheese and ½ cup of the milk in the container of an electric blender* and whirl until smooth. Add the remaining milk, the instant pudding and rum; whirl until smooth. Spoon half the cream cheese mixture into the prepared pan. Top evenly with the bite-size pineapple pieces. Spoon the remaining cream cheese mixture over. Cover and chill until firm, for about 3 hours.
3. To serve, remove the sides of the pan. Place the cake on a serving plate. Top with the reserved halved pineapple slices and the toasted coconut. Garnish with whipped cream, if you wish.

*Note: You also may use an electric mixer, but the blender produces a smoother filling.*

# Cookies

## Old-Fashioned Butter Cookies

Bake at 400° for 7 to 9 minutes.
Makes 6 dozen cookies.

*Nutrient Value Per Cookie: 46 calories, 1 g protein, 3 g fat,
5 g carbohydrate, 17 mg sodium, 11 mg cholesterol.*

1   **cup (2 sticks) unsalted butter,
     at room temperature**
1   **cup unsifted 10X (confectioners'
     powdered) sugar**
1   **egg**
1½  **teaspoons vanilla**
2½  **cups unsifted all-purpose flour**
½   **teaspoon salt
     Pink Cream Filling (optional; see
     Pastel Creams, page 176)**

1. Beat together the butter, 10X
   (confectioners' powdered) sugar, egg and
   vanilla in a large bowl with an electric
   mixer at medium speed until smooth and
   fluffy, for 4 minutes.
2. Stir together the flour and the salt in a
   small bowl. Add to the butter mixture
   and beat at low speed until combined.
3. To shape the cookies: For *pressed
   cookies*, spoon the dough into the press.
   Press the desired shapes onto ungreased
   baking sheets. For *slice and bake
   cookies*, refrigerate the dough, wrapped,
   for 45 minutes. Divide the dough in half.
   Shape each half on wax paper into a 6-
   inch log and wrap. Chill in the
   refrigerator for 1 hour or in the freezer
   for 30 minutes. Slice the cookies ⅛ inch
   thick and place on ungreased baking
   sheets.
4. Preheat the oven to hot (400°).
5. Bake the cookies, pressed or sliced, in the
   preheated hot oven (400°) for 7 to 9
   minutes, depending on the shape, or until

set and lightly browned around the
edges; the tops should not brown. Let the
cookies stand on the sheet for 1 minute.
Transfer the cookies with a metal spatula
to a wire rack to cool. Pipe on Pink
Cream Filling, if you wish. Store in a
tightly covered container.

## Almond Bites

Bake at 400° for 9 minutes.
Makes about 5 dozen cookies.

*Nutrient Value Per Cookie: 60 calories, 1 g protein, 4 g fat,
6 g carbohydrate, 20 mg sodium, 13 mg cholesterol.*

Preheat the oven to hot (400°). Prepare 1
recipe of Old-Fashioned Butter Cookies
*(recipe, at left)* with the following changes:
Substitute 1 teaspoon of almond extract for
the vanilla in Step 1. Spoon the dough into a
cookie press fitted with a flower plate.
Press the cookies onto ungreased baking
sheets. Garnish with ½ cup of sliced
almonds. Bake in the preheated hot oven
(400°) for 9 minutes, or until set and lightly
browned around the edges.

## Espresso Dreams

Bake at 400° for 8 to 9 minutes.
Makes 4 dozen cookies.

*Nutrient Value Per Cookie: 78 calories, 1 g protein, 5 g fat,
8 g carbohydrate, 25 mg sodium, 16 mg cholesterol.*

Preheat the oven to hot (400°). Prepare 1
recipe of Old-Fashioned Butter Cookies
*(recipe, page 173)* with the following
changes: Stir together 1½ teaspoons of
instant espresso powder and ½ teaspoon of

1. Old-Fashioned Butter Cookies
2. Almond Bites
3. Espresso Dreams
4. Apricot Thumbprints
5. Almond Crescents
6. Madeleines
7. Chocolate Ribbons
8. Peanut Butter Cookies
9. Chocolate Mint Bars
10. Pastel Creams
11. Lemon Pistachio Slices

ground cinnamon with the flour and the salt in Step 2. Wrap the dough; refrigerate for 45 minutes. Pour ½ cup of ground pecans, almonds or walnuts into a bowl. Shape the dough into 1-inch balls, roll in the nuts to coat and place on ungreased baking sheets. Flatten each to a ¼-inch thickness; garnish with a pecan half. Bake in the preheated hot oven (400°) for 8 to 9 minutes, or until set and lightly browned around the edges.

## Apricot Thumbprints

Bake at 400° for 9 to 10 minutes.
Makes 4 to 5 dozen cookies.

*Nutrient Value Per Cookie: 58 calories, 1 g protein, 3 g fat, 8 g carbohydrate, 28 mg sodium, 12 mg cholesterol.*

Preheat the oven to hot (400°). Prepare 1 recipe of Old-Fashioned Butter Cookies *(recipe, page 173)* with the following changes: Reduce the butter to ½ cup (1 stick). Beat together 4 ounces of cream cheese and 1 teaspoon of grated orange rind with the butter mixture in Step 1. Wrap the dough; refrigerate for 45 minutes. Shape into 1-inch balls, place them on ungreased baking sheets and flatten to a ¼-inch thickness. Make an indentation in each cookie with your thumb. Spoon ¼ teaspoon of apricot preserves into each indentation. Bake in the preheated hot oven (400°) for 9 to 10 minutes, or until set and lightly browned around the edges.

**Note:** *Cherry Bow Ties, Gumdrop Carnival Cookies and Question Mark Cookies are not pictured.*

# Almond Crescents

Bake at 400° for 8 to 9 minutes.
Makes 4 dozen crescents.

*Nutrient Value Per Crescent: 78 calories, 1 g protein, 5 g fat, 8 g carbohydrate, 25 mg sodium, 16 mg cholesterol.*

Preheat the oven to hot (400°). Prepare 1 recipe of Old-Fashioned Butter Cookies *(recipe, page 173)* with the following changes: Stir together ½ teaspoon of ground cinnamon, ½ teaspoon of ground nutmeg and ¼ teaspoon of ground allspice with the flour and the salt in Step 2. Wrap the dough and refrigerate for 45 minutes. Pour ½ cup of ground almonds, walnuts or pecans into a shallow bowl or pie plate. Shape the dough into 1-inch balls and roll in the nuts to coat. Place 2 inches apart on ungreased baking sheets. Flatten slightly and turn the ends down to form half-moon shapes. Bake in the preheated hot oven (400°) for 8 to 9 minutes. While still warm, but not hot, roll the crescents in *sifted* 10X (confectioners' powdered) sugar, if you wish. Roll again in 10X sugar when cool.

# Madeleines

Bake at 375° for 15 to 17 minutes.
Makes 21 to 24 cakes.

*Nutrient Value Per Cake: 149 calories, 2 g protein, 8 g fat, 18 g carbohydrate, 50 mg sodium, 32 mg cholesterol.*

Preheat the oven to moderate (375°). Prepare 1 recipe of Old-Fashioned Butter Cookies *(recipe, page 173)* with the following changes: Beat together 2 teaspoons of grated orange rind with the butter, sugar, egg and vanilla in Step 1. Do not chill the dough. Push the dough into individual molds in 2 small madeleine pans*. Smooth the tops even with the tops of the molds, using the flat side of a knife. Bake in the preheated moderate oven (375°)

for 15 to 17 minutes, or until the edges of the cakes are golden brown. Invert the cakes onto a wire rack to cool, fluted side up. Prepare the Glaze: Stir 2½ to 3 teaspoons of orange juice into ½ cup of 10X (confectioners' powdered) sugar in a small bowl until the glaze is a good spreading consistency. Brush the glaze over the madeleines. Garnish with diced candied orange peel, using about ¼ teaspoon for each madeleine.

*\*Note: A madeleine pan has 12 individual large or small molds shaped like a scallop shell. We used the large size. The pans are available in better department stores and in cookware specialty stores.*

# Chocolate Ribbons

Bake at 400° for 5 to 7 minutes.
Makes 6 dozen ribbons.

*Nutrient Value Per Ribbon: 67 calories, 1 g protein, 4 g fat, 7 g carbohydrate, 17 mg sodium, 11 mg cholesterol.*

Preheat the oven to hot (400°). Prepare 1 recipe of Old-Fashioned Butter Cookies *(recipe, page 173)* with the following changes: Add 3 ounces (3 squares) of semisweet chocolate, melted and cooled, to the butter mixture in Step 1. Spoon the dough into a cookie press fitted with a plate for ribbon strips. Press ribbons of dough, about 4 inches long, onto ungreased baking sheets. Bake in the preheated hot oven (400°) for 5 to 7 minutes, or until set and very lightly browned. Prepare the Chocolate Glaze: Heat together 6 ounces (6 squares) of semisweet chocolate and 1½ tablespoons of vegetable shortening in a small saucepan over low heat until melted and well combined. Dip the ends of the ribbons into the glaze, place the ribbons on wax paper or aluminum foil and let them stand until the glaze sets.

## Peanut Butter Cookies

Bake at 375° for 9 minutes.
Makes 3½ to 4 dozen cookies.

*Nutrient Value Per Cookie: 68 calories, 2 g protein, 4 g fat, 7 g carbohydrate, 40 mg sodium, 12 mg cholesterol.*

Preheat the oven to moderate (375°). Prepare 1 recipe of Old-Fashioned Butter Cookies *(recipe, page 173)* with the following changes: Reduce the butter to ½ cup (1 stick). Beat together ½ cup of creamy peanut butter and an additional ½ teaspoon of vanilla with the butter, sugar and egg in Step 1. Reduce the flour to 2 cups in Step 2. Do not chill the dough (it will dry out). Shape the dough into 1-inch balls and place 2 inches apart on ungreased baking sheets. Flatten to a ¼-inch thickness and make a crisscross pattern on the top of each cookie with the tines of a fork. Bake in the preheated moderate oven (375°) for 9 minutes, or until set and lightly browned around the edges.

## Chocolate Mint Bars

Bake at 400° for 18 to 20 minutes.
Makes 3 dozen bars.

*Nutrient Value Per Bar: 130 calories, 1 g protein, 7 g fat, 16 g carbohydrate, 39 mg sodium, 22 mg cholesterol.*

Preheat the oven to hot (400°). Prepare 1 recipe of Old-Fashioned Butter Cookies *(recipe, page 173)* with the following changes: Substitute 1 cup of firmly packed light brown sugar for the 10X (confectioners' powdered) sugar and add another ½ teaspoon of vanilla. Beat together with the butter and the egg in Step 1. Spread the dough in an ungreased 13 x 9 x 2-inch baking pan. Bake in the preheated hot oven (400°) for 18 to 20 minutes, or until set and lightly browned around the edges. While the dough is

baking, unwrap one 6- or 7-ounce package of individually wrapped crème de menthe wafer candies. Arrange the candies evenly over the top of the hot cake. Let stand for 5 minutes to soften. Spread the melted chocolate over the cake. Let stand until the frosting sets. Cut into 36 bars.

## Pastel Creams

Bake at 400° for 6 to 7 minutes.
Makes 3 dozen sandwiches.

*Nutrient Value Per Cookie: 235 calories, 3 g protein, 12 g fat, 30 g carbohydrate, 80 mg sodium, 47 mg cholesterol.*

Preheat the oven to hot (400°). Prepare 1 recipe of Old-Fashioned Butter Cookies *(recipe, page 173)* with the following changes: Add 6 drops of red food coloring to the butter mixture in Step 1. Shape the dough for *slice and bake cookies* in Step 3. Bake in the preheated hot oven (400°) for 6 to 7 minutes, or until set and lightly browned around the edges. Prepare the *Pink Cream Filling:* Stir together 1½ cups of 10X (confectioners' powdered) sugar, 2 tablespoons of melted butter, 3 to 4 drops of red food coloring and 1½ to 2 tablespoons of milk until smooth and a good spreading consistency. Spread filling on the flat side of half the cookies and top with the remaining cookies. Spoon the remaining filling into a pastry bag fitted with a small writing tip and pipe a spiral on top of each cookie.

## Lemon Pistachio Slices

Bake at 400° for 6 to 7 minutes.
Makes 5 dozen cookies.

*Nutrient Value Per Cookie: 77 calories, 1 g protein, 4 g fat, 9 g carbohydrate, 20 mg sodium, 13 mg cholesterol.*

Preheat the oven to hot (400°). Prepare 1 recipe of Old-Fashioned Butter Cookies *(recipe, page 173)* with the following changes: Beat together 1 tablespoon of grated lemon rind with the other ingredients in Step 1. Shape the dough for *slice and bake cookies* in Step 3. Bake in the preheated hot oven (400°) for 6 to 7 minutes, or until set and lightly browned around the edges. When cool, spread with the following glaze: Stir together 1½ cups of *un*sifted 10X (confectioners' powdered) sugar, 1 tablespoon of melted butter and up to 2 tablespoons of lemon juice to make a glaze with a good spreading consistency. Spread over the cookies. Sprinkle with chopped pistachio nuts, using about ⅔ cup in all.

---

## Food for Thought . . .

**Maraschino Cherries** *These decorative cherries are made from sweet, light colored cherries. They are bleached, pitted and steeped in a colored sugar syrup. Maraschino cherries here are unlike their European predecessors. Italians soak white, sweet cherries in a cherry liqueur called "maraschino," made from the marasca cherry. The French also soak cherries in a sugar syrup and call them maraschino. Americans developed their own recipe for making maraschino cherries based on the European techniques.*

### ◀◀ Cherry Bow Ties

Bake at 400° for 8 minutes.
Makes 5 dozen bow ties.

*Nutrient Value Per Bow Tie: 57 calories, 1 g protein, 3 g fat, 6 g carbohydrate, 20 mg sodium, 13 mg cholesterol.*

Preheat the oven to hot (400°). Prepare 1 recipe of Old-Fashioned Butter Cookies

*(recipe, page 173)* with the following changes: Shape the dough for *slice and bake cookies* in Step 3. Place the slices 1 inch apart on ungreased baking sheets. With your fingers, pinch together the top and bottom of each dough circle to make a bow tie shape. Press a drained maraschino cherry half or candied cherry half into the center of each bow tie. Bake in the preheated hot oven (400°) for 8 minutes, or until set and lightly browned around the edges.

### ◀◀ Question Mark Cookies

Bake at 400° for 10 to 11 minutes.
Makes 2 dozen cookies.

*Nutrient Value Per Cookie: 172 calories, 2 g protein, 10 g fat, 19 g carbohydrate, 50 mg sodium, 32 mg cholesterol.*

Preheat the oven to hot (400°). Prepare 1 recipe of Old-Fashioned Butter Cookies *(recipe, page 173)* with the following changes: Spoon the dough into a cookie press fitted with a ¾-inch star plate*. Press question marks, about 3 inches long, onto an ungreased baking sheet, adding an extra knob at each straight end for a question mark dot. Press a jelly candy into each knob (you'll need 2 dozen candies). Bake in the preheated hot oven (400°) for 10 to 11 minutes, or until set and lightly browned around the edges. When the cookies are cool, melt together 4 ounces (4 squares) of semisweet chocolate with 1 tablespoon of vegetable shortening in a small saucepan over low heat. Spread the curled half of each cookie with the chocolate. Place on wax paper and refrigerate for 10 to 15 minutes to set the glaze. Do not refrigerate the cookies; store them at room temperature.

***Note:** You can use a ½-inch star plate for a greater yield.*

## Food for Thought . . .

**Macadamia Nuts** *The edible seeds of silk oak trees that are native to Australia but now grow in Hawaii and California, macadamia nuts have a flavor similar to that of the Brazil nut. They are white, crisp, sweet and high in oil content.*

*Macadamia nuts have round shiny brown shells about an inch in diameter. Because they are very thick and difficult to crack, macadamia nuts seldom are sold in the shell. Most macadamia nuts are sold in cans shelled, roasted and salted.*

## Gumdrop Carnival Cookies

Bake at 400° for 7 to 9 minutes.
Makes 4 dozen cookies.

*Nutrient Value Per Cookie: 90 calories, 1 g protein, 4 g fat, 13 g carbohydrate, 27 mg sodium, 16 mg cholesterol.*

Preheat the oven to hot (400°). Prepare 1 recipe of Old-Fashioned Butter Cookies *(recipe, page 173)* with the following changes: Wrap the dough and chill in the refrigerator for 45 minutes. Spread ¼ cup of colored sugar crystals in a shallow dish, if you wish. Shape the dough into 1-inch balls, tucking a gumdrop into each ball (you'll need a total of 48 gumdrops). Roll the balls in the sugar crystals, if you wish. Bake in the preheated hot oven (400°) for 7 to 9 minutes, or until set and lightly browned around the edges.

## Macadamia Lace Cookies

Bake at 375° for 8 to 10 minutes.
Makes 2 to 2½ dozen cookies.

*Nutrient Value Per Cookie: 107 calories, 1 g protein, 7 g fat, 11 g carbohydrate, 6 mg sodium, 19 mg cholesterol.*

1    egg
½    teaspoon vanilla
½    cup (1 stick) unsalted butter, melted and cooled to room temperature
1    cup firmly packed light brown sugar
1½   cups old-fashioned rolled oats
1    jar (3½ ounces) macadamia nuts, chopped

1. Preheat the oven to moderate (375°). Line a baking sheet with aluminum foil and lightly butter the foil. Set aside.
2. Beat together the egg, vanilla and butter in a large bowl until smooth. Add the brown sugar and beat until smooth. Stir in the oats and the macadamia nuts.
3. Drop the batter by teaspoonfuls, 2 inches apart, onto the foil-lined baking sheet. Place no more than 6 cookies on the sheet. Press the batter flat.
4. Bake in the preheated moderate oven (375°) until golden brown around the edges, for about 8 to 10 minutes. Cool the cookies completely on the foil. Carefully peel away the foil. Repeat for all the cookies, cooling the baking sheet under cold water before reusing it.

## Food for Thought . . .

**Unsweetened Chocolate** *The basic chocolate from which all other chocolate products are made. Roasted cocoa beans are pressed until the cocoa butter liquefies; the resulting liquor is poured into molds to harden into 1-ounce cakes of chocolate. Semisweet chocolate is a blend of sugar, cocoa butter and unsweetened chocolate.*

## The Ultimate Brownie

Bake at 350° for 25 minutes.
Makes 24 squares.

*Nutrient Value Per Brownie: 248 calories, 3 g protein, 13 g fat, 33 g carbohydrate, 46 mg sodium, 59 mg cholesterol.*

1¾  **cups unsifted all-purpose flour**
¼  **teaspoon salt**
2  **cups sugar**
½  **cup (1 stick) unsalted butter or margarine, softened**
4  **eggs**
1  **teaspoon vanilla**
4  **squares (1 ounce each) unsweetened chocolate, melted and cooled**
1  **cup coarsely chopped, toasted walnuts***
  **Icing (recipe follows)**

1. Preheat the oven to moderate (350°). Grease a 15 x 10 x 1-inch jelly-roll pan.
2. Combine the flour and the salt in a small bowl. Set aside.
3. Beat together the sugar, butter or margarine, eggs and vanilla in a large bowl until well blended. Add the melted chocolate and blend thoroughly. Blend in the flour mixture. Stir in the walnuts. Spread the batter in the prepared pan.
4. Bake in the preheated moderate oven (350°) for 25 minutes, or until firm on top and the edges begin to pull away from the sides of the pan. Cool in the pan on a wire rack.
5. Prepare the Icing.
6. Spread the brownies with the Icing. Let stand until firm. Cut into 24 squares.

***Note:** To toast walnuts, spread them in a jelly-roll pan. Bake at 325°, stirring often, until browned, for about 20 minutes.*

***Icing:*** Beat together 1½ cups of *sifted* 10X (confectioners' powdered) sugar, 3 tablespoons of hot water, 2 squares (1 ounce each) of melted and cooled unsweetened chocolate, 2 tablespoons of melted butter, 2 teaspoons of light corn syrup and 1 teaspoon of vanilla in a small bowl. Beat until well blended and smooth. *Makes about 1 cup.*

---

### Food for Thought . . .

**Brownies** *An American original! Legend has it that the first brownies were salvaged from a fallen chocolate cake. Whatever their origin, these chewy bars are a favorite anytime.*

## Blondies

Bake at 350° for 35 minutes.
Makes 24 blondies.

*Nutrient Value Per Blondie: 231 calories, 2 g protein, 12 g fat, 29 g carbohydrate, 138 mg sodium, 44 mg cholesterol.*

2¼  **cups unsifted all-purpose flour**
1  **teaspoon baking powder**
¼  **teaspoon salt**
1  **cup (2 sticks) butter or margarine, softened**
2  **cups firmly packed light brown sugar**
2  **eggs**
2  **teaspoons vanilla**
1  **cup pecans, chopped**
1  **cup flaked coconut**

1. Preheat the oven to moderate (350°). Grease a 13 x 9 x 2-inch baking pan.
2. Stir together the flour, baking powder and salt in a small bowl until well mixed. Set aside.
3. Beat together the butter or margarine and the brown sugar in a large bowl until light and fluffy. Beat in the eggs, one at a time, until well blended. Mix in the vanilla. Stir in the flour mixture until well blended. Fold in the pecans and the coconut until well mixed. Spread the batter evenly with a rubber spatula in the prepared pan.
4. Bake in the preheated moderate oven (350°) for 35 minutes, or until the top springs back when lightly touched with your fingertip. Cool in the pan on a wire rack. Cut into 24 blondies.

# Pies, Tarts & Fruits

## Lattice Cherry Pie

*You can use the flaky pie crust recipe with our fresh cherry filling — or any fruit filling you like.*

Bake at 400° for 40 to 45 minutes.
Makes 8 servings.

*Nutrient Value Per Serving: 557 calories, 6 g protein, 27 g fat, 75 g carbohydrate, 46 mg sodium, 34 mg cholesterol.*

2⅔  **cups all-purpose flour**
     **Pinch of salt**
  1  **cup vegetable shortening**
  7  **to 8 tablespoons cold lemon-lime soda**
      **OR: cold water**
     **Fresh Cherry Filling (recipe,**
      **page 182) OR: 1 can (21 ounces)**
      **cherry pie filling**
  1  **egg, beaten with a pinch of salt**

### CRUMBLING CRUST

*If the edge of your pie crust crumbles, break off the entire edge and, when ready to serve, pipe a pretty border of whipped cream around the edge. This trick works well with pies that are to be served cold or at room temperature. A warm pie will melt the whipped cream.*

1. Combine the flour and the salt in a medium-size bowl. Add the shortening and blend with a pastry blender or two knives until the mixture resembles bread crumbs.
2. Slowly add the soda or water (soda makes a flakier crust), mixing with a fork just until the dough forms a ball that leaves the side of the bowl. If necessary, add 1 to 2 teaspoons more liquid.
3. Divide the dough in half. Shape each half into a flattened ball. Wrap in plastic wrap and refrigerate for 1 hour.
4. Preheat the oven to hot (400°).
5. Roll out half the dough to a 14-inch circle on a lightly floured surface, with a lightly floured rolling pin. Loosely fold the circle in quarters, place in the center of a 10-inch pie pan and unfold. Gently ease the dough around the pan, using a floured ball of dough to work the circle into the bottom edge of the pan.
6. Place the Fresh Cherry Filling or canned pie filling in the bottom crust.
7. Roll out the remaining dough to an 11-inch round. Cut into fourteen ½-inch-wide strips, using a pastry wheel or a knife.
8. Place 7 strips horizontally and 7 strips vertically across the filling, to make a lattice. Cut the ends to fit the pan. Fold the bottom crust edge over the strips to

*(from top, left to right) Fresh Strawberries in Liqueur, Fresh Kiwi Slices in Liqueur, Fresh Raspberries in Liqueur (recipes, page 191); Blueberry Cream Tartlet, Strawberry Cream Tartlet, Kiwi Cream Tartlet, Raspberry Cream Tartlet (recipes, page 182); Lattice Cherry Pie (recipe, page 180); Blueberry Spice Muffins (recipe, page 37), Peach Pecan Muffins (recipe, page 38)*

make a high edge. Pinch to seal, then flute the edge all around. Brush the edge and the lattice with the beaten egg and salt.

9. Bake in the preheated hot oven (400°) for 40 to 45 minutes, or until the crust is brown and the filling bubbles up. Cool the pie on a wire rack. Serve warm or at room temperature.

***Fresh Cherry Filling:*** Wash, drain and pit 4 cups of fresh sour cherries. Place in a large bowl and sprinkle with 2 tablespoons of kirsch. Combine 3 tablespoons of quick-cooking tapioca and 1¼ cups of sugar in a small bowl and gently mix into the cherries. Let stand for 15 minutes. Stir and taste the juices, adding a few drops of red food coloring, if you wish, and more sugar, if necessary. Cool the filling completely before spooning into the bottom crust. *Makes enough for one 10-inch pie.*

## DARK EDGES

*If your pie's edges are baking faster than the rest of the pie, take a sheet of aluminum foil slightly larger than the pie and fold it in half. Cut out a semicircle the same diameter as the pie filling. Unfold the leftover rim of foil, place it over the edge of the crust and continue baking the pie.*

## Fresh Fruit Tartlets

*This rich, lemon-scented dough complements any fruit.*

Bake at 400° for 10 minutes.
Makes about 2 dozen tartlets.

*Nutrient Value Per Serving: 321 calories, 6 g protein, 12 g fat, 46 g carbohydrate, 103 mg sodium, 163 mg cholesterol.*

- **4    cups all-purpose flour**
- **1    cup (2 sticks) butter or margarine**
- **4    egg yolks, slightly beaten**
- **1    tablespoon water**
- **¼    teaspoon grated lemon rind**
- **1    cup sugar**
  **Pastry Cream (recipe, page 183)**
  **Cut-up strawberries and peaches, whole raspberries, blackberries or blueberries, sliced kiwifruit**
  **Clear Glaze (recipe follows)**
  **Finely chopped blanched almonds**

1. Place the flour in a large bowl. Add the butter or margarine and knead into the flour with your fingertips until the mixture resembles bread crumbs. Make a well in the center.
2. Mix together the egg yolks, water, lemon rind and sugar; place in the well.
3. Start incorporating the flour into the yolk mixture, working it in gradually so the dough will be smooth. (The dough should be made quickly with a minimum of handling, to make a tender crust.)
4. Roll out the dough to a ¼-inch thickness on a lightly floured surface. Cut out dough rounds with a 3-inch fluted round cutter and place in individual tartlet pans. Prick holes all over the rounds with a fork. Line the pans with aluminum foil and fill with raw beans or rice. (This process, called "baking blind," prevents the dough from shrinking during baking.)
5. Meanwhile, preheat the oven to hot (400°).
6. Bake in the preheated hot oven (400°) for 5 minutes, or until the dough is set. Remove the foil and the beans or rice. Continue baking the tartlet shells for 5

minutes more, or until the dough is light brown. Cool the shells completely on wire racks.

7. Fill the shells with a small amount of the Pastry Cream, then top with your choice of cut-up fruit. Carefully brush with the Clear Glaze. Adhere the finely chopped almonds to the border of each tartlet.

*Clear Glaze:* Combine 1 cup of water and ¾ cup of sugar in a small saucepan. Cook over medium heat, stirring frequently, until the sugar dissolves. Remove the saucepan from the heat. Stir in ½ cup of kirsch or white rum. *Makes enough for 2 dozen tartlets.*

# Pastry Cream

Makes about 1 quart.

- *1   quart milk*
- *1   vanilla bean, sliced in half*
- *1   cup all-purpose flour*
- *1   cup sugar*
- *8   egg yolks*

1. Heat the milk and the vanilla bean in a medium-size saucepan over medium heat until the mixture begins to boil. Remove the saucepan from the heat.
2. Blend the flour, sugar and egg yolks in a medium-size bowl. Gradually pour in the hot milk mixture, stirring constantly with a wire whisk. Return the mixture to the saucepan. Place the saucepan over medium heat.
3. Bring the mixture to boiling over medium heat, stirring rapidly with a whisk and cooking only until the cream is thick and smooth.
4. Immediately pour the pastry cream through a fine sieve into a shallow container. Cover the surface directly with plastic wrap (this prevents a skin from forming on the top). Refrigerate to cool completely. Beat with a wire whisk to lighten before spooning the pastry cream into the tartlet shells.

## DOUGHS AND DON'TS

*Here are a few tips to help make your pastry flaky, light and picture-perfect.*
- *Handle pastry dough as little as possible; unlike bread dough, pastry dough that is overhandled will become tough. As soon as the dough holds together, form a ball, divide it in half and shape one half into a round about 1 inch high on a lightly floured pastry cloth. Roll out the round to the size specified in the recipe. Repeat with the remaining dough.*
- *Always roll dough from the center to the edge so that the crust will be even in size and thickness. As you roll out the dough, turn it gently to prevent sticking.*
- *Use the pie plate as a size guide. Turn it upside-down on the rolled dough and check the dough size for additional rolling needed. As a general rule, it's best to roll out the dough 2 inches larger than the pie plate.*
- *Fold the rolled pastry in half over the rolling pin, lay one half over the pie plate to help center it and flip the other half over the rest of the pie plate.*
- *Be sure to fit the dough loosely in the pie plate. If the dough is stretched taut, it will shrink during baking and break.*
- *For lattice pies as well as pastry shells, turn under the edges of the dough and pinch them to form a stand-up edge. There is no need to seal in the juices as there is with most two-crust pies.*
- *The trimmings from pastry can be rerolled, cut and sprinkled with sugar and cinnamon for an extra treat.*
- *To catch any runovers during baking, place a sheet of aluminum foil on the oven rack below the pie.*

# A PLAN FOR PERFECT PASTRY

## Starting From Scratch

**1.** Cut the cold vegetable shortening into the all-purpose flour and salt in a large bowl with a pastry blender or two knives. Keep cutting in the vegetable shortening until the mixture is crumbly and the shortening is evenly distributed. *Note: This step is crucial to insure a light and flaky pastry after baking.*

**2.** Stir in the ice-cold water, 1 tablespoon at a time, with a fork, adding just enough water to moisten the mixture.

**3.** Keep mixing the dough with a fork, just until the pastry forms a ball that leaves the side of the mixing bowl clean. Divide the ball in half.

**4.** Fit a stocking onto your rolling pin and sprinkle flour over your pastry cloth. *Note: A set of stocking and pastry cloth is not expensive and can be found in the housewares department of most stores.*

**5.** Flour the pastry cloth lightly by sprinkling flour on the cloth and rolling pin over the cloth to coat both evenly.

**6.** Shape the pastry for the bottom crust into a 1-inch-thick round and place the ball on the pastry cloth. Start from the center and roll the pastry evenly with a circular motion, so the pastry will retain its circular shape, to the desired diameter. As you roll out the dough, turn it gently to prevent it from sticking. Use a pie plate for a good size guide, turning the plate upside down on the rolled dough. Check the size of the dough to see if additional rolling is needed.

**7.** Using the pastry cloth, lift and fold the rolled out pastry at the center of the circle over the rolling pin and transfer the pastry to the pie plate. Be careful not to tear the dough.

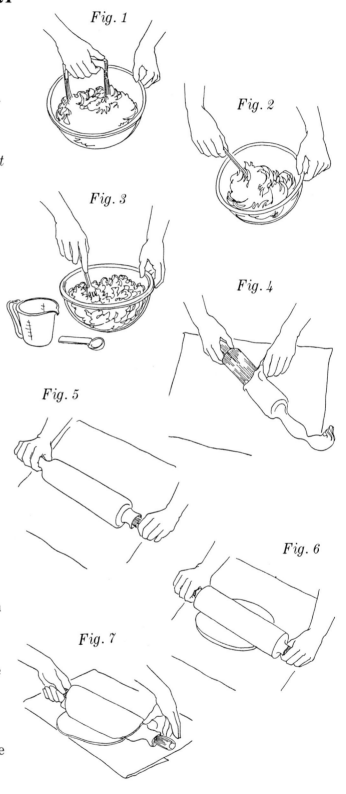

Fig. 1

Fig. 2

Fig. 3

Fig. 4

Fig. 5

Fig. 6

Fig. 7

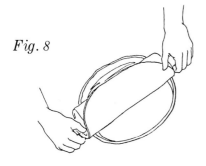

*Fig. 8*

*Fig. 9*

8. Gently unroll the pastry into the pie plate. Be sure to fit the dough loosely in the pie plate. If the dough is stretched too much, it will shrink during the baking and break.

**9.** Trim the edge of the pastry to ½ inch and roll the edge with your fingers to make a smooth edge. Choose any of the edges on the next page to add the finishing touch to your pastry.

## The Winning Edge

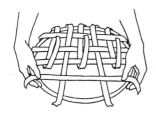

*Lattice Top* Roll the remaining half of the Flaky Pastry dough or other dough being used, to a 12 x 8-inch rectangle. Cut the rectangle lengthwise into ½-inch strips. Weave the strips into a lattice over the pie filling. Trim the overhang even with the bottom crust; pinch to seal the edge. Turn the sealed edge *under* and pinch again to make a stand-up edge; flute.
*Note: You may find it easier to weave the lattice on a piece of wax paper or heavy-duty aluminum foil, and then place it over the filling. Also, using a pastry wheel will make pretty, unusually-shaped lattice strips.*

*Rope Edge* Press the pie rim firmly between the thumb and forefinger of your right hand, pressing down and to the right with your thumb. Continue pressing, turning the pie clockwise as you do, until the entire rim is finished.
*Note: Lefthanded people should reverse hands.*

*Scalloped Edge* Place your left thumb and forefinger on the outside of the pie rim. With a teaspoon, press the inside of the rim between your fingers, forming a large, rounded scallop. Repeat the scallops about every inch around the pastry rim.

---

## Food for Thought . . .

**Rhubarb** *Rhubarb is the stems of a hardy vegetable, native to Mongolia, that is used like a fruit. Only the rhubarb stems or stalks are edible; the large, green leaves are poisonous.*

*Fresh rhubarb is marketed from February to June. Buy fresh, firm, crisp stalks that are either pink or cherry red in color. Refrigerate them and use as soon as possible. One pound of fresh rhubarb will yield about 2 cups cooked.*

---

## Strawberry Rhubarb Pie

Bake at 400° for 50 to 60 minutes.
Makes 8 servings.

*Nutrient Value Per Serving: 402 calories, 3 g protein, 18 g fat, 56 g carbohydrate, 304 mg sodium, 10 mg cholesterol.*

1    **package (11 ounces) pie crust mix**
1    **cup sugar**
1/3  **cup all-purpose flour**
     **Grated rind of 1 orange**
2½   **cups fresh strawberries**
2½   **cups cut fresh or frozen rhubarb, thawed**
¼    **cup orange juice**
1    **tablespoon butter**

1. Prepare the pie crust mix following the package directions. Shape the pastry into a ball. Wrap in wax paper and refrigerate for 30 minutes.
2. Preheat the oven to hot (400°).
3. Divide the pastry in half. Roll out one half to a 12-inch circle on a lightly floured surface. Fit into a 9-inch pie plate.
4. Combine the sugar, flour and orange rind in a large bowl. Toss with the strawberries, rhubarb and orange juice. Scrape into the bottom crust. Dot with the butter.
5. Roll out the remaining pastry to an 11-

inch circle. Place over the filling. Seal the edges, trim and flute. Cut slits in the top crust for vents.
6. Bake in the preheated hot oven (400°) for 50 to 60 minutes, or until the top is nicely browned. If the edges brown too quickly, cover them with aluminum foil. Cool on a wire rack. Serve at room temperature.

---

## Strawberry Kropsua

*This Finnish dessert pancake will collapse as soon as it emerges from the oven, so don't be alarmed. After standing a few minutes, the pancake's custardlike interior becomes even tastier. You may substitute your favorite fruit preserves for the Strawberry Topping, if you wish.*

Bake at 425° for 20 minutes.
Makes 6 servings.

*Nutrient Value Per Serving: 254 calories, 8 g protein, 7 g fat, 39 g carbohydrate, 165 mg sodium, 148 mg cholesterol.*

**Strawberry Topping:**
1    **pint strawberries, rinsed and hulled**
2    **to 3 tablespoons granulated sugar**
1    **tablespoon brandy OR: red wine**
½    **teaspoon vanilla**

**Kropsua (Pancake):**
3    **eggs**
¼    **cup granulated sugar**
¼    **teaspoon salt**
2    **cups milk**
1    **teaspoon vanilla**
1    **cup unsifted all-purpose flour**
1    **teaspoon vegetable oil**
1    **tablespoon 10X (confectioners' powdered) sugar**
     **Thin curls of lemon peel, for garnish (optional)**

1. Prepare the Strawberry Topping: Cut the strawberries in half and place in a bowl. Add the sugar, brandy or wine and the vanilla. Stir until the sugar dissolves. Cover the bowl and set aside.
2. Preheat the oven to hot (425°).
3. Place a 9- or 10-inch well-seasoned cast iron skillet in the preheated hot oven (425°) for 10 minutes.

4. Meanwhile, prepare the Kropsua: Beat together the eggs, sugar and salt in a large bowl with an electric mixer. Beat in the milk and the vanilla. Gradually whisk in the flour until the batter is smooth and well blended.

5. Using a pot holder, remove the preheated skillet from the oven and brush with the oil. Pour in the batter.

6. Bake in the preheated hot oven (425°) for 20 minutes, or until the Kropsua is puffed and golden. Remove the skillet to a wire rack and let stand for 10 minutes. Dust the Kropsua with the 10X (confectioners' powdered) sugar, sprinkling through a sieve. Serve hot with the Strawberry Topping. Garnish with thin curls of lemon peel, if you wish.

# Lime Chiffon Pie

Bake crust at 400° for 25 to 30 minutes.
Makes 8 servings.

*Nutrient Value Per Serving: 284 calories, 6 g protein, 12 g fat, 39 g carbohydrate, 201 mg sodium, 159 mg cholesterol.*

### Pie Crust:
1    cup unsifted all-purpose flour
2    teaspoons sugar
1/4  teaspoon salt
6    tablespoons cold butter
4    to 5 tablespoons ice water

### Lime Filling:
1    envelope unflavored gelatin
1/2  cup cold water
4    egg yolks
1    cup sugar
1/2  cup lime juice (4 to 6 limes)
1    tablespoon grated lime rind
2    drops green food coloring (optional)
6    egg whites

    Strips of lime peel, for garnish

1. Prepare the Pie Crust: Combine the flour, sugar and salt in a medium-size

bowl. Cut in the butter with a pastry blender until the butter is the size of peas. Add the ice water, a tablespoon at a time, stirring with a fork until the dough forms a ball. Wrap in plastic wrap and refrigerate for 30 minutes.

2. Preheat the oven to hot (400°).

3. Roll out the dough to an 11-inch circle on a lightly floured surface. Fit the circle into a 9-inch pie plate. Trim and flute the edges and prick the bottom and the sides with a fork. Line the bottom and the sides of the crust with aluminum foil. Weight down the foil with 3 cups of dried beans or uncooked rice.

4. Bake in the preheated hot oven (400°) for 20 minutes. Remove the foil and the beans or rice. Bake for 5 to 10 minutes more, or until the crust is golden brown. Cool the crust completely on a wire rack.

5. Prepare the Lime Filling: Sprinkle the gelatin over 1/4 cup of the cold water in a small bowl. Let stand to soften for at least 2 minutes. Mix together the egg yolks, 1/2 cup of the sugar, the lime juice and the remaining 1/4 cup of cold water in a small saucepan. Bring just to boiling over medium heat, stirring constantly. Immediately remove from the heat. Add the softened gelatin and stir until completely dissolved, for about 1 minute. Add the lime rind, and food coloring, if you wish. Pour the lime mixture into a bowl. Chill, stirring every 15 minutes, for 45 minutes, or until it is the consistency of unbeaten egg whites. Remove from the refrigerator. (If the mixture becomes too firm, place the bowl in a larger bowl of hot water for a few seconds.)

6. Beat the egg whites in a large bowl with an electric mixer until soft peaks form. Gradually beat in the remaining 1/2 cup of sugar, 1 tablespoon at a time. Continue beating until stiff, shiny peaks form. Thoroughly mix about 1 cup of the beaten egg whites into the lime mixture. Gently fold in the remaining egg whites. Spoon into the prepared pie crust. Refrigerate for at least 5 hours, or overnight. Garnish with lime peel, if you wish.

## Food for Thought . . .

*Orange* This popular citrus fruit probably originated in southern Asia or China. The Spanish introduced oranges to Florida in the 16th century and to California in the 18th century. Oranges are classified into three types: sweet, sour and mandarin. There are numerous varieties within each type.

Sweet oranges are the most popular for general eating because the pulp is sweet and juicy. The best known varieties include navel, Valencia, Jaffa and blood oranges. The navel orange is seedless and available in quantity from November to May. Valencia oranges are shipped from Florida, February to June, and from California from late April to October. Jaffa and blood oranges are in season from mid-March to May. Blood oranges have a red or red and white streaked pulp. Hamlin is an excellent juice orange from Florida, available October to December.

Fresh oranges are available every month of the year, although the peak supply is in the market from December to March. Choose oranges that are heavy for their size. Skin color is not an indication of ripeness, because some ripe oranges have a tinge of green. Some oranges are artificially dyed to improve their appearance; such fruit must be stamped "color added." Oranges are sold by weight or piece.

Oranges will last at room temperature for up to a week. However, for best results, store them in the vegetable compartment or in a plastic bag in the refrigerator.

Oranges are an excellent source of vitamin C. A 2½-inch tangerine contains 46 calories; a 3½-inch navel orange contains 87 calories.

---

### Orange Math

- 2 to 4 medium-size oranges = 1 cup of juice
- 1 medium-size orange = 4 teaspoons of grated rind
- 1 medium-size tangerine = 3 to 4 tablespoons of juice or 2 to 3 teaspoons of grated rind

---

## Caramel Oranges

Bake at 325° for 1 hour.
Makes 6 servings.

*Nutrient Value Per Serving: 286 calories, 1 g protein, 0 g fat, 79 g carbohydrate, 15 mg sodium, 0 mg cholesterol.*

| | |
|---|---|
| 3 | **large navel oranges, unpeeled** |
| 2 | **teaspoons salt** |
| ⅔ | **cup water** |
| 1½ | **cups sugar** |
| ⅓ | **cup light corn syrup** |
| ⅓ | **cup white wine vinegar** |
| | **Sweetened whipped cream OR: vanilla ice cream (optional)** |

1. Place the whole oranges in a saucepan. Cover with cold water and stir in the salt. Bring to boiling and boil for 30 minutes. Drain well. Return the oranges to the saucepan, cover with cold water and let stand for 30 minutes. Drain and let stand until completely cool, for 30 minutes.
2. Preheat the oven to slow (325°).
3. Combine the ⅔ cup of water with the sugar, corn syrup and vinegar in a large saucepan. Bring to boiling. Lower the heat and simmer for 5 minutes. Cut each orange crosswise into 6 slices and add to the syrup. Increase the heat and boil for 15 minutes (do not let the mixture become too thick).

4. Pour the oranges and the syrup into a 15 x 10 x 1-inch jelly-roll pan.
5. Bake in the preheated slow oven (325°) for 1 hour. Cool. Serve chilled with whipped cream or vanilla ice cream, if you wish.

## Piña Colada Bundles

Toast coconut at 350° for 7 to 9 minutes. Makes 8 servings.

*Nutrient Value Per Serving: 250 calories, 7 g protein, 8 g fat, 38 g carbohydrate, 96 mg sodium, 116 mg cholesterol.*

**Crêpes:**
3   eggs
1   cup milk
⅔   cup unsifted all-purpose flour
1   teaspoon vanilla

**Coconut Rum Sauce:**
1½  cups shredded coconut
2   cups milk
4   teaspoons cornstarch
1   tablespoon dark rum
¼   cup sugar
½   teaspoon vanilla

1   can (20 ounces) crushed pineapple in unsweetened pineapple juice, drained
8   strips string licorice candy (each 8 inches long)

1. Prepare the Crêpes: Combine the eggs, milk, flour and vanilla in the container of an electric blender or a food processor. Cover and whirl until smooth. Pour into a medium-size bowl.
2. Preheat the oven to moderate (350°).
3. Heat a 10-inch nonstick skillet (with an 8-inch bottom surface) over medium-high heat. Pour a scant ¼ cup of the batter into the pan, swirling the pan as you pour to coat the bottom evenly with the batter. The crêpe should set at once. Cook until the surface looks dry and the edges are lightly browned. Turn over. Cook for 30 seconds more, or until lightly browned. Turn out onto a plate. Repeat to make 8 crêpes, stirring the batter occasionally. Stack the crêpes.
4. Prepare the Coconut Rum Sauce: Toast the coconut on a baking sheet in the preheated moderate oven (350°) for 7 to 9 minutes, or until well toasted. Reserve ½ cup. Combine the remaining coconut with the milk in a medium-size saucepan. Bring to boiling. Remove from the heat, cover the saucepan and let stand for 30 minutes. Strain through a fine sieve. Return the milk to the saucepan and discard the coconut in the sieve. Dissolve the cornstarch in the rum in a small cup. Stir into the milk. Add the sugar. Bring to boiling over medium-high heat, stirring constantly with a whisk. Cook for 1 minute. Remove from the heat. Stir in the vanilla. Set aside, uncovered.
5. Mix together the pineapple, the reserved ½ cup of coconut and 2 tablespoons of the Coconut Rum Sauce in a bowl. Place about 2 tablespoons of the pineapple mixture in the center of each crêpe. Bring the crêpe edges up around the filling and tie into a bundle with a string of licorice.
6. For each serving, pour a scant ¼ cup of the sauce on an individual dessert plate. Place a bundle in the center.

### Food for Thought . . .

**Cornstarch** *A fine, white powder ground from the endosperm, or starchy portion, of a corn kernel, cornstarch is used as a thickener in puddings, gravies and sauces. It also is used in baking cakes and some cookies.*

## Fresh Fruits in Liqueur

*Use as a topping for ice cream, ice cream-filled crêpes or pancakes. Or serve icy cold with a swirl of lightly whipped cream.*

Makes 8 servings.

*Ingredients vary too much to provide nutrient analysis.*

This is a flexible recipe, depending on the fruit or combination of fruits you have on hand. Use whole berries, washed and hulled if necessary (raspberries and blueberries are a delicious team); peeled and sliced kiwifruit, peaches, nectarines or plums; peeled and sectioned oranges; mango or papaya slices; pineapple spears or fans. Place about 4 cups of cut-up fruit in a glass jar or bowl. Pour about 1 cup of liqueur over. Tart fruit may require the addition of sugar. Toss the fruit gently and refrigerate for at least 1 hour to let the flavors blend. Some suggested combinations: cassis on berries; rum and Grand Marnier on peaches; kirsch and peach-flavored liqueur on peaches or nectarines.

### Food for Thought . . .

***Blackberries*** *Commonly found in most of the Northern Hemisphere, blackberries grow wild on long, prickly stems (canes) along the edges of woods and in fields. The purplish-black berries become plump and juicy when they ripen in late summer and early fall. Ripe berries should detach easily from the stem when picked.*

*The blackberries found in the market from May to August almost all are cultivated. Look for bright, plump, firm berries. Check to see that there are no stains on the cartons, indicating crushed or bruised fruit. The berries should be free from dirt or any adhering caps, and from mold or decay. Very soft berries are overripe; blackberries with a red hue are hard and underripe. Use fresh berries within 2 days. Store them, unwashed, in the refrigerator.*

*Wash blackberries in a bowl of cold water just before using; do not soak the berries. Use your hands to gently lift the berries out of the water to avoid crushing them. Drain them on paper toweling.*

### Food for Thought . . .

***Raspberries*** *Red raspberries are the most familiar type, but there are black, amber, yellow and purple raspberries as well. Red and black raspberries are found growing wild in many parts of the country; the other varieties generally are grown in home gardens. The only type grown commercially are red raspberries. Because they bruise easily, raspberries must be harvested carefully by hand, which contributes to their expense when marketed fresh.*

*Fresh raspberries are in the market from mid-April to November, with peak supplies available in June and July. Select berries that are firm, brightly colored and well-shaped. Before storing raspberries, sort them and place them in a single layer in a pan lined with paper toweling. Refrigerate the berries and use them within 2 days.*

*Wash raspberries in a bowl of cold water just before using; do not soak the berries. Use your hands to gently lift the berries out of the water to avoid crushing them. Drain the berries on paper toweling.*

## Food for Thought . . .

**Blueberries** *Small, dark purple berries with very small seeds, blueberries are the fruit of a bush found in North America, Europe and Asia. In some parts of America they are called huckleberries, although huckleberries actually are a wild variety of blueberry found throughout New England, Pennsylvania and Virginia. They are also known as "bilberries," "whinberries" and "whortleberries"—but they're all varieties of the blueberry.*

*Fresh blueberries are marketed from May to August. Buy plump, firm berries that are uniform in size. Blueberries sometimes are covered with a waxy, white bloom that is a natural protective coating. A dull appearance or soft, juicy berries indicate old berries. Blueberries have a short refrigerator life—1 to 2 days—so use them quickly after purchasing; they also can be frozen.*

### LUSCIOUS LIQUEURS

**Cassis** *is a liqueur made from black currants. Crème de cassis is a sweeter version of cassis. One part cassis mixed with 8 parts chilled, dry white wine makes a refreshing drink.*

**Grand Marnier** *is an orange-flavored liqueur. It is quite sweet, with a strong taste, and therefore generally is served after a meal with coffee, or over ice cream or pound cake as a sauce.*

**Kirsch** *is a colorless liqueur distilled from the fermented juice and pits of small black cherries. Kirsch often is used in cheese fondues and desserts.*

# Tulip Cups with Strawberries and Zabaglione

**It's important to add the ingredients in the order indicated and to stir with a wooden spoon. This recipe actually makes 9 tulip cups—just in case one crumbles.**

Bake tulips at 400° for 6 to 8 minutes.
Makes 8 servings.

*Nutrient Value Per Serving: 181 calories, 3 g protein, 7 g fat, 27 g carbohydrate, 82 mg sodium, 105 mg cholesterol.*

### *Nonstick vegetable cooking spray*

**Tulip Cups:**
2   egg whites
½   cup sugar
½   teaspoon vanilla
    Pinch salt
¼   cup (½ stick) butter, melted
⅓   cup unsifted all-purpose flour
1   tablespoon water

**Zabaglione:**
3   egg yolks
¼   cup sugar
¼   cup orange-flavored liqueur
1   tablespoon water

2   pints strawberries, washed, hulled and cut in half

1. Preheat the oven to hot (400°). Spray four 15½ x 10½ x 1-inch jelly-roll pans with nonstick vegetable cooking spray. Trace two 6-inch circles, 2 inches apart, on each pan.
2. Prepare the Tulip Cups: Mix together the egg whites, sugar, vanilla and salt in a bowl with a wooden spoon. Stir in the melted butter (it should be very warm). Add the flour, stirring until well mixed. Add the water and stir until smooth. The batter will be thin.
3. Spoon 2 tablespoons of the batter in the center of each circle on one pan; the batter will spread while baking. Bake only 2 Tulip Cups, or crêpes, at a time.
4. Bake in the preheated hot oven (400°) for 6 to 8 minutes, or until the crêpes have a 1½-inch brown edge. Immediately

## Food for Thought . . .

**Strawberries** *The luscious strawberries we indulge in today originally were cultivated from North and South American species during the 18th and 19th centuries. They are a hybrid of a Virginia wild strawberry that was taken to Europe in the 17th century, and of a plump red berry cultivated by the Indians of Chile. French explorers returned to their homeland with the strawberry plants from Chile. The Chilean berry was crossed with the wild Virginia berry and the descendants of those hybrids were brought to America in the mid-19th century.*

*Strawberry plants actually belong to the rose family. The plants will grow wild in temperate zones, and Europeans prefer the wild berry, called the Alpine strawberry, to the cultivated varieties. The French call those tiny, wild berries fraises des bois, or "strawberries of the woods."*

*Strawberries are an excellent source of vitamin C, contain iron and are low in calories. One cup of fresh, whole strawberries has only about 60 calories.*

*Fresh strawberries are marketed year-round in major cities, but are most plentiful in May and June. Look for fully ripened, bright red berries (strawberries do not ripen after being picked). Use strawberries as soon as possible after purchase. To store the berries, remove them from their container and arrange them in a single layer on a baking sheet or other shallow pan for refrigeration. They will keep for several days in the refrigerator. Never wash strawberries or remove their caps before storing.*

*Strawberries are delicate and require gentle handling. To wash them, place the berries in a colander or large strainer and rinse with a gentle spray of cool water. Remove the caps after washing, if the recipe so directs, and gently pat the berries dry with paper toweling. Serve strawberries whole, halved or sliced.*

### Strawberry Math

- *1 pint of strawberries = 3¼ cups of whole berries or 2¼ cups of sliced berries*
- *1 bag (20 ounces) of frozen strawberries = 4 cups of whole berries or 2½ cups of sliced berries*
- *1 package (10 ounces) of frozen sliced strawberries = 1¼ cups of berries in syrup*

remove from the pan with a metal spatula sprayed with nonstick vegetable cooking spray. To form the Cups: Place each crêpe on an inverted glass or Styrofoam® cup measuring 3 to 3½ inches high, with a 1¾- to 2-inch base. Then place a small bowl (4- to 5-inch diameter) over each crêpe. Remove the Cups to a wire rack to cool. The Tulip Cups can be made ahead and stored in an airtight container at room temperature, or in the freezer.

5. Prepare the Zabaglione: Combine the egg yolks, sugar, liqueur and water in the top of a double boiler. Place over barely simmering (*not* boiling) water. Cook, stirring constantly and vigorously with a whisk or electric hand mixer, for 3 to 5 minutes, or until the mixture is thick and smooth and mounds when dropped from a spoon. (The mixture will be very foamy and thin at first.) Immediately pour into a bowl. Use warm, or refrigerate for up to 3 hours.

6. Fill each Tulip Cup with about ½ cup of the strawberries. Spoon the Zabaglione over the top. Serve immediately.

# Cool Sensations

⟪⟪ ⵘ

## Irish Coffee Mousse with Praline

Makes 6 servings.

*Nutrient Value Per Serving: 408 calories, 9 g protein, 25 g fat, 35 g carbohydrate, 73 mg sodium, 197 mg cholesterol.*

*Praline:*
**Butter**
½   **cup sugar**
2   **tablespoons water**
½   **cup blanched whole almonds**

*Mousse:*
1   **cup milk**
2½  **tablespoons instant espresso granules**
1   **envelope unflavored gelatin**
3   **tablespoons Irish whiskey**
1   **teaspoon vanilla**
3   **eggs, separated**
6   **tablespoons sugar**
1   **cup heavy cream**

1. Prepare the Praline: Butter a baking sheet well. Combine the sugar and the water in a small, heavy saucepan. Cook over high heat, stirring just until the sugar dissolves. Continue cooking, without stirring, until the sugar begins to turn light brown. Add the almonds and cook until the mixture is medium brown. Quickly pour onto the prepared baking sheet. Let cool and harden, for about 1 hour. Break the praline into large pieces. Process in the container of a food processor until broken into small pieces, about ⅛ inch. Or place the praline in a plastic bag and crush with a rolling pin. Set aside in an airtight container.
2. Prepare the Mousse: Combine the milk and the instant espresso in a medium-size saucepan. Warm over medium heat, stirring to dissolve the instant espresso. Remove from the heat.
3. Sprinkle the gelatin over the Irish whiskey and the vanilla in a small bowl. Let stand to soften, for about 5 minutes.
4. Beat the egg yolks and 4 tablespoons of the sugar in a medium-size bowl until creamy, for 1 minute. Stir in a little of the hot milk mixture, then stir the egg yolk mixture into the saucepan. Cook over medium-low heat, stirring constantly, until the mixture thickens slightly and coats a metal spoon, for about 6 minutes; do not boil. Add the softened gelatin mixture. Cook for 1 minute, stirring constantly, until the gelatin dissolves. Strain into a large bowl. Set aside.
5. Beat the egg whites in a medium-size bowl until foamy. Add the remaining 2 tablespoons of sugar, beating until stiff peaks form. Fold into the warm custard. Set the bowl into a larger bowl of ice and water. Let the mixture cool, stirring gently every 2 to 3 minutes, until thick and almost set, for 10 minutes.
6. Beat the cream in a small bowl until stiff. Fold into the custard mixture.
7. Spoon about ¼ cup of the mousse into each of six wine or parfait glasses. Sprinkle 1 teaspoon of the praline mixture over the mousse. Repeat twice more, ending with the praline mixture.

---

## Food for Thought . . .

*Praline Originally an almond candy made in France, praline was introduced to Louisiana by French colonists in the 1700's. Instead of almonds, they used pecans and brown sugar to form the sweet patties.*

### ⧯ ⧨ ⑂

## *Blueberry Lemon Swirl*

Makes 6 servings.

*Nutrient Value Per Serving: 244 calories, 6 g protein, 2 g fat, 52 g carbohydrate, 57 mg sodium, 91 mg cholesterol.*

| | |
|---|---|
| 1 | **package unflavored gelatin** |
| ¼ | **cup cold water** |
| 1 | **bag (1 pound) unsweetened frozen blueberries** |
| 1¼ | **cups sugar** |
| 1 | **cinnamon stick** |
| ½ | **teaspoon vanilla** |
| 2 | **egg yolks** |
| ¼ | **cup lemon juice** |
| ¼ | **cup water** |
| 2 | **teaspoons grated lemon rind** |
| 6 | **egg whites** |
| | **Lemon twists and blueberries, for garnish (optional)** |

1. Sprinkle the gelatin over the cold water in a small cup. Let stand for at least 2 minutes to soften.
2. Combine the blueberries, ¼ cup of the sugar and the cinnamon stick in a medium-size saucepan. Bring to boiling over medium heat. (The berries will create their own liquid.) Cook, stirring occasionally, for 4 to 5 minutes. Strain through a fine sieve over a small bowl; press out all the liquid from the berries with the back of a wooden spoon. You will need 1¼ cups of blueberry juice. Return the juice to the saucepan. Add half the softened gelatin. Heat over low heat, stirring constantly, until the gelatin is dissolved, for about 1 minute. Stir in the vanilla. Pour the blueberry mixture into a medium-size bowl. Set aside.
3. Mix together the egg yolks, ½ cup of the sugar, the lemon juice, water and lemon rind in a medium-size saucepan. Cook over medium heat, stirring constantly, just until the mixture begins to boil. Remove from the heat. Add the remaining gelatin. Stir constantly until the gelatin is completely dissolved, for about 1 minute. Pour the lemon mixture into another medium-size bowl.
4. Place both bowls in the refrigerator. Chill for about 45 minutes, stirring every 15 minutes, until the mixtures are the consistency of unbeaten egg whites. Remove the bowls from the refrigerator. (If the gelatin becomes too firm, place the bowl in a larger bowl of hot water for a few seconds.)
5. Beat the egg whites in a medium-size bowl until soft peaks form. Gradually beat in the remaining ½ cup of sugar, 1 tablespoon at a time. Continue beating until stiff, shiny peaks form.
6. Divide the beaten egg whites in half. Thoroughly mix about ½ cup of the beaten whites from one half into the blueberry mixture. Gently fold in the remaining part of the half. Thoroughly mix about ½ cup of the beaten whites from the second half into the lemon mixture. Gently fold in the remaining egg whites.
7. Pour the blueberry mixture into a large bowl. Pour the lemon mixture on top of the blueberry mixture. To create swirls, fold or stir *only* 2 times with a rubber spatula. Immediately pour the mixture into a 6½-cup clear soufflé dish or bowl. Refrigerate for 8 hours, or overnight. Garnish with lemon twists and blueberries, if you wish.

# Orange Soufflé

**Low in calories, light and luscious.**

Bake at 350° for 35 to 40 minutes.
Makes 8 servings.

*Nutrient Value Per Serving: 158 calories, 4 g protein, 4 g fat, 27 g carbohydrate, 64 mg sodium, 140 mg cholesterol.*

| | |
|---|---|
| 1 | **teaspoon butter** |
| 1 | **teaspoon sugar** |

**Soufflé:**

| | |
|---|---|
| ½ | **cup milk** |
| ⅓ | **cup sugar** |
| 2 | **tablespoons cornstarch** |
| 4 | **eggs, separated** |
| 2 | **tablespoons orange-flavored liqueur** |
| 3 | **teaspoons grated orange rind** |
| 1 | **teaspoon vanilla extract** |
| | **Pinch salt** |

**Orange Sauce:**

| | |
|---|---|
| 1⅓ | **cups orange juice** |
| ⅓ | **cup sugar** |
| 1 | **tablespoon cornstarch** |
| 1 | **tablespoon orange-flavored liqueur** |
| 1 | **teaspoon grated orange rind** |

1. Place the oven shelf in the lowest position. Preheat the oven to moderate (350°). Butter the bottom and sides of a 6-cup glass soufflé dish. Sprinkle the bottom and sides with the 1 teaspoon of sugar.
2. Prepare the Soufflé: Mix together the milk, sugar and cornstarch in a saucepan until no lumps of cornstarch remain. Bring to boiling over medium heat, stirring constantly with a wooden spoon. Cook for 1 minute, stirring. Remove from the heat.
3. Mix together the egg yolks, liqueur, orange rind and vanilla in a large bowl. Whisk the cornstarch mixture into the orange mixture until smooth.
4. Beat together the egg whites and the salt in a medium-size bowl with an electric mixer until stiff, shiny peaks form. Thoroughly mix about ½ cup of the beaten egg whites into the orange mixture. Gently fold in the remaining egg whites. Pour into the prepared soufflé dish. Form a "top hat" by running a spatula around in a circle about ½ inch from the edge.
5. Bake on the lowest oven shelf in the preheated moderate oven (350°) for 35 to 40 minutes, or until the soufflé is puffed and browned.
6. While the soufflé is baking, prepare the Orange Sauce: Mix together the orange juice, sugar and cornstarch in a saucepan. Bring to boiling, stirring constantly with a wooden spoon. Cook for 1 minute, stirring constantly. Remove from the heat. Stir in the liqueur and the orange rind. Serve warm with the soufflé.

## JUICY FRUIT

*To get the most juice from citrus fruit, store the fruit at room temperature. Before squeezing, roll the fruit firmly between your hand and the counter.*

## Chocolate Mousse

*Make this dessert with heavy cream for a rich, velvety texture — or without it for fewer calories.*

Makes 6 servings.

*Nutrient Value Per Serving: 332 calories, 5 g protein, 25 g fat, 23 g carbohydrate, 127 mg sodium, 176 mg cholesterol.*

| | |
|---|---|
| 6 | **ounces semisweet chocolate** |
| 1/4 | **cup (1/2 stick) butter, cut into small pieces** |
| 3 | **tablespoons strong brewed coffee** |
| 2 | **to 3 tablespoons brandy OR: orange or raspberry-flavored liqueur** |
| 3 | **eggs** |
| 1 | **egg white** |
| 2 | **tablespoons sugar** |
| 1/8 | **teaspoon cream of tartar** |
| 1/3 | **cup cold heavy cream** |

1. Combine the chocolate, butter and coffee in the top of a double boiler. Melt the chocolate and the butter over hot water, stirring, until smooth. Stir in the brandy or liqueur. Remove from the heat and let cool slightly.
2. Separate the eggs: Break one egg over a small bowl so the white falls in the bowl while the yolk stays in the shell. Pour the yolk from one shell to another until all the white drops in the bowl. Put the yolk in a medium-size bowl. Transfer the white to a second medium-size bowl. Repeat with the rest of the eggs. Add the extra white.
3. Beat the yolks with an electric mixer at low speed until blended. Gradually beat in the sugar. Increase the speed to high and beat until the mixture is pale yellow and forms a ribbon when the beaters are lifted, for 4 to 5 minutes.
4. Stir the melted chocolate mixture into the

## Food for Thought . . .

**Mousse** *The French word for froth, mousse must be both light and frothy. This is accomplished by folding beaten egg whites or whipped cream into the sweet mixture.*

yolk mixture until blended thoroughly.

5. Beat together the egg whites and the cream of tartar at low speed with clean beaters until foamy. Increase the speed to high and beat until stiff, shiny peaks form. Do not overbeat or the whites will become grainy.

6. Stir one third of the beaten whites into the chocolate mixture to lighten.

7. Scoop the remaining whites on top of the chocolate mixture and fold in: Cut the spatula from the top center of the mixture down to the bottom of the bowl. Bring the spatula toward you against the side of the bowl and up to the left and out, turning the chocolate mixture from the bottom of the bowl up over the whites. Continue folding, rotating the bowl, until no white streaks remain.

8. Beat the cream in a chilled bowl with chilled beaters until soft peaks form; begin at low speed and increase the speed as the cream thickens. (For fewer calories, omit the cream and set the mousse as in Step 9.)

9. Fold the whipped cream into the chocolate mixture following the folding technique described in Step 7. To set, spoon the chocolate mixture into a serving bowl, or into individual soufflé dishes or ramekins. Cover and refrigerate until firm, for at least 2 hours.

## STIFF STUFF: WHIPPING CREAM

*Place the beaters, bowl and heavy cream in the refrigerator to chill for 1 hour. Beat the cream in the chilled bowl until stiff peaks form. For sweetened whipped cream, fold into the whipped cream 2 tablespoons of 10X (confectioners' powdered) sugar for each cup of heavy cream used.*

## TURN UP THE VOLUME: BEATING EGG WHITES

*Room temperature egg whites yield the most volume. Remove eggs from the refrigerator about 1 hour before beating. Separate the eggs while still cold, making sure absolutely no yolk gets into the whites—fat from the yolk will decrease the volume of the whites. Allow the whites to come to room temperature before beating.*

## WE ALL SCREAM FOR ICE CREAM!

*Ice cream—America's favorite—the perfect blending of milk, cream, sweetening and flavor to a silken smoothness.*

*"Premium" marked on an ice cream carton means the ice cream contains extra milkfat and higher-quality ingredients. It also usually has less air whipped in during the freezing. Premium ice cream, thus, is richer and higher in cost.*

*French or French Custard ice cream contains more eggs or egg yolks than other frozen desserts. Most homemade ice creams fall into this category.*

*Diabetic or Dietetic ice cream contents vary from state to state, but all diabetic ice creams are artificially sweetened.*

*Ice Milk Contains fewer milk solids but usually more sugar than ice cream. Many weight watchers think that ice milk has considerably fewer calories than ice cream. Here's the not-so-happy truth: ½ cup of vanilla ice milk has 152 calories; the same amount of vanilla ice cream has 193 calories.*

*Soft Frozen Custard is creamy soft and smooth, with extra eggs or egg yolks, and often is whipped to incorporate more air.*

*Sherbet is a mixture of, originally, water but more often today, milk with sweetener, fruit or juice and, sometimes, gelatin and/or egg whites for smoothness.*

## Old-Fashioned French Vanilla Ice Cream

Makes 12 half-cup servings.

*Nutrient Value Per ½ Cup: 265 calories, 4 g protein, 19 g fat, 20 g carbohydrate, 130 mg sodium, 196 mg cholesterol.*

- 6 **egg yolks, slightly beaten**
- 1 **cup sugar**
- ½ **teaspoon salt**
- 2 **cups milk**
- 2 **cups heavy cream**
- 2 **tablespoons vanilla**

1. Combine the egg yolks, sugar, salt and milk in a heavy 2-quart saucepan. Cook over medium heat, stirring constantly, until the custard mixture thickens enough to lightly coat a spoon; do not let the mixture boil, or it will curdle. Strain the custard through a sieve into a large bowl, and cool.
2. Stir the cream and the vanilla into the custard mixture. Cover and chill.
3. Place the custard mixture in the container of an ice cream maker. Freeze following the manufacturer's directions.

***Old-Fashioned Chocolate Ice Cream:*** Add 9 ounces of bittersweet chocolate, grated, to the hot custard in Step 1 above. Stir until completely melted and smooth.

## Mango Ice Cream

Makes 1½ quarts.

*Nutrient Value Per ½ Cup: 202 calories, 1 g protein, 15 g fat, 18 g carbohydrate, 16 mg sodium, 54 mg cholesterol.*

- ¾ **cup sugar**
- ⅓ **cup water**
- ⅛ **teaspoon cream of tartar**
- 1 **large ripe mango (1 pound)**
- 1 **teaspoon grated lime rind**
- 1 **tablespoon lime juice**
- 2 **cups heavy cream, whipped**

1. Combine the sugar, water and cream of tartar in a medium-size, nonaluminum saucepan. Bring to boiling. Lower the heat and simmer, uncovered, for about 5 minutes. Cool.
2. Peel the mango with a paring knife. Remove and discard the pit. Cut the mango into small pieces and place in the container of an electric blender or a food processor. Cover and whirl until a smooth purée. Transfer to a large bowl. Add the sugar syrup, lime rind and lime juice. Fold in the whipped cream. Pour the mixture into an ice cream maker. Freeze following the manufacturer's directions. Or pour into a 9 x 9 x 2-inch square pan. Cover with plastic wrap and freeze until firm, for about 3 hours.

## Food for Thought . . .

**Mango** *A juicy, refreshing tropical fruit native to East India, mangoes are flat or round in shape and have a yellow-orange to red skin when ripe.*

*Mangoes are in season from January to September. They now are grown in southern Florida, California, Hawaii and Mexico. They are picked green but will ripen if left at room temperature (the green skin turns yellow-orange when ripe). Once mangoes are ripe, they should be refrigerated. In India, both green and ripe mangoes are used to make chutney and pickles.*

*To peel a mango, cut only the skin with the tip of a knife, starting at the stem and circling the fruit several times. Peel the skin in sections. The flesh will cling to the large flat seed. Cut the flesh to free it from the seed, or scoop out the flesh with a spoon. Use mangoes in fruit compotes, salads or chutney.*

## Ice Cream Bombe

Makes 10 servings.

*Nutrient Value Per Serving: 237 calories, 3 g protein, 9 g fat, 36 g carbohydrate, 87 mg sodium, 39 mg cholesterol.*

¼ **cup finely chopped maraschino cherries**
2 **tablespoons candied lemon peel OR: orange peel**
2 **tablespoons finely chopped candied pineapple**
1 **quart chocolate ice cream**
1 **pint orange sherbet**
1 **pint chocolate ice cream Whipped cream, for garnish**

1. Combine the maraschino cherries, candied lemon or orange peel and candied pineapple in a small bowl. Set aside.
2. Place an 8-cup ice cream mold or metal bowl in the freezer. Soften the 1 quart of chocolate ice cream in the refrigerator for about 30 minutes.
3. Pack the softened ice cream into the chilled mold to make a 1- to 1½-inch-thick layer. Smooth the surface with a large spoon. Place the mold in the freezer for 2 hours, or until the ice cream is firm.
4. Soften the orange sherbet in the refrigerator for about 30 minutes. Transfer to a small bowl and fold in the candied fruit mixture. Spread the orange sherbet over the chocolate layer in the mold, smoothing the surface. Freeze until firm, for about 2 hours.
5. Soften the 1 pint of chocolate ice cream in the refrigerator for about 30 minutes. Pack into the mold, pressing firmly. Cover the surface of the mold with plastic wrap. Freeze for 2 hours, or until firm.
6. To unmold the bombe, immerse the mold in a large bowl of hot water for 5 to 10 seconds and quickly invert onto a chilled serving plate. If not ready to serve, place the plate in the freezer.
7. To serve, decorate the bombe with rosettes of whipped cream and cut with a long, sharp knife dipped in warm water.

CHAPTER 7

# On The Light Side

*It's de-light-ful eating when you try these wonderful waist-watching recipes.*

*Chicken with Sweet Pepper Sauce (recipe, page 202)*

**D**ieting.

It seems to be on everyone's mind, whether they're on a diet, thinking about it, or just coming off one. We often think of dieting in terms of things we can't have; this chapter stresses foods you *can* eat, and how to reduce calories in everyday meals.

Briefly, here's how we categorize the low-calorie dishes in this chapter:
- Low-cal main dishes: under 300 calories.
- Low-cal side dishes: under 100 calories.
- Low-cal desserts: under 150 calories.

And since there's no point in serving low-calorie dishes if they don't appeal to your taste buds, we always stress the "good" in good eating. For instance, there's Turkey Fajitas with Coriander Purée *(recipe, page 204)*, Spiced Basmati Rice *(recipe, page 217)* and Strawberry Raspberry Tart *(recipe, page 225)*.

Also included is must-know information on healthy eating, so that you can continue good habits long after the weight you wanted to shed is gone. We offer meat alternatives, such as Santa Maria Beans *(recipe, page 214)*, and include more complex carbohydrates such as Whole Wheat Spaghetti with Red Clam Sauce *(recipe, page 213)*. This chapter can help you continue good nutrition habits for a lifetime—and instill good habits in your family. ∎

# Main Dishes

## Chicken with Sweet Pepper Sauce

Makes 6 servings.

*Nutrient Value Per Serving: 195 calories, 35 g protein, 5 g fat, 2 g carbohydrate, 222 mg sodium, 85 mg cholesterol.*

**Sweet Pepper Sauce:**
3   whole sweet red peppers
¾   cup chicken broth
3   cloves garlic, peeled and sliced
      Salt or salt substitute, to taste
      Freshly ground pepper, to taste

1   tablespoon olive oil
3   whole chicken breasts (1 pound each),
      boned, skinned and split
      Watercress sprigs, for garnish

1. Prepare the Sweet Pepper Sauce: Preheat the broiler to high. Roast the red peppers under the broiler, turning with tongs from time to time, until they are charred all over, for about 15 to 20 minutes. Transfer the peppers with the tongs to a paper bag, close the bag and let stand for 10 minutes, so the trapped steam loosens the pepper skins and makes them easier to peel off.
2. Meanwhile, bring the broth to boiling in a small saucepan over medium heat. Add the garlic and lower the heat. Cook for 5 minutes. Remove from the heat.
3. Peel, seed and coarsely chop the peppers. Place them in the container of a food processor or an electric blender. Add the hot broth mixture, cover and process until puréed.
4. Transfer the sauce to a small saucepan. Season with the salt and the pepper. Cover and keep warm over low heat.
5. Sauté the chicken breasts, part at a time, in the oil in a large, nonstick sauté pan over medium heat for 3 to 5 minutes per side.
6. To serve, spoon some of the warm sauce onto a heated serving platter and top with the sautéed chicken breasts. Spoon the remaining sauce over the chicken. Garnish with watercress sprigs.

## Chicken Italia

Makes 6 servings.

*Nutrient Value Per Serving: 304 calories, 31 g protein, 17 g fat, 5 g carbohydrate, 173 mg sodium, 95 mg cholesterol.*

1   small cauliflower (1 to 1¼ pounds),
      cut into 1½-inch flowerets
      (about 3 cups)
1   chicken (3 to 3½ pounds), trimmed of
      fat and cut into eighths
3   cloves garlic, peeled and left whole
1   tablespoon extra-virgin olive oil
½   cup red wine vinegar
1   tablespoon chopped fresh rosemary
⅛   teaspoon crushed red pepper flakes
½   cup chopped, peeled tomatoes
      (about ½ pound)
2   tablespoons capers, drained and
      rinsed
2   tablespoons finely chopped flat-leaf
      Italian parsley
      Additional finely chopped flat-leaf
      Italian parsley (optional)

1. Cook the cauliflower in boiling water to cover in a small saucepan for 1 minute. Drain and set aside.

2. Sauté the chicken and the garlic in the oil in a large, nonstick skillet over medium-high heat. Cook, stirring the chicken pieces often, for 10 to 15 minutes, or until the chicken just begins to brown. Pour off the fat from the skillet.

3. Add the vinegar, rosemary and red pepper flakes. Bring to boiling, lower the heat and simmer, covered, for 3 minutes. Uncover and cook for 1 minute more so the vinegar evaporates.

4. Add the tomatoes, capers and parsley. Bring the sauce to boiling, lower the heat and add the cauliflower. Cover and simmer, stirring the mixture occasionally, for 15 to 20 minutes, or until the chicken no longer is pink near the bone and the cauliflower is fork-tender.

5. Sprinkle with additional chopped parsley, if you wish. To reduce the calories, remove the skin before eating the chicken.

## Microwave Instructions
*(for a 650-watt variable power microwave oven)*

**Ingredient Changes:** Eliminate the olive oil. Reduce the vinegar to 3 tablespoons and reduce the rosemary to 1½ teaspoons.

**Directions:** Place the chicken pieces, skin side up, in a microwave-safe 13 x 9-inch baking pan. Add the garlic. Cover with wax paper. Microwave at full power for 10 minutes. Tuck the cauliflower pieces between the chicken. Combine the 3 tablespoons of vinegar, the 1½ teaspoons of rosemary, the red pepper flakes, tomatoes, capers and parsley. Spoon the mixture over the chicken. Cover with microwave-safe plastic wrap, turned back at one corner to vent. Microwave at full power for 6 minutes, rotating the dish one half turn after 3 minutes. Let stand for 3 minutes.

## Food for Thought . . .

**Chicken** *Perfectly suited to most dietary needs, chicken provides complete protein at a moderate cost. It is a short-fibered meat and easy to digest. Consumers who are watching nutrition as well as calories naturally turn to chicken in their diet. Here are a few of the reasons:*
- *Chicken contains fewer calories than most meats. A 3½-ounce serving of broiled chicken (without the skin) has only about 136 calories. That same 3½ ounces, however, provides 31.2 grams of protein, or 52% of the average adult daily requirement. It also provides vitamin A, thiamine, riboflavin, niacin, iron and phosphorous.*
- *Here's some heartening news: Chicken is lower in fat than most red meats. Three ounces of broiled chicken with the skin yields about 9 grams of fat; an equal portion of other meats has double or triple the fat content. Chicken skin contains only about 17% fat, a small amount compared to the flavor it offers. Interestingly, two thirds of the fat present is unsaturated—good news for people concerned with their cholesterol intake.*
- *For calorie-wise eating, enhance the flavor of chicken by adding herbs and spices, such as rosemary, tarragon, dill or pepper.*
- *Team chicken with low-calorie vegetables, such as broccoli, tomatoes or zucchini.*
- *Cook chicken in low-cal ways— poached in broth, broiled or sautéed in a nonstick pan—instead of frying it in fatty oils.*
- *If you're really counting calories, don't eat the skin.*

## Rosemary Chicken and Potatoes

Bake at 400° for 30 to 40 minutes.
Makes 6 servings.

*Nutrient Value Per Serving: 302 calories, 27 g protein, 9 g fat, 29 g carbohydrate, 82 mg sodium, 72 mg cholesterol.*

1 **chicken (3 pounds), trimmed of fat and cut into eighths**
1 **tablespoon extra-virgin olive oil**
5 **cloves garlic, unpeeled**
1 **cup dry white wine**
2 **to 3 tablespoons chopped fresh rosemary**
2 **bay leaves**
¼ **to ½ teaspoon coarsely ground black pepper**
4 **cups ¼-inch-thick slices peeled all-purpose potatoes (about 2 pounds) Chicken broth or water, as necessary**

1. Preheat the oven to hot (400°).
2. Sauté the chicken in the oil in an ovenproof, nonstick Dutch oven over medium-high heat, turning the chicken often, for 10 to 15 minutes, or until the chicken begins to brown. Drain off all the fat from the pan.
3. Peel 2 of the garlic cloves and finely chop them. Leave the remaining 3 cloves whole and in their thin white skins. Add all the garlic to the pan along with the wine, rosemary, bay leaves and black pepper. Bring to boiling, lower the heat, cover and simmer for 5 minutes. Add the potato slices and gently stir to combine. Cover the pan.
4. Bake in the preheated hot oven (400°) for 10 minutes. Carefully uncover and stir the chicken-potato mixture. Add the broth or water, if necessary, to prevent sticking or scorching. Cover and bake for 20 to 30 minutes more, or until the potatoes are tender. Continue to check the mixture as it cooks, adding the broth or water as necessary to prevent sticking or scorching. The consistency of this dish should be rather dry. Remove the bay leaves and the whole cloves of garlic before serving, if you wish. To reduce the calories, remove the skin before eating the chicken.

## Turkey Fajitas with Coriander Purée

*Cooked chicken breast can be substituted for the turkey breast.*

Makes 6 servings.

*Nutrient Value Per Serving: 205 calories, 21 g protein, 4 g fat, 21 g carbohydrate, 115 mg sodium, 40 mg cholesterol.*

6 **flour tortillas**
¾ **pound cooked turkey breast, cut into julienne strips**
¼ **cup fresh lime juice**
2 **teaspoons finely chopped garlic**
½ **teaspoon ground cumin Nonstick vegetable cooking spray**
1 **red onion, thinly sliced**
1 **sweet red or green pepper, halved, seeded and cut into strips**
½ **cup Coriander Purée (recipe, page 206)**

1. Preheat the oven to slow (300°). Warm the tortillas in the oven while making the filling.
2. Combine the turkey, lime juice, garlic and cumin in a large bowl. Cover and marinate for at least 1 hour.
3. Spray a large, nonstick skillet with nonstick vegetable cooking spray and place over medium-high heat. Sauté the onion and the red or green pepper for 3 to 5 minutes, or until wilted.
4. Add the turkey and the marinade. Cook, tossing constantly with a nonstick spatula, for 5 minutes.
5. Spoon 2 tablespoons of the turkey mixture onto each tortilla and drizzle with the Coriander Purée. Roll up the tortilla.

*Turkey Fajitas with Coriander Purée*

## Food for Thought . . .

*Coriander* *Fresh coriander (also called cilantro and Chinese or Japanese parsley) is a fragrant herb with a pungent flavor native to southern Europe. The leaves are oval and flat, with a toothed edge. The tiny, beige seeds are similar in taste to anise and cumin; they are sold whole or ground.*

*Fresh coriander is sold by the bunch. If possible, buy it with the roots intact. Store coriander in the refrigerator with the roots in water and the leaves covered with damp paper toweling. Rinse thoroughly just prior to using.*

*Use coriander as you would parsley, although more sparingly.*

# Coriander Purée

Makes 6 servings.

*Nutrient Value Per Serving: 11 calories, 1 g protein, 1 g fat, 1 g carbohydrate, 74 mg sodium, 1 mg cholesterol.*

¼   **cup chicken broth**
1   **cup fresh coriander**
2   **tablespoons grated Parmesan cheese**
2   **cloves garlic**
⅛   **teaspoon leaf oregano, crumbled**
     **Salt or salt substitute, to taste**
     **Freshly ground pepper, to taste**

1. Bring the broth to boiling in a small saucepan.
2. Meanwhile, combine the coriander, Parmesan cheese, garlic and oregano in the container of an electric blender or a food processor. Process for 30 seconds, or until chopped.
3. With the motor running, pour the broth through the feed tube. Continue blending to make a smooth paste. Season with the salt and the pepper.
4. Place in a small bowl, cover and refrigerate.

## CUTTING CALORIES?

*"Dieting" is such a negative-sounding word. It seems to stress what you can't do and what you can't have. We prefer an approach that stresses culinary creativity: Don't give up your favorite foods, just make them less fattening! Slowly but surely the extra pounds will disappear.*

*Here's our basic approach to cutting calories in five easy steps:*

*1. Eat what you want, but always avoid a high-calorie food when there's a lower-calorie version available. Use frozen lowfat yogurt or sorbets instead of ice cream, part skim cheese instead of whole milk cheese, water-packed tuna instead of oil-packed, low-calorie jams and salad dressings instead of their high-calorie counterparts. This principle should be applied to every meal, every day, even on "special occasions."*

*2. Every calorie counts! It's the total calorie count per day that should concern you, and there's no such thing as a calorie difference too slight to bother with. Over the years those "slight" differences add up.*

*3. The best diet is a well-balanced diet. That must include the basic food groups. This is not a quick weight-loss scheme, so you can't afford to shortchange nutrition.*

*4. Make low-calorie cooking a test of your culinary skill! You'll be suprised at the fun you can have cheating your favorite recipes out of those extra calories.*

*5. Think of cutting calories as a "change for life" program that starts immediately and goes on indefinitely. Once you've retrained your tastebuds, those old, fatty foods should be gone forever—leaving you fit for life.*

# Vegetable Ham Salad

*Fresh vegetables and smoked ham create a delicious
main-dish salad that won't weigh you down.*

Makes 4 servings.

*Nutrient Value Per Serving: 274 calories, 20 g protein, 16 g
fat, 15 g carbohydrate, 1,342 mg sodium, 48 mg cholesterol.*

**Sweet Pickle Mayonnaise Dressing:**

- ¼ **cup mayonnaise**
- 1 **tablespoon sweet relish**
- 1 **teaspoon dry mustard**
- 1 **teaspoon cider vinegar**

- 2 **large ripe tomatoes
  (about 10 ounces each)**
- ¾ **pound smoked ham, cut into ¼-inch
  pieces (about 3 cups)**
- 1 **small zucchini, cut into ¼-inch
  pieces (about 1 cup)**
- ½ **cup cooked corn**
- ¼ **cup chopped celery**
- ¼ **cup finely chopped red onion**
- 8 **lettuce leaves
  Parsley sprigs, for garnish
  (optional)**

1. Prepare the Sweet Pickle Mayonnaise
   Dressing: Stir together the mayonnaise,
   relish, mustard and vinegar in a medium-
   size bowl.
2. Core and chop 1 of the tomatoes into ¼-
   inch pieces and add to the dressing. Add
   the ham, zucchini, corn, celery and onion
   to the dressing. Toss to coat all the
   ingredients well.
3. Arrange the lettuce leaves on a serving
   platter. Spoon the salad over the leaves.
   Core and slice the remaining tomato.
   Garnish the salad with the tomato slices,
   and with parsley sprigs, if you wish.

## MEAT: A SLIM STORY

***When You Shop:*** *Choose meat
carefully and select only the leanest
cuts. Have fat trimmed by the butcher,
or trim it yourself. Don't buy
prepackaged hamburger meat; have it
ground to order from lean cuts.*
***When You Cook:*** *Bake or broil on a
rack so that melting fats can drain.
For stove-top cooking, a nonstick
skillet and one tablespoon of oil is all
that's needed for the leanest meats.
Fattier meats such as hamburger or
lamb chops, don't even need that—they
can sauté in their own fat. Better yet,
broil them. Overcooking, not lack of
fat, robs meat of moisture, so invest in
a meat thermometer. When you slow-
simmer meat in a sauce or a stew, first
brown the meat under the broiler
instead of in the pot. Make the sauce or
stew a day ahead and refrigerate it,
then lift the hardened fat off the
surface. Fat adds calories but no
flavor to sauces and stews.*
***When You Serve:*** *Decide in advance
what constitutes a proper size meat
serving and prepare only that much.
This keeps a lot of leftovers from
"going to waist."*
***Pound for Pound:*** *Beef, lamb, pork
and ham are high-calorie main courses
compared to veal, poultry, liver and
seafood. Try this technique for cutting
calories: Every time you pick up a
pound of the high-calorie meats, pick
up an equal amount from the lower-
calorie group—for each pound of
hamburger, buy an equal amount of
chicken. For each pound of pork chops,
buy the equivalent of scallops or liver.
This self-enforced widening of your
main course repertoire can cut your
caloric intake dramatically!*

## Light Ham Casserole

*A stick-to-your-ribs dish that uses lowfat turkey ham and skim milk.*

Bake, covered, at 425° for 30 minutes, then uncovered for 5 minutes.
Makes 8 servings.

*Nutrient Value Per Serving: 278 calories, 18 g protein, 9 g fat, 31 g carbohydrate, 700 mg sodium, 16 mg cholesterol.*

| | |
|---|---|
| 2 | pounds all-purpose potatoes, peeled and cut into 1½-inch cubes |
| 1 | cup chopped onion |
| 1 | cup chopped sweet red pepper |
| 1 | tablespoon vegetable oil |
| 5 | tablespoons all-purpose flour |
| ½ | teaspoon pepper |
| ¼ | teaspoon leaf marjoram, crumbled |
| 2½ | cups skim milk |
| 2 | tablespoons Dijon-style mustard |
| 1 | cup shredded sharp Cheddar cheese (4 ounces) |
| 1 | bag (1 pound) frozen unthawed baby carrots |
| 12 | ounces 92% to 95% fat-free turkey ham slices, cut into 2 x ½-inch strips |
| ¼ | cup chopped parsley |

1. Preheat the oven to hot (425°).
2. Cook the potatoes in boiling water to cover in a large saucepan for 10 minutes, or until almost fork-tender. Drain.
3. Sauté the onion and the red pepper in the oil in a nonstick Dutch oven over medium-high heat until softened, for 2 to 3 minutes. Stir in the flour, pepper and marjoram. Add the milk. Bring to boiling. Lower the heat and simmer, stirring, until thickened, for 2 minutes.
4. Stir in the mustard and all but 1 tablespoon of the Cheddar cheese. Cook, stirring, until the Cheddar cheese melts. Remove from the heat. Gently fold in the potatoes, carrots, ham and parsley. Pour into a 4-quart casserole dish. Cover tightly with aluminum foil.
5. Bake in the preheated hot oven (425°) for 30 minutes. Sprinkle with the reserved tablespoon of Cheddar cheese. Bake, uncovered, for 5 minutes, or until bubbly.

## Spinach-Topped Sole

*A spicy spinach-and-potato mixture is used to sauce low-cal fish fillets.*

Bake at 375° for 10 to 15 minutes.
Makes 4 servings.

*Nutrient Value Per Serving: 218 calories, 35 g protein, 3 g fat, 10 g carbohydrate, 274 mg sodium, 82 mg cholesterol.*

| | |
|---|---|
| 4 | firm white fish fillets, such as sole or flounder (about 1½ pounds total) |
| 1 | medium-size all-purpose potato, peeled and cut into ¼-inch cubes |
| 1 | clove garlic, finely chopped |
| 1 | teaspoon vegetable oil |
| ⅛ | teaspoon ground coriander |
| ⅛ | teaspoon ground ginger |
| ⅛ | teaspoon salt |
| | Pinch ground hot red pepper |
| 1 | pound fresh spinach, stemmed, washed and coarsely chopped |
| ¼ | cup water |

1. Preheat the oven to moderate (375°).
2. Fold each fillet in half crosswise. Arrange in a shallow baking pan.
3. Bake in the preheated moderate oven (375°) for 10 to 15 minutes, or until the fish is easily flaked with a fork.
4. Meanwhile, sauté the potato with the garlic in the oil in a large, nonstick skillet. Add the coriander, ginger, salt and ground hot red pepper; sauté for 2 minutes.
5. Stir the spinach and the water into the potato mixture. Cover and cook over medium-high heat until the potatoes are tender, for about 10 minutes. Add additional water if the mixture becomes too dry.
6. Lift the fish out of the pan with a slotted spatula. Drain briefly on paper toweling. Transfer to individual plates and top with the spinach mixture.

## *Red Snapper in Tomato Herb Sauce*

Bake at 400° for 10 minutes; broil for 5 minutes.
Makes 6 servings.

*Nutrient Value Per Serving: 179 calories, 32 g protein, 2 g fat, 6 g carbohydrate, 104 mg sodium, 56 mg cholesterol.*

**6  red snapper fillets (about 2 pounds)**
**1  pound ripe plum tomatoes, peeled, seeded and chopped**
**1  large yellow onion, sliced**
**2  tablespoons fresh lime juice**
**¼  cup dry white wine**
**½  cup fresh basil, chopped**
    **Salt or salt substitute, to taste**
    **Freshly ground pepper, to taste**

1. Preheat the oven to hot (400°).
2. Place the fillets, skin side down, in a shallow baking dish. Add the tomatoes, onion, lime juice, wine and half the basil. Season with the salt and the pepper.
3. Bake in the preheated hot oven (400°) for 10 minutes, or until the fish is barely opaque.
4. Finish cooking the fish under the broiler, 2 inches from the source of the heat, until the onion browns and the fish flakes when lightly touched with a fork, for about 5 minutes.
5. Sprinkle the fish with the remaining basil.

## TO COOK A FISH . . .

*Delicate fish must be watched very carefully to avoid overcooking. As a general rule, cook fish 10 minutes for every 1 inch of thickness. The fish should change from a translucent off-white to a solid opaque white, and the flesh should flake when lightly touched with a fork.*

# Spicy Shrimp

**A spicy simmering liquid provides the pickling base for the shrimp.**

Makes 6 servings.

*Nutrient Value Per Serving: 75 calories, 13 g protein, 1 g fat, 3 g carbohydrate, 184 mg sodium, 93 mg cholesterol.*

**Simmering Liquid:**
- 1½  cups white vinegar
- 2  onions, peeled and sliced
- 10  whole cloves
- ¾  teaspoon black peppercorns
- 1  tablespoon sugar
- 1  teaspoon salt or salt substitute
- 1¼  teaspoons crushed red pepper flakes
- ½  teaspoon liquid red pepper seasoning

- 1  pound shrimp, peeled and deveined
- ½  sweet red pepper, seeded and chopped, for garnish
- ½  sweet yellow pepper, seeded and chopped, for garnish
  Fresh coriander, for garnish

1. Prepare the Simmering Liquid: Combine the vinegar, onion, cloves, peppercorns, sugar, salt or salt substitute, red pepper flakes and liquid red pepper seasoning in a large stainless steel or enamel saucepan. Bring to boiling over medium heat. Lower the heat and simmer for 10 minutes.
2. Add the shrimp to the Simmering Liquid and bring to boiling again. Lower the heat and simmer for 2 minutes more, or just until the shrimp are pink. (Do not overcook shrimp or they will be tough and dry.) Remove the saucepan from the heat.
3. Let the shrimp cool in the Simmering Liquid. Transfer the shrimp and the liquid to a glass bowl. Cover and refrigerate for at least 3 hours, or overnight. (The shrimp will be tangier if they are left to marinate overnight.)
4. To serve, drain the Simmering Liquid from the shrimp. (Reserve the liquid to use for refrigerating any leftover shrimp.) Skewer the shrimp with toothpicks or short wooden skewers, piercing each shrimp from the tail through to the head. Place the shrimp on a serving platter and garnish each shrimp with the red and yellow peppers and the fresh coriander.

## POACHING PLUSES

*Poaching is a cooking method in which foods are cooked in simmering, not boiling, liquid. Fish, chicken, eggs and fruit are the foods most commonly poached. The texture of such foods is preserved by a simmering liquid.*

## FANCY FLUTING

*Fluted vegetables and lemons add a decorative touch to your dinner table. Use a lemon zester to remove 3 to 5 evenly spaced narrow strips of peel or skin. Hold the top and bottom of the vegetable with one hand and turn it away from the zester, held in the other hand. Cut carrots and celery into 3-inch lengths before fluting.*

# Poached Salmon with Fluted Vegetables

*Gently simmered vegetables and poached fish — now that's light and easy cooking at its best.*

Makes 4 servings.

*Nutrient Value Per Serving: 240 calories, 25 g protein, 8 g fat, 20 g carbohydrate, 91 mg sodium, 63 mg cholesterol.*

4   **small new potatoes,** un**peeled and fluted**
3   **medium-size carrots, peeled, fluted and sliced ¼ inch thick**
2   **celery ribs, fluted and sliced ¼ inch thick**
½   **small onion, cut in wedges**
1   **lemon, fluted**
1   **pound salmon fillet**
4   **sprigs of parsley, for garnish**

1. Boil the potatoes for 12 to 15 minutes, or until tender.
2. In another pan, cook the carrots in 4 cups of boiling water for 3 minutes. Add the celery and the onion and cook for 5 minutes more, or until the vegetables are barely tender. Remove the vegetables with a slotted spoon, saving the broth in the pan. Keep the vegetables warm.
3. Cut 4 slices off the lemon for garnish. Squeeze the remainder and add to the broth.
4. Bring the liquid to a slow simmer and add the salmon. Gently poach for 3 to 5 minutes, or just until the salmon flakes. Cut the salmon into 4 slices.
5. Serve the salmon with the vegetables. Garnish each salmon slice with a fluted lemon slice and a parsley sprig.

## THE CALCIUM CONNECTION

| Milk Group | mgs calcium |
|---|---|
| Buttermilk, 1 cup | 285 |
| Cheese, American, 1 oz | 174 |
| Cheese, Cheddar, 1 oz | 204 |
| Cheese, ricotta, part skim, 1 oz | 337 |
| Cheese, Swiss, 1 oz | 272 |
| Ice cream, vanilla, ½ cup | 88 |
| Milk, 1 cup | 291 |
| Milk, lowfat (2%), 1 cup | 297 |
| Milk, skim, 1 cup | 302 |
| Yogurt, fruit, lowfat, 1 cup | 345 |
| Yogurt, plain, lowfat, 1 cup | 415 |

| Meat Group | |
|---|---|
| Beans, dried, cooked, 1 cup | 90 |
| Oysters, raw, 7 to 9 | 113 |
| Salmon, canned with bones, 3 oz | 167 |
| Sardines, with bones, 3 oz | 372 |
| Shrimp, canned, 3 oz | 99 |
| Tofu (bean curd), 4 oz* | 240 |

*Note: Only tofu processed with calcium sulfate is a source of calcium.*

| Fruit-Vegetable Group | |
|---|---|
| Beet greens, ½ cup | 72 |
| Bok choy, ½ cup | 126 |
| Broccoli, stalk, ½ cup | 68 |
| Collards, from raw, ½ cup | 179 |
| Collards, from frozen, ½ cup | 149 |
| Kale, from raw, ½ cup | 103 |
| Kale, from frozen, ½ cup | 79 |
| Mustard greens, ½ cup | 97 |
| Spinach, ½ cup | 84 |

| Grain Group | |
|---|---|
| Cornbread, 2½" x 2½" x 1½" | 94 |
| Pancakes, two, 4-inch diameter | 116 |
| Waffles, 7-inch diameter | 179 |

*Information courtesy of the National Dairy Council*

---

▬▬▬

## *SPICE UP THE SAUCE*

*Try sprucing up the flavor of our Easy Spaghetti Sauce by adding:*
- *Chopped fresh basil, savory and marjoram*
- *Red pepper flakes and chopped roasted red pepper*
- *Diced prosciutto and peas*
- *Sautéed slices of sweet and/or hot Italian sausage*
- *Chopped toasted walnuts and diced mozzarella cheese*
- *Tuna, capers and black olives*
- *Mussels and clams steamed in the sauce*
- *Blanched broccoli flowerets and chunks of zucchini*
- *Sautéed mushrooms and fresh thyme*

## *Easy Spaghetti Sauce*

*Start with our basic recipe below, then try some of the delicious add-ins to give you more variety.*

Makes 3½ cups (4 servings).

*Nutrient Value Per ½ Cup Serving: 79 calories, 1 g protein, 4 g fat, 10 g carbohydrate, 425 mg sodium, 0 mg cholesterol.*

| | |
|---|---|
| 1 | **medium-size onion** |
| 1 | **carrot** |
| 1 | **stalk celery** |
| 2 | **cloves garlic** |
| 2 | **tablespoons olive oil** |
| 1 | **can (28 ounces) whole tomatoes in purée** |
| 1 | **cup water** |
| ¾ | **teaspoon salt** |
| ½ | **teaspoon ground pepper** |
| ½ | **teaspoon leaf basil, crumbled** |
| ½ | **teaspoon leaf oregano, crumbled** |
| | **Bay leaf** |
| | **Chopped parsley (optional)** |

1. Coarsely chop the onion. Coarsely chop the carrot and the celery together. Then place the onion in the container of an electric blender and finely chop. Scrape the onion out of the blender and set aside. Repeat with the garlic, then with the carrot and the celery together.
2. Heat the oil in a large skillet. Add the onion and sauté until softened but not brown, for 4 to 5 minutes. Add the garlic and sauté for 1 minute. Add the carrot and celery and sauté until softened, for 1 to 2 minutes.
3. Add the tomatoes with their purée, the water, salt, pepper, basil, oregano and bay leaf. Bring the mixture to boiling. Reduce the heat and simmer, uncovered, for 10 minutes.
4. Place a food mill or fine sieve over a bowl. Pour the tomato mixture into the food mill and force through (if using a sieve, force through with the back of a wooden spoon). Discard any solids left in the mill.
5. Return the sauce to the skillet. Simmer for 10 to 15 minutes, or until the sauce reaches the desired consistency. Remove the bay leaf. Just before serving, stir in chopped parsley, if you wish.

## Food for Thought . . .

**Protein** *Made up of amino acids, protein is a component of all body cells, antibodies and enzymes, and is essential for the growth, repair and maintenance of cells. Proteins from most animal sources usually are complete, having all the amino acids needed for a healthy diet, while proteins from plant sources usually are incomplete and need to be paired with other complementary plant proteins to provide all the necessary amino acids. The National Academy of Sciences recommends a daily intake of 44 grams of protein for the average woman and 56 grams for the average man.*

## Whole Wheat Spaghetti with Red Clam Sauce

*A down-home, slightly chunky tomato sauce.*

Makes 6 servings.

*Nutrient Value Per Serving: 307 calories, 19 g protein, 3 g fat, 52 g carbohydrate, 253 mg sodium, 21 mg cholesterol.*

- 2 **medium-size carrots, peeled and finely diced**
- 2 **teaspoons olive oil**
- 1 **medium-size clove garlic, finely chopped**
- 1 **can (28 ounces) crushed tomatoes in purée**
- 1 **can (6½ ounces) finely chopped clams**
- 2 **teaspoons dried basil, crumbled OR: 2 tablespoons chopped fresh basil**
- ¼ **teaspoon fennel seed, crushed**
- 12 **ounces whole wheat spaghetti**

1. Cook the carrots in the oil in a large pan over medium-low heat, stirring frequently, for 8 minutes, or until they are tender.
2. Add the garlic and cook for 1 minute, stirring constantly. Add the tomatoes with their purée and let the sauce come to a boil. Lower the heat.
3. Drain the clams, pressing out all the water. Reserve ¼ cup of the clams for garnish and stir the remainder into the tomatoes along with the basil and the fennel. Let the mixture bubble gently for 1 minute, stirring frequently.
4. While the sauce is cooking, cook the spaghetti until it is *al dente*, firm but tender. Drain the spaghetti in a colander.
5. Divide the spaghetti among 6 individual plates and top with the tomato sauce. Garnish with the reserved clams.

◄◄ 💲

# Santa Maria Beans

*The authentic Pinquito bean is small and pink and is available only in the Santa Maria area of California. Pinto beans make a good substitute.*

Makes 24 servings (4 quarts).

*Nutrient Value Per Serving: 227 calories, 10 g protein, 9 g fat, 28 g carbohydrate, 390 mg sodium, 10 mg cholesterol.*

2    **packages (1 pound each) Pinquito beans OR: pinto beans, picked over, rinsed and drained (4½ cups)**
1½   **quarts cold water**
2    **cans (16 ounces each) whole tomatoes, undrained**
1    **ham hock (1 pound), cracked**
2    **large white onions, chopped**
2    **cups bottled mild chili salsa**
½    **pound salt pork, cut into 4 pieces**
2    **teaspoons leaf oregano, crumbled**
¼    **teaspoon crushed red pepper flakes**

1. Combine the Pinquito or pinto beans and the water in a large kettle or Dutch oven. Soak overnight. Do not drain.
2. Add the tomatoes with their liquid, the ham hock, onion, salsa, salt pork, oregano and red pepper flakes to the beans. Bring to boiling and cook for 5 minutes. Lower the heat and simmer, uncovered, for 6 hours, or until the beans are tender. Add water as necessary to keep the beans covered by 2 inches.

*Note: These beans are best made a day ahead and refrigerated overnight to develop the flavors. The beans freeze well for up to 6 months.*

## *Food for Thought . . .*

**Cholesterol** *A fat-like substance, cholesterol is obtained through the diet as well as manufactured by the body. It is necessary for hormones and cell membranes. High levels of serum cholesterol are a risk factor for hardening of the arteries and heart disease. Cholesterol comes from animal sources, such as egg yolks, organ meats, whole milk products, butter and lard. The American Heart Association recommends no more than 300 milligrams of cholesterol daily for healthy men and women.*

## *CHOLESTEROL CONTROL*

• *Reduce your intake of saturated fats, such as butter, cheese, heavy cream and fatty meats.*
• *Limit your use of whole eggs, either by themselves or in cooking.*
• *Increase your consumption of complex carbohydrates and high fiber foods.*
• *Satisfy your snack cravings with fruit and other naturally sweet foods. Avoid candy, cakes, pies and soft drinks for snacking.*
• *Cut down on the amount of fat you use in cooking by using nonstick vegetable cooking spray and nonstick cookware and utensils.*
• *Do not eat fried or deep-fried foods.*
• *Broil, roast on a rack, steam, poach or stir-fry foods using very little oil.*
• *Trim fat before and after cooking, and remove poultry and fish skin.*
• *Chill soups and stews so the excess fat rises to the top; remove the fat with a spoon and discard.*

# Vegetables & Accompaniments

### ⬇ ⟪ ♆ 💲

## Minted Sugar Snap Peas

Makes 8 servings.

*Nutrient Value Per Serving: 78 calories, 3 g protein, 4 g fat, 9 g carbohydrate, 280 mg sodium, 0 mg cholesterol.*

2   **tablespoons vegetable oil**
2   **pounds fresh sugar snap peas, strings removed**
¼   **cup water**
2   **tablespoons chopped fresh mint**
1   **teaspoon salt**
¼   **teaspoon pepper**

1. Heat the oil in a 12-inch skillet over high heat. Add the peas and stir-fry for 1 to 2 minutes, or until well coated with oil.
2. Add the water, mint, salt and pepper. Lower the heat to medium-high. Cover and cook for 1 minute. Uncover and stir-fry for 3 to 5 minutes, or until the peas are crisp-tender.

***To Make Ahead:*** You may remove the strings from sugar snap peas the day before.

### ⬇ ♆

## Asparagus with Gruyère

*A vertical asparagus steamer cooks this spring delicacy to perfection.*

Makes 6 servings.

*Nutrient Value Per Serving: 44 calories, 5 g protein, 2 g fat, 4 g carbohydrate, 18 mg sodium, 5 mg cholesterol.*

2   **pounds fresh asparagus**
¼   **cup grated Gruyère cheese (1 ounce)**
    **Salt or salt substitute, to taste**
    **Freshly ground pepper, to taste**

1. Cut the bottom 2 inches from the asparagus spears, if they are woody. If the spears are young and tender, just trim the bottoms. Use a swivel-bladed peeler to shave off the tough outside layer.
2. Place the trimmed asparagus in a large saucepan of boiling water. When the water returns to boiling, cook the asparagus for 3 minutes more, or until crisp-tender. Drain the asparagus. (Or use a vertical asparagus steamer.)
3. Arrange the asparagus spears, overlapping, in a 9 x 13-inch baking dish and sprinkle with the Gruyère cheese. Season with the salt or salt substitute and the pepper.
4. Broil the asparagus until the Gruyère cheese bubbles.

# THE VEGETABLE BIN

Here's the lowdown on some popular vegetables, with cooking tips to preserve their maximum flavor, color and nutrient value.

**Asparagus:** Iron, vitamins A and C; 11 calories per ½ cup. Steam over medium heat for 5 to 10 minutes until asparagus bends slightly.

**Beans (green and yellow):** Vitamin A; 15 calories per ½ cup. Steam; stir-fry.

**Beets:** Vitamins A and C; 40 calories per ½ cup. Microwave; grill; steam; serve raw. Wash first; leave nutrient-packed skin intact.

**Bok Choy:** Vitamin C, calcium; 15 calories per cup. Serve raw; stir-fry; sauté; separate leaves from stem, cook separately.

**Broccoli:** Vitamins A and C, calcium, fiber; 32 calories per stalk. Blanch to crisp-tender; microwave; steam; stir-fry; serve raw.

**Carrots:** Vitamin A; 50 calories per cup, sliced. Steam; stir-fry; microwave; serve raw.

**Cauliflower:** Vitamin C, iron; 27 calories per cup. Microwave; steam; stir-fry; serve raw.

**Cucumbers:** Some vitamins and minerals; 25 calories each. Scrub skin (peel if waxed), serve raw.

**Lettuce:** Darker leaves contain vitamins A, C and E; about 15 calories per head. Best served raw.

**Mushrooms:** Trace vitamins and minerals; 20 calories per cup. Best served raw; may be sautéed.

**Onions:** Some vitamin C; 40 calories per dry-skinned onion; 9 calories per green onion. Cook chopped onion, covered, to mellow flavor.

**Peas:** Protein, iron, vitamins A and C; snow peas: 40 calories per ½ cup; garden peas: 60 calories. Stir-fry snow peas; blanch snow peas in boiling water for 1 minute; hold blanched peas under cold running water to stop cooking. Steam fresh peas.

**Peppers (sweet):** Vitamins A and C, phosphorous, iron; 15 calories each. Best served raw, unpeeled.

**Potatoes:** Vitamins C and B1, iron, protein; average-size potato contains approximately 90 calories. Best cooked and served in skin.

**Spinach:** Vitamins A and C, iron, calcium; 14 calories per cup. Serve raw in salads; cook briefly in non-aluminum pan to retain color.

**Zucchini:** Vitamins A and C; 14 calories per ½ cup. Serve raw; steam lightly.

---

## Snap Peas with Balsamic Vinegar

Makes 6 servings.

*Nutrient Value Per Serving: 48 calories, 3 g protein, 0 g fat, 9 g carbohydrate, 5 mg sodium, 0 mg cholesterol.*

1½  **pounds snap peas OR: snow peas**
2    **tablespoons balsamic vinegar**
     **Salt or salt substitute, to taste**
     **Freshly ground pepper, to taste**

1. Trim the stem ends from the peas.
2. Place enough water to cover the peas in a large saucepan. Bring to boiling over medium heat and add the salt or salt substitute and the peas.
3. Return to boiling over medium heat. Lower the heat and simmer for 5 minutes, or until the peas are crisp-tender; drain well. Return to the pan.
4. Add the vinegar, salt or salt substitute and the pepper. Toss over low heat to blend. Adjust the seasonings, if necessary. Serve the peas immediately.

## String Bean Vinaigrette

Makes 6 servings.

*Nutrient Value Per Serving: 64 calories, 2 g protein, 4 g fat, 6 g carbohydrate, 7 mg sodium, 0 mg cholesterol.*

½  **pound green string beans, trimmed**
½  **pound yellow string beans, trimmed**
1  **large sweet red pepper, halved, seeded and thinly sliced into ¼-inch-wide strips**
¼  **cup sliced green onion**
2  **tablespoons snipped chives**
2  **tablespoons red wine vinegar**
1  **tablespoon olive oil**
1  **clove garlic, finely chopped**
⅛  **teaspoon chili powder**
3  **tablespoons sliced almonds, toasted**

1. Cook the green and yellow string beans in boiling water to cover in a large saucepan for 4 to 5 minutes, or until crisp-tender. Drain and place in a large bowl. Add the red pepper. Cover and chill.
2. Combine the green onion, chives, vinegar, oil, garlic and chili powder in a jar with a tight-fitting lid. Shake the dressing and pour over the vegetables. Toss to coat all the ingredients well. Sprinkle with the almonds.

## Spiced Basmati Rice

*Basmati rice has a special fragrance and flavor.*

Makes 6 servings.

*Nutrient Value Per Serving: 227 calories, 49 g protein, 0 g fat, 50 g carbohydrate, 278 mg sodium, 0 mg cholesterol.*

2  **cups basmati rice**
¾  **teaspoon salt or salt substitute**
1  **cinnamon stick**
1  **teaspoon ground cumin**
1  **bay leaf**
2⅔  **cups water**

1. Rinse the rice several times and place in a medium-size bowl. Add 1 quart of cold water and let stand for 30 minutes. Drain the rice.
2. Combine the rice, salt or salt substitute, cinnamon stick, cumin, bay leaf and water in a medium-size, heavy-bottomed saucepan. Bring to boiling over medium heat. Cover tightly and lower the heat to very low. Cook for 20 minutes.
3. Uncover, gently toss the rice with a fork and cover again. Cook slowly for 5 to 10 minutes more, or until the rice is tender and the liquid is absorbed.

## Ricotta Dip

*This dip also is a good filling for hollowed cherry tomatoes.*

Makes 6 servings.

*Nutrient Value Per Serving: 124 calories, 10 g protein, 7 g fat, 7 g carbohydrate, 105 mg sodium, 25 mg cholesterol.*

2  **cups part-skim ricotta cheese**
1  **cup finely chopped seeded tomato**
¼  **cup finely chopped fresh basil**
¼  **cup finely chopped red onion**
1  **teaspoon red wine vinegar**
¼  **teaspoon leaf thyme, crumbled**
¼  **teaspoon crushed red pepper flakes**
   **Salt or salt substitute, to taste**
   **Freshly ground pepper, to taste**

1. Combine the ricotta cheese, tomato, basil, onion, vinegar, thyme, red pepper flakes, salt or salt substitute and the pepper in a medium-size bowl.
2. Mix together until all the ingredients are well blended.
3. Chill and serve with assorted raw vegetables.

# UNUSUAL PRODUCE CAN LIVEN UP A MEAL
### And, happily, it is as close as your supermarket. The chart below will make you an instant expert on some of the variety items.

| Product | Description/Flavor | Recommended Uses | Basic Preparation |
|---|---|---|---|
| **Black Radish** | Black-skinned tuber, shaped like a turnip. Its white flesh has a sharp, radish flavor. | Use in salads, stir-fries, sauces. Sprinkle shreds on Oriental dishes for garnish. | Peel and shred or mince. Flavor is fairly sharp, so add and taste frequently. |
| **Boniatos** | A version of the sweet potato with white, sweet-tasting flesh and pale red skin. | Use in casseroles or pies, or cook and glaze with a little butter and brown sugar. | Cook as you would sweet potatoes: bake, boil or steam. |
| **Cactus Leaves** | Pads of Nopal cactus. | Use in salads, salsa, or as called for in Mexican recipes. | Remove thorns with a potato peeler. Slice or dice, serve raw, or boil 10 minutes. |
| **Chayote Squash** | Pear-shaped, green or white skin. Flavor is a cross between apple and cucumber. | Great in spicy sauces, or cheese or tomato dishes. | Bake halves at 375° for 30 minutes, or steam or boil ¼-inch chunks 15 minutes, or till tender. |
| **Cherimoya** | Has green multi-faceted skin. White flesh with black seeds, flavor is a mix of papaya, banana and pineapple. | Cut into wedges and eat like a papaya, discarding seeds. Or, add peeled and chopped fruit to compote or salad. | Ripen at room temperature for a few days till fruit yields to gentle pressure. |
| **Chiles, dried** | Dried Anaheim chiles. Red color and mild chile flavor. | Try in marinades or salad dressing, in stuffings, in cheese or egg dishes. | Soak in warm water for 1 hour to soften. Slit; cut off stems. |
| **Anaheim Chiles, Fresh** | Mild-flavored large green chile peppers. Shape is elongated. | Perfect for stuffing with meat or cheese, or in classic Chiles Rellenos. Chop into cornbread batter. | When handling fresh chilies, wear rubber gloves, or wash your hands thoroughly with soap and water immediately after handling. Chiles contain an oily substance that can cause a burning sensation—especially in eyes, on lips and fingers. The seeds and veins are the hottest parts; to tone down the hotness, discard those portions. To peel, place whole chiles on a broiler pan. Place pan about 4″ from heat source; broil till charred, turning frequently. Steam in paper bag for 15 minutes; skins will slip off easily. |
| **Jalapeño Chiles, Fresh** | Medium to small green or reddish-green chiles with a hot flavor. | Since these peppers are so hot, use sparingly to spark Mexican recipes, or egg- or tomato-based dishes. | |
| **Serrano Chiles, Fresh** | Small green to greenish-red chiles that pack a hot, pungent flavor. | Super-hot, these chiles are excellent in Mexican sauces, relishes and chile—but taste carefully as you go. | |
| **Yellow Chiles, Fresh** | Medium-size bright yellow chiles with a sunny-sweet, yet spunky flavor. Almost as mild as Anaheim chiles. | Great chopped into salads, meat stuffings, relishes, or salsas. Often pickled. | |

| Product | Description/Flavor | Recommended Uses | Basic Preparation |
|---------|-------------------|------------------|-------------------|
| **Dried Oriental Mushrooms** | Abalone, oyster, shiitake and wood ear are dried mushroom varieties. | Use in salads, stir-fries, fish and poultry dishes. Or sauté by themselves for an elegant side dish. | Reconstitute in warm water to cover, 30 minutes. Cut off tough stems; discard. Use as recipe directs. |
| **Enoki Mushrooms** | Slender white Oriental mushrooms with a bean sprout-like stem and tiny white cap. | Team with steamed vegetables or stir-fries; sauté to use as a plate garnish. | Trim off bottom half of stems; rinse and pat dry. Eat raw, or cook 1-2 min. |
| **Finnish Potatoes** | A yellow-skinned variety of white potato, pale yellow interior, buttery potato flavor. | Use as regular potatoes. Try these low-cal toppings: plain yogurt, sliced green onion, fresh herbs. | Prepare as you would regular potatoes. (About 100 calories per potato.) |
| **Hot House Cucumber** | Same flavor as regular cucumber, but this variety is seedless, has no bitterness. | Sprinkle over baked potatoes, broiled meats; mix with plain yogurt and fresh dill. | No need to peel; just slice or chop and serve following suggestions at left. |
| **Jicama** | Brown-skinned with white flesh. Slightly sweet flavor. Called the "Mexican potato." | Enjoy raw as a vegetable dipper, or grated over Mexican or Oriental dishes. | Peel according to package directions; serve raw or cooked. |
| **Kabocha Squash** | A Japanese variety of squash with a pale green-grey shell; flattened ball shape. | Takes well to stuffings, glazes, and mashed or puréed mixtures. | Bake halves or quarters at 375° cut-side down on baking sheet, 40-60 min. |
| **Plantains** | This "green banana" is served as a vegetable. Has a mild, potato-like flavor. | Add to meat dishes or casseroles. Great puréed in a creamy soup. | Bake, boil and mash, sauté or fry. |
| **Quince** | A green- to golden-colored fruit that resembles a misshapen apple or pear. | Stuff like a squash, or in compotes, with chicken or fish dishes. | Peel and chop before cooking until tender. |
| **Sapote** | Fruit shaped like stemless pippin apple, similar to cherimoya in flavor. | Enjoy out of hand, or in compotes, with chicken or fish dishes. | Peel and chop before adding to prepared dishes. |
| **Tamarindos** | A pod from the tamarind tree, pulp that tastes like apricots, dates and lemon. | Excellent in curries and chutneys. Use pulp in fruit dressings. | Soften pulp in water, remove seed, then remove pulp before cooking. |
| **Taro Root** | A root similar to the potato. Highly digestible. | Cook and mash with potatoes as a side dish. | Scrub well. Do not eat raw. Cook in boiling water to cover 40 min. |
| **Tomatillos** | Tomato that can be yellow-green to purple in color. Tastes similar to green plums. | For Mexican salads, salsas, sandwich fillings or dips. | Remove the papery covering; dice raw. Or cook up in a flavorful green sauce. |

Information courtesy of Frieda's Finest/Produce Specialties.

# Salads

## Food for Thought . . .

**Herb** The word "herb" comes from the Latin "herba", meaning grass. At one time, herb was spelled without the "h" and pronounced just as it was spelled. After the 16th century, the "h" was added, yet the pronunciation remained the same until the 1800's, when the English added the "h" sound. Today, both pronunciations are acceptable.

Herbs are the leaves of aromatic plants and shrubs. Known to mankind for thousands of years, herbs are used to add flavor to foods, and are known for their fragrance and medicinal properties.

Most herbs are classified into one of three families: The mint family (Labiatae) includes basil, lavender, marjoram, the mints, rosemary, sage, savory and thyme. The composite family (Compositae) includes tarragon, chamomile and yarrow. The umbel family (Umbelliferae), which is characterized by feathery or finely cut foliage and flowers borne on umbels, includes anise, angelica, caraway, chervil, coriander, dill, fennel and parsley.

Moderation is the rule when cooking with herbs, fresh or dried. Herbs should be used to enhance the flavor of a dish, not to overwhelm it; you can always add more, if you wish. Herbs are an excellent way to add flavor without calories.

## HERB LORE

• When substituting dried herbs for fresh, use 1 teaspoon of dried herbs for each tablespoon of fresh.

• When using dried herbs, crush the leaves in the palm of your hand just before adding to the recipe.

• Herbs in leaf form have a fresher flavor than ground herbs.

• Get to know the flavor of an herb by using it alone in a recipe. Then try blending several together.

• If you grow your own herbs, pick them just before the flowers open to get the best flavor. Wash the herbs and pat them dry with paper toweling. Tie them in small bunches and hang them to dry in a cool, airy place. When the bunches are brittle and dry, store them in tightly covered containers.

• To dry herbs in a microwave oven, remove the leaves from the stems and measure out 1½ to 2 cups. Spread the leaves on a double thickness of paper toweling. Microwave on high for 4 to 6 minutes. Stir the leaves several times during the drying. When the herbs are dry, store them in tightly covered containers.

• You can freeze herbs and use them without defrosting. Use the same amount as you would of fresh herbs.

• To make herb butter, use 1 tablespoon of chopped fresh herbs to ½ cup (1 stick) of butter.

• To make herb vinegar, use 1 cup of fresh, bruised leaves (dill, tarragon, basil or thyme are best) to 1 pint of white wine vinegar and steep for 2 weeks.

# *AN HERB FOR ALL SEASONINGS*

### *Basil*
Sweet, strong and aromatic. Clove-like in taste. Great with tomatoes, fish or eggs.

### *Bay Leaf*
Whole or ground leaves add a pungent flavor to long-simmered dishes. Use in soups, stews.

### *Chervil*
One of the *fines herbes*. More delicate leaves than parsley. Good in egg dishes.

### *Chives*
Slender, hollow stems with a mild onion flavor. Use with eggs, potatoes, cottage cheese, fish dishes.

### *Dill*
The feathery, fragrant fronds are great with fish, cucumbers, eggs or sour cream.

### *Fennel*
The feathery leaves are used fresh only. The seeds are dried. Use the leaves in fish or egg dishes.

### *Marjoram*
Sweet-scented, more delicate than oregano but interchangeable. Use in sausages, stews or tomato dishes.

### *Mint*
Many varieties, all having a refreshing aroma and taste. Use for fruit cups, jelly, in salads or marinades.

### *Oregano*
Pungent cousin of marjoram; flavor similar but stronger. Use with tomato dishes, pizza or eggplant.

### *Parsley*
Most common of all herbs; has curly or flat leaves. The main herb in *bouquet garni* and *fines herbes*.

### *Rosemary*
Fragrance like sun-warmed pine needles. Use in tomato or spaghetti sauces and marinades for meats.

### *Sage*
Very aromatic and fragrant. Has great affinity for pork, duck or goose, even cheese.

### *Savory*
Use winter savory for stews or stuffing, summer savory for green beans, eggs or fish.

### *Tarragon*
Has an anise-like flavor; essential in Bearnaise sauce. Add to eggs, fish and chicken, or use in vinegar.

### *Thyme*
Tiny fragrant leaves are nice in soups, stews, chowders or stuffing.

## Couscous Salad

*Couscous, made from semolina, is very quick to prepare.*

Makes 6 servings.

*Nutrient Value Per Serving: 215 calories, 7 g protein, 5 g fat, 35 g carbohydrate, 4 mg sodium, 0 mg cholesterol.*

2½ cups water
1 tablespoon olive oil
⅛ teaspoon crushed red pepper flakes
  Salt or salt substitute, to taste
1½ cups couscous
¼ cup fresh lemon juice
½ cup finely chopped parsley
¼ cup finely chopped mint
1 firm, ripe tomato, peeled, seeded and chopped
1 green onion, trimmed and chopped (about ¼ cup)
¼ cup pine nuts (pignoli), lightly toasted
  Freshly ground pepper, to taste

1. Combine the water, oil, red pepper flakes and salt or salt substitute in a medium-size saucepan and bring to boiling over medium heat.
2. Add the couscous and stir with a fork. Cover tightly and remove from the heat. Let stand for 5 minutes, or until the water is absorbed. Fluff the grains with the fork again, to eliminate any lumps.
3. Blend in the lemon juice, parsley, mint, tomato, green onion, pine nuts and pepper. Taste and adjust the seasonings, if necessary. Serve the salad at room temperature, or refrigerate it and serve it chilled, if you wish.

## Orange, Fennel and Onion Salad

Makes 6 servings.

*Nutrient Value Per Serving: 60 calories, 1 g protein, 2 g fat, 10 g carbohydrate, 10 mg sodium, 0 mg cholesterol.*

3 navel oranges, peeled, pith removed and sliced
1 medium-size red onion, thinly sliced
½ cup thinly sliced fennel
½ cup finely chopped mint
⅛ teaspoon crushed red pepper flakes
1 tablespoon olive oil
1 teaspoon red wine vinegar
  Salt or salt substitute, to taste
  Freshly ground pepper, to taste

1. Divide the orange, onion and fennel slices among 6 individual salad plates. Sprinkle with the mint and the red pepper flakes.
2. Combine the oil, vinegar, salt or salt substitute and the pepper in a small bowl. Drizzle the dressing over the salads.

# De-light-ful Desserts

⚡ ◀◀ 🍸 💲

## Pear Champagne Sorbet

Makes 6 servings.

*Nutrient Value Per Serving: 145 calories, 0 g protein, 0 g fat, 31 g carbohydrate, 9 mg sodium, 0 mg cholesterol.*

**1    can (29 ounces) pear halves, in heavy syrup**
**2    tablespoons sugar**
**1    tablespoon lemon juice**
**1    cup champagne**
      **Sprigs of fresh mint, for garnish (optional)**

1. Drain the pears, reserving 1 cup of the syrup. Dissolve the sugar in the reserved pear syrup. Add the lemon juice.
2. Purée the pears in the container of an electric blender or a food processor until very smooth, for about 30 seconds. Mix with the champagne and the syrup mixture in a large bowl. Pour into the container of an ice cream maker. Freeze following the manufacturer's directions. Garnish each serving with a mint sprig, if you wish.

---

### SO EASY SORBET

*Pour the fruit mixture into a 13 x 9 x 2-inch metal pan and cover with plastic wrap. Freeze until the mixture is firm 1½ inches from the edges, for about 1½ hours. Scrape the mixture into a large bowl and beat it at low speed until slushy. Pour the mixture back into the pan and cover. Freeze again until almost firm, for about 30 minutes. Beat again and return the mixture to the pan. Freeze until just firm, for about 2 hours.*

### LOW-CAL COOKING: TOOLS OF THE TRADE

**Calorie Charts & Guides:** *If you're serious about losing weight, one of the best ways to keep track of your food intake is by using calorie charts. After a few weeks of conscientious counting, you'll be able to do a quick calorie count for 90 percent of the foods you eat.*

*Try to look for a calorie guide that includes brand names, and lists specific products, convenience foods and mixes. The U.S. Department of Agriculture publishes a large handbook, The Composition of Foods, that includes calorie counts as well as other nutritional information— a worthwhile investment.*

**Weights & Measures:** *Invest in an accurate set of measures and a postal scale. Most dieters have no idea how small a 3- or 4-ounce serving of meat is! After a week of weighing and measuring your food, you'll develop a fairly accurate "eye" and won't need to measure everything you cook.*

**The Proper Equipment:** *A nonstick skillet is an absolute necessity to cut down on the use of fatty oils, as is a rack-equipped broiling pan so meats don't simmer in their own fat.*

**A Home Research Center:** *Become a collector of low-calorie cookbooks (borrow them from the library to try them first). Cookbooks for diabetics and heart patients are full of good hints, too. And most makers of low-calorie food brands publish recipe booklets that are yours for the writing.*

## THE HEALTHY SNACK BAR

*Vegetables and fruits make deliciously healthy and relatively low-cal snacks and hors d'oeuvres. Try the following at your next feast—and keep some on hand in the refrigerator, ready for munching at any time.*

- *Leeks, peeled, split and trimmed*
- *Sweet green pepper, cut into squares*
- *Radishes, halved*
- *Cherry tomatoes, halved*
- *Carrots, peeled and cut in slices or sticks*
- *Cauliflower, separated into flowerets*
- *Pineapple, cut into thin slices*
- *Apples, cut into wedges*
- *Zucchini, cut into spears*
- *Turnips, cut into slices*
- *Celery, cut into 1-inch pieces*
- *Kiwi, peeled and cut into slices*
- *Peas, raw*
- *Endive, separated into leaves*
- *Small whole cooked beets, cut into sticks*
- *Mushroom caps, cooked or raw*
- *Chinese snow peas*
- *Sweet red pepper, cut into squares*
- *Sugar snap peas, blanched*
- *Broccoli, separated into flowerets*
- *Orange slices, whole or halved*

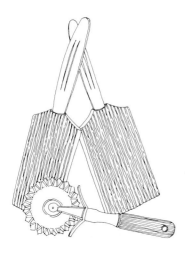

## Orange Sponge Cake with Raspberry Sauce

*A delicious make-ahead—and it's low-calorie.*

Bake at 400° for 12 to 14 minutes.
Makes 12 servings.

*Nutrient Value Per Serving: 91 calories, 3 g protein, 2 g fat, 15 g carbohydrate, 46 mg sodium, 91 mg cholesterol.*

**Nonstick vegetable cooking spray**

**Orange Sponge Cake:**
- 4   **eggs, separated**
- 1/8 **teaspoon salt**
- 1/4 **cup sugar**
- 1/2 **teaspoon grated orange rind**
- 1   **teaspoon orange juice**
- 2/3 **cup sifted all-purpose flour**

**Raspberry Sauce:**
- 3   **cups fresh raspberries, washed and hulled**
- 1/4 **cup 10X (confectioners' powdered) sugar**
- 1   **teaspoon raspberry brandy (optional)**
- 12  **raspberries, for garnish (optional)**

1. Preheat the oven to hot (400°). Spray the bottom of a 9 x 9 x 2-inch square baking pan with nonstick vegetable cooking spray. Line the bottom with aluminum foil and spray the foil.
2. Prepare the Orange Sponge Cake: Beat the egg whites with the salt in a large bowl until the whites are fluffy. Gradually beat in the sugar until the whites form stiff, shiny peaks.
3. Beat together the egg yolks, orange rind and orange juice in a second large bowl until well combined. Fold 1/2 cup of the beaten whites into the yolk mixture. Fold in the remaining whites. Then fold in the flour, 1 tablespoon at a time. Spread the batter evenly into the pan.
4. Bake in the preheated hot oven (400°) for 12 to 14 minutes, or until the top springs back when touched with your fingertip.

5. Loosen the cake around the edges of the pan with a knife and invert it onto a wire rack. Remove the pan and the foil. Invert the cake again so the golden side is on top. Cool the cake to room temperature on the rack.
6. Prepare the Raspberry Sauce: Combine the raspberries, 10X (confectioners' powdered) sugar and, if you wish, the raspberry brandy in the container of an electric blender or a food processor. Cover and whirl until the mixture is smooth. (The sauce can be made a day ahead, covered and refrigerated.)
7. To serve, cut the cake into 12 equal pieces and set on individual dessert plates. Spoon a generous 2 tablespoons of the sauce over each piece, and garnish each serving with a raspberry, if you wish.

## ◀◀ ▮ 💲
# *Strawberry Raspberry Tart*

*For a slightly sweeter taste, add a little sugar substitute to the cooled filling.*

Bake crust at 400° for 10 to 12 minutes. Makes 10 servings.

*Nutrient Value Per Serving: 126 calories, 1 g protein, 7 g fat, 15 g carbohydrate, 119 mg sodium, 3 mg cholesterol.*

½  *of 11-ounce package pie crust mix*
2  *pint baskets strawberries, hulled*
5  *tablespoons low-sugar raspberry preserves or jam*

1. Preheat the oven to hot (400°).
2. Prepare the pie crust mix following the package directions for a single 9-inch crust. Line a 9-inch tart pan with a removable bottom with the dough. Prick the bottom with a fork. Refrigerate for 10 minutes to set.
3. Bake in the preheated hot oven (400°) for 10 to 12 minutes, or until pale golden. Transfer to a wire rack to cool.
4. Reserve 1 pint of the strawberries for garnish. Halve the remaining berries.

5. Combine the halved strawberries with the raspberry preserves or jam in a saucepan. Bring to boiling. Lower the heat and simmer, stirring occasionally, until the berries have softened, for about 7 minutes.
6. Strain the berries over a bowl. Transfer the berries to a small bowl. Pour the fruit syrup back into the saucepan. Cook over low heat, stirring constantly, until thickened to a jamlike consistency, for about 5 minutes. Add the thickened syrup to the cooked berries in the small bowl. Cool to room temperature.
7. Spread the cooked berry mixture into the tart shell. Refrigerate, lightly covered, until ready to serve. (The tart may be kept overnight.)
8. Just before serving, remove the outer ring from the tart pan. Cut the reserved pint of strawberries into ½-inch-thick slices and arrange them on the tart.

## ◀◀
# *Honey Spiced Peaches*

*When peaches aren't in season, use the poaching liquid to prepare firm, ripe pears.*

Makes 6 servings.

*Nutrient Value Per Serving: 107 calories, 1 g protein, 0 g fat, 28 g carbohydrate, 5 mg sodium, 0 mg cholesterol.*

2  *cups dry white wine*
   *OR: white grape juice*
1  *bay leaf*
12  *whole allspice berries*
12  *whole black peppercorns*
2  *whole cloves*
3  *tablespoons honey*
6  *large, ripe but firm peaches, skinned, halved and pitted*

1. Combine the wine or grape juice, the bay leaf, allspice, peppercorns, cloves and honey in a medium-size, non-aluminum saucepan. Bring to boiling over medium heat, stirring until the honey dissolves.
2. Add the peaches to the spiced syrup and

lower the heat. Simmer, stirring occasionally, just until the peaches are tender but still retain their shape, for about 5 minutes. Strain, reserving the poaching liquid. Place the peaches and spices in a medium-size bowl.

3. Boil the reserved poaching liquid until it is reduced by half, for about 10 minutes. Carefully pour the liquid over the peaches in the bowl and cool to room temperature. Refrigerate, covered, for at least 4 hours, or overnight.

---

## Food for Thought . . .

**Honey** *Honey was the only known sweetener prior to the extraction of sugar from sugar cane, which began in the 15th century. Honey is made by honeybees from flower nectar. The bees collect the nectar and store it in their honey sacs, where it is converted into a sweet liquid. This liquid is deposited in honeycombs, where it undergoes chemical changes to become honey.*

*Honey is flavored and colored by the flowers used to produce it. Clover, sage, orange and alfalfa blossom are the most common kinds of honey. It is sold as a liquid or still in the honeycomb.*

*Honey can be substituted for sugar in most recipes by reducing the amount of liquid called for in the recipe by 1/4 cup for each cup of honey used. Its sweetening capacity is comparable to that of sugar.*

*Store honey at room temperature in a tightly covered container. Cold temperatures increase crystallization. To liquify crystallized honey, place the jar in a pan of warm, not hot, water until the honey returns to its liquid state.*

---

## Berries in Cinnamon Yogurt

*Plain yogurt, pleasantly spiced, makes a versatile dessert topping base.*

Makes 6 servings.

---

*Nutrient Value Per Serving: 63 calories, 2 g protein, 14 g carbohydrate, 1 g fat, 16 mg sodium, 1 mg cholesterol.*

---

| | |
|---|---|
| 1/2 | cup plain lowfat yogurt |
| 1 | teaspoon honey |
| 1/2 | teaspoon ground cinnamon |
| 1 | pint blueberries, rinsed |
| 1 | pint raspberries, rinsed |
| 6 | sprigs fresh mint, for garnish |

1. Mix together the yogurt, honey and cinnamon in a small bowl until well blended (this can be done in advance). Cover and refrigerate the spiced yogurt.
2. When ready to serve, divide the blueberries and the raspberries among 6 individual bowls. Top with the spiced yogurt and garnish with a mint sprig.

---

### FRESH IDEAS FOR YOGURT

*Use plain lowfat yogurt as a base for a variety of fruit and spice combinations. Yogurt mixed with crushed raspberries and a teaspoon or two of raspberry liqueur can be layered with sliced ripe peaches or nectarines to make a delectable melba-like dessert. Or, for a tropical touch, purée fresh mango cubes with lime juice and lime rind, stir into yogurt and use as a dip for other fresh fruits.*

*Berries in Cinnamon Yogurt*

# CHAPTER 8

# Microwave Miracles

*This is the dawning of the age of the microwave—a marvel of quick cooking.*

*"Roasted" Lamb Chop(s) (recipe, page 233); Baby Carrots and Green Beans (recipe, page 252); "Roasted" New Potatoes (recipe, pages 253-254); Minted Pea Purée in Tomato Cups (recipe, page 257)*

By now, you've read articles and seen books that sing the praises of the microwave oven. You know it's efficient, clean, cool and saves incredible amounts of time. But if you're still a Doubting Thomas about using your microwave for something other than boiling water, reheating food or melting butter, these recipes are for you. Taste and ye shall believe.

The point of this chapter is to introduce you to the recipe diversity a microwave oven offers. Try Chicken El Calvador *(recipe, page 242)*, Paella Mariscos *(recipe, page 246)*, or Black 'n White Cheesecake *(recipe, page 262)* with Strawberry Sauce *(recipe, page 261)*. Now that's using your microwave to its fullest potential!

In addition to all the recipes in this chapter, you'll find microwave adaptations of many recipes throughout this book. Whether you're a newcomer to the microwave oven, or an experienced cook looking to expand your microwave repertoire, you'll find these recipes and tips invaluable. Read the helpful hints throughout this chapter before you use your microwave again.

Remember: A microwave oven can cut your kitchen work into a fraction of its usual load. So invest some time in learning how to make a microwave work for you—and make it easy on yourself. ■

# Appetizers

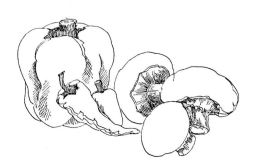

## Confetti Peppers

Microwave at full power for 7 to 8 minutes.
Makes 20 appetizers.

*Nutrient Value Per Appetizer: 28 calories, 2 g protein,
2 g fat, 1 g carbohydrate, 36 mg sodium, 6 mg cholesterol.*

**5    small sweet peppers, red, green
        and/or yellow
½    cup chopped onion (1 medium-size
        onion)
2    ounces chopped mushrooms
        (about ½ cup)
1    cup shredded Cheddar cheese
        (about 4 ounces)
        Crumbled bacon, sliced green onion
        and sliced pimiento, for garnish**

1. Cut the peppers into quarters, then core
   and seed them. Place the peppers on an
   11-inch microwave-safe quiche pan or
   platter. Cover with microwave-safe
   plastic wrap. Microwave at full power for
   3 minutes, rotating the dish one quarter
   turn after 2 minutes. Cool slightly.
2. Combine the onion and the mushrooms in
   a 9-inch microwave-safe pie plate. Cover
   with microwave-safe plastic wrap.
   Microwave at full power for 2 minutes.
3. Spoon the onion-mushroom mixture onto
   the pepper quarters. Sprinkle with the
   Cheddar cheese. Microwave, uncovered,
   at full power for 2 to 3 minutes, or until
   the Cheddar cheese melts. Garnish with
   crumbled bacon and sliced green onion
   and pimiento, if you wish.

## MICROWAVE MAGIC: HOW DOES IT WORK?

*Microwaves reflect off the sides, top
and bottom of the oven cavity,
penetrating the cookware and causing
the water molecules in food to vibrate
rapidly (about 450 million times per
second), which results in friction. In
turn, the friction creates heat and it is
this internal heat that cooks the food.*

*A microwave oven should be
operated only when food or liquid is on
the static tray or turntable, and the
door is closed. Extensive damage
and/or arcing (similar to a fireworks
display) can result from microwaves
bouncing around an empty oven.*

*A microwave oven cooks food from
the outside—top, bottom and sides—
in. Microwave-safe utensils transmit
but, as a rule, do not absorb
microwave energy. As a result, the
cookware remains cool to the touch,
unless the food becomes so hot that it
transfers heat to the cooking container.*

*From top: Confetti Peppers, Chicken Pumpkin Mousse (recipe, page 232)*

# Chicken Pumpkin Mousse

Microwave at three quarters power for 7 to 8 minutes.
Makes 4 servings.

*Nutrient Value Per Serving: 221 calories, 12 g protein, 15 g fat, 12 g carbohydrate, 703 mg sodium, 194 mg cholesterol.*

> **Tomato Salsa (recipe follows)**
> 1 **skinless, boned chicken breast half, (4 to 4½ ounces), cut into 1-inch chunks**
> 2 **eggs**
> 1 **cup solid-pack pumpkin purée**
> ½ **cup heavy cream**
> ¾ **teaspoon salt**
> ½ **teaspoon ground cumin**
> ⅛ **teaspoon pepper**
> **Coriander sprigs, for garnish**

1. Prepare the Tomato Salsa.
2. Purée the chicken with 1 of the eggs in the container of a food processor or an electric blender. Add the remaining egg, the pumpkin purée, cream, salt, cumin and pepper and whirl until smooth. Pour into a 1½-quart microwave-safe bowl. Cover with microwave-safe plastic wrap. Microwave at three quarters power for 3 minutes, stirring after each minute.
3. Spoon the mixture into 4 buttered 6-ounce microwave-safe custard cups and smooth the tops. Cover each cup with vented, microwave-safe plastic wrap. Microwave at three quarters power for 4 to 5 minutes, or until almost set, rotating each cup one quarter turn after 2 minutes. Let stand, covered, 10 minutes.
4. To serve, unmold each mousse onto a plate and garnish with the coriander sprigs. Serve with the Tomato Salsa.

**Tomato Salsa:** Drain 1 can (16 ounces) of whole tomatoes; chop coarsely. Place them in a small bowl. Stir in 3 tablespoons of chopped canned green chili peppers, 2 tablespoons of chopped green onion, 1 tablespoon of chopped cilantro or parsley and, if you wish, ⅛ teaspoon of salt.

## Food for Thought . . .

**Pumpkin** *The fruit of a vine of the gourd family that was native to Central America and grown by American Indians long before the first colonists landed in this country. Indians boiled and baked pumpkins, and also dried them to use in the winter. Although pumpkins are used primarily to make pies, they also can be served as a vegetable and used to make soups or breads. Pumpkins are a good source of vitamin A, with only 33 calories in a 3½-ounce serving.*

*Pumpkins are in season from September to December. The size and shape of a pumpkin does not affect its taste, but the smaller the pumpkin, the more tender the flesh. A 5-pound pumpkin will yield about 4½ cups of mashed, cooked pumpkin. When serving it as a vegetable, allow ½ to ¾ pound per serving. Fresh pumpkin can be stored in a dry, well-ventilated place for several months.*

## THE DISH TEST

*Most dishes and utensils safe for use in a microwave are clearly marked. If you don't know whether or not a plate of glass, china or pottery is microwavable, try this test:*

*Put the dish in question into the microwave next to a 1-cup glass measure filled with cool water. Microwave at full power for 1 minute. If the water warms up but the test dish remains cool, the dish is safe for microwave use.*

*If the dish is warm, it can be used, but only for short periods of heating. If the dish gets hot, do not use it in the microwave for any purpose.*

# Main Dishes

## "Roasted" Lamb Chops

*A browning tray is essential to the success of this recipe. The tray's special coating absorbs microwaves when preheated. This makes the cooking surface very hot so it can brown and crisp food.*

Microwave at full power for 6 to 7 minutes.
Makes 4 servings.

*Nutrient Value Per Serving: 315 calories, 35 g protein, 18 g fat, 0 g carbohydrate, 85 mg sodium, 128 mg cholesterol.*

8  rib lamb chops (about 6 ounces each), trimmed
1½  tablespoons olive oil
1  teaspoon leaf thyme, crumbled
   Salt and pepper, to taste

1. Place a browning tray in the microwave and heat for 6 minutes at full power (or following the manufacturer's directions).
2. Coat the lamb chops on both sides with the oil. Rub on the thyme and sprinkle with the salt and pepper. Working in batches, if necessary (depending on the size of the oven and browning tray), place the chops on the preheated browning tray.
3. Microwave at full power for 5 minutes. Turn and microwave for 1 to 2 minutes more, or until done to taste. Cover and let stand for 3 minutes before serving.

## Pinto Beans Picante

*The beans need no soaking with this microwave technique. They take an hour, but that's still half or a third of the time needed on top of the stove.*

Microwave at full power for 1 hour, 22 minutes.
Makes 8 servings (about 8 cups).

*Nutrient Value Per Serving: 281 calories, 14 g protein, 9 g fat, 36 g carbohydrate, 436 mg sodium, 11 mg cholesterol.*

½  pound sliced lean bacon
1  pound dried pinto beans
8  cups water
3  cloves garlic, finely chopped
1  teaspoon salt

1. Cut the bacon into ½-inch squares. Place in a 3-quart microwave-safe casserole dish.
2. Microwave at full power for 7 minutes, stirring after 5 minutes. If the bacon was fatty, pour off and discard all but 3 to 4 tablespoons of the fat.
3. Rinse the pinto beans, picking them over for any discolored ones. Add to the casserole dish with the water and the garlic.
4. Microwave at full power for 15 minutes. Stir and microwave for 1 hour more, stirring every 15 minutes, and adding the salt during the last 15 minutes. Let stand at least 10 minutes before serving.

# MARVELOUS MICRO-GRILLING

By using your microwave oven to help speed up barbecue cooking time, you can achieve perfectly barbecued food in record time!

Knowing which foods to precook, and for how long, can make delicious barbecued food available to you any night of your busy week.

## Chicken

• Arrange chicken parts in a microwave-safe baking dish with the meatiest portions toward the outside of the dish. Cover the dish loosely with heavy-duty plastic wrap and cook in your microwave according to the chicken cooking guide, page 242.

• Place the chicken, while still hot, over hot coals on a grill that's been sprayed with nonstick cooking spray for fast and easy clean-up.

• For the best flavor, baste the chicken frequently with your favorite barbecue sauce.

• Check for doneness by removing one piece of the chicken from the grill, letting it stand for a few minutes, and cutting into it to see if the juices run clear. The perfectly grilled chicken is crisp-skinned, juicy inside and permeated with smoky flavor.

## Italian Sausage

• Place hot or sweet Italian sausage in a microwave-safe dish. Prick with a fork in several places.

• Cover the dish loosely with wax paper and cook at full power for about 7 minutes per pound, or until almost no pink remains. Drain and cut into 3- or 4-inch pieces.

• Cook over hot coals for about 15 minutes, turning the pieces frequently.

## Spare Ribs

• For about 3 pounds of ribs, place a large-size oven cooking bag in a microwave-safe baking dish. Add barbecue sauce (bottled or your own recipe), then the ribs.

• Squeeze the bag a few times to coat the meat, then tie with string or a non-metal twist-tie. Make several small slits in the bag near the top.

• Cook at half power for about 30 minutes, or until the meat is just about tender. To ensure even cooking, turn the bag over and rotate once during the cooking time.

• Remove the ribs from the bag and place them over hot coals for about 25 minutes, turning them frequently and basting with the sauce left in the cooking bag.

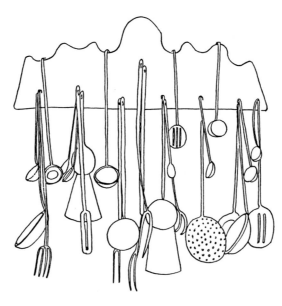

## Vegetables

• Whole potatoes can be scrubbed, dried and placed on paper toweling. For four large Idaho potatoes, cook at full power for about 10 minutes. Wrap the whole potatoes in heavy-duty aluminum foil and bury them in hot coals until fork tender. Or slice the potatoes in half, baste them with butter or barbecue sauce and place them, cut side down, on the grill. Cook over hot coals, turning and basting a few times, until the potatoes are tender.

• To prepare moist, fresh-flavored corn on the cob, sprinkle sparingly with water or brush the ears with melted butter. Wrap the ears in microwave-safe plastic wrap, twisting the ends loosely so that a small amount of steam can escape. Cook for 6 to 8 minutes (for four ears) at full power just until tender. You may eat the corn this way, or remove the plastic, wrap in aluminum foil and place the corn directly on the hot coals for 5 to 10 minutes to get a fresh-from-the-grill flavor.

• Cut three small, unpeeled eggplants (about 6 ounces each) in half. Place them on a microwave-safe plate. Cover the plate loosely with microwave-safe plastic wrap and cook the 6 halves at full power for 3 minutes. Brush the eggplant halves with olive oil and sprinkle them with chopped fresh basil. Grill the eggplant, cut side down, for about 10 minutes, or until very tender. The eggplant should be tender enough to scoop out of its shell to eat.

• "Stubborn" foods, such as onions and sweet peppers, can be softened slightly in the microwave before being threaded onto skewers to cook as shish kebab.

**Note:** Always cut vegetables into even-size pieces before microwaving, and remember that foods continue to cook for a few minutes after they've been removed from the oven. As a rule, 30 seconds to 1 minute at full power is perfect for six small, whole white onions or a cut-up sweet green pepper.

## MICRO-EASE

• *Cover dishes of vegetables, fish, poultry and other foods that benefit from moisture cooking (steam) with microwave-safe plastic wrap, and fold back a small corner of the wrap to vent. This allows the steam to escape, preventing burns that might occur when the wrap is removed. Remove plastic wrap by lifting the corner farthest away from you; do not cut or puncture the wrap.*

• *Revive lumpy white or brown sugar by placing it in a microwave-safe dish with an apple slice. Cover, vent and microwave at full power for 15 seconds. The moisture from the apple should soften the sugar.*

• *Tortilla shells and pita bread become more pliable and easier to fill when softened first. Wrap in plastic wrap and microwave at full power for 30 seconds, or until warm. Leave them wrapped until ready to fill—they harden as they cool.*

• *To melt 1 ounce of chocolate or butter, cover a small glass custard cup with vented plastic wrap. Microwave at half power until the chocolate or butter just begins to melt. Remove from the microwave and let stand. The plastic wrap will hold in enough heat to completely melt the chocolate or butter without cooking.*

• *For delicious scrambled eggs, melt 2 tablespoons of butter in a ½-quart glass casserole dish. Beat 8 eggs with ½ cup of milk, pour into the casserole dish and cover with vented plastic wrap. Microwave at full power for 4½ to 5 minutes, or until the eggs are set but still moist; stir twice. Sprinkle with ½ cup of shredded Cheddar cheese. Let stand, covered, for 2 minutes to melt the cheese.*

*Beef Enchiladas, Enchilada Sauce (recipe, page 240), Chicken Tacos (recipe, page 243), Pinto Beans Picante (recipe, page 233), Spanish Rice (recipe, page 244)*

# Beef Enchiladas

*Prepare the enchilada sauce and the beef filling ahead of time and you can have a terrific South-of-the-Border feast ready in minutes. (Shredded Chicken Filling, page 241, can be used here in place of beef.)*

Microwave at full power for 15 to 16 minutes.
Makes 8 servings.

---

*Nutrient Value Per Serving: 528 calories, 25 g protein, 40 g fat, 20 g carbohydrate, 695 mg sodium, 89 mg cholesterol.*

---

½   **cup vegetable oil**
8   **corn tortillas (6-inch)**
1½  **cups hot Enchilada Sauce**
      **(recipe, page 240)**
2   **cups Shredded Beef Filling**
      **(recipe at right)**
1   **cup thinly sliced green onions**
24  **pitted ripe olives**
1   **cup shredded mild Cheddar cheese**
      **(4 ounces)**
1   **cup shredded Monterey Jack cheese**
      **(4 ounces)**
1   **cup dairy sour cream**
8   **radishes**

1. Place the oil in a shallow 7- or 8-inch round microwave-safe casserole dish.
2. Microwave at full power for 5 minutes, or until hot.
3. Remove from the oven and, with tongs, dip in one tortilla, turning it once, until it sizzles and softens, for about 30 seconds on each side. Place on paper toweling and repeat with a second tortilla. (Usually the oil remains hot enough to sizzle two.) Reheat the oil for 2 minutes and repeat, until all the tortillas are done, stacking them between paper toweling to absorb excess oil.
4. If the Enchilada Sauce has cooled, heat it for about 1 minute at full power (it should be in a container wide enough to dip a tortilla into). Dip a tortilla into the sauce and place it in a microwave-safe shallow, oblong casserole dish (or browning tray).
5. Arrange ¼ cup of the Shredded Beef Filling along the lower third of the tortilla, add 2 tablespoons of the green onion and 2 of the olives. Roll up to enclose the filling. Repeat, placing the enchiladas in a row. Top with the Cheddar and Monterey Jack cheeses.
6. Microwave at full power for 4 minutes, or until hot and the Cheddar and Monterey Jack cheeses have melted.
7. Serve hot with the remaining 8 olives, the sour cream and radishes. Serve with Pinto Beans Picante *(recipe, page 233)* and Spanish Rice *(recipe, page 244)*, if you wish.

# Shredded Beef Filling

*Use this tasty filling in tacos or enchiladas. The tender shreds of beef normally would take about 3 hours of simmering; here, they are ready in about an hour.*

Microwave at full power for 5 minutes, then at half power for 55 minutes.
Makes 2 cups.

---

*Nutrient Value Per Serving: 189 calories, 13 g protein, 15 g fat, 0 g carbohydrate, 140 mg sodium, 49 mg cholesterol.*

---

1¼  **pounds beef chuck, cut into 1½-inch**
      **cubes**
1   **cup canned beef or chicken broth**
1   **bay leaf**
1   **clove garlic, finely chopped**

1. Combine the beef, beef or chicken broth, bay leaf and garlic in a 2-quart microwave-safe casserole dish.
2. Microwave at full power for 5 minutes.
3. Reduce the power to half and microwave for 30 minutes, stirring every 10 minutes. Let stand for 10 minutes.
4. Microwave at half power for 15 minutes more. Let stand for 10 minutes.
5. When the beef is cool enough to handle, tear into shreds with your fingers and return to the casserole dish. Cover with heavy-duty plastic wrap and microwave at half power for 10 minutes.

# *MAXIMIZE YOUR MICROWAVE*

These pointers will help you to use your microwave oven to its maximum potential.

### *Basic Know-How*

*1.* Make sure the cookware rests on a solid, heatproof surface during the standing or resting time specified in the recipe.

*2.* Set a timer for the minimum cooking time called for in a recipe. Check the doneness of the food, then microwave for the additional time, if necessary.

*3.* When frequent stirring is necessary for a dish, leave a wooden spoon or microwave-safe utensil in the dish in the oven.

*4.* When cooking uniform pieces of food, such as meatballs or chicken wings, arrange them in a circle for even cooking.

*5.* Do not use gold- or silver-trimmed dishes in a microwave oven; arcing may occur. Arcing is an electrical current that flows from the oven wall to any metal in the oven, causing a light flash and a popping sound. This may cause damage to the magnetron tube, the interior oven wall or the cookware. If arcing occurs, turn off the power immediately.

*6.* To prevent damage to your microwave if accidently turned on, always keep a glass measure or bowl containing about 1 cup of water in the oven.

*7.* Microwaving works especially well with foods that have a naturally high moisture content, such as fish, poultry, fruits and vegetables.

*8.* Dense foods, such as potatoes, will take longer to cook in a microwave oven than lighter-textured foods, such as a cake.

### *Meat, Fish and Poultry*

*9.* Cook clams and mussels in their shells: Place them on a microwave-safe pie plate, hinged side toward the outside of the plate, and cover loosely with wax paper. For three 5-ounce clams, microwave at full power for 3 to 5 minutes, or until the shells open.

*10.* If your roast beef is too rare, microwave the slices right on the dinner plate until the desired doneness is reached.

*11.* For one-step cooking and draining of excess fat, crumble ground meat into a microwave-safe plastic colander set in a casserole dish. The fat will drain into the casserole dish during cooking.

*12.* For no-fuss hors d'oeuvres: Wrap pineapple chunks or water chestnuts in bacon and fasten with a wooden pick. Place them on paper toweling. Microwave at full power until the bacon is thoroughly cooked.

*13.* For an instant hot dog in a warm bun, lightly score a fully cooked frankfurter and place it in the bun. Wrap loosely in paper toweling and microwave at full power for 30 to 45 seconds.

*14.* For barbecued spareribs and chicken, microwave until tender, then grill for a charcoal flavor and a crisp exterior *(see Marvelous Micro-Grilling, page 234).*

*15.* Boneless meats cook more evenly than meats on the bone, because bones attract more microwave energy than meat does.

### *Fruits and Vegetables*

*16.* To get the maximum amount of juice from citrus fruits, microwave at full power for 15 to 30 seconds before squeezing.

*17.* Peel, core and pierce whole fruit, such as apples, before microwaving, to allow steam to escape and avoid spattering.

*18.* When microwaving cabbage-family vegetables, such as fresh broccoli or cauliflower, cover loosely with wax paper for better flavor and color.

*19.* For an easy single serving of frozen vegetables: Put ½ cup of frozen vegetables with 1 tablespoon of water in a custard cup; cover with wax paper. Microwave at full power for 1½ to 2 minutes.

*20.* To quickly cook crisp frozen hash brown or French fried potatoes, first partially thaw them in the microwave, following the package directions, then fry or bake them conventionally to finish.

*21.* To plump dried fruit, place it in a bowl, sprinkle with water and microwave at full power for 15 to 30 seconds.

**22.** To dry fresh herbs, wash and pat dry on paper toweling. Spread 1½ cups (without stems) on a double thickness of paper toweling and microwave at full power for 4 to 5 minutes, stirring several times.

**23.** Pierce the skin of a medium-size (1¼ pounds) acorn squash and microwave at full power for 4 minutes. Cut in half, remove the seeds and microwave for another 4 minutes. Let stand for 5 minutes.

**24.** Cook broccoli or asparagus with the tender flower ends pointing toward the center and the stem ends pointing out.

### Quick Cooking Tips

**25.** Microwave cold bacon slices in their package at full power for 30 to 45 seconds to separate.

**26.** To soften ice cream for easier scooping, microwave the container at one third power for 20 to 40 seconds.

**27.** Soften a stick of butter at half power for 45 to 55 seconds; remove the wrapper first.

**28.** To soften cream cheese, remove the foil wrapper and wrap in wax paper. Microwave at one third power for 1½ to 2 minutes for 3 ounces, 3 to 4 minutes for 8 ounces.

**29.** Double paper muffin-pan liners to help absorb excess moisture when microwaving.

**30.** Loosen hard brown sugar: Add an apple slice or a few drops of water to the box; microwave at full power for a few seconds.

**31.** To melt chocolate, microwave it in a microwave-safe cup at full power for 45 to 60 seconds per ounce.

**32.** To make chocolate curls, heat a block of chocolate, unwrapped, on a microwave-safe plate at half power for 8 to 12 seconds. Scrape off curls with a vegetable peeler.

**33.** To "toast" coconut, spread out 1 cup of shredded coconut on a microwave-safe pie plate. Microwave at full power for 2 to 3 minutes, stirring several times.

**34.** To make chocolate syrup, combine 1¼ cups of granulated sugar, 1 cup of unsweetened cocoa powder, ¾ cup of water and ⅛ teaspoon of salt in a 1-quart measuring cup. Microwave at full power for 2 minutes, or until the mixture boils; stir.

Continue cooking for 2 minutes more, stirring every 30 seconds; don't let the mixture boil over. Stir in ½ teaspoon of vanilla. To serve, stir 2 tablespoons of the syrup into an 8-ounce glass of milk. When refrigerated, tightly covered, syrup will keep for up to 1 month.

**35.** For fried or poached eggs, always pierce the yolks with a wooden pick *before* microwaving, to prevent bursting.

**36.** Heat water for tea, instant coffee or cocoa directly in the cup. A 6-ounce cup of water microwaved at full power will be steaming after 1¼ to 2 minutes.

**37.** Toast 2 slices of bread in a toaster or toaster oven. Place a slice of cheese on one slice; spread with mustard, if you wish, then top with the remaining slice. Place the sandwich on a paper plate; microwave at three quarters power for 15 to 20 seconds, or until the cheese melts.

### Warming Up Foods

**38.** Microwave rolls in a napkin-lined basket at full power for 15 to 30 seconds, depending on the size and number of rolls.

**39.** Microwave sandwiches wrapped in paper toweling to absorb excess moisture.

**40.** Heat pancake syrup in its container with the cap removed, or in a serving pitcher, at full power for 15 seconds.

**41.** Heat gravy in a serving bowl or gravy boat at full power for 45 to 60 seconds.

**42.** To warm a 12-ounce jar of sundae topping, remove the lid and microwave at full power for 45 to 60 seconds.

**43.** Reheat fast food in its own wrapping at full power. If it has a foil top, remove the top and cover loosely with wax paper. Reheat a fast food hamburger in its plastic package at full power for 20 to 40 seconds.

**44.** To crisp and renew the flavor of day old cookies, crackers or potato chips, microwave at full power for 5 to 15 seconds.

**45.** To warm a slice of fruit pie, microwave at full power for 15 to 20 seconds.

**46.** Reheat popped corn at full power for 15 to 20 seconds per cup.

## JUST THE FACTS, MA'AM: MICROWAVE BASICS

- *Microwave cooking involves cooking with time, not temperature. The amount of time required to cook food is directly related to the food's starting temperature, volume and density.*
- *The colder the food, the longer it takes to cook, heat or defrost.*
- *As the food volume increases, the cooking, heating or defrosting time increases—two potatoes take longer to bake than one.*
- *The more dense a food item, the longer it takes to cook, heat or defrost. A 1-pound piece of meat takes longer to cook than a 1-pound loaf of bread, because meat is denser than bread.*

- *Stirring foods, such as scrambled eggs or puddings, keeps the cooking even by mixing the cooked outside portion with the center.*
- *Food continues to cook after being removed from microwave, so a standing time is necessary. Standing time allows the heat to be conducted toward the center.*
- *Microwaves cook the outer section of food first, so the center takes the longest to cook. When arranging food on a plate or in cookware, place the largest, thickest portion of the food toward the outside of the dish.*

## Enchilada Sauce

*This simple sauce can be made from ingredients usually kept on hand in the pantry.*

Microwave at full power for 7 minutes.
Makes 1½ cups (enough for 8 enchiladas).

*Nutrient Value Per Serving: 47 calories, 2 g protein, 3 g fat, 3 g carbohydrate, 241 mg sodium, 0 mg cholesterol.*

1½ **tablespoons vegetable oil**
2 **tablespoons all-purpose flour**
1 **clove garlic, finely chopped**
3 **tablespoons chili powder**
½ **teaspoon ground cumin**
½ **teaspoon leaf oregano, crumbled**
¼ **teaspoon salt**
1½ **cups chicken stock or canned broth**

1. Stir together the oil, flour and garlic in a 1-quart microwave-safe casserole dish.
2. Microwave at full power for 1 minute, or until hot.
3. Stir in the chili powder, cumin, oregano, salt and stock or broth.
4. Microwave at full power for 6 minutes, or until the sauce has thickened, stirring every 2 minutes.

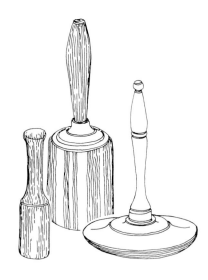

## Hot Pita Pockets

Microwave at full power for 14 to 17 minutes.
Makes 8 servings.

*Nutrient Value Per Serving: 298 calories, 17 g protein, 10 g fat, 36 g carbohydrate, 680 mg sodium, 37 mg cholesterol.*

- ½    **pound lean ground beef**
- ½    **pound lean ground pork**
- 2    **tomatoes, diced**
- ½    **cup bottled hot barbecue sauce**
- 2    **tablespoons Worcestershire sauce**
- 1    **teaspoon chili powder**
- ¼    **teaspoon ground cumin**
- ⅛    **teaspoon leaf oregano, crumbled**
- 2    **green onions, sliced**
- 1    **small zucchini, cut into julienne strips**
- ½    **small sweet red pepper, cut into julienne strips**
- 1    **clove garlic, finely chopped**
- 2    **tablespoons water**
- 4    **large whole wheat pita breads, halved**
        **Shredded lettuce**
- ½    **cup shredded Cheddar cheese, for garnish**
- 12    **pitted black olives, sliced, for garnish**

1. Crumble the beef and the pork into a microwave-safe 2-quart casserole dish. Cover with microwave-safe plastic wrap. Microwave at full power for 4 to 6 minutes, or until the meat turns brown, stirring twice. Remove from the oven. Drain off any fat, if necessary.
2. Stir in the tomatoes, barbecue and Worcestershire sauces, chili powder, cumin and oregano. Cover tightly with microwave-safe plastic wrap. Microwave at full power for 5 to 6 minutes, or until boiling, stirring twice. Remove from the oven.
3. Combine the green onion, zucchini, red pepper, garlic and water in a microwave-safe 1½-quart casserole dish. Cover tightly with microwave-safe plastic wrap. Microwave at full power for 5 minutes, or until the vegetables are crisp-tender. Remove from the oven and drain. Stir into the meat mixture.
4. To serve, line each pita half with the shredded lettuce. Ladle in some of the meat mixture. Garnish with the Cheddar cheese and the olives.

---

### HOW TO JULIENNE VEGETABLES

*Cut the vegetable into 1½-inch lengths. Stand the sections on a cut side. Slice each one into ¼-inch widths, then turn and cut into matchstick lengths.*

---

## Shredded Chicken Filling

**This moist and tender filling is perfect for tacos or enchiladas.**

Microwave at full power for 7 minutes.
Makes 2 cups.

*Nutrient Value Per ¼ Cup: 98 calories, 20 g protein, 1 g fat, 0 g carbohydrate, 145 mg sodium, 49 mg cholesterol.*

- 1½    **pounds skinless, boned chicken breast halves**
- ¾    **cup chicken stock or canned broth**
- 1    **bay leaf**
- 1    **clove garlic, finely chopped**
        **Pinch of salt, to taste**

1. Place the chicken in a 1- or 2-quart microwave-safe casserole dish. Add the stock or broth, the bay leaf and garlic. Cover with heavy-duty plastic wrap, turned back on one side to vent.
2. Microwave at full power for 5 minutes. Turn the pieces of chicken, cover, and microwave for about 2 minutes more, until done. Let stand for 5 minutes.
3. When cool enough to handle, tear the chicken into shreds with your fingers and return to the broth. Add the pinch of salt.

## Chicken El Calvador

Microwave chicken at full power for 6 to 8 minutes; microwave apple sauce at full power for 3 to 5 minutes.
Makes 4 servings.

*Nutrient Value Per Serving: 573 calories, 41 g protein, 36 g fat, 23 g carbohydrate, 475 mg sodium, 164 mg cholesterol.*

2  **tablespoons fine dry bread crumbs**
1  **tablespoon finely chopped parsley**
1  **teaspoon paprika**
4  **skinless, boned chicken breast halves (about 1¼ pounds)**
3  **tablespoons margarine, melted**
1  **cup finely chopped, peeled tart apple (1 large apple)**
1  **cup chopped pecans**
½  **cup shredded Swiss cheese (2 ounces)**
½  **teaspoon onion salt**
1  **egg, slightly beaten**

Apple Sauce:
¾  **cup apple juice**
1  **tablespoon apple brandy OR: apple jack**
2  **teaspoons cornstarch**

**Apple wedges, for garnish (optional)**

1. Combine the bread crumbs, parsley and paprika in a small bowl and set aside.
2. Pound the chicken breasts between 2 sheets of microwave-safe plastic wrap to a thickness of ⅜ inch. Remove the top sheet. Brush the top surfaces of the chicken with 1 tablespoon of the margarine. Sprinkle with the bread crumb mixture. Lift the chicken pieces carefully and place into four 10-ounce microwave-safe custard cups, crumbed sides against the cup, allowing the sides to overlap the top edge, if necessary.
3. Combine the apple, pecans, Swiss cheese, onion salt, egg and the remaining 2 tablespoons of margarine in a medium-size bowl and mix lightly. Spoon the stuffing into the prepared custard cups;

fold any overhanging chicken over the tops. Cover each with microwave-safe plastic wrap, turned back on one side to vent.
4. Place the custard cups in a circle in the microwave oven. Microwave at full power for 6 to 8 minutes, rotating each cup one quarter turn every 3 minutes. Let stand, covered, on a solid surface for 5 minutes.
5. Prepare the Apple Sauce: Combine the apple juice, apple brandy or jack and the cornstarch in a 2-cup microwave-safe measure and mix until smooth. Microwave, uncovered, at full power for 3 to 5 minutes, or until the mixture thickens and boils, stirring once. Remove from the oven and whisk until smooth.
6. To serve, unmold each custard cup onto an individual plate. Garnish with apple wedges, if you wish. Serve with the Apple Sauce.

### POULTRY FOR ONE

*Dinner for one? No problem—it's easy to cook just the amount of chicken needed for a single serving. Here are recommended times for cooking chicken parts in the microwave. Arrange the part or parts on a microwave roasting rack with the meatier areas toward the outside, and cover with wax paper.*

| Parts | Power | Minutes |
|---|---|---|
| 1 breast half | Full | 4-6 |
| 1 thigh | Three quarters | 4-5 |
| 1 leg-thigh combination | Three quarters | 7-9 |
| 2 breast halves | Full | 8-10 |
| 2 thighs | Three quarters | 6-8 |
| 2 leg-thigh combinations | Three quarters | 9-13 |

Chart courtesty of The National Broiler Council

## CHICKEN COOKING GUIDE

| | Microwave Cooking | Grilling Time (Approximate) | Standing Time (Approximate) |
|---|---|---|---|
| **Broiler/Fryer** (2-4 pound) | 3 minutes at High, additional 10-12 minutes at Medium High | 20 minutes | 10 minutes |
| **Oven Stuffer Roaster*** (5-7 pounds) | 3 minutes at High and 6-8 minutes per pound at Medium High | 60 minutes | 10 minutes |
| **Cornish Game Hens*** | 10-12 minutes at Medium High | 15 minutes | 5 minutes |
| **Broiler Parts** | 10-12 minutes, at Medium High | 15 minutes | 5 minutes |
| **Roaster Parts** | 2-4 minutes at High, additional 14-16 minutes at Medium High | 20 minutes | 5 minutes |

*For whole roaster, meaty portion of thigh should register 185° F. on a meat thermometer, after grilling. Chart courtesy of Perdue Farms.

## Chicken Tacos

*Make your own taco shells in the microwave (or substitute store-bought ones). You can substitute the Shredded Beef Filling (recipe, page 237) for the chicken, if you wish.*

Microwave at full power for 19 minutes.
Makes 8 servings.

*Nutrient Value Per Serving: 258 calories, 26 g protein, 10 g fat, 14 g carbohydrate, 288 mg sodium, 64 mg cholesterol.*

½   **cup vegetable oil**
8   **corn tortillas (6-inch)**
2   **cups Shredded Chicken Filling (recipe, page 241)**
1   **cup shredded romaine or iceberg lettuce**
1   **cup diced ripe tomatoes**
4   **ounces shredded mild Cheddar cheese (1 cup)**
  **Taco sauce, to taste**

1. Place the oil in a shallow 7- or 8-inch round microwave-safe casserole.
2. Microwave at full power for 5 minutes.
3. Remove from the oven and, with tongs, dip one tortilla in. Turn the tortilla from side to side until it stiffens (it should be sizzling as it fries or the oil is not hot enough). As it stiffens, hold it with the tongs so that it bends in half to make a taco shell. Continue holding the shell until the sizzling subsides. Drain the shell on paper toweling. Heat the oil for about 2 minutes longer for each tortilla and make all of the shells.
4. Place ¼ cup of the Shredded Chicken Filling in each taco shell (if desired, the shells can be heated for a minute). Add 2 tablespoons each of the lettuce, tomatoes and Cheddar cheese to each shell. Top with the taco sauce.

# Spanish Rice

*This festive rice dish makes good use of the microwave.*

Microwave at full power for 21 minutes.
Makes 4 cups (8 servings).

*Nutrient Value Per Serving: 122 calories, 3 g protein, 2 g fat, 21 g carbohydrate, 373 mg sodium, 0 mg cholesterol.*

- 1   tablespoon vegetable oil
- 1   cup long-grain white rice
- 1   sweet red pepper, cut into
  ¼ x 2-inch strips
- 1   medium-size onion, chopped (½ cup)
- 1   clove garlic, finely chopped
- 2   tablespoons chili powder
- ¼   teaspoon ground cumin
- ½   teaspoon salt
- ¼   cup tomato sauce
- 1¾  cups chicken stock or canned broth

1. Stir together the oil and the rice in a 2-quart microwave-safe casserole dish.
2. Microwave at full power for 2 minutes. Stir and microwave at full power for 2 minutes more, or until golden brown. Stir in the red pepper, onion and garlic and microwave for 2 minutes.
3. Stir in the chili powder, cumin, salt, tomato sauce and stock or broth. Cover with heavy-duty plastic wrap.
4. Microwave at full power for 10 minutes. Stir and microwave for about 5 minutes more. Let stand, covered, for 5 minutes.

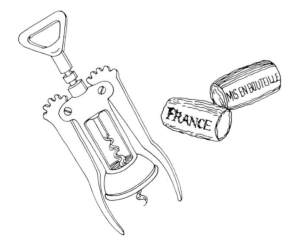

# Poached Salmon Steaks

Microwave at full power for 9 to 11 minutes.
Makes 4 servings.

*Nutrient Value Per Serving: 203 calories, 28 g protein, 9 g fat, 2 g carbohydrate, 131 mg sodium, 78 mg cholesterol.*

- ½   cup water
- ½   cup dry white wine OR: dry vermouth
- 1   medium-size onion, sliced thin
- 1   lemon, sliced thin
- ¼   teaspoon salt
- ½   teaspoon peppercorns
- 2   sprigs fresh dill
  OR: ½ teaspoon dillweed
- 2   sprigs parsley
- 4   salmon steaks (½ inch thick)
  Lemon wedges, for garnish,
  (optional)
  Dill sprigs, for garnish
  (optional)
  Horseradish Cream Sauce
  (recipe, page 255)

1. Put the water, wine or vermouth, onion, lemon, salt, peppercorns, dill and parsley in a 9-inch square or round glass dish. Cover with heavy-duty plastic wrap, turned back at one corner to vent.
2. Microwave at full power for 3 minutes, or until boiling.
3. Carefully slip the salmon steaks into the hot liquid, putting the thickest part toward the edges of the dish. Cover again with vented plastic wrap.
4. Microwave at full power for 6 to 8 minutes, or until the fish is opaque and flakes easily when lightly touched with a fork. Rotate the dish once while cooking. Let stand, covered, for 5 minutes.
5. Carefully lift the steaks from the cooking liquid and place on a serving platter. Garnish with lemon wedges and dill sprigs, if you wish. Serve hot, at room temperature or chilled. Pass the Horseradish Cream Sauce at the table.

2. Pour the remaining onion-garlic mixture, the wine and salt into the container of an electric blender, cover and whirl until puréed. Set aside.
3. In the same baking dish, combine the remaining 1 tablespoon of oil, the carrots and celery. Cover with microwave-safe plastic wrap, turned back at one corner to vent. Microwave at full power for 2½ minutes, stirring once. Mix in the puréed onion mixture and the reserved tablespoon of onion-garlic mixture. Fold the fish fillets in half lengthwise and place on top of the vegetables, with the thickest part of the fillets toward the outside of the dish.
4. Cover with microwave-safe plastic wrap vented at one corner. Microwave at full power for 7 to 8 minutes, or until the fish flakes easily when lightly touched with a fork, rotating the dish one quarter turn after 3 and 5 minutes. Let stand on a solid surface for 5 minutes. Garnish with chopped parsley, if you wish.

## Poached Red Snapper and Vegetables

*Fish and vegetables—all in one dish.*

Microwave at full power for 11½ to 12½ minutes.
Makes 4 servings.

*Nutrient Value Per Serving: 274 calories, 36 g protein, 9 g fat, 10 g carbohydrate, 430 mg sodium, 64 mg cholesterol.*

2 **tablespoons vegetable oil**
1 **cup chopped onion (1 large onion)**
1 **clove garlic, finely chopped**
¼ **cup dry white wine**
½ **teaspoon salt**
3 **medium-size carrots, cut into matchstick pieces**
3 **stalks celery, cut into matchstick pieces**
4 **red snapper fillets (about 1½ pounds)**
 **Chopped parsley, for garnish (optional)**

1. Combine 1 tablespoon of the oil, the onion and garlic in a microwave-safe shallow baking dish, about 12 x 8 x 2 inches. Microwave, uncovered, at full power for 2 minutes, stirring once. Lift out about 1 tablespoon of the onion-garlic mixture and reserve.

### POWER PLAY: FOOD AT ITS LEVEL BEST

*(based on a 600- to 700-watt oven)*

**Full power** or **high (10)** or **100% power:** *Meat patties, chicken parts, fish, sauces, candy, cut-up vegetables, cakes, baked apples.*
**Three quarters power** or **medium-high (7)** or **70% power:** *Whole chicken, loaf-shaped foods, whole vegetables, rolls, muffins, omelets.*
**Half power** or **medium (5)** or **50% power:** *Roasts, bread, poached eggs.*
**One third power** or **low/defrost (3)** or **30% power:** *Defrosting, custards, stewing and braising of meats.*
**One fifth power** or **warm (2)** or **20% power:** *Proofing bread, reheating.*

## *Paella Mariscos*

Microwave at full power for 7 to 11 minutes, then at half power for 19 to 23 minutes. Makes 4 servings.

*Nutrient Value Per Serving: 434 calories, 28 g protein, 11 g fat, 55 g carbohydrate, 1,332 mg sodium, 89 mg cholesterol.*

- ¾ **cup sliced fresh mushrooms**
- 1 **medium-size onion, chopped (½ cup)**
- 2 **cloves garlic, finely chopped**
- 3 **tablespoons margarine**
- 1 **cup uncooked long-grain white rice**
- ½ **teaspoon leaf thyme, crumbled**
- ½ **teaspoon grated orange rind**
- 1 **teaspoon salt**
- ¼ **teaspoon pepper**
- 4 **strands saffron, crushed**
- 1¼ **cups chicken broth**
- ½ **cup hot tap water**
- ½ **cup tomato purée**
- ½ **pound fresh scallops, rinsed**
- ½ **pound shrimp, shelled and deveined**
- 1 **package (10 ounces) frozen peas, partially thawed**

1. Combine the mushrooms, onion, garlic and margarine in a 2- or 3-quart microwave-safe casserole dish. Cover with heavy-duty plastic wrap, turned back on one side to vent.
2. Microwave at full power for 2 to 4 minutes, or until the onion is tender. Stir.
3. Add the rice, thyme, orange rind, salt, pepper, saffron, broth, water and tomato purée. Stir, cover again with vented plastic wrap and elevate the flat-bottomed dish on an inverted saucer.
4. Microwave at full power for 5 to 7 minutes, or until bubbly.
5. Reduce the power to half and microwave for 15 to 17 minutes, or until the rice is tender.
6. Stir in the scallops, shrimp and peas. Cover again with vented plastic wrap.
7. Microwave at half power for 4 to 6 minutes, or until the shrimp turn pink, the scallops become opaque and the peas are tender. Let stand, covered, for 3 minutes.

## Bay Scallop Salad

*A deliciously easy salad—the scallops are prepared quickly in the microwave oven.*

Microwave at full power for 4 minutes.
Makes 4 main-dish salads.

---

*Nutrient Value Per Serving: 131 calories, 22 g protein, 1 g fat, 8 g carbohydrate, 303 mg sodium, 37 mg cholesterol.*

---

½  **cup low-sodium chicken broth, defatted**
2  **tablespoons white wine vinegar**
½  **cup parsley leaves, chopped**
1  **clove garlic, chopped**
¼  **teaspoon leaf tarragon, crumbled**
⅛  **teaspoon sugar**
1  **pound bay scallops**
1½ **pounds bok choy, cut into ½-inch-wide strips (about 9 cups)**
    **Tomato slices, for garnish (optional)**

1. Stir together the broth, vinegar, parsley, garlic, tarragon and sugar in a 2-cup glass measure. Cover and refrigerate the dressing for at least 1 hour for the flavors to develop.
2. Arrange the scallops in a microwave-safe 9-inch pie plate with the thickest, meaty areas toward the outside of the plate. Completely moisten microwave-safe paper toweling and squeeze out. Place over the pie plate.
3. Microwave at full power for 2 minutes. Give the plate one quarter turn. Cook at full power for 2 minutes more, or until the scallops are opaque and firm, but not rubbery. Transfer with a slotted spoon to a large bowl.
4. Add the bok choy and the dressing. Toss to coat all the ingredients well. Serve immediately. Garnish with tomato slices, if you wish.

### Food for Thought . . .

**Bok Choy** *The cabbage of South China, bok choy is a very green leaf cabbage that has succulent white ribs stemming from a bulbous base. It is very crisp with very little bitterness, and is somewhat similar in appearance to romaine lettuce.*

## EQUIVALENTS IN MICROWAVE COOKING TIMES

*The recipes in this book were tested in a 600- to 700-watt microwave oven. Consult the chart below if you have a lower-power unit.*

| 600- to 700-watt oven | 500- to 600-watt oven | 400- to 500-watt oven |
|---|---|---|
| 15 seconds | 18 seconds | 20 seconds |
| 30 seconds | 35 seconds | 45 seconds |
| 1 minute | 1 minute, 15 seconds | 1 minute, 30 seconds |
| 2 minutes | 2 minutes, 30 seconds | 2 minutes, 50 seconds |
| 3 minutes | 3 minutes, 30 seconds | 4 minutes, 15 seconds |
| 4 minutes | 4 minutes, 50 seconds | 5 minutes, 45 seconds |
| 5 minutes | 6 minutes | 7 minutes |
| 6 minutes | 7 minutes, 15 seconds | 8 minutes, 30 seconds |
| 8 minutes | 9 minutes, 30 seconds | 11 minutes, 15 seconds |
| 10 minutes | 12 minutes | 14 minutes |

## Lasagna Florentine

*An easy-to-prepare, delicious vegetarian lasagna that is cooked completely in the microwave—that means no precooking of noodles is needed.*

Microwave at full power for 8 minutes, then at half power for 30 to 35 minutes.
Makes 8 servings.

*Nutrient Value Per Serving: 430 calories, 25 g protein, 21 g fat, 37 g carbohydrate, 687 mg sodium, 96 mg cholesterol.*

| | |
|---|---|
| 1 | *jar (14 ounces) prepared spaghetti sauce* |
| 1 | *can (16 ounces) whole tomatoes, undrained* |
| ½ | *cup water* |
| 1 | *container (15½ ounces) ricotta cheese* |
| 1 | *package (16 ounces) mozzarella cheese, shredded (about 4 cups)* |
| 1 | *egg* |
| ¼ | *teaspoon garlic powder* |
| 9 | *uncooked lasagna noodles* |
| 1 | *package (10 ounces) frozen chopped spinach, thawed and well drained* |
| 3 | *tablespoons grated Parmesan cheese* |

1. Combine the spaghetti sauce, tomatoes with their liquid and the water in a bowl. Stir to blend and break up the tomatoes. Set aside.
2. Combine the ricotta cheese, ½ cup of the mozzarella cheese, the egg and garlic powder in a small bowl and mix well.
3. Spread one third of the spaghetti sauce mixture in the bottom of a microwave-safe baking dish, about 12 x 8 x 2 inches. Place 3 lasagna noodles on top of the sauce. Spread half the ricotta mixture over the noodles. Layer with half the spinach and 1 cup of the mozzarella cheese. Repeat the layers (sauce, noodles, ricotta mixture, spinach and mozzarella cheese). Cover with the remaining noodles and pour on the remaining sauce mixture.
4. Cover the dish with microwave-safe plastic wrap, turned back at one corner to vent. Microwave at full power for 8 minutes. Rotate the dish one half turn. Microwave at half power for 30 to 35

minutes, or until the noodles are tender, turning the dish another half turn after 15 minutes. Sprinkle the top evenly with the Parmesan cheese and the remaining mozzarella cheese. Cover the dish again with plastic wrap and let stand on a solid surface for 10 minutes before serving.

## Codfish Gumbo

*Here's a browned Louisiana roux made in the microwave.*

Microwave at full power for 40 to 43 minutes.
Makes 8 servings.

*Nutrient Value Per Serving: 663 calories, 45 g protein, 32 g fat, 46 g carbohydrate, 1,311 mg sodium, 113 mg cholesterol.*

| | |
|---|---|
| ⅔ | *cup all-purpose flour* |
| ½ | *cup vegetable oil* |
| 2 | *cups finely chopped onion* |
| 2 | *cups finely chopped sweet green pepper* |
| 2 | *cups finely diced celery* |
| 1 | *tablespoon finely chopped garlic* |
| 1 | *bay leaf* |
| ½ | *teaspoon leaf thyme, crumbled* |
| ½ | *teaspoon leaf oregano, crumbled* |
| ½ | *teaspoon black pepper* |
| ½ | *teaspoon ground hot red pepper* |
| 1 | *teaspoon salt* |
| 2 | *cups chicken broth* |
| 2 | *bottles (8 ounces each) clam juice* |
| 1 | *can (16 ounces) whole tomatoes, drained* |
| 1 | *pound green beans, cut into 1-inch pieces* |
| 1 | *pound kielbasa (smoked sausage), cut into ¼-inch slices* |
| 3 | *codfish steaks (about 1 pound each)* |
| 4 | *cups cooked white rice* |

*Codfish Gumbo*

1. Stir together the flour and the oil in a 3-quart microwave-safe casserole dish.
2. Microwave at full power for 10 to 12 minutes, or until the flour is deep golden brown, stirring twice.
3. Add the onion, green pepper and celery, tossing to coat.
4. Microwave at full power for 4 minutes, stirring once. Add the garlic and microwave for 2 minutes more. Stir in the bay leaf, thyme, oregano, black pepper, ground hot red pepper and salt. Microwave for 4 minutes, stirring once. Stir in the broth and the clam juice.
5. Microwave at full power for 6 minutes, or until thickened, stirring every 2 minutes. Cut up the tomatoes and stir them in along with the green beans; cover.
6. Microwave at full power for 3 to 4 minutes more. Remove from the oven and let stand for 10 minutes, then add the kielbasa.
7. Microwave at full power for 4 minutes. Add more salt, if you wish.
8. Remove and discard the skin and bones from the cod and cut the steaks into 2-inch pieces. Add them to the casserole dish and cover with heavy-duty plastic wrap, turned back on one side to vent.
9. Microwave at full power for 7 minutes, or until the fish is cooked, stirring gently once or twice. Serve hot, over the white rice.

# Hearty Gazpacho

*The bulgur wheat gives this dish enough substance to double as a salad.*

Microwave at full power for 9 minutes, then at half power for 7 to 8 minutes.
Makes 6 servings.

*Nutrient Value Per Serving: 192 calories, 4 g protein, 7 g fat, 28 g carbohydrate, 520 mg sodium, 0 mg cholesterol.*

3 tablespoons olive oil
¼ cup sliced green onions, both white and green parts
¼ cup diced sweet green pepper
1 cup bulgur
1 can (6 ounces) spicy-hot tomato-vegetable juice
1 can (10½ ounces) condensed beef broth
Juice of 1 lime
1 teaspoon leaf thyme, crumbled
¼ teaspoon garlic powder
1 large tomato, chopped
1 medium-size cucumber, peeled and chopped
¼ cup chopped fresh parsley
Cucumber slices, lime slices and parsley sprigs, for garnish (optional)

1. Place the oil in a shallow, round microwave-safe casserole dish, about 9 inches in diameter. Stir in the green onion, green pepper and bulgur. Cover with microwave-safe plastic wrap. Microwave at full power for 3 minutes.
2. Add the vegetable juice, broth, lime juice, thyme and garlic powder. Cover with microwave-safe plastic wrap, turned back on one side to vent. Microwave at full power for 6 minutes. Then microwave at half power for 7 to 8 minutes, or until the bulgur is tender. Mix in the tomato, cucumber and parsley. Let stand, covered, on a solid surface for 5 minutes. Garnish with cucumber slices, lime slices and parsley sprigs, if you wish.

## Food for Thought . . .

**Bulgur** *Sometimes called parboiled wheat, bulgur is whole wheat that has been cooked, dried, partially debranned and cracked into coarse fragments. Bulgur makes delicious salads or soups and is a good alternative to rice or potatoes in a menu. The making of bulgur is our oldest recorded use of wheat. This ancient food originated in the Near East. To rehydrate bulgur, soak it in twice its volume of boiling water and let it stand until all the water has been absorbed, or until the particles are tender; drain off the excess water. Store bulgur in an airtight container in a cool place, and use within 6 months.*

# Stuffed Shells Marinara

*While the pasta is cooking on the stove top, microwave the sauce and make the cottage cheese filling.*

Microwave at full power for 12 minutes, then at half power for 8 to 10 minutes.
Makes 4 servings.

*Nutrient Value Per Serving: 277 calories, 22 g protein, 3 g fat, 41 g carbohydrate, 1,518 mg sodium, 7 mg cholesterol.*

24 jumbo pasta shells (½ of a 12-ounce box)
2 green onions, finely chopped
1 can (16 ounces) peeled tomatoes, drained
1 tablespoon leaf basil, crumbled
1 teaspoon salt
1 pound lowfat cottage cheese
½ teaspoon salt
2 tablespoons grated Parmesan cheese
1 tablespoon chopped parsley
Ground nutmeg, to taste

*Stuffed Shells Marinara*

1. Cook the pasta shells conventionally, following the package directions (about 9 to 10 minutes), and drain. Do not overcook, or the shells will fall apart.
2. Put the green onion in a 2-quart microwave-safe mixing bowl and cover with wax paper.
3. Microwave at full power for 2 minutes, stirring once.
4. Stir in the tomatoes, mashing slightly with a spoon. Add the basil and the 1 teaspoon of salt. Cover with wax paper.
5. Microwave at full power for 10 minutes, stirring once. Let the sauce stand uncovered.
6. Mix together the cottage cheese, the ½ teaspoon of salt, the Parmesan cheese, parsley and nutmeg.

7. Fill the shells with the cottage cheese mixture, placing the filled shells in a single layer in an 8- or 9-inch round glass dish. Spoon the sauce over the shells and cover with wax paper.
8. Reduce the power to half and microwave for 4 minutes. Rotate the dish one half turn. Microwave at half power for 4 to 6 minutes more, or until hot.

# Vegetables & Accompaniments

## Baby Carrots and Green Beans

*Cut the vegetables into uniform-size pieces for fast, even cooking.*

Microwave at full power for 5 minutes. Makes 4 servings.

*Nutrient Value Per Serving: 83 calories, 1 g protein, 6 g fat, 8 g carbohydrate, 89 mg sodium, 16 mg cholesterol.*

½ **pound baby (Belgian) carrots**
¼ **pound small green beans**
1 **cup water**
2 **tablespoons butter, sliced**
**Salt and pepper, to taste**

1. Using a swivel-bladed vegetable peeler, peel the carrots, leaving the stems on. Trim the ends of the green beans and, if you wish, cut the beans lengthwise, French-style.
2. Combine the carrots and the green beans with the water in a 2-quart microwave-safe casserole dish. Cover with heavy-duty plastic wrap, turned back on one side to vent.
3. Microwave at full power for 5 minutes, stirring after 2½ minutes. Let stand, covered, for 3 minutes. Taste for doneness. If you prefer, cook longer.
4. Drain the vegetables and toss with the butter and the salt and pepper. Serve hot.

## Parslied New Potatoes

*To reheat these from room temperature, cover with wax paper and microwave at half power for 3 to 4 minutes. Stir gently once or twice while reheating.*

Microwave at full power for 11 to 13 minutes. Makes 4 servings.

*Nutrient Value Per Serving: 190 calories, 3 g protein, 9 g fat, 26 g carbohydrate, 96 mg sodium, 23 mg cholesterol.*

12 **small new potatoes**
¼ **cup water**
3 **tablespoons butter**
1 **clove garlic, crushed**
1 **tablespoon finely chopped fresh parsley**
**Freshly ground black pepper, to taste**

1. Wash the potatoes well. Cut off the ends, or peel a ½-inch strip around the middle of each. Put the potatoes and the water in a 2-quart microwave-safe casserole dish. Cover with heavy-duty plastic wrap, turned back on one side to vent, or the casserole lid.
2. Microwave at full power for 10 to 12 minutes. Stir once during the cooking. Drain and let stand.
3. Microwave the butter and the garlic in a 1-cup glass measure at full power for 1 minute, or until the butter is melted. Remove the garlic butter and stir in the parsley and the pepper. Pour over the potatoes and serve.

## CATCH THE MICRO-WAVE!

• Always stir food in the oven from the outside toward the center of the dish.

• Set a kitchen timer to remind you to stir or rotate food.

• For the most accurate time setting on a dial-type microwave, turn the dial past the time desired, then bring it back to the correct number.

• When removing a cover or microwave-safe plastic wrap from a dish that's been in the oven, lift the far corner first so steam escapes away from you.

• Rule of thumb: Food that requires covering in a conventional oven also should be covered for microwaving.

• To avoid boil-overs with liquid foods, such as soups and sauces, use a container that holds two or three times more liquid than the amount you are cooking.

• Foods that have been coated with crumbs will be crisper if they're placed on a microwave roasting rack.

• Dense foods will cook more evenly if the cooking dish is placed on an inverted saucer.

• To find out if a heated plate is hot enough to serve, carefully put your hand carefully under the center bottom of the plate. If the plate feels warm to the touch, the food should be heated through.

• Fish fillets cook more evenly if you fold under any thin portions, so the fillet is a uniform thickness all over.

• When cooking a whole chicken or turkey, remove the accumulated juices from the dish, or the microwaves will be attracted to the juices rather than to the bird.

• Cool baked goods on a heatproof countertop or other solid surface, rather than on a wire rack. The held-in heat helps to finish cooking the food.

## Food for Thought . . .

**New Potatoes** *These are not a particular variety of potato, but simply young potatoes that are shipped directly from the field after harvesting. They are small in size with a thin skin. Available from March to August. "New" potatoes are not placed in storage because they do not store well; buy only the amount you need.*

## "Roasted" New Potatoes

*The microwave browning tray is good for "roasting" potatoes.*

Microwave at full power for 8 minutes.
Makes 4 servings.

*Nutrient Value Per Serving: 150 calories, 2 g protein, 7 g fat, 20 g carbohydrate, 280 mg sodium, 0 mg cholesterol.*

12   **small new red-skinned potatoes (1 pound), quartered**
2    **tablespoons olive oil**
½    **teaspoon salt**
¼    **teaspoon pepper**

1. Place the browning tray in the microwave and heat at full power for 6 minutes (or following the manufacturer's directions).
2. Toss together the potatoes, oil, salt and pepper in a bowl. Arrange the potatoes

on the preheated browning tray, cut sides down.
3. Microwave at full power for 4 minutes. Turn so the other cut side is down and microwave for 4 minutes more. Cover and let stand for 10 minutes.

🔥🍸

# Zucchini Nests

*Another time, substitute shredded carrots for zucchini, if you wish.*

Microwave at full power for 8 minutes.
Makes 4 to 6 servings.

---

*Nutrient Value Per Serving: 136 calories, 3 g protein, 12 g fat, 7 g carbohydrate, 124 mg sodium, 31 mg cholesterol.*

---

2    **pounds very firm zucchini**
¼    **cup (½ stick) butter**
1    **teaspoon freshly ground white pepper**
1    **teaspoon leaf tarragon, crumbled**
       **Cocktail onions (optional)**

1. Wash and dry the zucchini. Cut in half lengthwise and remove any seeds. Coarsely shred the zucchini in the container of a food processor or with a grater. Put the shredded zucchini in a 2-quart microwave-safe casserole dish and cover with heavy-duty plastic wrap, turned back on one side to vent.
2. Microwave at full power for 7 minutes, or until crisp-tender. Stir gently once while cooking.
3. Dot with the butter.
4. Microwave, uncovered, at full power for 1 minute, or until the butter starts to melt. Sprinkle with the white pepper and the tarragon and toss lightly. Serve in mounds, with cocktail onions in each, if you wish.

## NATURE'S BEST CLEANER: BAKING SODA

*Baking soda safely cleans all the spatters and spills that can accumulate in a microwave. Just mix 2 tablespoons of baking soda with 2 cups of warm water and sponge down the interior. For stubborn stains, sprinkle on dry baking soda, rub lightly with a moist sponge, rinse and buff dry. Baking soda is an effective and non-abrasive cleanser; unlike many cleaning powders and liquids, it won't scratch or erode the delicate interior of the microwave. To neutralize food odors, leave a small dish of baking soda inside the microwave. Remember to remove the baking soda before using the oven.*

🔥📶💲

# Toasty Zucchini

Microwave at full power for 16 minutes.
Makes 6 servings.

---

*Nutrient Value Per Serving: 186 calories, 11 g protein, 9 g fat, 15 g carbohydrate, 338 mg sodium, 111 mg cholesterol.*

---

4    **ounces fresh mushrooms, sliced**
1    **tablespoon dry white wine**
⅛    **teaspoon salt**
       **Nonstick vegetable cooking spray**
1    **pound zucchini**
4    **cups ½-inch bread cubes***
1    **small tomato, cored, seeded and diced**
2    **cloves garlic, finely chopped**
⅛    **teaspoon pepper**
½    **cup grated Parmesan cheese**
2    **eggs, slightly beaten**
4    **ounces Monterey Jack cheese, cut into ½-inch cubes**

1. Combine the mushrooms, wine and salt in a small bowl. Stir and set aside.
2. Lightly spray a microwave-safe baking

dish, about 10 x 6 x 2 inches, with nonstick vegetable cooking spray.

3. Coarsely grate the unpeeled zucchini into a large bowl. Stir in the bread cubes, tomato, garlic, pepper, Parmesan cheese, eggs and Monterey Jack cheese. Let stand for a few minutes for the bread to absorb the liquid. Stir in the undrained mushrooms. Spoon the mixture into the prepared dish and pack lightly.

4. Cover with microwave-safe plastic wrap, turned back at one corner to vent. Microwave at full power for 16 minutes, rotating the dish one quarter turn every 4 minutes. Let stand on a solid surface for 3 minutes. Serve warm.

*Note:* Use day old sour dough or French bread. White bread also can be used, but lightly toast it first.

# Horseradish Cream Sauce

*Typically with a microwave sauce, the components are combined and heated in the same container.*

Microwave at full power for 4 to 5 minutes. Makes about 1¾ cups.

*Nutrient Value Per 1 Tablespoon: 23 calories, 1 g protein, 1 g fat, 2 g carbohydrate, 17 mg sodium, 13 mg cholesterol.*

| | |
|---|---|
| 1 | **large egg** |
| 1½ | **cups milk** |
| 2 | **tablespoons cornstarch** |
| 2 | **tablespoons grated fresh horseradish** |
| ¼ | **cup white vinegar** |
| 1 | **tablespoon sugar** |
| 2 | **tablespoons butter** |

1. Mix together the egg and the milk in a 1½-quart microwave-safe casserole dish. Whisk in the cornstarch, horseradish, vinegar and sugar.

2. Microwave at full power for 4 to 5 minutes, or until thickened. Whisk twice during the cooking.

3. Stir in the butter until melted. Serve warm, or at room temperature.

## CONSIDER THE COVER

*Wax Paper: Forms a loose cover. It holds in the heat, speeds up the cooking and prevents spattering when cooking foods that do not steam to tenderize. Use wax paper when microwaving fish, lasagna, some types of casseroles, corn on the cob or crispy-coated chicken, when proofing yeast dough or melting butter.*

*Plastic Wrap (microwave-safe): Forms a tight cover to hold in moisture during microwaving, similar to conventional steaming, poaching or stewing. Use plastic wrap when microwaving vegetables, some types of casseroles, fish, and leftovers. Fold back one edge to form a narrow vent to allow steam to escape. Wait until the standing time is complete before removing. Carefully remove plastic wrap away from you to avoid steam burns.*

*Aluminum Foil: Shields areas of food that tend to cook too rapidly. Areas such as corners of cakes or bar cookies, fatty areas of meat, drumstick ends, wings and the breastbone of turkey or chicken should be covered with bits of foil to prevent overcooking. When defrosting, foil also can shield the outer edges, which may begin to cook before the center is defrosted. Foil also is used to cover foods to hold in heat after microwaving. To help prevent "arcing"—and damage to the oven— when you microwave with foil, cover no more than half the food with foil, leaving at least half exposed so the food can absorb the microwaves. Press the foil smoothly to the food. Do not let the foil get nearer than 1 inch to the inside walls of the microwave oven.*

*No Cover: Baked items and all other foods that are left uncovered when cooked in a conventional oven. This includes whole vegetables, such as potatoes or squash.*

# HOLDING TIME

Foods will stay warm for up to one hour after standing time. The length of time depends on proper wrapping and the food's ability to retain heat. Large, dense items tightly wrapped in aluminum foil will stay hot longest. The chart below will help you determine the holding time for your food.

## LONG HOLDING TIME:
30 to 60 minutes

**Baked Beans,** dish tightly wrapped
**Cauliflower,** whole, dish tightly wrapped
**Corn on the Cob,** in husk, tightly wrapped individually
**Ham,** tented
**Onions,** wrapped individually or dish tightly wrapped
**Pork (or well done roast beef),** at least 2 inches in diameter, tented
**Potatoes,** baked, individually wrapped
**Potatoes,** scalloped, dish tightly wrapped
**Stuffed Peppers,** individually wrapped or full dish tightly wrapped
**Sweet Potatoes,** whole, individually wrapped
**Turkey,** tented
**Winter Squash,** casserole dish tightly wrapped
**Winter Squash,** large individually wrapped

## MEDIUM HOLDING TIME:
15 to 30 minutes

**Broccoli,** dish tightly wrapped
**Carrots,** whole, dish tightly wrapped
**Casseroles,** dish tightly wrapped
**Cauliflower,** dish tightly wrapped
**Chicken,** tented
**Corn on the Cob,** in husk or husked, loosely wrapped individually
**Ham Slice,** 1 inch or thicker, dish tightly wrapped
**Meatloaf,** tightly wrapped
**Potatoes,** mashed, dish tightly wrapped
**Rice,** fluffed with fork, dish tightly wrapped
**Roasts,** beef, not well done, 4 pounds or more, tented
**Roasts,** weighing 2 to 4 pounds, tented
**Winter Squash,** small, individually wrapped

## SHORT HOLDING TIME:
5 to 10 minutes

**Beans (green or wax),** dish tightly wrapped
**Carrots,** sliced, dish tightly wrapped
**Chops,** dish tightly wrapped or stacked and wrapped
**Corn,** whole kernel, tightly wrapped
**Fish Fillets,** dish tightly wrapped or stacked and wrapped
**Hamburgers,** dish tightly wrapped or stacked and wrapped
**Mushrooms,** dish tightly wrapped
**Peas,** dish tightly wrapped

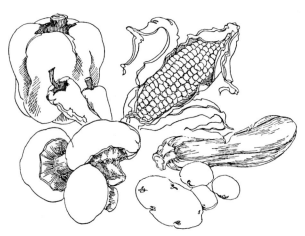

# ⬛⬛⬛⬛⬛
## Curried Vegetable Salad

Microwave vegetables at full power for 12 to 16 minutes; microwave dressing at half power for 1½ to 2 minutes.
Makes 6 servings.

*Nutrient Value Per Serving: 164 calories, 6 g protein, 4 g fat, 27 g carbohydrate, 69 mg sodium, 11 mg cholesterol.*

- **1½ pounds red-skinned potatoes, unpeeled and diced**
- **2 tablespoons butter or margarine, softened**
- **2 cups cauliflower flowerets (about 8 ounces)**
- **1 cup cross-cut green beans (about 4 ounces)**
- **6 asparagus spears, cut into ½-inch-thick slices (about ½ pound)**
- **¼ cup diced sweet green pepper**
- **¼ cup diced sweet red pepper**

**Curried Dressing:**
- **½ cup plain yogurt**
- **1 to 2 tablespoons grated lime rind**
- **1 to 1½ tablespoons lime juice**
- **1½ teaspoons curry powder**
- **Lettuce leaves (optional)**

1. Combine the potatoes and the butter or margarine in a 3-quart microwave-safe casserole dish. Cover with microwave-safe plastic wrap. Microwave at full power for 7 to 9 minutes, or until the potatoes are tender, gently shaking the dish twice. Remove with a slotted spoon; set aside.
2. Add the cauliflower to the casserole dish. Cover with plastic wrap. Microwave at full power for 2 minutes, or until crisp-tender. Add to the potatoes.
3. Add the green beans to the casserole dish. Cover with plastic wrap. Microwave at full power for 1 to 2 minutes, or until crisp-tender. Add to the potato mixture.
4. Add the asparagus and the green and red peppers to the casserole dish. Cover with plastic wrap. Microwave at full power for 2 to 3 minutes, or until crisp-tender. Add to the potatoes.

5. Prepare the Curried Dressing: Combine the yogurt, lime rind, lime juice and curry powder in a 1-cup microwave-safe measure. Cover with plastic wrap. Microwave at half power for 1½ to 2 minutes, or until warm. Whisk until smooth. Stir half the dressing into the vegetable mixture.
6. Arrange the vegetable mixture on lettuce leaves, if you wish. Pass the remaining dressing.

# ⬛⬛
## Minted Pea Purée in Tomato Cups

Microwave at full power for 5 minutes.
Makes 24.

*Nutrient Value Per Serving: 20 calories, 1 g protein, 1 g fat, 2 g carbohydrate, 46 mg sodium, 3 mg cholesterol.*

- **1 package (10 ounces) frozen peas**
- **2 tablespoons butter**
- **2 tablespoons water**
- **3 tablespoons chopped fresh mint OR: 1 teaspoon dried mint**
- **¼ teaspoon salt**
- **24 cherry tomatoes (1 pint), rinsed**

1. Combine the peas, butter and water in a 1-quart microwave-safe casserole dish.
2. Microwave at full power for 4 minutes, stirring once.
3. Stir in the mint and the salt. Purée the pea mixture in the container of an electric blender or a food processor.
4. Slice off the tops (about ¼ inch) from the cherry tomatoes. With a small spoon, scoop out the insides and let the shells drain upside down on paper toweling. (The vegetables can be made ahead to this point.)
5. With a small spoon or with a pastry bag fitted with a ¼-inch star or plain tip, pipe the pea purée into the tomatoes, mounding it slightly. Place in a small, shallow microwave-safe dish.
6. Microwave at full power for 1 minute. Serve hot.

# Sweet Treats

◀◀◀ 🍷

## Diplomat Pudding

*Originally this soft, molded dessert, which closely resembles an English trifle, was served with a light custard sauce. No less impressive, this quickly prepared contemporary version may be garnished colorfully with whipped cream, slivered almonds and maraschino cherries. Allow several hours for the dessert to cool completely.*

Microwave at full power for 14 to 16 minutes.
Makes 8 servings.

*Nutrient Value Per Serving: 536 calories, 9 g protein, 17 g fat, 89 g carbohydrate, 213 mg sodium, 158 mg cholesterol.*

| 1 | **cup peach jam** |
| 1 | **frozen pound cake, thawed (about 10 ounces) OR: 2 packages (3 ounces each) ladyfingers** |
| 2 | **tablespoons unsalted butter** |
| 1 | **can (12 ounces) evaporated milk** |
| 1 | **cup water** |
| 1 | **vanilla bean (about 1 inch long) OR: 1 teaspoon vanilla** |
| 4 | **eggs** |
| 1 | **cup granulated sugar** |
| 1 | **tablespoon grated orange rind** |
| 1 | **teaspoon grated lemon rind** |
| 1 | **cup plump, moist raisins** |
| | **Julienned lemon rind, for garnish (optional)** |

1. Press the jam through a mesh strainer, discarding the remaining solids.
2. Cut the cake into ½- to ¾-inch-thick slices. Halve 5 slices on the diagonal. Spread one side of all the slices with the sieved jam. Set aside. (If using ladyfingers, split both packages of the cakes in half. You should have 40 halves.

Spread the cut side of the cakes with jam. Set aside.)
3. Microwave the butter in a 2½-quart microwave-safe soufflé dish at full power for 2 minutes, or until melted. Brush the butter along the bottom and sides of the dish. Set aside.
4. Place the evaporated milk, water and vanilla bean in a 1-quart glass dish. If using vanilla extract, do not add it yet.
5. Microwave, uncovered, at full power for 4 minutes. (Or, using a probe, heat the milk until scalded, 180°.)
6. Whisk the eggs and the sugar in a separate large bowl. Slowly whisk the scalded milk into the egg mixture. Add the orange and lemon rinds and remove the vanilla bean. (If using vanilla extract, add it now.)
7. Jam side up, place the diagonally sliced cake, or 10 ladyfingers, in the prepared dish. Sprinkle with a few raisins and about ¾ cup of the custard mixture. Repeat the layers twice more, ending with a layer of cake. Pour the remaining custard mixture over all. Press the cake gently with the tines of a fork to help it absorb the custard mixture.
8. Place the soufflé dish in a glass pie plate. Pour 1½ cups of water into the glass pie plate only.
9. Microwave at full power, uncovered, for 8 to 10 minutes, or until a probe inserted into the pudding's center reaches 150°. Carefully remove the pudding from the oven. Cool. Invert onto a large serving platter. Garnish with julienned lemon rind, if you wish.

*Diplomat Pudding, Honeyed Fruit Compote (recipe, page 260), Rice Pudding Crown (recipe, page 260)*

### ◤ ◀◀ ⊤
## Honeyed Fruit Compote

*A fine finale eaten plain, chilled compote also can be served over angel or pound cake. With a dash of ginger, it can accompany a cold meat platter.*

Microwave at full power for 12 to 15 minutes, then at one third power for 3 to 4 minutes.
Makes 8 servings.

*Nutrient Value Per Serving: 250 calories, 3 g protein, 0 g fat, 64 g carbohydrate, 16 mg sodium, 0 mg cholesterol.*

| | |
|---|---|
| 1 | cup dried apricots (from a 6-ounce bag) |
| 1 | cup dried apples |
| 1 | cup dried peaches |
| 1 | cup large prunes, unpitted |
| ¼ | cup light raisins |
| ¼ | cup dark raisins |
| 2 | thin slices lemon |
| 4 | cups orange juice |
| 1 | teaspoon light-colored honey |
| 1 | to 2 teaspoons superfine sugar |

1. Using floured scissors, cut the apricots, apples and peaches into bite-size pieces and place in a 3- to 4-quart microwave-safe bowl.
2. Add the prunes, light and dark raisins, lemon slices and orange juice. Toss together. Cover the bowl with a doubled piece of wax paper.
3. Microwave at full power for 12 to 15 minutes, or until the liquid barely boils.
4. Reduce the power to one third and microwave for 3 to 4 minutes, or until the fruit is soft, but not mushy. Add the honey and the sugar. Taste and add more honey and sugar, if necessary. Cool slightly, or chill before serving.

### ◤ ◀◀ ⊤
## Rice Pudding Crown

*This microwave adaptation cooks in about half the time (21 to 23 minutes) of the conventionally baked old-fashioned dessert. Kiwifruit and red grapes add a touch of distinction.*

Microwave at full power for 8 minutes, then at half power for 13 to 15 minutes.
Makes 6 servings.

*Nutrient Value Per Serving: 194 calories, 4 g protein, 5 g fat, 34 g carbohydrate, 151 mg sodium, 17 mg cholesterol.*

| | |
|---|---|
| 2 | cups milk |
| ¼ | cup sugar |
| ½ | teaspoon ground cinnamon |
| ¼ | teaspoon salt |
| 2 | cups cooked rice |
| 2 | kiwifruit, peeled and chopped |
| ½ | cup halved red grapes, seeded if necessary |
| 1 | tablespoon butter |
| | Kiwi slice and additional red grapes, for garnish |

1. Combine the milk, sugar, cinnamon and salt in a 2-quart microwave-safe container.
2. Microwave at full power for 5 minutes. Stir in the rice. Cover with heavy-duty plastic wrap.
3. Microwave at full power for 3 minutes and stir.
4. Reduce the power to half and microwave for 13 to 15 minutes, or until the mixture thickens. Stir 2 or 3 times during the cooking. Let stand for 10 minutes.
5. Stir in the kiwifruit, grapes and butter. Pack the pudding into a greased 4-cup mold. Unmold onto a serving platter. Garnish with a slice of kiwi and additional red grapes.

1. Place the egg yolks and the maple syrup in a medium-size microwave-safe bowl. Beat with an electric mixer at medium speed for 3 to 4 minutes, or until the mixture is thickened and frothy.
2. Microwave, uncovered, at half power for 3 minutes.
3. Increase the power to three quarters and microwave for 2½ minutes. Stir once or twice during the cooking. (The mixture will barely coat a wooden spoon.)
4. To cool, place the bowl containing the mixture in a larger pan of ice cubes or crushed ice, or chill in the refrigerator.
5. Meanwhile, in a large separate bowl, beat the 3 cups of heavy cream with the electric mixer at high speed until soft peaks form. Add the vanilla and the salt. Beat until stiff peaks form.
6. Pour the cooled custard mixture through a fine-meshed sieve into the beaten cream. Blend well with the electric mixer at low speed, or use a wooden spoon. Pour into individual, long-stemmed dessert dishes and freeze for 3 hours, or until firm.
7. Garnish each serving with a dollop of the whipped cream and a toasted pecan half. The mousse also may be frozen in a freezer-safe 2-quart glass serving dish.

*Frozen Maple Mousse*

## Frozen Maple Mousse

Microwave at half power for three minutes, then at three quarters power for 2½ minutes.
Makes 6 servings.

*Nutrient Value Per Serving: 791 calories, 6 g protein, 65 g fat, 48 g carbohydrate, 99 mg sodium, 535 mg cholesterol.*

| | |
|---|---|
| 7 | **large egg yolks, at room temperature** |
| 1¼ | **cups pure maple syrup** |
| | **Ice** |
| 3 | **cups chilled heavy cream** |
| 2 | **teaspoons vanilla** |
| | **Pinch salt** |
| 1 | **cup heavy cream, whipped, for garnish** |
| | **Toasted pecan halves, for garnish** |

## Strawberry Sauce

*Serve as a topping on fruit or ice cream, or with the Black 'n White Cheesecake (recipe, page 262).*

Microwave at full power for 6 to 8 minutes.
Makes about 1 cup.

*Nutrient Value Per Serving: 65 calories, 0 g protein, 0 g fat, 17 g carbohydrate, 3 mg sodium, 0 mg cholesterol.*

| | |
|---|---|
| 1 | **package (10 ounces) frozen strawberries, thawed** |
| 2 | **tablespoons cornstarch** |
| 2 | **tablespoons sugar** |
| 1 | **jar (8 ounces) currant jelly** |

1. Purée the strawberries in the container of an electric blender or a food processor.

2. Combine the cornstarch and the sugar in a 1-quart glass bowl. Add the strawberry purée and the currant jelly, mixing thoroughly.
3. Microwave at full power for 6 to 8 minutes, or until thickened and clear, stirring halfway through the cooking time. Serve warm.

## THE MICROWAVE BAKERY: IT CAN BE DONE!

*Turning out delicious baked products from a microwave oven probably is more a matter of expectation than expertise. If you know what to expect from your microwave oven, you can get the best results possible with no disappointments. Here are some tips on what to look for:*

*• Choose glass bakeware so that you can see the food as it cooks—you'll be able to check for doneness by just looking at the bottom.*

*• The test for doneness is different than in conventional baking. In most cases, baked goods still will be underdone at the center when they come out of the microwave; they will finish cooking and firm up during the standing time.*

*• Cakes, whether from a mix or from scratch, tend to rise higher in the microwave than in a conventional oven. Underfill cake pans slightly, using the extra batter for cupcakes.*

*• Avoid the urge to cut or slice until the baked goods are completely cooled.*

*• For a "browner" look to baked goods, you can substitute brown sugar for some of the granulated sugar in most recipes, and whole wheat flour for not more than ¼ of the all-purpose flour.*

# Black 'n White Cheesecake

*Use the special springform pan (directions, page 263) when microwaving this cheesecake.*

Microwave at full power for 1¾ minutes, then at half power for 6 to 7 minutes, then at three quarters power for 11 to 13 minutes.
Makes 12 servings.

*Nutrient Value Per Serving: 562 calories, 8 g protein, 31 g fat, 67 g carbohydrate, 292 mg sodium, 142 mg cholesterol.*

2 tablespoons butter
24 chocolate wafer cookies, crushed (1¼ cups)
3 packages (8 ounces each) cream cheese
¾ cup sugar
3 eggs
2 teaspoons vanilla
¾ cup dairy sour cream
3 squares (1 ounce each) unsweetened chocolate
½ cup sugar
Strawberry Sauce (recipe, page 261)
Fresh raspberries, for garnish

1. Microwave the butter in a 2-cup glass measure at full power for 45 seconds, or until melted.
2. Add the cookie crumbs and blend well. Press the crumb mixture onto the cardboard bottom in a microwave-safe springform pan (see box, page 263).
3. Microwave at full power for 1 minute, rotating the pan halfway through the cooking.
4. Microwave the unwrapped cream cheese in a glass mixer bowl at half power for 3 to 3½ minutes, or until softened.
5. Beat with an electric mixer until creamy. Add the ¾ cup of sugar and beat well. Add the eggs and the vanilla and beat until smooth. Add the sour cream and beat until smooth.
6. Microwave the unwrapped chocolate squares in a 4-cup glass measure at half power for 3 to 3½ minutes, stirring halfway through the cooking.

*Black 'n White Cheesecake with raspberries and Strawberry Sauce (recipe, page 261)*

7. Blend in the ½ cup of sugar. Remove 1½ cups of the cream cheese mixture and blend into the chocolate mixture. Whisk vigorously until very smooth. Pour the chocolate batter on top of the light batter. Dip a rubber spatula into the mix and gently swirl to create a marbled effect. Carefully pour into the prepared pan.

8. Microwave at three quarters power for 11 to 13 minutes, rotating the pan every 2 minutes. Let stand until cool. Refrigerate until chilled.

9. Use the plastic sling to remove the cheesecake from the pan. Cut the cake into 12 wedges. Spoon 2 tablespoons of the Strawberry Sauce onto each of 12 individual plates. Place a wedge of cheesecake, garnished with fresh raspberries, onto each plate.

### MICROWAVE SPRINGFORM PAN

*To make a springform pan for your microwave, cut a 24-inch piece of heavy-duty plastic wrap. Fold it in half lengthwise and drape it across the sides and bottom of a 9 x 2½-inch plastic round layer-cake pan. Cut a circle of corrugated cardboard to fit the bottom of the pan and place it on top of the plastic wrap "sling," so that the baked cheesecake can be lifted easily from the pan. Spray the cardboard with nonstick vegetable cooking spray.*

# *The Party Line*

*Celebrate good times—with spirited sippers, special dinners, birthday cakes!*

*Orange Cream Tart with Fresh Fruit (recipe, pages 286-287); Chilled Asparagus with Horseradish Vinaigrette (recipe, page 284); Dilled Borsht (recipe, page 280); Herbed Capon with Brown Rice Stuffing and Roasted Potatoes (recipe, pages 281-282); Wheat Germ Brioche (recipe, page 285)*

S pecial occasions call for special food—and whether you've got a birthday, anniversary or celebratory dinner, you'll find food in this chapter to fill the bill.

For example, buffets are a great way to invite a group over without the preparations for a sit-down dinner. And buffets let you offer a more diverse selection of food. Glazed Ham Loaves *(recipe, page 272)*, Crunchy Chicken Casserole *(recipe, page 275)*, and finger-licking Apricot Bonbons *(recipe, page 279)* all go well together on the buffet table.

When the occasion calls for a sit-down dinner, we've got one already planned out. It features Herbed Capon with Brown Rice Stuffing *(recipe, page 281)*, Chilled Asparagus with Horseradish Vinaigrette *(recipe, page 284)* and Orange Cream Tart with Fresh Fruit *(recipe, page 286)*.

If you want to add a special spirited sipper to a get-together, you can choose From Russia With Love *(recipe, page 268)*, or Blue Heaven *(recipe, page 269)*. There's also a plethora of wonderful desserts to top off any meal or serve together at a Dessert Party.

Are there children in your life? Take a look at our special KidCakes. They're whimsical as well as delicious—Clarence the Circus Bear *(recipe, page 298)* would agree! ■

# Spirited Sippers

## THE PARTY BAR

*Few things can be more embarrassing than having your bar "run dry" in the middle of your party. To make sure you don't get caught short, follow our handy charts to select alcohol and figure out how much you'll need to have on hand.*
*Some points to remember:*
*• Check with your liquor store to see if they will take back unopened bottles.*
*• If your party is going to run 3 hours or longer, always have coffee on hand.*
*• It's fine to ask a friend or family member to tend the bar if the party is fairly intimate, but hire a professional bartender if you're having a crowd.*
*• Stock up on all-purpose wineglasses and 8-ounce highball glasses. Figure that at a 2-hour party, each guest may use 2 to 3 glasses.*
*• Necessary equipment: bottle opener, cocktail shaker, corkscrew, cutting board, juicer, paring knife, shot glass, strainer, tongs and scoops.*

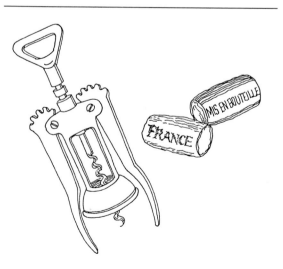

## THE BUYER'S GUIDE

Liquor and wine have gone metric—here's a rundown on what's what.

| Metric measure replaces: | U.S. measure |
|---|---|
| 500 milliliters or ½ liter (16.9 oz) | the pint |
| 750 milliliters (25.4 oz) | the fifth |
| 1 liter (33.8 oz) | the quart |
| 2 liters (67.6 oz) | the ½ gallon |
| 4 liters (135.2 oz) | the gallon |

Below is a chart indicating how many drinks you should get from bottles of liquor or wine. If you're serving wine with dinner, however, figure on fewer glasses to a bottle: 5 to 6 to a liter (quart); 3 to 4 to a 750-milliliter (fifth).

### Number of drinks per bottle

| | 1 liter | 750 milliliter |
|---|---|---|
| whiskey, gin, vodka (mixed drinks, highballs: 1½-oz servings) | 22 | 17 |
| table wines (red, white, rosé: 4- to 5-oz servings) | 6-8 | 5-6 |
| sherry (3-oz servings) | 11 | 8 |
| cordials (1-oz servings) | 33 | 25 |
| champagne, sparkling wine (4- to 5-oz servings) | 6-8 | 5-6 |

*Note: Keep in mind that people are drinking lighter these days. However, as a general rule, figure 2 drinks per person for the first 2 hours, 1 drink per person after that.*

*Orange Sunset, Perfectly Peachy, Mint Magic, Chocolate Supreme, Blue Heaven, From Russia With Love, Strawberry Kiss (recipes, pages 268-269)*

## SET 'EM UP!

1. One liter each bourbon, gin, scotch*, vodka*, sweet and dry vermouth
   *Two liters for 20 or more guests*
2. Two to three 6-packs beer
3. One 750-milliliter brandy
4. Two 750-milliliter liqueurs (Grand Marnier, Bailey's Irish Cream, Amaretto, etc.)
5. Two to four quarts seltzer
6. One quart each cola, diet soda, ginger ale, tonic water, orange juice, tomato juice
7. One bottle Bloody Mary mix
8. Three limes, one lemon
9. Green olives, pearl onions
   *Two liters for 20 or more guests*

| A WINE GUIDE | | |
|---|---|---|
| No. Of Guests | Bottles White (750 ml) | Bottles Red (750 ml) |
| 4 | 2 | 1 |
| 6 | 2 | 2 |
| 10 | 4 | 2 |
| 12 | 6 | 2 |
| 30 | 9 | 4 |
| 40 | 13 | 6 |

*Note: If you're using wine coolers, plan on two to three 6-packs for 8 to 12 guests, and at least 1 pound of ice per person.*

## Orange Sunset

*Substitute tangerine juice for a more tart flavor.*

Makes 1 drink.

*Nutrient Value Per Serving: 153 calories, 1 g protein, 0 g fat, 13 g carbohydrate, 2 mg sodium, 0 mg cholesterol.*

| | |
|---|---|
| ½ | cup orange juice |
| 2 | or 3 dashes orange bitters |
| 1½ | ounces (1 jigger) gin |
| | Ice cubes |
| | Orange slice, for garnish (optional) |
| | Maraschino cherry, for garnish (optional) |

Combine the orange juice, bitters and gin in a shaker glass. Cover and shake. Pour over the ice in a large sherry glass. Garnish with an orange slice and a maraschino cherry, if you wish.

*Note: For a non-alcoholic version of this drink, substitute ¼ cup of tonic water for the gin. Besides tangerine juice, pink grapefruit juice can be used as a substitute for the orange juice.*

## From Russia with Love

*Limonnaya lemon vodka, from Stolichnaya, is the only Russian lemon vodka available in the United States today.*

Makes 1 drink.

*Nutrient Value Per Serving: 146 calories, 0 g protein, 0 g fat, 13 g carbohydrate, 4 mg sodium, 0 mg cholesterol.*

| | |
|---|---|
| 1½ | ounces (1 jigger) Limonnaya vodka |
| ½ | cup prepared lemonade |
| ½ | cup crushed ice |
| | Maraschino cherry, for garnish (optional) |

Combine the vodka and the lemonade in a shaker glass. Cover and shake. Pour over the ice in a large wine glass. Garnish with a maraschino cherry, if you wish.

## Perfectly Peachy

*There's nothing quite like the taste of fresh peaches.*

Makes 1 drink.

*Nutrient Value Per Serving: 153 calories, 1 g protein, 1 g fat, 21 g carbohydrate, 1 mg sodium, 0 mg cholesterol.*

| | |
|---|---|
| ½ | ripe peach, peeled and pitted |
| ½ | cup crushed ice |
| | Juice of ½ lime |
| 1½ | ounces (1 jigger) peach-flavored liqueur |
| | Lime wedge, for garnish (optional) |

1. Slice the peach directly into the container of an electric blender and add the ice. Cover and blend at high speed until the mixture is smooth.
2. Add the lime juice and the peach-flavored liqueur. Cover and blend until smooth. Pour into a wine glass. Garnish with a lime wedge, if you wish.

*Note: For a non-alcoholic version of this drink, substitute ¼ cup of orange juice for the peach-flavored liqueur.*

## Mint Magic

*Even the color is cooling.*

Makes 1 drink.

*Nutrient Value Per Serving: 187 calories, 0 g protein, 0 g fat, 21 g carbohydrate, 3 mg sodium, 0 mg cholesterol.*

| | |
|---|---|
| 1½ | ounces (1 jigger) green crème de menthe |
| ½ | cup seltzer |
| | Ice cubes |
| | Fresh mint sprig, for garnish (optional) |

Combine the crème de menthe and the seltzer in a shaker glass. Cover and shake. Pour over the ice in a julep glass. Garnish with a mint sprig, if you wish.

# Chocolate Supreme

*A chocolate milk shake——for adults only!*

Makes 1 drink.

*Nutrient Value Per Serving: 605 calories, 13 g protein, 23 g fat, 64 g carbohydrate, 238 mg sodium, 94 mg cholesterol.*

- **2    scoops chocolate ice cream**
- **1    cup milk**
- **1½  ounces (1 jigger) crème de cacao**

Combine the ice cream, milk and crème de cacao in the container of an electric blender. Cover and blend until smooth. Pour into a tall glass.

**Note:** *For a non-alcoholic drink, substitute chocolate syrup for the crème de cacao.*

# Strawberry Kiss

*Just a touch of strawberries gives this drink a rosy glow.*

Makes 1 drink.

*Nutrient Value Per Serving: 239 calories, 1 g protein, 0 g fat, 22 g carbohydrate, 12 mg sodium, 0 mg cholesterol.*

- **4    to 6 strawberries**
- **½   cup crushed ice**
- **1    cup dry white wine**
- **1½  tablespoons sugar**

1. Reserve 1 of the strawberries for garnish. Hull and halve the remainder into the container of an electric blender. Add the ice, wine and sugar. Cover and blend at high speed until the mixture is smooth.
2. Pour into a large glass. Garnish with the reserved strawberry.

**Note:** *For a non-alcoholic version of this drink, substitute seltzer for the wine.*

# Blue Heaven

*This cool, blue elixir will spirit you off into the horizon.*

Makes 1 drink.

*Nutrient Value Per Serving: 124 calories, 0 g protein, 0 g fat, 14 g carbohydrate, 0 mg sodium, 0 mg cholesterol.*

- **1½  ounces (1 jigger) Parfait Amour liqueur**
-      **Crushed ice (optional)**
-      **Lemon peel, for garnish**

Pour the liqueur straight up or, if you wish, over crushed ice. Garnish with the lemon peel.

# Margaritaville

Makes 4 servings.

*Nutrient Value Per Serving: 241 calories, 0 g protein, 0 g fat, 31 g carbohydrate, 0 mg sodium, 0 mg cholesterol.*

-      **Lemon juice**
-      **Coarse salt**
- **1    can (6 ounces) frozen limeade concentrate**
- **¾   cup tequila**
- **¼   cup triple sec (orange-flavored liqueur)**
- **2½  to 3 cups crushed ice**
-      **Lime slices, for garnish (optional)**

1. Chill the container of an electric blender or a food processor. Pour a little lemon juice into a saucer. Spread the coarse salt in a second saucer.
2. Dip the rims of 4 margarita glasses or wine glasses into the lemon juice, then into the salt; gently shake off excess salt. Refrigerate for about 15 minutes to dry.
3. Combine the limeade, tequila, triple sec and ice in the chilled blender or food processor container. Cover and whirl until slushy.
4. Pour the margarita into the prepared glasses. Garnish each with a lime slice, if you wish.

# FRUIT OF THE VINE: A MINI-GUIDE TO WINE

### The Wine Cellar
Wine can be served before meals, with them and after—or savored by itself, just like any other beverage. Before a meal, many people prefer a dry to medium-sweet wine, such as sherry, vermouth or any of the aperitif wines. All of these wines should be served chilled, on the rocks or with soda. Champagne and other not-too-sweet sparkling wines also make excellent before-dinner drinks. The reason for not choosing a very sweet wine is that the before-dinner drink should lead into the first course, which is not sweet. Thus, a very sweet before-dinner drink is like starting the meal with dessert.

For an informal occasion or an everyday-type meal, try a modest, inexpensive wine, known in France and Italy as *vin ordinaire* and *vino da tavola* (meaning "plain" and "table" wine). Serve one of the many white, rosé, blush or red wines available, choosing the type that best complements the main dish. Finer wines, and the unusually fine wines called "great," are for special occasions. For a more formal occasion, some people like to serve a different wine with each course. Generally, a dryish white wine is served with a first dish of fish or seafood, and a more robust red wine with the meat. But lately, even those who entertain a great deal are serving only one wine throughout the meal.

### Which Wine With What?
Selecting the best wine to complement your meal can be confusing. However, taking the time to experiment with some of the more traditional food and wine combinations can allow you to discover which wines go particularly well with which foods—simply because both taste better when served together.

*The Rule of Order:* White before red and dry before sweet is the basic rule, just as fish comes before the meat, and dessert at the end of a meal. But, of course, you can follow a dry red dinner wine with a sweet white wine or champagne for dessert.

*Hors d'Oeuvres and Soup:* For the first course, serve the same wine you have selected to serve with the entrée.
*Fish:* Dry white wine or dry sherry.
*Shellfish:* Dry or medium-dry (not sweet) white wine, or a light red wine.
*Poultry:* Depending on the fashion in which the dish is prepared, a light or full red or a white wine is appropriate. The richer the food, the more robust the flavor of the wine should be. Cold chicken takes a light white wine; roast chicken, a fuller one or a light red wine; *coq au vin* (chicken in wine) is both prepared in and served with red wine; chicken served with a cream sauce takes a full white wine; roast duck or goose, a full white or medium-full red wine. If a dish is prepared with a certain wine, the same wine should be served with the meal.
*Veal and Pork:* Full white wine, light red wine or a rosé.
*Beef and Lamb:* Full red wine.
*Ham:* Full white wine, medium-full red wine or a good quality rosé.
*Venison and Game:* Full red wine is good with venison. For the more delicate game birds, such as pheasant, dove and quail, use a full white wine. For wild duck, use a medium-full red.
*Dessert:* Sweet wine for cakes, puddings and fruits, except acid citrus fruits. Champagne is another good choice—not the extra-dry variety, but one that is just a bit sweet.
*Nuts and Cheese:* Port, sweet sherry or Madeira.
*Exceptions to the Rule:* Do not serve wine with highly spiced foods, such as curry or Mexican food—beer is a better complement to them—or with vinegary foods, such as salads, which can make the wine taste sour. If you are serving cheese with wine (a delicious combination), be careful in your selection of cheeses: A too-strong cheese will overwhelm the wine.

### The Wine Service

The classic rule is as follows: To bring out their full flavor, white wines should be served chilled and red wines at room temperature. But this rule needs some clarification: "Chilled" means cool in the mouth—slightly chilled, but not icy, with a temperature of around 45° to 50°. If you chill a white wine too much, or freeze it, you destroy the flavor. You can properly chill white wines, including champagnes and rosés, by refrigerating them for one to two hours—never put them in the freezer! (White aperitif or dessert wines are the exception, as they often are served on the rocks.) If time is a problem, fill an ice bucket or a large pot with water and ice, and leave the bottle in it for about 20 minutes. This also is a good method to use when serving a crowd.

"Room temperature," at which red wines should be served, refers to a range between 60° and 68°. If the wine is very warm, you can bring down the temperature by standing the wine near an open window for 10 to 15 minutes, depending on the weather, or by putting it in the refrigerator for five minutes before serving. But never heat a chilled bottle of red wine; this ruins the wine. Let the bottle stand until it has returned to the proper temperature.

A good bottle of red wine should be uncorked one to two hours before it is consumed. This is called "letting the wine breathe," and allows the full flavor of the wine to develop.

Most of the wines we choose to serve with casual or everyday meals do not require anything beyond pouring—and domestic gallon and half-gallon table wines are an excellent value. But all wine should be served at the right temperature to best enhance the flavor of your meal. Just remember this basic rule: Extremes of heat or cold destroy the flavor of food *and* wine.

### The Wine List

*Dinner Wines:* These wines, served primarily with meals, may be white, rosé or red, dry or sweet. Dinner wines account for the majority of all wines produced in the world, and are available in an enormous range of flavors and qualities.

*Sparkling Wines:* These wines usually are reserved for festive occasions. Champagne is the best know variety of sparkling wine, but there are many others, such as sparkling Burgundy, for example.

*Fortified Wines:* These wines have been made stronger and longer-lasting by the addition of brandy. Sherry, port and Madeira are the best known varieties. Fortified wines can be sweet or dry; the sweet varieties generally are served with dessert, and the dry as apéritifs (before-dinner drinks).

*Aromatized Wines:* These red or white wines are fortified *and* flavored with herbs, seeds and/or spices. Vermouth is the best known. Aromatic wines often are combined with liquors for cocktails, but they can be served alone as apéritifs.

### The Wine Store

Always lay down wine bottles on their sides to store them; this keeps the cork moist. If the cork dries out, air will get into the bottle and spoil the wine.

Wine should be stored in a cool, dark place. The ideal temperature is about 55° to 60°. It is important that the temperature be steady all year round, never varying more than a few degrees. Unless you are equipped with good storage conditions, don't buy more wine than you will drink within a reasonable period—wine doesn't keep well.

# *Entertaining Ideas: Beautiful Buffet*

## BUFFET SAVVY

- *The buffet table should have plenty of room for your guests to move around it easily.*
- *Arrange the table for easy serving and traffic flow: plates first, entrées and accompaniments next, tableware and napkins last.*
- *Wrap each set of tableware in a napkin for easy carrying.*
- *The bread basket and butter plate should be placed next to each other, and the butter should be at room temperature for easy spreading.*
- *Place the correct serving utensils next to each dish.*
- *Be sure there is plenty of table and seating space for each guest. Card tables and tray tables work very well.*
- *If you choose to seat guests at the dining table, set the table with napkins and tableware beforehand, so your guests won't have to pick them up at the buffet.*

## Glazed Ham Loaves

Bake at 350° for 45 minutes.
Makes 10 servings.

*Nutrient Value Per Loaf: 391 calories, 19 g protein, 15 g fat, 44 g carbohydrate, 1,229 mg sodium, 116 mg cholesterol.*

1½  **pounds ground cooked ham**
½  **pound ground beef**
1  **cup finely crushed saltine crackers without salted tops (about 2½ ounces)**
1  **cup milk**
2  **eggs**
2  **tablespoons white wine vinegar**
2  **tablespoons granulated sugar**
1  **tablespoon all-purpose flour**
1  **tablespoon dry mustard**
1  **cup catsup**
1  **cup firmly packed light brown sugar**

1. Preheat the oven to moderate (350°). Lightly grease a large baking pan.
2. Combine the ham, beef, cracker crumbs, milk, eggs, vinegar, granulated sugar, flour and mustard in a bowl. Divide the mixture into 10 portions and shape each into a 5 x 2 x 2-inch loaf. Arrange in the prepared pan.
3. Bake in the preheated moderate oven (350°) for 30 minutes.
4. Meanwhile, prepare the glaze: Combine the catsup and the brown sugar in a medium-size bowl. Spoon the glaze over the ham loaves. Bake for 15 minutes more. Spoon the leftover sauce from the pan into a sauceboat and serve with the ham loaves.

## Microwave Instructions
*(for a 650-watt variable power microwave oven)*

*Nutrient Value Per Serving: 336 calories, 19 g protein, 15 g fat, 30 g carbohydrate, 1,084 mg sodium, 116 mg cholesterol.*

**Ingredient Changes:** Decrease the catsup and the brown sugar each to ½ cup.

**Directions:** Combine the ingredients for the ham loaves as in Step 2 of the above recipe. Shape into 10 balls using a 1-cup measure. Space the ham balls evenly in a microwave-safe 12-inch quiche dish. Cover with microwave-safe plastic wrap, turned back slightly on one side to vent. Microwave at full power for 8 minutes. Rearrange the balls in the dish, placing the balls that were in the center at the outside rim of the dish. Cover again with the plastic wrap. Microwave at full power for 7 minutes. Meanwhile, combine the ½ cup of catsup and the ½ cup of brown sugar. Spoon the glaze over the loaves. Microwave, uncovered, at full power for 2 minutes. Serve the remaining sauce from the dish with the loaves.

## Italian Roast Beef

Bake at 300° for 20 to 23 minutes per pound for medium-rare.
Makes 6 to 8 servings.

*Nutrient Value Per Serving: 607 calories, 33 g protein, 51 g fat, 2 g carbohydrate, 228 mg sodium, 138 mg cholesterol.*

1    **boneless sirloin roast (4 pounds)**
2    **cloves garlic, sliced**
¼    **teaspoon coarsely ground black pepper**
1    **cup beef broth**
½    **cup chopped onions**
¾    **teaspoon Italian seasoning**

1. Preheat the oven to slow (300°). Cut small slashes around the roast and insert the garlic slices. Sprinkle the roast with the black pepper. Insert a meat thermometer so it reaches the center of the meat.

2. Place the meat in a roasting pan. Add the broth to the pan and sprinkle the onion and the Italian seasoning over the meat.

3. Roast in the preheated slow oven (300°) for 20 to 23 minutes per pound for medium-rare (140° on the meat thermometer), or for 24 to 28 minutes per pound for medium (160° on the meat thermometer). Baste occasionally.

4. Remove the roast and let stand for 15 minutes before carving. Slice thinly, reserving ¼ of the meat uncut for Chopped Beef Salad Sandwiches *(recipe, below)*, if you wish. Serve with the pan juices.

## Chopped Beef Salad Sandwiches

Makes 4 servings.

*Nutrient Value Per Serving: 420 calories, 21 g protein, 35 g fat, 4 g carbohydrate, 345 mg sodium, 82 mg cholesterol.*

2    **green onions, quartered**
¾    **pound cooked beef, cut into ¾-inch cubes (from Italian Roast Beef; recipe, at left)**
⅓    **cup mayonnaise**
2    **tablespoons sweet pickle relish**
1    **tablespoon lemon juice**
½    **teaspoon dry mustard**
¼    **teaspoon salt**
     **Rolls or bread**

1. Finely chop the green onion in the container of a food processor. Add the beef and process just until finely chopped, for three 1-second pulses.

2. Combine the mayonnaise, relish, lemon juice, mustard and salt in a medium-size bowl. Add the beef mixture and stir until blended. Serve on rolls or bread.

# 🎴 Rigatoni with Meatballs

Makes 6 servings.

*Nutrient Value Per Serving: 875 calories, 38 g protein, 54 g fat, 58 g carbohydrate, 1,418 mg sodium, 187 mg cholesterol.*

**Meatballs:**

- ¾ **pound ground beef**
- ¼ **cup cracker crumbs**
- 2 **tablespoons grated Romano cheese**
- 1 **egg**
- 1 **small clove garlic, finely chopped**
- 1 **tablespoon chopped fresh parsley leaves**
- ¼ **teaspoon salt**
- ⅛ **teaspoon pepper**

**Meat Sauce:**

- 1 **tablespoon olive oil**
- 6 **sweet Italian sausages (about 1 pound)**
- ¼ **cup finely chopped celery**
- 2 **tablespoons finely chopped onion**
- 1 **clove garlic, finely chopped**
- 8 **ounces ground beef**
- 1 **can (15 ounces) tomato sauce**
- 1 **can (6 ounces) tomato paste**
- 2¼ **cups water**
- 2 **tablespoons grated Romano cheese**

- 12 **ounces rigatoni or pasta of your choice**

1. Prepare the Meatballs: Combine the beef, cracker crumbs, Romano cheese, egg, garlic, parsley, salt and pepper in a medium-size bowl and mix well. Shape into twelve 2-inch balls and set aside.
2. Prepare the Meat Sauce: Heat the oil in a large saucepot. Add the sausages and cook until browned, for about 10 minutes. Transfer with a slotted spoon to a plate and set aside. Add the celery, onion and garlic to the pot. Cook for 3 minutes. Add the beef. Cook, stirring to break up the meat, until browned, for about 5 minutes.
3. Stir in the tomato sauce, tomato paste, water and Romano cheese. Bring to boiling. Reduce the heat to low. Add the meatballs and the sausages and simmer, partially covered, for 1 to 1½ hours, or until the desired consistency. (The sauce can be prepared up to 2 days in advance.)
4. Cook the pasta in a large pot of lightly salted boiling water just until *al dente*, firm but tender. Drain the pasta in a colander.
5. Remove the meatballs and the sausages from the sauce and set aside. Spoon half the sauce into a serving bowl. Add the pasta to the bowl and toss to coat with the sauce. Pour the remaining sauce over the pasta. Serve immediately with the meatballs and the sausages.

# 🎴 💲 Classic Lasagna

Bake at 375° for 50 to 60 minutes.
Makes 8 servings.

*Nutrient Value Per Serving: 466 calories, 28 g protein, 26 g fat, 30 g carbohydrate, 913 mg sodium, 114 mg cholesterol.*

- 1 **pound ground beef**
- 1 **can (35 ounces) tomatoes, drained and chopped**
- 1 **can (6 ounces) tomato paste**
- ½ **teaspoon garlic powder**
- 8 **lasagna noodles**
- 1½ **cups cottage cheese**
- ½ **cup grated Parmesan cheese**
- 1 **egg**
- 2 **tablespoons dried parsley flakes**
- ½ **teaspoon salt**
- ½ **teaspoon pepper**
- 8 **ounces mozzarella cheese, shredded**

1. Cook the beef in a large saucepan, stirring to break up the meat, until browned, for about 10 minutes. Add the tomatoes, tomato paste and garlic powder. Simmer for 40 minutes, or until thickened.
2. Meanwhile, cook the lasagna noodles in a large pot of lightly salted boiling water just until *al dente*, firm but tender. Drain the noodles in a colander.
3. Preheat the oven to moderate (375°). Lightly grease a 13 x 9 x 2-inch baking pan.

4. Stir together the cottage cheese, Parmesan cheese, egg, parsley flakes, salt and pepper in a medium-size bowl until well blended.
5. Spoon approximately one third of the sauce into the prepared baking dish. Top with 4 noodles, half the cheese mixture, half the remaining sauce and half the mozzarella cheese. Repeat the layers, starting with the noodles and ending with the mozzarella cheese.
6. Cover the pan with aluminum foil and seal tightly.
7. Bake in the preheated moderate oven (375°) for 50 to 60 minutes, or until heated through. Cool on a wire rack for 10 minutes before cutting and serving.

## Food for Thought . . .

**Mozzarella** *A cheese of Italian origin, mozzarella is a semisoft cheese made from whole or skim milk. It is mild tasting and melts easily. It often is used on pizza and eggplant dishes, but mozzarella also can be used in salads and sandwiches.*

*Mozzarella is an unripened cheese made in an unusual process. Usually, the curd is drained from the whey, then pressed, ripened or aged to make cheese. For mozzarella, the curd just is pulled in scalding hot water and kneaded.*

*Mozzarella is available fresh, smoked or rolled with sausage or ham in a variety of shapes.*

# Crunchy Chicken Casserole

Bake at 350° for 30 to 40 minutes.
Makes 12 servings.

*Nutrient Value Per Serving: 493 calories, 20 g protein, 40 g fat, 15 g carbohydrate, 670 mg sodium, 150 mg cholesterol.*

| | |
|---|---|
| 2 | **cans (10¾ ounces each) condensed cream of chicken soup, undiluted** |
| 1½ | **cups mayonnaise** |
| 1 | **tablespoon prepared mustard** |
| 1 | **tablespoon Worcestershire sauce** |
| 1 | **package (7 ounces) low-salt potato chips, crushed** |
| ½ | **cup slivered almonds** |
| 4 | **cups cubed cooked chicken** |
| 2 | **cups diced celery** |
| ¼ | **cup finely chopped onion** |
| 4 | **hard-cooked eggs, sliced** |

1. Preheat the oven to moderate (350°). Lightly butter a 13 x 9 x 2-inch ovenproof casserole dish.
2. Combine the condensed soup, mayonnaise, mustard and Worcestershire sauce in a medium-size bowl. Reserve 1 cup of the potato chips and 2 tablespoons of the slivered almonds for the top of the casserole.
3. Place half the remaining potato chips in the bottom of the casserole dish, spreading them evenly. Layer half each of the chicken, celery, onion, eggs and remaining almonds. Spread half the mayonnaise mixture on top. Repeat the layers, ending with the reserved potato chips and almonds.
4. Bake in the preheated moderate oven (350°) for 30 to 40 minutes, or until heated through.

## Microwave Instructions
*(for a 650-watt variable power microwave oven)*

**Directions:** Follow the directions in Step 2 of the above recipe. Assemble the casserole as in Step 3 in a microwave-safe baking dish, about 12½ x 8½ inches. Cover with wax paper. Microwave at full power for 14 minutes, rotating the dish one quarter turn after 7 minutes. Let stand for 2 minutes.

# Ham and Cheese Surprise

Bake at 350° for 20 to 25 minutes.
Makes 12 servings.

*Nutrient Value Per Serving: 463 calories, 24 g protein, 26 g fat, 33 g carbohydrate, 1,285 mg sodium, 89 mg cholesterol.*

12   **Kaiser rolls**
¾   **cup (1½ sticks) butter, softened**
⅓   **cup horseradish mustard**
2   **tablespoons finely chopped onion**
2   **teaspoons poppy seeds**
1½  **pounds thinly sliced boiled ham**
12   **slices Swiss cheese (about 12 ounces)**

1. Preheat the oven to moderate (350°).
2. Slice the rolls and set aside. Combine the butter, mustard, onion and poppy seeds in a small bowl.
3. Spread the butter mixture on the cut sides of the rolls.* Divide the ham and the Swiss cheese evenly among the rolls. Wrap individually in aluminum foil, sealing tightly. Place the rolls on a baking sheet.
4. Bake in the preheated moderate oven (350°) for 20 to 25 minutes, or until heated through. Serve immediately.

*\*Note: Save any remaining butter mixture for another use.*

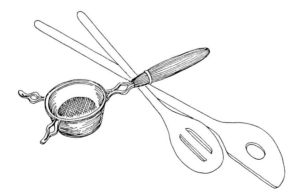

# Cherry Custard Pie

Bake at 375° for 45 minutes.
Makes 8 servings.

*Nutrient Value Per Serving: 302 calories, 7 g protein, 15 g fat, 34 g carbohydrate, 138 mg sodium, 184 mg cholesterol.*

¼   **cup plus 2 tablespoons granulated sugar**
1   **can (16 ounces) dark, sweet, pitted cherries, drained**
1½  **cups milk**
1   **cup heavy cream**
4   **eggs**
1   **teaspoon vanilla**
1   **cup unsifted all-purpose flour**
¼   **teaspoon salt**
1   **tablespoon superfine sugar, for garnish**

1. Preheat the oven to moderate (375°).
2. Butter a 10-inch pie plate and sprinkle with 1 tablespoon of the granulated sugar, tilting the plate to coat the bottom and sides. Place the cherries evenly in the plate and sprinkle with 1 tablespoon of the granulated sugar.
3. Place the remaining ¼ cup of granulated sugar, the milk, cream, eggs, vanilla, flour and salt in the container of an electric blender or a food processor. Cover and whirl until the batter is smooth. Pour the batter over the cherries in the pie plate. Place on a baking sheet.
4. Bake in the preheated moderate oven (375°) for 45 minutes, or until puffed, golden and springy to the touch. Cool on a wire rack for 15 minutes. Dust the top of the pie with the superfine sugar and serve immediately, or slightly warm.

⦀ ❢ 💲

## Lemon Cheesecake

Bake at 350° for 35 minutes.
Makes 10 servings.

*Nutrient Value Per Serving: 312 calories, 4 g protein, 19 g fat, 31 g carbohydrate, 267 mg sodium, 80 mg cholesterol.*

**Crust:**
1¼ **cups graham cracker crumbs**
⅓ **cup sugar**
⅓ **cup melted butter**

**Filling:**
3 **packages (3 ounces each) cream cheese**
2 **tablespoons butter**
½ **cup sugar**
2 **tablespoons flour**
⅔ **cup milk**
¼ **cup lemon juice**
1 **egg**

1. Preheat the oven to moderate (350°). Lightly grease a 10-inch glass pie plate.
2. Prepare the Crust: Combine the cracker crumbs, sugar and butter in a bowl. Reserve ¼ cup. Press the remaining mixture into the prepared pie plate.
3. Prepare the Filling: Beat together the cream cheese and the butter in a bowl with an electric mixer until smooth. Add the sugar, flour, milk, lemon juice and egg. Mix until blended, for 2 minutes. Pour into the crust and sprinkle with the reserved crumb mixture.
4. Bake in the preheated moderate oven (350°) for 35 minutes. Cool on a wire rack. Refrigerate. Serve cold, or at room temperature.

⦀ ❢ 💲

## Chocolate Zucchini Cake

Bake at 350° for 1 hour and 10 minutes.
Makes 12 servings.

*Nutrient Value Per Serving: 485 calories, 5 g protein, 29 g fat, 55 g carbohydrate, 351 mg sodium, 88 mg cholesterol.*

2½ **cups unsifted all-purpose flour**
3 **tablespoons unsweetened cocoa powder**
1 **teaspoon baking soda**
½ **teaspoon baking powder**
½ **teaspoon salt**
½ **teaspoon ground cinnamon**
1 **cup butter or margarine, softened**
1¾ **cups sugar**
½ **cup vegetable oil**
2 **eggs**
1 **teaspoon vanilla**
½ **cup sour milk***
2 **cups grated zucchini (about 6 ounces)**
½ **cup semisweet chocolate pieces**
**Whipped cream, for garnish**

1. Preheat the oven to moderate (350°). Grease and flour a 13 x 9 x 2-inch baking pan.
2. Sift together the flour, cocoa, baking soda, baking powder, salt and cinnamon onto wax paper.
3. Beat together the butter or margarine, sugar and oil in a large bowl with an electric mixer at high speed for 2 minutes. Add the eggs and the vanilla and beat for 2 minutes more, or until light and fluffy. Beat in the flour mixture alternately with the sour milk in 3 additions at very low speed until combined. Stir in the zucchini. Scrape the batter into the prepared pan. Sprinkle the chocolate pieces evenly over the top.
4. Bake in the preheated moderate oven (350°) for 1 hour and 10 minutes, or until a wooden pick inserted in the center of the cake comes out clean. Cool in the pan on a wire rack. To serve, cut into 12 squares and top with the whipped cream.

***Note:** To make sour milk, combine ½ teaspoon of distilled white vinegar with ½ cup of milk.*

## Caramel Pecan Rolls

Bake at 425° for 25 minutes.
Makes 3 dozen rolls.

*Nutrient Value Per Roll: 184 calories, 3 g protein, 7 g fat, 27 g carbohydrate, 170 mg sodium, 12 mg cholesterol.*

### Dough:

1¾ **cups milk**
½ **cup water**
2 **tablespoons granulated sugar**
2 **teaspoons salt**
3 **tablespoons vegetable shortening**
2 **packages active dry yeast**
5½ **to 6 cups unsifted all-purpose flour**

### Caramel Mixture:

1 **cup firmly packed light brown sugar**
½ **cup (1 stick) butter or margarine, softened**
2 **tablespoons corn syrup**
1 **cup pecan halves**

### Cinnamon Sugar:

½ **cup granulated sugar**
1 **teaspoon ground cinnamon**

4 **tablespoons (½ stick) butter, softened**

1. Prepare the Dough: Combine the milk, water, sugar, salt and shortening in a small saucepan. Heat, stirring, just until the shortening is melted. Pour into a large bowl. Cool to very warm (90°). Sprinkle on the yeast and stir to dissolve. Let stand until bubbly, for about 10 minutes.
2. Add 2½ cups of the flour to the yeast mixture. Beat with an electric mixer at low speed for 30 seconds. Scrape down the sides of the bowl. Beat at high speed for 3 minutes. Stir in enough of the remaining flour with a wooden spoon to make a soft dough.
3. Turn out the dough onto a floured board. Knead until smooth and elastic, for about 5 minutes, adding more flour as necessary to prevent sticking. Place the dough in an oiled large bowl and turn the oiled side up. Cover and let rise in a warm place, away from drafts, for 30 minutes, or until almost doubled in bulk.
4. Meanwhile, prepare the Caramel Mixture: Lightly grease three 9-inch round layer-cake pans. Combine the brown sugar, butter or margarine and corn syrup in a small saucepan. Cook over low heat, stirring, until blended. Divide evenly among the baking pans. Sprinkle the pecans evenly over the Caramel Mixture.
5. Prepare the Cinnamon Sugar: Combine the sugar and the cinnamon in a small bowl.
6. Punch down the dough and divide into 2 equal portions. Roll out each portion on a lightly floured surface to a 12 x 10-inch rectangle. Spread each portion with 2 tablespoons of the softened butter and sprinkle evenly with the Cinnamon Sugar. Beginning with the long side, roll up each portion, jelly-roll fashion. Cut crosswise into 1-inch slices. Place the slices, cut side down, in the prepared pans, using 8 slices per pan. Cover and refrigerate for 2 to 24 hours.
7. When ready to bake, remove the rolls from the refrigerator and let stand for 25 minutes. Meanwhile, preheat the oven to hot (425°).
8. Bake in the preheated hot oven (425°) for 25 minutes, or until golden on top. Cool in the pans on a wire rack for 5 minutes. Invert the rolls onto a serving plate and serve warm.

## 🍸💲

# Caramel Brownies

*These brownies are the gooey variety.*

Bake at 350° for 24 minutes.
Makes 24 brownies.

*Nutrient Value Per Brownie: 245 calories, 3 g protein, 13 g fat, 31 g carbohydrate, 277 mg sodium, 18 mg cholesterol.*

1 **package (18¼ ounces) dark chocolate cake mix**
¾ **cup (1½ sticks) butter or margarine, melted**
⅔ **cup evaporated milk**
1 **package (12 ounces) caramels**
1 **package (6 ounces) semisweet chocolate pieces**

1. Preheat the oven to moderate (350°). Lightly grease and flour a 13 x 9 x 2-inch baking pan.
2. Mix together the cake mix, butter or margarine and ⅓ cup of the evaporated milk in a medium-size bowl. Spread half the mixture (1½ cups) evenly in the prepared pan.
3. Bake in the preheated moderate oven (350°) for 6 minutes. Meanwhile, melt the caramels with the remaining ⅓ cup of evaporated milk in a small saucepan over low heat.
4. Sprinkle the chocolate pieces over the baked mixture, then drizzle the caramel mixture on top. Crumble the remaining cake mixture on top of the caramel.
5. Bake in the preheated moderate oven (350°) for 18 minutes more. Let cool completely in the pan on a wire rack. Cut into 24 bars and serve cold.

## 🍸💲

# Apricot Bonbons

Makes about 5 dozen.

*Nutrient Value Per Bonbon: 85 calories, 1 g protein, 4 g fat, 11 g carbohydrate, 29 mg sodium, 3 mg cholesterol.*

1 **package (14 ounces) flaked coconut**
1 **package (6 ounces) dried apricots, finely chopped**
1 **can (14 ounces) sweetened condensed milk (not evaporated)**
1 **bag (12 ounces) white coating chocolate, for dipping**

1. Combine the coconut, apricots and condensed milk in a large bowl. Cover with plastic wrap and refrigerate for 4 hours, or overnight.
2. Roll the chilled coconut mixture into balls, using a scant measuring tablespoon per ball, and place on a piece of wax paper. Return to the refrigerator.
3. Set the chocolate to melt in a bowl that just fits over a pan of simmering water. Remove from the heat. Stir occasionally until the chocolate is smooth.
4. Line baking sheets with wax paper. Using a fork, spear the balls and dip into the melted chocolate, turning until evenly coated. Place on the lined baking sheets and refrigerate until hardened. Store in a tightly covered container.

---

## Food for Thought . . .

**Caramel** *This can be either a chewy candy or sugar that has been heated until it melts into a brown syrup. Caramel syrup is used to coat molds for custards or flans. Caramel candy is made of sugar, cream, butter and flavoring.*

# Entertaining Ideas: Special Sit-Down Dinner

## Dilled Borscht

Makes 8 servings.

*Nutrient Value Per Serving: 80 calories, 5 g protein, 2 g fat, 12 g carbohydrate, 490 mg sodium, 4 mg cholesterol.*

- 3    cups chicken broth
- 1¾   pounds beets (about 8 medium-size beets), stems removed, scrubbed, peeled and diced OR: 1 can (1 pound) sliced beets, drained and liquid reserved
- 1¼   cups buttermilk
- 1¼   cups plain lowfat yogurt
- 1    tablespoon chopped fresh dill
- 1    tablespoon lemon juice
- ⅛    teaspoon freshly ground pepper
       Additional plain lowfat yogurt OR: dairy sour cream, for garnish (optional)
       Dill sprigs, for garnish (optional)

1. If using fresh beets, bring the broth to boiling in a large saucepan over high heat. Add the beets and return to boiling. Lower the heat, cover and simmer for 25 minutes, or until the beets are tender. If using canned beets, combine the liquid from the can with enough broth to make 3 cups and combine with the beets in a bowl.
2. Place the beets with the broth, working in batches if necessary, in the container of an electric blender (for smoother consistency) or a food processor. Cover and whirl until puréed.
3. Pour the purée into a large bowl. Whisk in the buttermilk, yogurt, dill, lemon juice and pepper until well blended. Cover and chill for several hours, or overnight.
4. Just before serving, whisk the borscht a few times until blended and smooth. Pour into chilled serving bowls. If you wish, garnish with additional plain lowfat yogurt, or sour cream, and fresh dill sprigs.

## Microwave Instructions
*(for a 650-watt variable power microwave oven)*

**Directions:** Trim the beet greens to about 1 inch and scrub the beets well. Place the beets in a microwave-safe 1½-quart casserole dish. Pour in ½ cup of water. Cover and microwave at full power for 18 to 23 minutes, or until the beets are tender. (If the beets vary in size, check periodically for the tenderness of the smaller ones.) Let cool slightly. Trim the ends and slip off the skins. Coarsely chop into the container of an electric blender or a food processor and add 2 cups of the broth. Cover and whirl until smooth and puréed. Pour into a large bowl. Whisk in the remaining 1 cup of broth, the buttermilk, yogurt, dill, lemon juice and pepper. Cover, chill and serve as in the above recipe.

## ⫘ 🍴
# *Herbed Capon with Brown Rice Stuffing and Roasted Potatoes*

Roast at 425° for 15 minutes, then at 325°
for 2½ hours.
Makes 8 servings.

*Nutrient Value Per Serving of Capon with Potatoes: 678 calories, 67 g protein, 27 g fat, 39 g carbohydrate, 476 mg sodium, 190 mg cholesterol.*

*Nutrient Value Per Serving of Stuffing: 162 calories, 6 g protein, 7 g fat, 19 g carbohydrate, 427 mg sodium, 18 mg cholesterol.*

*Nutrient Value Per Serving of Gravy: 91 calories, 2 g protein, 7 g fat, 5 g carbohydrate, 138 mg sodium, 6 mg cholesterol.*

**Brown Rice Stuffing:**
- 1   medium-size onion, chopped
- ¼   cup chopped sweet red pepper
- 2   to 3 medium-size mushrooms, chopped (1 cup)
- 2   tablespoons butter or margarine
- ½   cup uncooked brown rice
- 1   can (8 ounces) pineapple tidbits in natural juices, drained, coarsely chopped and juice reserved
    Chicken broth, homemade or canned
- ¼   teaspoon leaf marjoram, crumbled
- ¼   teaspoon leaf thyme, crumbled
- ¼   teaspoon freshly ground pepper
- ⅛   teaspoon salt
- 5   ounces boiled or smoked ham, chopped (1 cup)
- ¼   cup golden raisins
- ¼   cup chopped pistachio nuts

**Capon:**
- 1   capon (about 8 pounds) OR: 6- to 8-pound roasting chicken, thawed if frozen, with giblets reserved
- 1½   teaspoons leaf marjoram, crumbled
- 1½   teaspoons leaf thyme, crumbled
- 1¼   teaspoons salt
- ½   teaspoon freshly ground pepper
- 1   tablespoon butter or margarine, melted

- 3   to 3½ pounds small (1 to 2 inches in diameter) red-skinned potatoes (about 24)

**Herbed Giblet Gravy:**
- 3½   cups water
    Giblets reserved from bird
- ⅔   cup defatted pan drippings
- 4   tablespoons fat from pan drippings, butter or margarine
- ½   cup finely chopped shallots
- ¼   teaspoon leaf marjoram, crumbled
- ¼   teaspoon leaf thyme, crumbled
- ¼   cup all-purpose flour
- ½   teaspoon salt
- ⅛   teaspoon freshly ground pepper

**Garnish:**
  Watercress sprigs
  Sweet red and yellow pepper strips

1. Prepare the Brown Rice Stuffing: Sauté the onion, red pepper and mushrooms in the butter or margarine in a medium-size saucepan over medium heat, stirring occasionally, for 5 minutes. Add the brown rice and sauté, stirring occasionally, for 5 minutes, or until lightly golden. Place the pineapple liquid in a measuring cup. Add enough broth to make 1¼ cups. Add to the rice along with the marjoram, thyme, pepper and salt. Bring to boiling. Reduce the heat to low, cover and simmer for 50 minutes, or until the liquid is absorbed and the rice is tender. Stir in the ham, raisins, pistachio nuts and reserved pineapple tidbits.

2. Meanwhile, prepare the Capon: Preheat the oven to hot (425°). Remove the neck and reserve the giblets. Rinse the bird well inside and out with cold water. Pat dry with paper toweling. Starting from the edge of the cavity, gently loosen and lift the skin covering the breasts and legs, being careful not to tear the skin. Carefully rub the meat with a combination of ½ teaspoon *each* of the marjoram and the thyme. Carefully press the skin back into place.

3. Sprinkle the inside of the body and neck cavities with ¼ teaspoon of the salt and

¼ teaspoon of the pepper. Spoon the stuffing loosely into both cavities. Tie the legs to the tail with string and skewer the neck skin to the back. Place the bird on a rack in a roasting pan. Brush the bird with the melted butter or margarine and sprinkle with the remaining 1 teaspoon *each* of marjoram and thyme, the remaining 1 teaspoon of salt and ¼ teaspoon of pepper.

4. Roast the bird, uncovered, in the preheated hot oven (425°) for 15 minutes. Reduce the oven temperature to slow (325°). Roast for 2½ hours, or until a meat thermometer inserted in the thickest part of the thigh, without touching the bone, reaches 180°. Baste the bird frequently with the pan drippings. If the bird browns too quickly, cover with aluminum foil.

5. About 1½ hours before the bird is done, prepare the potatoes for roasting: Using a channeling knife or swivel-bladed vegetable peeler and beginning on the top side of each potato, peel one long continuous strip around each entire potato. Rinse the potatoes and dry well with paper toweling. Place the potatoes in a single layer in the pan drippings, turning to coat. Continue cooking until the bird and the potatoes are done.

6. While the potatoes are roasting, begin to prepare the Herbed Giblet Gravy:

Bring the water to boiling in a large saucepan over high heat. Add the reserved giblets and return to boiling. Reduce the heat and simmer for 15 to 20 minutes. Remove the giblets and, when cool enough to handle, chop them. Reserve the chopped giblets and the broth separately.

7. When the bird and the potatoes are done, remove the bird to a warm platter and let stand for 20 minutes before carving. Remove the potatoes to a warm bowl and cover.

8. Strain the drippings from the roasting pan into a 4-cup glass measure. Skim off the fat and reserve 4 tablespoons (or add enough melted butter or margarine, if necessary, to make 4 tablespoons). You should have at least ⅔ cup of pan drippings without the fat. Add enough reserved broth from Step 6, or water or chicken broth, if necessary, to make 4 cups.

9. Heat the reserved fat in a medium-size saucepan. Add the shallots, marjoram and thyme. Sauté for 1 to 2 minutes, or until the shallots are tender. Stir in the flour and cook, stirring constantly, for 2 minutes. Gradually stir in the broth-pan drippings mixture. Cook over medium heat, stirring constantly, until the mixture thickens and boils. Lower the heat, stir in the reserved chopped giblets and simmer for 5 minutes. Stir in the salt and the pepper. Pour into a gravy boat and keep warm.

10. Place the bird on a serving platter. Garnish the platter with the potatoes, watercress sprigs and red and yellow pepper strips. Serve with the gravy.

11. To store the leftovers, remove the stuffing from the bird and refrigerate separately.

⫸ 𝖸 $

# Crumb-Topped Leeks

*A buttery cheese sauce adds the special touch to this savory dish.*

Bake at 350° for 30 minutes.
Makes 8 servings.

---

*Nutrient Value Per Serving: 205 calories, 6 g protein, 10 g fat, 24 g carbohydrate, 405 mg sodium, 27 mg cholesterol.*

---

**16**  **medium-size leeks (about 5 pounds)**
**1**   **cup chicken broth**
**2**   **large cloves garlic, finely chopped**
**¼**  **teaspoon leaf thyme, crumbled**
**3**   **tablespoons butter or margarine**
**3**   **tablespoons all-purpose flour**
**¼**  **teaspoon freshly ground pepper**
    **Chicken broth**
**½**  **cup half-and-half**
**¼**  **cup shredded Swiss cheese**
**¼**  **cup freshly grated Parmesan cheese**

**Topping:**
**½**  **cup fresh whole wheat bread crumbs (1½ slices)**
**1½** **tablespoons freshly grated Parmesan cheese**
**1**   **tablespoon butter or margarine, melted**

1. Remove yellow or limp leaves from the leeks. Cut off the coarser green leaves at the top and the stringy roots, leaving each leek about 7 inches long. Slit lengthwise to within 1 inch of the root end. Soak in water and wash well under running water, spreading out the leaves to remove all the grit.
2. Preheat the oven to moderate (350°).
3. Bring the 1 cup of broth to boiling in a large skillet or Dutch oven over high heat. Add the leeks and return to boiling. Lower the heat to medium, cover and cook for 10 to 15 minutes, or until tender. Drain and reserve the cooking broth.
4. Sauté the garlic and the thyme in the butter or margarine in a medium-size saucepan over medium-low heat for 1 minute, or until the garlic is tender, but not brown. Stir in the flour and the

pepper and cook, stirring, for about 2 minutes.
5. Add enough additional chicken broth to the reserved cooking broth to make 1 cup. Gradually add to the flour mixture along with the half-and-half. Cook, stirring constantly, for 3 to 5 minutes, or until smooth and thickened. Remove from the heat and stir in the Swiss cheese and the ¼ cup of Parmesan cheese.
6. Spoon half the sauce over the bottom of a lightly greased 2-quart shallow baking dish. Arrange the leeks over the top of the sauce and spoon the remaining sauce on top.
7. Prepare the Topping: Combine the bread crumbs, Parmesan cheese and melted butter or margarine in a bowl and toss together. Sprinkle over the leeks.
8. Bake in the preheated moderate oven (350°) for 30 minutes, or until bubbly.

**To Make Ahead:** Assemble the dish the day before and refrigerate. Set the dish in the oven to bake for about 45 minutes before serving.

---

## Food for Thought . . .

**Leeks** *A member of the onion family, the leek resembles an overgrown green onion with flat, coarse leaves. The pale ivory stalk is surprisingly tender and pleasantly mild-tasting. Leeks often are used in delicate soups and in salads.*

## Food for Thought . . .

**Balsamic Vinegar** *A rich-flavored red wine vinegar aged in wooden casks.*

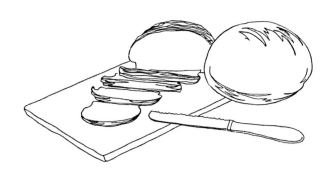

## Chilled Asparagus with Horseradish Vinaigrette

Makes 8 servings.

*Nutrient Value Per Serving: 90 calories, 3 g protein, 8 g fat, 3 g carbohydrate, 140 mg sodium, 0 mg cholesterol.*

| | |
|---|---|
| 2½ | **pounds fresh asparagus** |
| ½ | **teaspoon salt** |
| ¼ | **cup olive oil** |
| ¼ | **teaspoon Oriental sesame oil\*** |
| 1 | **tablespoon balsamic vinegar OR: white wine vinegar** |
| 1 | **tablespoon bottled horseradish, drained** |
| ⅛ | **teaspoon freshly ground pepper** |
| 2 | **tablespoons coarsely chopped pine nuts (pignoli), toasted Lemon twists, for garnish (optional)** |

1. Wash, trim and, if you wish, cut the asparagus into halves or thirds. Bring 1 inch of water to boiling in a large skillet or Dutch oven. Add ¼ teaspoon of the salt and the asparagus. Cover and cook for 3 to 5 minutes, or until the asparagus is crisp-tender. Drain in a colander.
2. Combine the olive and Oriental sesame oils, balsamic or white wine vinegar, horseradish, pepper and the remaining ¼ teaspoon of salt in a large bowl. Whisk together vigorously until well blended

Add the asparagus and toss together until well combined. Cover and chill for several hours, or overnight, tossing occasionally.
3. Just before serving, sprinkle with the pine nuts. Garnish with lemon twists, if you wish.

**\*Note:** *Oriental sesame oil has more flavor and is darker in color than regular sesame oil. It can be found in the Oriental food section of many supermarkets or in Oriental specialty food stores.*

## Food for Thought . . .

**Brioche** *A yeast bread of French origin, brioche usually is served as a bun or roll with morning coffee. It also can be hollowed and filled with a creamy meat or fish mixture. Brioche is characterized by its knob, a small round ball of dough on top. It has a rich brown crust, golden interior and buttery flavor. Brioche can be baked in different shapes, but typically is baked in one large or several individual, fluted brioche pans. It is thought that the first brioche might have been made in Brie, hence the name.*

# 🍺 🍸 💲
## *Wheat Germ Brioche*

Bake at 375° for 12 to 15 minutes.
Makes 2 dozen brioche.

---

*Nutrient Value Per Brioche: 169 calories, 6 g protein, 10 g
fat, 14 g carbohydrate, 113 mg sodium, 89 mg cholesterol.*

---

| | |
|---|---|
| 2 | **cups** unsifted all-purpose flour |
| 2 | **cups** unsweetened wheat germ |
| 3 | **tablespoons** sugar |
| 1 | **teaspoon** salt |
| 1 | **cup (2 sticks)** unsalted butter or margarine, melted |
| 1 | **envelope** active dry yeast |
| ¼ | **cup** warm water (105° to 115°) |
| 6 | **eggs** |
| 1 | **egg white** |
| 1 | **tablespoon** cold water |

1. Stir together the flour and the wheat germ on wax paper until combined; set aside.
2. Combine 2 tablespoons of the sugar and the salt in a large bowl. Stir in the butter or margarine and cool to lukewarm.
3. Meanwhile, sprinkle the yeast over the warm water and the remaining 1 tablespoon of sugar in a small cup and stir to dissolve. ("Warm water" should feel comfortably warm when dropped on your wrist.) Let stand until the yeast mixture is bubbly, for about 5 minutes.
4. Add the whole eggs, yeast mixture and 3 cups of the flour mixture to the cooled butter mixture in a large bowl. Beat with an electric mixer at medium speed until blended and smooth, for about 4 minutes. With a wooden spoon, mix in enough of the remaining flour mixture to form a soft dough.
5. Cover the dough with greased wax paper. Let rise in a warm place, away from drafts, until doubled in bulk, for about 1 to 1½ hours.
6. Stir down the dough. Cover with greased aluminum foil or plastic wrap and refrigerate overnight.

7. Grease 24 brioche pans, each measuring 2¾ to 3 inches in diameter, or 2½-inch muffin-pan cups. Place the pans on a baking sheet. Turn out the dough onto a lightly floured board. Cut the dough into fourths using a lightly floured knife. Cut three of the fourths into 8 equal pieces. Shape into balls, each about 1½ inches in diameter. Place one ball into each prepared brioche pan.* Lightly flour your index finger and make a deep depression in the center of each ball. Cut the remaining fourth of dough into 24 pieces. Roll each piece into a ball, about 1 inch in diameter, and place 1 ball into each depression. Cover with lightly greased wax paper. Let rise in a warm place, away from drafts, until doubled in bulk, for about 45 minutes to 1 hour.
8. When ready to bake, preheat the oven to moderate (375°).
9. Lightly beat together the egg white and the cold water in a small cup. Lightly brush each brioche with the mixture.
10. Bake in the preheated moderate oven (375°) for 12 to 15 minutes, or until browned. Remove the brioche from the pans at once. Serve warm, or cool on wire racks.

*\*Note: If you do not have 24 brioche pans, cover and refrigerate the remaining dough while one batch is baking. Proceed as directed in the recipe.*

**To Make Ahead:** Cool the baked brioche completely. Place in a tightly sealed container and freeze. To serve, thaw the desired number of brioche. Wrap securely in aluminum foil and heat in a preheated moderate oven (350°) for 10 to 15 minutes, or until heated through.

## Food for Thought . . .

**Kiwifruit** *A light brown, fuzzy, egg-shaped fruit that tastes like a strawberry, kiwi usually is imported to our country from New Zealand; however, kiwi now is being cultivated in California as well. The flesh of the kiwifruit is a soft, bright green and is dotted with small, edible black seeds. It can be peeled and sliced, or left unpeeled, halved and eaten with a spoon. Kiwifruit actually is a type of gooseberry, native to China and introduced to New Zealand in 1906. The merchandisers felt that "kiwi" was a more marketable name because of its association with the New Zealand kiwi bird.*

*Kiwifruit grows on a tree and is harvested from June to March. For the best eating, ripe kiwi should be as soft as a ripe pear. If the fruit is firm, ripen it at room temperature, then refrigerate. It can be eaten out-of-hand after peeling, sliced or halved and served topped with prosciutto or Westphalian ham for an appetizer. Include kiwi in fruit compotes or salads to add color and a tart taste.*

*Kiwifruit is a good source of vitamin C and contains only 36 calories per 3½ ounces.*

## Orange Cream Tart with Fresh Fruit

Bake crust at 400° for 25 minutes.
Makes 8 servings.

*Nutrient Value Per Serving: 351 calories, 5 g protein, 15 g fat, 52 g carbohydrate, 44 mg sodium, 167 mg cholesterol.*

**Orange Pastry:**
- 3 **tablespoons orange juice**
- 2 **tablespoons grated orange rind**
- 1 **egg yolk**
- 1¼ **cups unsifted all-purpose flour**
- ⅛ **teaspoon salt**
- ½ **cup (1 stick) unsalted butter or margarine, cut into ½-inch slices**

**Orange Cream:**
- ½ **cup sugar**
- ¼ **cup cornstarch**
- 1½ **cups orange juice**
- 3 **egg yolks**

**Fruit Topping:**
- 2 **navel oranges, peeled and cut into ¼-inch-thick slices**
- 2 **kiwifruit, peeled and cut into ¼-inch-thick slices**
- ½ **pint strawberries, hulled and cut into ¼-inch-thick slices**

**Glaze:**
- ¼ **cup orange marmalade**

1. Preheat the oven to hot (400°).
2. Prepare the Orange Pastry: Beat together the orange juice, orange rind and egg yolk in a small bowl and set aside.
3. Combine the flour and the salt in a medium-size bowl. Cut in the butter or margarine with a pastry blender or 2 knives until the mixture resembles coarse meal. Gradually add the juice-yolk mixture, stirring with a fork until the dough is soft enough to be gathered into a ball that doesn't stick to your fingers or the bowl.

4. Roll out the dough with a floured rolling pin on a lightly floured surface to a 13-inch circle. Roll the circle onto the rolling pin and unroll into an 11-inch round tart pan with a removable bottom. Trim the dough even with the edge of the pan. Prick the bottom all over with a fork. Line the crust with aluminum foil. Fill with pie weights or dried beans.

5. Bake the crust in the preheated hot oven (400°) for 20 minutes. Remove the aluminum foil and weights. Bake for 5 minutes more. Remove from the oven. If any bubbles have formed in the pastry, flatten gently with a wooden spoon. Cool completely in the pan on a wire rack.

6. Prepare the Orange Cream: Combine the sugar and the cornstarch in a medium-size saucepan. Gradually stir in the orange juice until well blended.

7. Cook, stirring constantly, over medium heat until the mixture thickens and bubbles. Continue cooking and stirring until the mixture is very thick, for about 2 minutes more.

8. Beat the egg yolks in a medium-size bowl until frothy. Slowly stir in half the orange mixture until blended. Return the entire mixture to the saucepan. Cook over low heat, stirring constantly, for 1 minute more; do not boil.

9. Remove from the heat. Place a piece of plastic wrap directly on the surface and cool completely at room temperature.

10. Remove the plastic wrap. Pour and spread the cooled cream filling in the cooled tart shell. Cover with plastic wrap and refrigerate for up to 1 hour before serving.

11. When ready to serve, arrange the Fruit Topping: Place the orange slices, overlapping, in a circle around the outer edge of the Orange Cream filling. Arrange the kiwi slices, overlapping, in a circle over the top half of the oranges. Fill in the center with overlapping circles of the strawberry slices.

12. Prepare the Glaze: Melt the orange marmalade in a small saucepan over low heat. Using the back of a spoon, force the marmalade through a sieve into a small bowl. Lightly brush the fruits carefully with just enough of the strained marmalade to give a shiny glaze. Refrigerate until ready to serve.

## Microwave Instructions
*(for a 650-watt variable power microwave oven)*

**Directions:** Follow the directions in Steps 1 to 5 of the above recipe. Then prepare the Orange Cream: Mix together the sugar and the cornstarch in a microwave-safe 8-cup measure. Gradually stir in the orange juice until smooth. Microwave, uncovered, at full power for 5 minutes, whisking well after 2½ minutes. Remove from the microwave and whisk well. Microwave, uncovered, at full power for 1 minute more. Beat the egg yolks in a small bowl and mix in some of the orange mixture. Stir back into the remaining orange mixture in the 8-cup measure. Microwave, uncovered, at full power for 30 seconds. Continue with Step 9 of the above recipe.

# Just Desserts Party

🍴 🍸 💲

## Pecan Autumn Leaf Cake

*A garnish of delicate chocolate leaves — perfect for a fall feast — tops off this classy cake.*

Bake at 350° for 25 minutes.
Makes 12 servings.

*Nutrient Value Per Serving: 602 calories, 6 g protein, 44 g fat, 51 g carbohydrate, 304 mg sodium, 200 mg cholesterol.*

| | |
|---|---|
| 1 | **cup sifted cake flour** |
| 1 | **cup pecan halves** |
| ½ | **teaspoon ground cinnamon** |
| ¾ | **cup (1½ sticks) butter, softened** |
| ½ | **cup firmly packed light brown sugar** |
| 6 | **eggs, separated** |
| ⅛ | **teaspoon salt** |
| ½ | **cup granulated sugar** |
| | **Chocolate Maple Leaves (recipe follows)** |
| | **Chocolate Bourbon Frosting (recipe, page 290)** |
| ½ | **cup coarsely chopped pecans** |

1. Preheat the oven to moderate (350°). Grease and flour two 8-inch round layer-cake pans.
2. In the container of an electric blender or a food processor, combine the flour, pecan halves and cinnamon. Cover and whirl at high speed for about 1 minute, or until the pecans are finely ground. Set aside.
3. Beat together the butter and the brown sugar in a large bowl with an electric mixer at medium speed until light and fluffy. Add the egg yolks, one at a time, beating well after each addition. Stir in the ground pecan mixture.
4. Using clean beaters, beat together the egg whites and the salt in a large bowl with the electric mixer at high speed until foamy white. Gradually beat in the granulated sugar. Beat until the

meringue stands in firm peaks. Stir one quarter of the meringue into the pecan batter until well blended. Fold in the remaining meringue until no streaks of white remain. Divide the batter evenly between the 2 prepared pans.
5. Bake in the preheated moderate oven (350°) for 25 minutes, or until the centers spring back when lightly pressed with your fingertip. Cool in the pans for 10 minutes. Turn out the layers onto wire racks to cool completely.
6. Meanwhile, prepare the Chocolate Maple Leaves.
7. Prepare the Chocolate Bourbon Frosting.
8. Fill and frost the cake layers with the Chocolate Bourbon Frosting. Sprinkle the top of the cake with the chopped pecans. Gently peel the Chocolate Maple Leaves off the aluminum foil. Place 9 around the outside of the cake and the remaining 3 in the center top of the cake.

**Chocolate Maple Leaves:** On a piece of stiff cardboard, trace and cut out one stencil in the shape and size of the maple leaf pictured *(page 290)*. Line a large baking sheet with aluminum foil and set aside. Melt 3 ounces (about ½ cup) of milk chocolate morsels or wafers, or 3 squares (1 ounce each) of semisweet chocolate, in the top of a double boiler or in a small bowl over hot water, stirring occasionally, until the chocolate

*Pecan Autumn Leaf Cake*

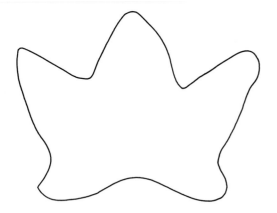

is smooth. Place the leaf stencil cutout on the lined baking sheet. Spoon about 1 teaspoon of the melted chocolate into the stencil cutout. With a small, thin metal spatula, smooth the chocolate into the leaf shape. Gently lift the stencil and scrape any excess chocolate from the cardboard back into the double boiler. Repeat 11 times to make a total of 12 chocolate leaves. Chill until firm. When hard, remove the baking sheet from the refrigerator. With a wooden pick or skewer, sketch veins onto each chocolate leaf.

**Chocolate Bourbon Frosting:** Combine ⅓ cup of sugar, ⅓ cup of water and 3 tablespoons of dark corn syrup in a small saucepan. Bring to boiling over medium heat, stirring constantly, until the sugar is completely dissolved. Remove from the heat and add 8 squares (1 ounce each) of semisweet chocolate, coarsely chopped. Cover and set aside for about 3 minutes. Whisk the chocolate until it is smooth, then cool completely. Stir in 1½ tablespoons of bourbon. Beat ¾ cup (1½ sticks) of softened butter or margarine in a small bowl until creamy and smooth. Gradually beat in the cooled chocolate mixture until smooth. If the frosting is too soft, refrigerate until it is a good spreading consistency.

## Individual Fruitcakes with Orange Sauce

Bake at 350° for 25 minutes.
Makes 12 servings.

*Nutrient Value Per Serving: 433 calories, 5 g protein, 15 g fat, 72 g carbohydrate, 231 mg sodium, 66 mg cholesterol.*

**Fruitcakes:**
1 cup fresh cranberries, halved
1 cup chopped pitted dates
½ cup raisins
1 cup orange-flavored liqueur
2 cups unsifted all-purpose flour
2 teaspoons baking powder
¼ teaspoon baking soda
¼ teaspoon salt
1 teaspoon ground cinnamon
¼ teaspoon ground nutmeg
⅛ teaspoon ground cloves
½ cup (1 stick) butter, softened
1 cup firmly packed light brown sugar
2 eggs, slightly beaten
½ cup orange juice
1 cup coarsely chopped walnuts

**Orange Sauce:**
½ cup sugar
1½ tablespoons cornstarch
1¼ to 1¾ cups orange juice
1 teaspoon grated orange rind

1. Prepare the Fruitcakes: Combine the cranberries, dates, raisins and liqueur in a large, nonmetal bowl and toss. Let stand at room temperature for 1 hour. Drain well, reserving the marinade for the Orange Sauce and the fruits for the Fruitcake.
2. Preheat the oven to moderate (350°). Grease and flour 12 tart pans, with a 3½-inch diameter and ½-cup capacity.
3. Sift together the flour, baking powder, baking soda, salt, cinnamon, nutmeg and cloves onto wax paper.
4. Beat together the butter and the brown sugar in a large bowl with an electric mixer until smooth and fluffy. Add the eggs and beat well.

5. Beat in the flour mixture alternately with the orange juice, beginning and ending with the flour. Fold in the reserved fruits and the walnuts. Spoon the batter evenly into the prepared pans. (The batter will come to the top edge of each pan.)

6. Bake in the preheated moderate oven (350°) for 25 minutes, or until a wooden pick inserted in the centers of the cakes comes out clean. Remove the cakes from the pans to wire racks to cool.

7. Prepare the Orange Sauce: Combine the sugar and the cornstarch in a medium-size saucepan. Add enough orange juice to the reserved fruit marinade to make 2 cups. Stir into the cornstarch mixture.

8. Bring to boiling. Lower the heat, simmer and stir for 1 minute, or until the mixture thickens slightly. Cool. Stir in the orange rind. Cover the surface with plastic wrap and refrigerate until chilled.

9. Serve the cakes with the Orange Sauce.

**《《 𝖸 $**

## Cappuccino Chocolate Cheesecake

Bake at 325° for 1 hour and 30 minutes.
Makes 20 servings.

*Nutrient Value Per Serving: 232 calories, 7 g protein, 13 g fat, 21 g carbohydrate, 122 mg sodium, 86 mg cholesterol.*

1½  **cups finely ground chocolate wafer cookie crumbs (about 30 cookies)**
⅛   **teaspoon ground cinnamon**
2   **containers (15 ounces each) whole milk ricotta cheese**
1   **cup sugar**
3   **tablespoons freeze-dried coffee granules**
2   **tablespoons all-purpose flour**
4   **eggs, separated**
3   **tablespoons coffee-flavored liqueur**
1   **tablespoon vanilla**
1   **container (16 ounces) dairy sour cream**
1   **square (1 ounce) semisweet chocolate, melted**

1. Preheat the oven to slow (325°). Grease a 9 x 3-inch springform pan.

2. Combine the cookie crumbs and the cinnamon. Press the mixture evenly into the bottom of the pan.

3. Combine the ricotta cheese, ¾ cup of the sugar, the coffee granules and flour in a food processor and whirl until smooth. Add the egg yolks, liqueur and vanilla. Whirl until the granules dissolve. Pour into a bowl. Whisk in the sour cream.

4. Beat the egg whites in a large bowl with an electric mixer until foamy. Beat in the remaining ¼ cup of sugar, a tablespoon at a time, until firm peaks form. Fold into the ricotta mixture. Ladle into the prepared pan.

5. Spoon the melted chocolate over the batter in 6 parallel lines. Swirl with a knife.

6. Bake in the preheated slow oven (325°) for 1 hour and 30 minutes; the center of the cake will move slightly when the pan is nudged. Turn off the oven and let the cake remain in the oven with the door closed for 30 minutes.

7. Remove from the oven and cool completely on a wire rack. Refrigerate overnight.

### Food for Thought...

***Ricotta*** *A soft, unripened white cheese originating in Italy, ricotta is made from skimmed sheep's buttermilk or the whey left over from other cheese, such as Pecorina Romano. American-made ricotta is made from whole or skimmed cow's milk, and is the consistency of a smooth cottage cheese, with the flavor of cream cheese.*

## Apricot Apple Tart

Bake crust at 425° for 12 minutes; bake tart at 350° for 45 minutes.
Makes 10 servings.

*Nutrient Value Per Serving: 255 calories, 3 g protein, 10 g fat, 40 g carbohydrate, 113 mg sodium, 53 mg cholesterol.*

### Crust:

1⅓ **cups unsifted all-purpose flour**
2   **tablespoons sugar**
½   **teaspoon salt**
8   **tablespoons (1 stick) unsalted butter, well chilled**
1   **egg yolk**
3   **to 4 tablespoons ice water**

### Filling:

4   **ounces dried apricots (about ¾ cup)**
1   **cup water**
1   **cinnamon stick**
2   **strips lemon zest, each about 2½ x ½ inches**
½   **cup sugar**
2   **tablespoons brandy**
3   **medium-size Golden Delicious apples (about 1¼ pounds)**

1. Prepare the Crust: Combine the flour, sugar and salt in a large bowl. Cut in the butter with a pastry blender until coarse crumbs form.
2. Mix together the egg yolk and 1 tablespoon of the ice water. Add to the flour mixture, stirring with a fork. Add additional ice water to form a soft dough. Wrap and refrigerate for 30 minutes.
3. Place the oven rack in the lowest position. Preheat the oven to hot (425°).
4. Roll out the dough on a lightly floured surface to a 14-inch circle. Fit loosely into an 11-inch fluted tart pan with a removable bottom. Fold under the overhang for a thick edge.
5. Bake in the preheated hot oven (425°) for 12 minutes. Remove to a wire rack. Lower the temperature to moderate (350°).
6. Prepare the Filling: Combine the apricots, water, cinnamon stick and lemon zest in a small saucepan. Bring to boiling. Lower the heat, cover and simmer for 10 minutes.
7. Discard the cinnamon stick and the lemon zest. Process the undrained apricots, the sugar and brandy in a food processor until puréed. Spread a thin layer of purée over the crust.
8. Peel, halve and core the apples. Slice each half crosswise into 8 slices. Place 5 halves around the edge of the tart and place one in the center. Slightly fan the halves. Spread the remaining purée evenly over the apples.
9. Bake in the preheated moderate oven (350°) for 45 minutes, or until the apples are tender. Cool on a wire rack.

## Pink Grapefruit Ice

Makes 8 servings (1 quart).

*Nutrient Value Per Serving: 129 calories, 1 g protein, 0 g fat, 32 g carbohydrate, 1 mg sodium, 0 mg cholesterol.*

5   **large pink grapefruits**
¾   **cup sugar**
2   **tablespoons grenadine syrup**

1. Halve the grapefruits. Squeeze out the juice and strain. You should have 4 cups.
2. Combine the sugar with 1 cup of the grapefruit juice in a saucepan. Heat over low heat, stirring constantly, just until the sugar is dissolved. Do not boil. Pour into a bowl. Add the remaining grapefruit juice and the grenadine. Refrigerate until chilled.
3. Transfer the mixture to the container of an ice cream maker. Freeze, following the manufacturer's directions, until the ice begins to stiffen. Remove the container and remove the dasher. Cover and freeze overnight.

## 🔻🍸💲
# *Lemon Dream Cake*

Bake at 350° for 20 to 25 minutes.
Makes 10 servings.

*Nutrient Value Per Serving: 540 calories, 6 g protein, 30 g fat, 64 g carbohydrate, 370 mg sodium, 172 mg cholesterol.*

### *Lemon Cake:*
- 3  cups sifted cake flour
- 3  teaspoons baking powder
- ¼  teaspoon salt
- ¾  cup (1½ sticks) butter, softened
- 1½  cups sugar
- 3  eggs, separated
- 3  teaspoons grated lemon rind
- 1  cup milk

### *Syrup:*
- ¼  cup fresh lemon juice
- ⅓  cup 10X (confectioners' powdered) sugar

### *Ginger Cream:*
- 1½  cups heavy cream
- 6  tablespoons 10X (confectioners' powdered) sugar
- 2  teaspoons fresh lemon juice
- 1½  teaspoons finely grated gingerroot
  OR: ¾ teaspoon ground ginger

1. Preheat the oven to moderate (350°). Grease three 8 x 1½-inch round layer-cake pans. Line the bottoms with wax paper. Grease the paper.
2. Prepare the Lemon Cake: Sift together the flour, baking powder and salt onto wax paper. Set aside.
3. Beat together the butter and the sugar in a large bowl with an electric mixer at high speed until fluffy. Beat in the egg yolks and the lemon rind. Beat in the flour mixture alternately with the milk, beginning and ending with the flour mixture.
4. Beat the egg whites in another bowl until soft peaks form; fold into the batter. Pour the batter into the prepared pans.
5. Bake in the preheated moderate oven (350°) for 20 to 25 minutes, or until a

## *BAKE-A-CAKE*

- *If you want your cake to have the best possible volume, shape and texture, use the exact ingredients, measurements and pan size called for in the recipe. And follow the recipe directions to the letter.*
- *Remember to preheat the oven to the proper temperature for 10 minutes before baking.*
- *The cake is done when:*
  —*It shrinks slightly from the sides of the pan.*
  —*A fingertip is pressed lightly on the top of the cake and the top springs back to shape.*
  —*A cake tester or wooden pick inserted near the center of the cake comes out clean, with no batter or moist particles clinging to it.*
- *The cake may turn out heavy and soggy if the oven temperature is too low.*
- *The cake may fall if the oven door is opened too soon, if the oven is too hot or if there is not enough flour in the batter.*

wooden pick inserted in the centers of the cakes comes out clean. Cool in the pans for 5 minutes. Invert onto wire racks, peel off the wax paper and cool.
6. Prepare the Syrup: Whisk the lemon juice into the 10X (confectioners' powdered) sugar in a bowl until smooth. Brush the sides and tops of the layers with the syrup.
7. Prepare the Ginger Cream: Combine the cream, 10X (confectioners' powdered) sugar, lemon juice and ginger in a large bowl. Beat with the electric mixer until stiff.
8. Stack and fill the cake layers with the Ginger Cream. Refrigerate until ready to serve.

# KidCakes

◧ ⵔ 💲

## Fantasy Carousel Cake

*A dream of a cake in pink and white, with gilded chargers or, if you prefer, miniature circus or zoo animals.*

Bake 10-inch round cake at 350° for 45 minutes; bake cupcakes at 350° for 20 minutes.
Makes 12 servings.

*Nutrient Value Per Serving: 765 calories, 3 g protein, 29 g fat, 126 g carbohydrate, 311 mg sodium, 69 mg cholesterol.*

| | |
|---|---|
| 1 | **package (18¼ ounces) yellow cake mix with pudding (plus eggs, oil and water called for on package label)** |
| ⅔ | **cup seedless raspberry jam** |
| 2 | **recipes Creamy White Frosting (recipe, page 301), made with almond flavoring** |
| | **Pink paste food coloring** |
| 4 | **wooden skewers (12-inch)** |
| 6 | **round red and white peppermint swirl candies** |
| 6 | **plastic straws (8-inch)** |
| 6 | **galloping horses\* or other circus or zoo animals (from plastic model or game set)** |
| 1 | **pink doily (12-inch)** |
| 1 | **piece pink construction paper** |

1. Preheat the oven to moderate (350°). Grease a 10-inch round layer-cake pan. Line the bottom with wax paper and grease the paper. Flour the wax paper and the pan. Grease and flour muffin-pan cups to make six 2½-inch cupcakes.
2. Prepare the cake mix following the package directions, using eggs, oil and water.
3. Remove ¾ cup of the batter and reserve. Pour the remaining batter into the 10-inch pan.

4. Bake in the preheated moderate oven (350°) for 45 minutes, or until a cake tester inserted in the center of the cake comes out clean. Cool the cake in the pan on a wire rack for 10 minutes. Turn out the cake onto the wire rack. Peel off the wax paper and let the cake cool completely. Leave the oven on.
5. Spoon the reserved ¾ cup of batter into the 6 prepared muffin-pan cups.
6. Bake in the preheated moderate oven (350°) for 20 minutes, or until a cake tester comes out clean. Cool the cupcakes in the pan on a wire rack for 10 minutes. Turn out onto the wire rack to cool completely.
7. Split the round cake in half horizontally with a serrated knife. Place the top half, cut side up, on a serving platter. Spread with the raspberry jam. Top with the second half, cut side down.
8. Prepare the Creamy White Frosting in a large bowl. Remove 2 cups to a small bowl, cover with plastic wrap and reserve.
9. Color the remaining white frosting bright pink with the pink food coloring. Beat to combine. Use two thirds of the pink frosting to frost the top and sides of the round cake.
10. Frost the tops of the 6 cupcakes with part of the remaining pink frosting. Thread all 6, tops to bottoms, on one of the 12-inch skewers, frosted tops down, leaving about 3 inches of skewer at the top. Push the cupcakes together firmly. The cupcake stack should be about 6 inches tall. Press the pointed end of the skewer into the center of the frosted round cake to make a center column.
11. Cut the ends from the remaining 3 skewers to make them 8 inches long.

*Fantasy Carousel Cake, Rum-Tum-Drum Cake (recipe, page 297) and Clarence the Circus Bear (recipe, page 298)*

Press them through the cupcakes around the long skewer and into the round cake to anchor the column.

12. Use the remaining pink frosting to frost the cupcake column, holding the end of the long skewer to steady the column.

13. Using a 2-inch round cookie cutter, mark a swag pattern around the side of the round cake by pressing the lower half of the cutter all around the top half of the side, leaving about a ½-inch space between each half circle. There should be about 12 half circles.

14. Spoon the reserved 2 cups of white frosting into a pastry bag fitted with a medium-size star tip. Pipe a star border around the cake base.

15. Using the star tip, pipe a decorative shell border around the top edge of the round cake. Pipe frosting along the half circle cookie cutter imprint lines to make swags. In the space between each swag, from a point two thirds down the side of the cake, pipe an elongated shell in one motion upward to the top edge of the cake to form a swag end. Pipe a rosette to cover the top of the swag end and join the curved swag sections.

16. Pipe a shell border around the base of the center column.

17. Place the 6 peppermint candies around the center of the column. Change the tip on the pastry bag to a large writing tip. Pipe a ring of small dots around each candy.

18. Stick the 6 plastic straws, spaced evenly around the column about 2 inches from the outside edge of the cake, 1 inch into the top of the round cake. Place a horse or other animal in front of each straw.

19. Cut the doily from the outside edge to the center. Overlap the edges about 2

____

### FROSTING FACTS

*• Cakes with a butter cream frosting can be left at room temperature. Cover the cut surface of the cake with plastic wrap and place it in a cake keeper, or invert a large bowl over the cake plate. The cake will keep for 2 to 3 days this way. (In hot weather, it is still best to refrigerate the cake.)*

*• Cakes with a cream frosting or filling should be refrigerated, with plastic wrap covering the cut part.*

*• Unfrosted cakes freeze best—for up to 4 months. Wrap the cake or cake halves in aluminum foil, plastic wrap or large, freezer-weight plastic bags, and freeze; thaw them at room temperature for 1 hour.*

*• Frosted cakes should be frozen on a piece of cardboard or a baking sheet until firm, then wrapped in aluminum foil, plastic wrap or very large, freezer-weight plastic bags. You can freeze frosted cakes for up to 3 months, and thaw them at room temperature for 2 hours.*

____

inches and tape together to form a roof. Center the doily over the tall skewer and push it down to the top of the straws. If the straws are too tall, snip with kitchen shears to even them up.

20. Make a flag from the pink construction paper and tape it to the skewer top.

*Note: We used model paints from a hobby store to paint the saddles.*

# Rum-Tum-Drum Cake

*An easy-to-decorate cake for wee ones.*

Bake at 350° for 25 minutes.
Makes 20 servings.

*Nutrient Value Per Serving: 664 calories, 4 g protein, 24 g fat, 110 g carbohydrate, 462 mg sodium, 82 mg cholesterol.*

- 1 **package (18¼ ounces) chocolate cake mix with pudding (plus eggs, oil and water called for on package label)**
- 1 **package (18¼ ounces) yellow cake mix with pudding (plus eggs, oil and water called for on package label)**
- 1 **recipe Decorator Frosting (recipe, page 298)**
- **Green paste food coloring**
- 2 **recipes Creamy White Frosting (recipe, page 301)**
- 1 **box (4 ounces) strawberry-flavored fruit roll-ups**
- 12 **green and white candy sticks (5 inches long)**
- 12 **yellow (or other color) jelly candies, from multicolored package (8 ounces)**
- 2 **breadsticks**

1. Preheat the oven to moderate (350°). Grease and flour two 9-inch round layer-cake pans.
2. Prepare the chocolate cake mix following the package directions, using eggs, oil and water. Pour the batter into the prepared pans.
3. Bake in the preheated moderate oven (350°) for 25 minutes, or until a cake tester inserted in the centers of the cakes comes out clean. Cool the cakes in the pans on wire racks for 10 minutes. Turn out onto the wire racks to cool completely.
4. Repeat with the yellow cake mix to make two 9-inch yellow cakes.
5. Meanwhile, make the letters: Use a ruler and a fork tine to draw two long parallel lines 1¼ inches apart on a large piece of wax paper. With the fork tine, write HAPPY BIRTHDAY between the parallel lines several times, leaving ½ inch between the letters. (Only one set of letters is needed, but it is best to have extra in case a letter breaks when being removed from the paper.)
6. Prepare the Decorator Frosting. Add the green food coloring to make the frosting bright green. Spoon the frosting into a pastry bag fitted with a medium-size writing tip. Trace the HAPPY BIRTHDAY lettering on the wax paper; the letters should be 1¼ inches high. Let dry. Place damp paper toweling over the tip opening and reserve the remaining green frosting.
7. When the cakes are cooled, prepare the Creamy White Frosting.
8. Place one chocolate cake layer on a serving platter. Frost the top with ½ cup of the white frosting. Top with a yellow cake layer. Frost as above. Top with the remaining chocolate cake layer. Frost. Top with the remaining yellow cake layer, flat side up. Frost the top and sides with the remaining white frosting, smoothing with a large, straight-sided cake spreader for a flat surface.
9. Open 4 packages (half the box) of fruit roll-ups. Cut each piece in half lengthwise. Line up the pieces end to end lengthwise, shiny side down, on wax paper, overlapping ends about ¼ inch to form a band 28 inches long. Fold down the top edge of the band almost to the center, pressing it firmly in place. Fold up the bottom edge of the band almost to the center and press it in place. The band now should be about 2 inches wide. Trim the wax paper even with the edges of the band. Place the band, wax paper side out, around the base of the cake. Trim off any excess band where the ends meet. Carefully peel off the wax paper, pressing the band firmly to the cake.
10. Repeat Step 9, but place the band around the top of the cake, overlapping the edge by about ¼ inch.

11. Cut the candy sticks to about 3½ inches in length. Place in a zigzag pattern around the side of the drum, with the ends meeting. Place a jelly candy at each of the points where 2 candy sticks meet. Use a drop of the reserved green decorator frosting to help the candy adhere, if necessary.

12. Carefully peel the dried letters from the wax paper. Place on the cake top to spell HAPPY BIRTHDAY. Place the 2 breadsticks on the cake for drumsticks. To store the cake, cover it, but do *not* refrigerate; refrigerator moisture will melt the candy sticks.

*Decorator Frosting:* Combine 1 cup of *un*sifted 10X (confectioners' powdered) sugar, ⅛ teaspoon of cream of tartar and 1 egg white in a small bowl. Beat with an electric mixer at high speed until stiff, for 3 to 5 minutes. *Makes about 1 cup.*

◄◄ ▼ 💲

## Clarence the Circus Bear

*The cakes may be baked ahead and frozen until the day of the party. Thaw the cakes completely before assembling.*

Bake chocolate bowl cake at 325° for 60 minutes; bake cupcakes at 350° for 20 minutes; bake 10-inch round cake at 350° for 45 minutes.
Makes 20 servings.

*Nutrient Value Per Serving: 615 calories, 4 g protein, 24 g fat, 98 g carbohydrate, 499 mg sodium, 95 mg cholesterol.*

1 *package (18¼ ounces) chocolate cake mix with pudding (plus eggs, oil and water called for on package label)*
1 *package (18¼ ounces) yellow cake mix with pudding (plus eggs, oil and water called for on package label)*
⅔ *cup seedless raspberry jam*
1 *recipe Creamy White Frosting (recipe, page 301)*
  *Yellow and red paste food coloring*
1 *recipe Chocolate Frosting (recipe, page 301)*
  *Doughnut-shaped sugar-coated jelly candies (2 yellow, 1 black, 1 red, from 8-ounce bag)*
1 *sugar ice cream cone*

1. Preheat the oven to slow (325°). Grease and flour a 1½-quart (6-inch diameter) ovenproof mixing bowl and muffin-pan cups to make twelve 2½-inch cupcakes.
2. Prepare the chocolate cake mix, using eggs, oil and water, following the package directions. Measure out 3½ cups of the batter and pour into the prepared bowl.
3. Bake in the preheated slow oven (325°) for 60 minutes, or until a cake tester inserted in the center of the cake comes out clean. Cool the cake in the bowl on a wire rack for 10 minutes. Turn out onto the wire rack to cool completely.
4. Increase the oven temperature to moderate (350°).
5. Spoon the remaining chocolate cake batter into the prepared muffin-pan cups, filling each two thirds full.

6. Bake in the preheated moderate oven (350°) for 20 minutes, or until a cake tester comes out clean. Cool in the pans on a wire rack for 10 minutes. Turn out onto the wire rack to cool completely. Leave the oven at 350°.

7. Meanwhile, grease a 10-inch round layer-cake pan. Line the bottom with a wax paper circle and grease the paper. Flour the wax paper and the pan.

8. Prepare the yellow cake mix, using eggs, oil and water, following the package directions. Pour into the prepared pan.

9. Bake in the preheated moderate oven (350°) for 45 minutes, or until a cake tester inserted in the center of the cake comes out clean. Cool in the pan on a wire rack for 10 minutes. Turn out onto the wire rack to cool completely. Carefully peel off the wax paper.

10. Split the round cake in half horizontally with a serrated knife. Place the top half, cut side up, on a serving platter. Spread with the raspberry jam. Top with the second half, cut side down.

11. Make the Creamy White Frosting. Remove ¾ cup of the frosting to a small bowl, cover with plastic wrap and reserve. Add the yellow food coloring to the remaining frosting to make a bright lemon yellow. Use to frost the top and sides of the round cake.

12. Center the chocolate head on the yellow cake. Gently place pieces of wax paper on top of the yellow frosting around the chocolate cake.

13. Make the Chocolate Frosting. Frost the top of one cupcake. Place the frosted top against the bottom of the chocolate head to form a muzzle. Frost the head and the muzzle with the Chocolate Frosting.

14. Cut one cupcake in half vertically. Place one half, cut side down, against the right top side of the head to form an ear. Repeat with the other cupcake half to make an ear on the left side. The remaining cupcakes may be frosted and frozen to use another time.

15. For an eye, cut a ¼-inch piece from the black doughnut-shaped candy. Insert the piece, cut side up, into one of the yellow doughnut-shaped candies. Cut the bottom from the yellow candy just below the flat edge of the black candy and discard the small yellow part. Place the eye on the right side of the head, just above the muzzle. Repeat for the left eye.

16. Cut half the black doughnut-shaped candy for a nose and press onto the top front of the muzzle. Cut the red doughnut-shaped candy in half for a mouth and press onto the bottom front of the muzzle.

17. Remove the pieces of wax paper from the yellow cake. Add the red food coloring to the reserved Creamy White Frosting. Spoon into a pastry bag fitted with a medium-size star tip. Pipe a ruffle around the side of the yellow cake.

18. Pipe a shell or star border at the base of the bear's neck.

19. While holding the tip of the ice cream cone, use a circular motion to pipe a border around the base of the hat. Place on the bear's head. Pipe a red tuft on the tip of the hat. Store the cake, covered, in a cool, dry place. Do *not* refrigerate or freeze the cake; this will make the colors run.

# FROSTING CAKE LAYERS

*Fig. 1*

*Fig. 2*

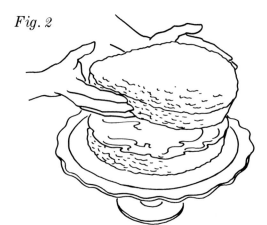

*Fig. 3*

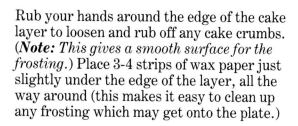

*Fig. 4*

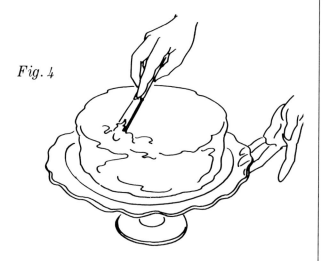

Rub your hands around the edge of the cake layer to loosen and rub off any cake crumbs. (**Note:** *This gives a smooth surface for the frosting.*) Place 3-4 strips of wax paper just slightly under the edge of the layer, all the way around (this makes it easy to clean up any frosting which may get onto the plate.)

Place the cake layer, rounded-side down, on a cake plate; spread, with a generous layer of frosting around the edge of the layer (Fig. 1). Place the second layer, rounded side up, over the filled layer (Fig. 2). Top a spatula with a generous amount of frosting and spread it in a swirling motion up the side to the top of the cake to cover and make a decorative edge to the cake (Fig. 3).

Spread the remaining frosting over the top of the cake, making swirling motions with the spatula for decorative finish (Fig. 4). Gently remove the wax paper strips.

***Baker's Tip:*** If there is a tear in the side of the cake, mix ½ cup of the prepared frosting with 3 tablespoons of the water to make a very thin mixture. Spread it over the broken surface to coat evenly; allow it to dry before frosting the cake.

# Creamy White Frosting

Makes about 2 cups.

*Nutrient Value Per ¼ Cup: 334 calories, 0 g protein, 13 g fat, 57 g carbohydrate, 1 mg sodium, 0 mg cholesterol.*

½  **cup vegetable shortening**
1  **box (1 pound) 10X (confectioners' powdered) sugar**
1  **teaspoon vanilla OR: ¼ teaspoon almond flavoring**
3  **to 4 tablespoons water**

Beat the shortening in a small bowl until creamy. With an electric mixer at low speed, beat in 1 cup of the 10X (confectioners' powdered) sugar. Beat in the vanilla or almond flavoring and 1 tablespoon of the water. Add the remaining 10X (confectioners' powdered) sugar alternately with enough of the remaining water, beating well after each addition, to make the frosting thick and creamy.

# Chocolate Frosting

Makes about 2 cups.

*Nutrient Value Per ¼ Cup: 331 calories, 1 g protein, 12 g fat, 58 g carbohydrate, 121 mg sodium, 32 mg cholesterol.*

1  **box (1 pound) 10X (confectioners' powdered) sugar**
¼  **cup unsweetened cocoa powder**
½  **cup (1 stick) butter, softened**
¼  **teaspoon vanilla**
3  **to 4 tablespoons milk**

1. Sift together the 10X (confectioners' powdered) sugar and the cocoa onto wax paper.
2. Beat the butter in a medium-size bowl with an electric mixer until soft and creamy. Beat in the vanilla.
3. Add the sugar mixture to the butter alternately with enough of the milk, beating well after each addition, to make the frosting thick and spreadable.

# Index

*Italicized* page numbers refer to photographs